EUROPE IN EXILE

EUROPE IN EXILE

European Exile Communities in Britain 1940–1945

EDITED BY MARTIN CONWAY AND JOSÉ GOTOVITCH

Berghahn Books
New York • Oxford

SOMA[ ]CEGES

First published in 2001 by

Berghahn Books

www.BerghahnBooks.com

© 2001 Martin Conway and José Gotovitch

Library of Congress Cataloging-in-Publication Data

Europe in exile : European exile communities in Britain, 1940–1945 /
edited by Martin Conway and José Gotovitc
p. cm.
Includes bibliographical references.
ISBN 1-57181-759-X (acid-free paper) – ISBN 1-57181-503-1
(pbk. : acid-free paper)
1. World War, 1939–1945--Refugees. 2. World War, 1939–1945--
Governments in exile. 3. Great Britain--Emigration and immigration--
History--20th century. 4. Europeans--Great Britain--History--20th
century. 5. Refugees--Great Britain--History--20th century. 6. Refugees--
Europe--History--20th century. I. Conway, Martin, 1960–
II. Gotovitch, José.

D809.G7 E93 2001
940.53'08691–dc21   2001025283

British Library Cataloguing in Publication Data
A catalogue record for this book is available
from the British Library.

Printed in the United States on acid-free paper.
ISBN 1-57181-759-X hardback
ISBN 1-57181-503-1 paperback

CONTENTS

Introduction   1
  José Gotovitch and Martin Conway

Part One: Pre-histories

1. British Government Policy Towards Wartime Refugees
   Colin Holmes   11

2. Pre-War Belgian Attitudes to Britain: Anglophilia and
   Anglophobia
   Jean Stengers   35

Part Two: The Belgian Example

3. Belgian Society in Exile: An Attempt at a Synthesis
   Luis Angel Bernardo y Garcia and Matthew Buck   53

4. Female Belgian Refugees in Britain during the Second
   World War: An Oral History
   Françoise Raes   67

5. The Reconstruction of Belgian Military Forces in Britain,
   1940–1945
   Luc De Vos   81

6. Belgian Military Plans for the Post-War Period
   Pascal Deloge   99

7. The Commission pour l'Etude des Problèmes d'Après-Guerre
   (CEPAG) 1941–1944
   Diane de Bellefroid   121

8. The Staff of the High Commissariat for National Security:
   A Socio-Professional Profile
   Eric Laureys   135

Part Three: The European Dimension

9. The Norwegian Armed Forces in Britain
   Chris Mann   153

10. The Czechoslovak Armed Forces in Britain, 1940-1945
    Alan Brown   167

11. The Social History of Polish Exile (1939-1945).
    The Exile State and the Clandestine State: Society,
    Problems and Reflections
    Jan E. Zamojski   183

12. France in Exile: The French Community in Britain,
    1940–1944
    Nicholas Atkin   213

13. Dutch Exiles in London
    N. David J. Barnouw   229

14. The Socialist Internationale: Society or Counter-Society?
    Herman Balthazar   247

15. Legacies of Exile: The Exile Governments in London
    during the Second World War and the Politics of
    Post-war Europe
    Martin Conway   255

Index   275

INTRODUCTION

MARTIN CONWAY AND JOSÉ GOTOVITCH

As these lines are being written, the entire world is once again confronted with the drama of large numbers of refugees fleeing their native lands which have been ravaged by conflicts. The force of the live television images transmitted most recently from Africa and Kosovo proves without any doubt and without any need for the slightest explanation the simple, brutal and terrifying reason for these population movements: the refugees are seeking simply to save their lives.

In 1940 Hitler's invasion of Western Europe similarly provoked millions of civilians to flee, motivated by a terror constructed or transmitted by previous generations and reinforced by the events of the 1914–18 conflict. For these refugees, the power of imagined horrors was just as strong, if not stronger, than the real images transmitted today. Terror certainly played a role in the decisions to flee: the memory of the crimes perpetrated by the *uhlans*, the sacking of Dinant, the burning of the library of the University of Louvain and the shootings by the so-called *francs-tireurs* caused many to flee from what they imagined to be the imminent prospect of direct brutality. But so too did the memories of the experience of exile during the First World War of the hundreds of thousands of Belgians who had spent the war years in exile in France and Britain, in a free society sheltered from the dangers of the military conflict.

Thus it was the First World War that for the first time created mass exile societies, which, beyond divisions of class and ideology, brought together national populations who lived together during the military conflict in the expectation of a return to their homeland after the military defeat of the enemy. In this respect, the exile societies of the First World War differed in their inclusive nature from those of the *émigrés* in Germany during the French Revolution, or, before them, those of the Huguenot refugees expelled from France on the basis of their religious belief. The exile communities of the 1914–18 conflict became in this way a 'model' that all those who participated in this experience of exile were nevertheless resolved never to have to relive.

Hitler's dreams of domination of the whole of Europe, as well as the Nazi racist ideology and its model of a prison-society, served, however, to transform both the scale and the nature of the fear that the German Reich inspired at the outbreak of the Second World War. To the primal and all too justified fear of violence was now added among the more aware sections of the population (who also possessed the material means of acting upon their convictions) the wish to escape at any price from Nazi domination, however 'pacific' in character its architects might claim it to be. The fall of France and the decision of Pétain to choose the path of collaboration effectively imprisoned some hundreds of thousands of European refugees, many of whom had taken refuge in France from countries already conquered 'surreptitiously' as a consequence of the Nuremberg racial laws, the *Anschluss*, the Munich agreement or the Nazi-Soviet Pact. Thus Britain became, or, rather, became once again, the only combatant and friendly country willing to serve as a place of exile and asylum.

It is necessary to emphasise the friendly element because for the unfortunate Europeans forced into exile there were other possibilities that they could try to exploit. Sweden became a place of refuge for some German Social Democrats. Switzerland opened its doors to a very few, albeit on certain strictly-defined conditions. North Africa, too, seemed briefly to offer the prospect of refuge, but one that proved to be an ephemeral mirage as a result of its harsh climate and the control of the Vichy regime that imposed a harsh regime of internment camps on the refugees. Others sought to cross the Pyrenees from France into Spain, a journey that would be imitated by many other resisters and escapees once the escape routes in Nazi-occupied Europe had been established. For many of these refugees, however, entry into Spain was via the Francoist camp at Miranda, an institution that became a place of sinister memory for almost two thousand Belgians as well as many Poles and French citizens who mistakenly believed that by arriving in officially-neutral Spain they had finally managed to escape from persecution.

The recently republished work by Varian Fry[1] has also rightly highlighted the importance of the United States as a place of exile, aided by its neutrality during the years 1940–41 and by the presence of various U.S. agencies in the unoccupied southern zone of France.

Exile in the U.S.A. had, however, a number of distinct characteristics. The particular role played by American Jewish organisations permitted the rescue of a good number of Jewish citizens not only from Austria and Germany in particular but also from the rest of Europe. In addition, the U.S. authorities deliberately sought to assist members of the European intelligentsia to find refuge in the United States. Finally, the decisions taken by numerous financial, industrial and commercial companies to locate their head offices and their capital reserves in the relative security of New York from 1939 onwards ensured that business leaders formed a prominent element of this European refugee population. For those who did not fit these criteria, Cuba and Mexico became alternative, and not entirely unpleasant, places of refuge in the New World.

But nowhere outside Britain did European exile take on such a structured form, which was rendered more official by the establishment in London of the legitimate or reconstituted governments of Belgium, the Netherlands, Czechoslovakia, Norway and Poland. In addition, it was in London that the Free French authorities found a home as well as numerous other committees claiming to speak on behalf of lands governed by the fascist forces.

Moscow, and, indeed, the USSR as a whole, also became a place of wartime refuge, albeit a much more ambiguous one and one that was often marked by tragedy. The Soviet occupation of the eastern territories of Poland led to the pure and simple murder of some tens of thousands of soldiers while many hundreds of thousands of others were deported to 'distant regions' of the USSR. Even so, the reversal of diplomatic and military fortunes protected these refugees, including many East-European Jews, from the Nazi massacres and genocide. Conscious of the need to prepare for the post-war world, the Soviet authorities recruited among the Polish and Czech refugees, as well as among those who had been 'forced' into exile, such as Hungarian, Romanian and even German prisoners of war, to form the leadership groups on whom they would rely on to establish their subsequent control of central and Eastern Europe.

Thus, to simplify greatly, it can be argued that the events of the war years served to prefigure the divisions of the postwar era. Already, long before the Cold War had begun to loom on the horizon, the exile communities of Europe had divided into two contrasting poles: around certain squares in central London what would become the 'Free World' was being constituted; while, further east, the Kremlin was using its pre-war and wartime refugees to put in place the 'Socialist world' of the future.

It is therefore easy to see the importance that the experience of exile between 1939 and 1945 holds for an understanding of the postwar world, and its implications at the governmental and diplomatic levels have been substantially examined in a number of earlier works. The purpose and, we hope, originality of this volume lies in its intention to look beyond the level of governmental authorities at the 'societies of exile'. Taking as its starting-point the largest exile population in wartime Britain, the Belgians, it seeks to look at the exile populations in the full diversity of their civilian and military dimensions. The challenge of this international research project was therefore to seek to explore the social composition and cultural values articulated by these thousands of exiles who shared in common only their arrival in Britain as a consequence of frequently very dissimilar choices, journeys and intentions.

Aspects of Exile

The diverse and multinational structure of the book takes as its starting-point the history of the Belgian refugee community in Britain, which was the focus of a research project directed jointly by the Faculty of Modern History of the University of Oxford, the Free University of Brussels (ULB) and the Centre d'Etudes et de Documentation Guerre et Sociétés Contemporaines (CEGES) of Brussels. In the opening chapter, Colin Holmes analyses the manner in which, in preparing to receive on its soil escapees from the looming European military conflict, Britain sought to reconcile its policy of strict immigration control, established after the First World War, with its unavoidable role as a place of refuge. Not surprisingly, it managed to do so only with considerable difficulty and at the price of numerous contradictions between the actions of the different branches of the state apparatus. Nevertheless, if one considers the large number of initiatives that the British succeeded in launching amidst the chaos of wartime, one is obliged to recognise that the British governmental system did succeed in adapting with remarkable flexibility to the impossible conditions of these gloomy times. It is, therefore, worth stressing that, in marked contrast to the memories of the Belgians who fled to France in 1940, the Belgian wartime refugees who managed to reach Britain have retained memories composed exclusively of gratitude and admiration for their British hosts. This is all the more remarkable given the fact that, as Jean Stengers makes clear in his contribution, anglophobia and anglophilia had both been present in Belgium since the nineteenth century, with the former often prevailing over the latter.

The purpose of the chapter by Luis Bernardo and Matthew Buck is to escape from the Belgian governmental offices in Eaton Square in London in order to explore the full social diversity of the Belgian refugee experience. It demonstrates how the scattered Belgian communities sought painstakingly to reconstruct their familiar and cherished structures of sociability through schools, churches, trade unions, lecture societies and musical concerts. Within this reconstituted and largely improvised society, it was the women who, consciously or by force of circumstance, were obliged to play the leading role. As the contribution by Françoise Raes demonstrates, these women, be they pillars of family life, workers or members of the auxiliary armed forces engaged on a path of feminist liberation, found themselves also obliged to adopt the more traditional roles of the (foreign) soldier's wife, and therefore also of the war widow. All aspects of the life of the Belgian community were inevitably dominated by the war. A new army was created that, as Luc De Vos stresses in his chapter, also acquired through its renovated structures and methods of fighting a new character that would form the basis of the Belgian army of the postwar era. Plans for the future constituted a major theme of the actions of the exile authorities, be it the military planning investigated by Pascal Deloge or that by the wide range of prominent Belgian exile figures brought together in the Commission pour l'étude des problèmes d'après-guerre (CEPAG) studied by Diane de Bellefroid. More than such planning, it was, however, the more immediate prospect of social and political troubles arising from the prospect of liberation that preoccupied the Belgian exile authorities. Like many of the other exile regimes, they were haunted by a 'fear of the return', both in terms of the material difficulties that it would present as well as the prospect of a rejection of their authority by the liberated population. They therefore sought to prepare their return with care, creating an Haut Commissariat à la Sécurité de l'Etat (HSCE) composed, as Eric Laureys stresses, of individuals whom the government believed it could count on as reliable.

This Belgian experience is then compared with those of the other European refugee populations. Military matters inevitably loom large in the case of the Norwegians and the Czechoslovaks, examined by Christopher Mann and Alan Brown respectively, as well as in the very particular war experience of the Poles, despite the remarkable range of Polish civilian exile activities examined in the contribution by Jan Zamojski. Even the Free French were first and foremost soldiers, though the dominating figure of General de Gaulle has overshadowed the history of the French civilian population, which, as Nick Atkin demonstrates, though small in number and highly fragmented, contained a number of prominent figures both of that time as well as of the future. Much the same was true of the Dutch exiles, among whom the presence of Queen Wilhelmina, as David Barnouw analyses in his contribution, dominated all of the imagery of the Netherlands at war.

A further and distinctive element of the exile communities in London was the presence of many of the leading figures of the pre-war Socialist Internationale. In his contribution, Herman Balthazar explores this microcosm of exile in which both British and Belgian figures played a leading role, as well as certain of the leading Socialist politicians of those countries, notably Germany and Austria, that had been conquered 'from the interior'. With its weaknesses and internal divisions, the wartime Internationale exemplified not only the tensions between patriotic loyalty and internationalism but also the hope for a better future based on world peace. In the final contribution, Martin Conway seeks to assess the impact which the wartime exile regimes had on post-war society, as it moved almost seamlessly from World War to Cold War. Though their immediate impact was in many cases limited, their long-term contribution could be argued to have been more significant.

Through their examination of these various aspects of exile, the essays in this volume seek to provide a new examination of the European exile societies of the war years, the existence of which has tended to be overlooked both in popular memory and in written accounts. Certainly, in comparison with the sufferings of the populations of occupied Europe, the communities on the other side of the Channel appear as privileged groups, about whose experiences for a long time it seemed almost indecent to speak. But, like all such human entities, the history of the European exile communities deserves to be examined, both because of its inherent value and the unique experience that it comprised. As in any such crisis situation, the destruction of the authority of traditional structures enabled patterns of behaviour to emerge that in more normal times would have remained hidden from view. For this reason, the phenomenon of exile, it can be argued, can be used by historians to study the 'mother society': the occupied country from which they sprang. Thus we believe that this volume of essays provides, however imperfectly, a contribution not merely to a neglected aspect of the history of the Second World War but also to the wider history of modern Europe.

Acknowledgements

This volume, and the conference upon which it is based, could not have come to fruition without the invaluable assistance of a large number of organisations and individuals. First and foremost, we are indebted to the Wiener-Anspach Foundation of Brussels, which, under the energetic leadership of its president Etienne Gutt, supported the conference held at Balliol College in Oxford in the autumn of 1998. In addition, the Foundation funded a two-year research project on the history of the Belgian refugees in Britain that enabled two researchers (Matthew Buck at the University of Oxford and Luis Bernardo at the Free University of Brussels) to undertake a comprehensive analysis of the history of the Belgian refugee experience in Britain that will result in the forthcoming publication of a joint-authored book in Belgium. Throughout their work, they were assisted by Baron Jean Bloch, president of the Fondation de la Mémoire, who through his expert advice, helped to design and structure the research project. The conference in Oxford was also made possible by valuable financial assistance from the British Council, the Belgian Ministry of Foreign Affairs, the Services Scientifiques, Techniques et Culturels of the Belgian Federal Government and the Regius Professor's Discretionary Fund of the Faculty of Modern History of the University of Oxford. For invaluable organisational assistance, we are grateful to Lut Van Daele, Tina Hodgkinson, Matthew Buck and Joseph Bord.

As editors, we are indebted to Marion Berghahn for her enthusiastic support for the project, to Christine Arthur for her expert and accomplished translation of the French-language contributions to the volume and to Alison Falby for her painstaking attention to the detail of the editorial work. Above all, we are grateful to all of our contributors for their commitment to this volume of collective research.

Note

1. V. Fry, *Surrender on Demand*, New York, 1945; published in French translation as *Le massacre des juifs*, Paris, 1999.

PART ONE

Pre-histories

1

BRITISH GOVERNMENT POLICY TOWARDS WARTIME REFUGEES

COLIN HOLMES

Arrivé à huit heures à Weymouth après une traversée qui avait duré neuf heures, nous débarquâmes à une heure et apprîmes que l'on avait l'intention de nous envoyer dans une ville industrielle du Lancashire; nous étions stupéfaits. Etre obligés de quitter les plages ensoleillés et l'air limpide de Guernsey pour aller vivre dans une atmosphère de fumée, de pluie et de brouillard, voilà un avenir peu attrayant.

A school essay on evacuation, written in December 1940, quoted in B.A. Read, *No Cause for Panic – Channel Islands Refugees 1940–45*

I had my trepidations for a long time.
But yesterday I could wait no more.
I went to the phone and dialled a number: my number!
At the other end of the line, in my house, I heard an unknown voice saying that I wasn't there. I asked him if he knew what had happened to me, where I was, and he said he had moved in recently and that he didn't know.
I know perfectly well where I am . . . I am not really here, and over there,
I am no more.

'Neither Here nor There', by Himzo Skorupan, in *The Bend in the Road: Refugees Writing*

'The refugee crisis is a major world issue of the 1990s.'[1] In other words, the problems of the uprooted have continued to attract attention, even if, as in the past, the precise definition of 'refugee' has proved slippery.[2] Much of this recent interest has focused on the world beyond Europe, which increasingly since 1945 has witnessed major refugee migrations. As a result, many African, Asian, and Middle Eastern nations now contain a far higher proportion of refugees relative to their populations, than any European state.[3] However, Europe has also witnessed the continual creation of refugees, evident most recently in the upheavals in the Balkans. Religious and racial antipathies in Europe have both contributed to such problems. So too have the ravages of war, even though some groups displaced from their homelands through wartime pressures would not technically count as refugees under certain definitions.[4]

In the case of wartime exiles, the events of 1939 to 1945 assumed a particular significance: 'All told the number of people displaced by the . . . war in Europe amounted to 30 million — a number that is unfathomable in terms of human lives'.[5] During these years, 'Frontiers where each immigrant had been carefully filtered were crossed by millions whose passports were guns and whose visas were bullets. They set in motion millions of others who marched unarmed between streams of blood and tears'.[6] Britain could not stand aside from such developments.

A Fascinating Mixture of Nationalities and Races

In 1940 Britain stood exposed to Nazi Germany's expansionist policies. One is reminded of an earlier conflict, recalled in Wordsworth's poetry, when the country had stood alone 'the last that dare to struggle with the foe', on that occasion in the shape of Napoleon's France.[7] In 1940 a literary evocation of the country's mood can be found in George Orwell's *The Lion and the Unicorn*, written during the Luftwaffe's aerial bombardment. This explained its arresting opening sentence: 'As I write, highly civilised human beings are flying overhead, trying to kill me!'[8] If Orwell's work carried signs of apprehension, it also contained seeds of hope. 'If we come through this war,' he wrote, 'the defeat in Flanders will turn out to have been one of the great turning points in English history.'[9] The War might lead to major structural changes and society might change for the better.

This remark on the defeat in Flanders reminds us once again that between 1939 and 1945 the history of Britain was inextricably linked with events in Europe. It has been suggested that during these years Britain 'experienced the most remarkable and large-scale migration of peoples in its history'. As a result of the arrival of peoples who had fled in the face of Nazism, the country became 'a fascinating mix of nationalities and races'.[10] That phenomenon, in which Europeans in exile featured prominently, certainly caught the attention of some observers who lived through the War, as a graphic description of wartime London clearly shows. The writer vividly recalled:

> French sailors with their red pompoms and striped shirts, Dutch police in black uniforms and grey-silver braid, the dragoon-like mortar boards of Polish officers, the smart grey of nursing units from Canada, the cerise berets and sky-blue trimmings of the new parachute regiments, the scarlet lining of our own nurses' cloaks, the vivid electric blue of Dominion air forces, sandy bush hats and lion-coloured turbans, the prevalent Royal Air Force blue, a few greenish-tinted Russian uniforms and the suave black and gold of the Chinese navy.[11]

London, then, even cosmopolitan London, looked different during the wartime years as a consequence of the arrival of military personnel from other countries.[12] One needs to take a wider perspective, however, and sweep up other groups in order to paint a fuller picture. Jews featured heavily in Europe's population movements during the War, particularly in consequence of their forced deportations to the death camps, but some Jews from continental Europe did manage to enter Britain. It has been suggested that a figure of 'no more that 10,000', would constitute 'a reliable estimate' of the net increase in the Jewish refugee population during the War.[13]

But what of the still broader picture? A history of the immigration service, written from an insider's perspective, captures the bustle of activity created by the outbreak of war: 'Overnight the whole complexion of work both at Headquarters and at the ports had changed completely and the Immigration Officer found himself with all sorts of new powers to enforce.'[14] Departures and arrivals both came under scrutiny and 1940 proved to be a particularly busy time for monitoring the latter. Indeed, fears surfaced in official circles that troop movements might become clogged up by the presence of the refugees.[15] One can find newspaper pictures at this time of Belgians in flight and numerous references to the arrival of Dutch exiles.[16] Press reports also dwelt on the preparations then under way to cope with this immigration.[17] However, it is far from easy to ascertain the precise scale of such movement.

It has been claimed that 60,000 alien refugees reached Britain between May 1940 and December 1943, a key period for immigration. However, this figure does not include Allied forces living in Britain.[18] Another more recent source has suggested that 'over 70,000 refugees arrived in Britain during the Second World War'.[19]

But is there any official estimate? In 1943 a parliamentary answer, which took account of the situation in 1939 as well as entry during the War, gave a figure of 150,000 refugees, including children, who were then living in Britain.[20] Then, three years later, the Aliens Department of the Home Office maintained in a report addressed to the Foreign Office on the number of wartime refugees that:

> If children are excluded, the number of refugees who were in Britain at the outbreak of war or who entered subsequently was not less than 150,000. Excluding children, some 70–80,000 German, Austrian and Czech refugees were residing in Britain by the outbreak of war in September 1939; and from May 1940 to December 1943 when the United Kingdom became the immediate base for the attack on Hitler's continental fortress, some 60,000 refugees entered the country.[21]

It can be understood why 1943 was used as the upper chronological limit in this report: after that date intending refugees were often advised to stay where they were and to await their fate at the end of the war. In other respects the Home Office memorandum is less than satisfactory: there is a vagueness as to which groups it counted. However, a figure of 150,000 refugees living in Britain during the war, almost half of whom entered the country in the course of the war, and of whom the Belgians numbered 15,000, would seem to be reasonable.

Contributions to the War Effort

Whatever the precise numbers, the presence of refugees sheltering from Nazi terror could be turned to Britain's advantage. Some 35,000 Polish military personnel were among the early arrivals. Following the defeat of Poland they had re-grouped initially in France and then, with the subsequent collapse of that country in the face of the German advance, had made their way to Britain.[22] Not that these refugees constituted the only exiles from Poland. In accordance with the terms of the Nazi-Soviet pact of 23 August 1939, a rapprochement that stunned Europe's other capitals, and following the German attack on Poland in the subsequent month, the eastern part of the Polish state had been annexed by the USSR, with German approval. The Soviet authorities subsequently killed leading members of the Polish elite in this part of the country; one recalls the Katyn forest massacre carried out by the NKVD, as we now know, on Stalin's orders. Moreover, some 1.5 million Poles found themselves deported to remote regions of the Soviet Union.[23] Some deportees did not survive but others did, and with the breakdown of the Nazi-Soviet pact following the German invasion of the Soviet Union on 22 June 1941, the Soviet Union suddenly became an ally in the war against fascism. In these circumstances, those Polish military personnel and their families who had been languishing in Soviet camps found themselves released and the Second Polish Army Corps subsequently emerged under the command of General Anders. These Poles, who had no love for the Soviet Union, made their way westwards and eventually swelled the ranks of Polish exiles in wartime Britain.[24]

The early Polish exiles soon aligned themselves with the British war effort and contributed to the defeat of the Luftwaffe in the Battle of Britain.[25] However, as yet, their role in that conflict has received much less emphasis than the activities of young Englishmen such as Richard Hillary, around whom a substantial mythology has been constructed.[26] In the Battle of Britain the Poles fought alongside Czech airmen who had also moved westwards when their country was annexed by Germany.[27] Later in the war, Polish airborne troops fought alongside other paratroop units at the disastrous Battle of Arnhem in 1944.[28] Once again their contribution has been relatively neglected. Confirming this, the report in *The Times* on the fortieth anniversary of the battle commented on the 'bravery and losses' of the Polish contingent but emphasised that such valour had often remained 'overlooked'.[29] Not that Arnhem stands alone in the wartime memory of exiled Poland. The savage Battle of Monte Cassino, in Italy, also remains a powerful and painful reminder of the Poles at war in the west.[30]

The Poles needed little encouragement to engage in the struggle against Nazism: the British state could rely throughout the war on their wholehearted involvement. Other groups of exiles, such as the French and the various sections of European exiles who worked in the Special Operations Executive (SOE), also made their own contributions to the war effort. Some forms of involvement, however, were more complex. For example, after 1941 and the USSR's entry into the war, Austrian Communists who were intended to become NKVD agents in Nazi-occupied Europe, came to Britain to be trained by SOE for their future activities.[31]

Even so, the government still came under pressure, particularly in the early days of the war, to squeeze as much military support as it could from all alien groups in Britain. Hence suggestions surfaced in spring 1940 that a foreign legion should be formed out of the able-bodied refugees. In *The Times*, where the proposal received serious consideration, a leader column emphasised that 'there can be little objection to the formation from among both Poles and more recent refugees of a Foreign Legion; and there will

certainly be a widespread desire among the refugees themselves to
serve in this way if circumstances prevent them from serving in any
other'.[32] The proposal received enthusiastic letters of support and
a plan to form such a military grouping was submitted to the War
Office. In discussion it was further suggested that the legion should
be opened up to foreigners who were not refugees but were nevertheless living in Britain, as well as the citizens of neutral
countries.[33]

However, the proposal proved superfluous. The British Government had already taken steps to ensure the enlistment of
appropriate aliens into the ranks of the military[34] and the contributions which Poles and Czechs, for example, had already made to the
Allied cause underlined the involvement of exiles in the war effort.
But nonetheless the proposal was interesting. It surfaced at a time
when an increasing number of refugees were arriving from Europe
and, as will become clear later, doubts had already begun to surface
about the loyalty even of friendly aliens. In other words, the episode
needs to be related to the issue of loyalty and seen as part of a public campaign directed towards the government to secure the
bonding of aliens to the Allied cause.

The contribution of exiles to the war effort cannot be discussed
exclusively with reference to warriors in the field. Polish successes in
cracking German code traffic that had begun before the war assisted
the wartime work of British codebreakers at Bletchley Park.[35]
Moreover, the influence of refugee scholars from Central Europe
also assumed a marked significance. The persecution practised by
the Nazis after 1933 resulted in a significant emigration of scientists
from the greater Germany, and amongst those who came to Britain
'a large number . . . obtained temporary research fellowships at
Cambridge, and at other British Universities'. Indeed, 'The U.K.,
perhaps more than any other country, was . . . able to provide short-
term support to large numbers of intellectual émigrés . . .'[36] The
impact of this migration touched many areas of intellectual life in
Britain, and in the case of Jewish refugees, who featured prominently among such exiles, these developments have already been
carefully recorded and well documented.[37] In particular, the specific
wartime contributions that arose from scientific research proved to
be extremely important, notwithstanding the barriers placed in the
path of refugee intellectuals. 'When the war started', it has been
written, 'most British physicists were put on to radar, which was
regarded as the most urgent and also the most confidential task.
Refugee scientists were excluded from this work and were thus free
to continue their research in nuclear physics which was not
expected to have any practical application to the war.'[38] This

observation, however, is characterised by a degree of over-statement: refugee scientists did not have a trouble-free life even when they worked on the uranium bomb project.[39] Hence an official could write in October 1940: 'We are in principle . . . strongly opposed on security grounds to the employment of aliens on work of a secret nature unless it can be shown that every effort has been made to obtain British personnel and that the technical branch concerned is of the opinion that it is in the national interest to make use of their services'. However, at the time that this remark was made aliens and recently-naturalised aliens had already made a significant contribution to the workings of the Marsh Committee on the uranium bomb project that had begun its deliberations in the spring of 1940.[40] This research proved to be of enormous significance, to the extent that the standard history of the development of atomic energy in Britain during the Second World War has remarked on 'the great debt which the British project owed to the refugee scientists'.[41]

Exiles from Europe buttressed the state in other ways in the fight against fascism, for example in the war's propaganda battles. The earlier world conflict between 1914 and 1918 had been remarkable for the intensity of the propaganda campaigns launched by the leading powers and the struggles between 1939 and 1945 continued in a similar vein but on a more extensive scale, with the resources of radio and the cinema assuming an increasing significance. It is in the former service that the involvement of European exiles can be traced, including groups, such as Hungarians, who have generally slipped through the historian's net in accounts of the British homefront.[42] Similar work was performed by Italian Jewish exiles whose history has also remained almost completely hidden.[43] But a more substantial and recognised contribution derived from the refugees who had migrated from the greater Germany. While the Nazis employed British renegades such as John Amery and Walter Purdy to transmit their radio propaganda as well as the American-born William Joyce, the British authorities drew on the expertise of *émigrés* from Central Europe.[44]

An Emphasis on Restriction

Notwithstanding such contributions, the relationship of refugees with the British Government proved to be far from universally comfortable. Immigration controls, internment and deportation are key issues that reveal a darker side. It has been estimated that before the war the total intake of refugees from the greater Germany was

56,000.[45] However, with the onset of the war, immigration policy was tightened: 'All visas granted to enemy nationals prior to the outbreak of war automatically ceased to be valid on 3 September 1939'.[46] Against this background, Sir John Anderson, the Home Secretary, assured the House of Commons in May 1940 that he had also amended the 1920 Aliens Order, with a view to requiring refugees from Belgium and Holland to comply with restrictions similar to those imposed on enemy aliens. Anderson then continued: 'I can assure the House that every practical step is being, and will be taken, to safeguard this country against the entry of enemy aliens.'[47] The fear of potential damage from enemy aliens can be appreciated, but the tough response also evident towards Belgian and Dutch refugees is more revealing of the Government's interest in controlling the flow of European traffic. At this juncture in the parliamentary proceedings one MP suggested that such refugees should be transferred ultimately to Dutch and Belgian territories overseas. However, not all MPs were keen to dump these exiles beyond Europe. With an eye on economic possibilities, and probably with an awareness of what had already occurred with Jewish women exiles from Central Europe, it was asked whether the Dutch and Belgian women refugees could be employed in domestic work; after all, many middle-class families were struggling to retain their 'girls' as other employment opportunities beckoned during the war years.[48]

There was, then, no easy entry into Britain for Europe's exiles. There was talk about possible assistance to Jewish refugees, for example at the Bermuda Conference in 1943, but it was essentially half-hearted stuff, lacking in firm resolve. And the enthusiasm on the part of the British Government for strict entry controls can be underlined by evidence drawn from Hungary. In spring 1944, as the Nazi grip tightened on Hungary, the Western Allies received a proposal known as the 'blood for trucks' deal, whereby the Nazis offered to allow Hungarian Jews and also Jews in neighbouring countries to emigrate, other than to Palestine, in exchange for military hardware that would then be deployed exclusively on the Eastern Front against the Red Army. The Germans also expressed an interest in receiving supplies of coffee, tea and cocoa. For a variety of reasons the Allies rejected the deal.[49] However, in summer 1944 the Hungarian Government, realising the near certainty of a German defeat, put forward an offer to allow the unconditional emigration of certain categories of Jewish refugees. This proposal posed a more formidable problem for the British Government: no strings were attached to the offer. Throughout these later discussions, however, the Government displayed a marked reluctance to provide a positive response. In the event, the scheme collapsed because the German Government refused to allow the emigration that the Hungarians had envisaged. The willingness of the British and American governments to discuss the proposal might have placed a brake on the deportation of Budapest's Jews to Auschwitz. But the discussions revealed once again the restrictive nature of British immigration policy.[50]

This emphasis on restriction can also be seen in British policy towards Jewish immigration into Palestine, where Britain had operated the League of Nations mandate since the end of the First World War. The strict nature of entry policy can be deduced from the May 1939 White Paper, which remained 'the formal basis of British policy in Palestine throughout the war'.[51] It recommended that Jewish immigration should continue for a further five years, subject to a maximum of 75,000 new immigrants.[52] In the event, the total Jewish immigration into Palestine fell short of that number during these years: only 60 percent, or thereabouts, of the vouchers were issued.[53] Moreover, there was no significant increase in the number of Jews admitted to Britain's colonial empire.[54]

The refugees who managed to enter Britain did not always find the unfettered freedom that they might have expected. Refugee scientists were not the only group to face restrictions. The employment of refugees from Holland, Belgium and Norway was the subject of a parliamentary question in 1940, when it became clear that after registering with the police they could be put on the employment register at local labour exchanges. However, the sting in the response to the question came in its tail, with the observation that, 'Subject to security considerations they will be submitted for employment for which no suitable British subjects are available'.[55] When refugees had arrived in Britain before the war it was never intended that they should displace British workers. That policy continued during the war. It also persisted in the postwar world, as the experiences of Polish European Volunteer Workers (EVWs) and Hungarian exiles made abundantly clear.[56]

But during the war certain aliens faced more than restrictions on employment. True, the forced marches and calculated murder that disfigured Europe during the war were off the agenda, but even so tensions arose. Internment and deportation were among the weightier issues that pressed on some exiles. There is no need here to recount these developments in detail. However, the unfolding outline of events should be recalled. Before the War, the British Government had concluded that some enemy aliens would have to be interned, and when hostilities began in 1939 a number of detentions occurred. In addition, on 4 September 1939 the government

announced a review of all German and Austrian nationals then living in Britain. As a result, an estimated 528 enemy aliens were
interned by January 1940. The major move on detention came later,
however, in spring 1940, as the Western European countries collapsed like a pack of cards in the face of the German armies'
advance. By the end of 1940 almost all enemy aliens regarded by the
authorities as dangerous had been interned. After 10 June 1940,
when Italy entered the war, Italians also became targets for internment. It has been estimated that 22,000 Germans and Austrians
finished up in camps, as did 4,300 Italians. The cull had been completed by summer 1940.

With this policy of internment in place, a process of deportation
began, mainly to Canada and Australia. However, this created its
own problems. The authorities had to contend with the consequences of alien deportees being robbed and generally ill-treated en
route to Australia, aboard the *Dunera*.[57] A greater tragedy occurred
on 2 July 1940 when the *Arandora Star* sank, with the loss of 650
lives. Many of the victims were Italians, the deaths of whom are
marked by a plaque at the magnificent St. Peter's Church in Hol-
born; the incident wounded the Italian minority in Britain deeply.[58]
The structure of internment proved to be short-lived, however. By
the end of July 1940 a White Paper laid down that certain classes of
internees could be released. This release programme accelerated
during the course of 1941, and by the end of August only two
camps remained on the Isle of Man. By the closing stages of the war
only a hard core of detainees languished in Britain's internment
camps.[59]

What are we to make of such developments? And what lay
behind them? In the case of immigration control, policy during the
Second World War can be traced back to the 1919 Aliens Act and
the associated Orders in Council. This legislation had granted the
state considerable powers relating to the entry, residence, employment and deportation of all aliens. The freedoms associated with
the Victorian world were swept away, and the 1919 Act continued
to exercise a tight grip on immigration policy from 1920 to 1971.[60]
The internment policy pursued during the war also had links with
the past. The First World War had witnessed the detention of enemy
aliens and files regarding this episode were taken down from the
shelves, dusted and perused to provide the framework for the policy that was followed during the later world conflict. Even the
location of the camps reflected continuity: the Isle of Man featured
as a major centre of detention in both World Wars.[61]

Nevertheless, historical precedent did not always guarantee the
consistent and smooth implementation of policy. Considerable

differences could open up between departments. As a result, it is mistaken, when considering wartime policy, to write of 'the bureaucratic machine of civil servants, security services, policemen and soldiers', as if they constituted a united and unified repressive force.[62] During the world conflict MI5 pressed the case for internment in the strongest terms, and its officers proved capable of discovering a dreaded fifth column lurking behind every alien. By contrast, the Home Office adopted a more liberal and restrained approach. This difference applied, incidentally, not only to the internment of enemy aliens but also to the detention of British fascists.[63] That fascists also had to face up to the prospect of internment underlines the fact that there was a general tightening of social and political control by the state during the Second World War. This happened to such an extent, indeed, that, according to one commentator, the battery of controls in Britain pressed more heavily on the population than did the rules and regulations imposed by other combatants on their respective populations, even including those in the USSR.[64]

This reference to Stalin's USSR serves as a reminder that public and official responses towards exiles in Britain were affected not only by national influences, such as the threat of German invasion, but also by international developments. Policy on internment swung wildly, both as circumstances changed in Europe and as the mood in Britain shifted from apprehension to the first stirrings of hope. Moreover, attitudes towards friendly aliens also mirrored such international shifts. Hence perceptions of Poles were affected by the changing image of the USSR. After 1941, a group that opposed the interests of the Soviet Union, or that wanted to distance itself from Stalin's Bear, was destined to encourage a degree of frustration. Polish anxieties in exile, which related to prewar national boundaries and the later treatment of Poles by Russians, with the Katyn forest massacre serving as a particularly deep wound, did not attract universal sympathy. 'Russia is wonderful', served as the theme of a Mass Observation survey report in 1943.[65] True, some uncertainty was noted in Home Intelligence reports, regarding, for example, the postwar aims of the Soviet Union and some short-term disquiet in 1944 at the Soviet refusal to assist the Warsaw uprising, but such issues remained significantly overshadowed by the 'unbounded admiration' for the Red Army's successes in the field.[66] Similar sentiments surfaced in official circles. After all, Churchill came to regard Stalin as someone who, with a little more sophistication, could be treated like a member of one's club. This was a dangerous illusion but a powerful one, and a view closely aligned to the generally warm image of 'Uncle Joe' and the USSR that began to exercise a grip on British public opinion after the Soviet Union became an ally.[67]

This all suggests that official policy and the wider currents of public opinion often swam together, and the claim is further underlined by the history of the imposition of internment and deportation. In April 1940, Mass Observation reported: 'IT IS BECOMING THE SOCIALLY DONE THING TO BE ANTI-REFUGEE'.[68] By May 1940, following news of collaboration with the Germans in Holland, the same organisation reported that anti-semitism and anti-alien sentiment had 'become the currency of respectable talk'.[69] Furthermore, newspapers such as the liberal *Manchester Guardian* and even the *Jewish Chronicle*, which had previously adopted a pro-refugee stance, fell in behind the policy of internment. The famed liberal tolerance that allegedly characterised British opinion had melted like spring snow to reveal a darker feelings lurking beneath the surface.[70] Such sentiment was supplemented by opinion in newspapers sympathetic to a Conservative position. The Kemsley, Beaverbrook and Rothermere presses maintained their hostility, which had been revealed in the 1930s, to refugees and thereby added to the pressures that encouraged the government to act.[71] In early 1940 even neutral aliens, such as the Italians, came under suspicion. A letter in *The Times* in the spring of that year began innocuously enough with the observation: 'In almost every town of any size in England there are bright-looking Italian cafés', but it then emphasised that in view of the links between Italy and Germany, 'the attractive little Italian cafe will be required to play its part in the wide reach of Hitler's elaborately complete system of espionage.' A wise step, therefore, would be to place 'all Italian restaurants and cafés out of bounds to members of our fighting services'.[72] Before 10 June, when Italy had entered the war and before the collective violence launched against the Italian communities in London and Edinburgh when it did do so, such suspicions had already become commonplace, and this helped to grease the wheels of the internment policy pursued against the Italian minority later in the year.[73]

However, public opinion did not always align itself with official policy. A Gallup poll in February 1943 on the question of admitting to Britain those Jews threatened with death in Europe, revealed that 78 percent of the sample supported their admission, whether on a temporary or a permanent basis. Such sentiment, however, did not influence the cautious outlook of the government, which continued to emphasise, even into the final year of the war, that the arrival of Jews would generate antisemitism and social unrest.[74]

Individual Cases

Thus far, individuals have barely been mentioned in these discussions. But now individual refugees will give testimony to their personal experiences. First, let us consider Reuben Ainsztein. When I first met him in London at a meeting of a Yad Vashem Committee, I was not fully aware of his background, and even after the publication in 1974 of his most important book, *Jewish Resistance in Nazi-Occupied Eastern Europe*, part of his life still remained in the shadows. Brought into the light it is, by any standards, a remarkable story. Born in Wilno in 1917, when the city survived under German occupation, he left it in 1936 because of the *numerus clausus* that controlled the entry of Jews into what was then a Polish university. He enrolled as a medical student in Brussels, and by 1938 had mastered English sufficiently to teach it, in order to finance his way through medical school. This mastery of English should be viewed as a part of a larger interest in England and Englishness. A 1981 article about him in *The Times* noted: 'From an early age he developed an obsession about England, nurtured by his wide and varied readings of English literature. He passionately longed to join the English-speaking world and was encouraged by the writings of Joseph Conrad to believe that he might do so.'[75] Conrad, it will be recalled, can be counted as the most Polish of English novelists.[76]

However, the British Government's tight immigration policy meant that Ainsztein could not satisfy the requirements for entry into Britainand he was also unsuccessful in his attempts to join the British Army. On the outbreak of war he appealed personally to Sir Samuel Hoare, the Secretary of State for Air, and received permission to join the RAF. Officials in Britain refused a visa, but they had not counted on Ainsztein's tenacity and determination. He travelled from Belgium to France, hoping to cross the Channel to no avail. He returned consequently to Belgium and lived for fifteen months under Nazi occupation. When the Nazis introduced the mandatory registration of Jews on 28 October 1941, he left once again, this time with the intention of crossing France and Spain in order to reach Portugal, en route, he hoped, to the elusive distant magnet of England. However, Spanish police detained him in 1942 and incarcerated him in a camp at Miranda de Ebro. There he remained for 14 months until, along with other inmates, he secured his release following a hunger strike. In June 1943 he sailed for Scotland on board an American liner. Once in Britain he achieved his ambition of joining the RAF and flew his first mission on 8 September 1944. Shot down on 15 January 1945, he parachuted into Belgium and eventually reached safety. What purchase here, has the hoary old

stereotype of Jews as cowards? After returning to Britain to conva-
lesce, he passed the remainder of the War in RAF intelligence.[77] It is
a stirring account that reminds us that behind the history of the legislation which restricted alien immigration and alongside the general
awareness of the contributions made by European exiles to the fight
against Nazism, there lie human stories of pain and hope, of rebuff
and determination and, in Ainsztein's case, of gritty satisfaction.

Reuben Ainsztein experienced difficulties in entering Britain. But
exiles who managed to enter the country more easily, if not with
effortless ease, could also experience problems. The career of Arnost
Kleinzeller provides a case in point. Born in 1914, Kleinzeller came
to Britain as a young refugee, financed by the Czech Refugee Trust
Fund. He became attached to the Department of Biochemistry at the
University of Sheffield where he worked under the supervision of Dr
Hans Krebs, himself a refugee from Nazism and, later, a recipient of
a Nobel Prize. Krebs had left Germany in 1933 and after a period in
Cambridge had been appointed head of the Department of Biochemistry at Sheffield in 1938.[78] In that fateful spring of 1940, which
has intruded so often into our discussion, Krebs contacted the Czech
Refugee Trust Fund in order to draw attention to Kleinzeller's difficulties. Why? Krebs stressed that the University buildings that
housed his Department had been declared a "special area", prohib-
ited to enemy aliens on grounds of security. Krebs continued: 'For
reasons which are obscure to me Dr. Kleinzeller is being treated as an
enemy alien although he is Czech and he had to interrupt his work
in the laboratory'. Krebs added that in view of Kleinzeller's difficulties attempts were under way to secure alternative laboratory
facilities.[79] By 2 July this problem had been solved.[80] So far so good.

However, by the autumn of 1940 a further difficulty had arisen.
Whereas another Czech postgraduate student apparently proceeded
smoothly on course, Kleinzeller hit more turbulence as a result of his
interest in aiding the war effort.[81] In order for Kleinzeller to continue
with his work the University needed to secure his clearance from the
Aliens War Services Department. However, it did not act. Other students also started to be caught in the net. By November 1940 Krebs's
exasperation became apparent when he wrote to Esther Simpson,
the saviour and patron of many refugees, in her capacity as General
Secretary of the Society for the Protection of Science and Learning:

> Since I wrote [last] conditions have grown worse in that a number of
> alien refugee students who were accepted by the University at the
> beginning of the session, with the special permission of the local police,
> have now been ordered by the Vice-Chancellor to discontinue their
> courses. A large number of my colleagues are most perturbed about
> this and steps are being organised to demand at least an explanation.[82]

In desperation Krebs also contacted Eleanor Rathbone M.P., another well-known defender of refugees' interests, emphasising, 'If the Government sets up a machinery in the form of the Alien War Services Department, to deal with the applications of aliens to work in special areas, it can hardly be their intention to prevent applications from being made'.[83]

We do not know precisely how the problem was solved. Krebs's correspondence on the matter dries up after Rathbone's sympathetic reply.[84] And, unsurprisingly, the official history of the University sheds no light on the episode.[85] We do know, however, that Kleinzeller remained in the University; he received his Ph.D. in 1941 for a thesis on intermediate metabolism. After the war Kleinzeller returned home, continued with his research, and for a time continued a correspondence with Krebs.[86] As late as 1995 he was known by the University of Sheffield to be living in Philadelphia.[87] The gaps in detail on the Kleinzeller affair are irritating and a sighting after 1995 would also be welcomed. But the significance of the tensions in 1940 and 1941 lies elsewhere and can be deduced from existing sources. Kleinzeller's experiences reveal that even friendly aliens who escaped internment in 1940 could nevertheless experience serious disruption to their lives during the dark, threatening days of the early stages of the war. Such episodes reveal how difficult some British authorities found it to distinguish between enemy aliens and friendly aliens. They all came from faraway countries of which little was known and could be lumped together as potentially dangerous. Such haziness mirrored the responses towards aliens in the First World War, when distinctions between Russian and German territories were not always sharply made and consistently maintained.[88] Finally, the problems faced by Kleinzeller also reveal the importance of local influences and, particularly, the power of the local state. In Sheffield the Chief Constable and Irvine Masson, the Vice-Chancellor of the University, who seems to have eaten out of the police chief's hand, made policy shifts on arbitrary and seemingly wrongheaded premises that guaranteed that researchers there of friendly alien status were treated differently from their contemporaries in Bristol, Cambridge and Liverpool, with Kleinzeller's case the most glaring and best known to us of such inconsistency.

Conclusions

The remark that 'studies of minorities in war remain relatively few despite the expansion of ethnic history',[89] even though the Holocaust is a noteworthy exception, brings several final thoughts to mind. As in previous wars the conflict between 1939 and 1945 succeeded in dividing 'them' from 'us' both in popular and official thought and action. At times it also underscored the belief that we often hate our enemies more than we love our friends. In the First World War the British Government had interned German nationals. It did so again in the later conflict. In the Great War, friendly aliens such as Russian Jews had come under attack; we have noted that between 1939 and 1945 friendly aliens once more ran into opposition. In the case of Belgians, memories derived from their presence during the Great War were revived and once more entered into circulation.[90] The distinctions between friendly aliens and enemy aliens were rarely coherently made and immigration debates are remarkable and fascinating in the way that they reveal this confusion. Moreover, such confusion sometimes spread into official initiatives. The policy of internment, for example, threw up a number of significant anomalies, most notably relating to the detention of well-known anti-Nazis such as Jürgen Kuczynski,[91] and also the seeming inability of the authorities to assess precisely the nationality of some aliens whose lives had been disrupted forever by the national boundary changes that followed the First World War.

In many respects one receives the impression that, once Edmund Burke's 'slender dyke' of the Channel had been crossed, all aliens could come under suspicion. That observation could certainly be supported by the events of the early stages of the war, especially during times of national crisis. In such circumstances responses and policies emerged that would suggest that Britain's fabled liberal toleration did not always prevail, and that in wartime the country did not always witness 'the triumph of decency over evil'.[92] That inference needs to be drawn even though various groups were allowed to re-group under the British Government's protection and hence survive the war, notably the Belgians, the Czechs, the Dutch, the French and the Poles. But internment and deportation provided the other side of the coin.

Even so, a rigid distinction between antipathy and sympathy would simplify unduly the wartime situation. Attitudes towards minorities are at all times full of ambiguity and ambivalence: hostility and toleration, antipathy and sympathy, whichever terms are used, were capable of co-existing simultaneously. Even groups such as the Czechs and the Dutch exiles who found much public sympathy and support also had their detractors who held unfavourable opinions. In some cases, of which the Poles provide an example, public opinion often divided along gender lines, with women holding a more positive view. The case of the Poles also demonstrates how images could change according to new circumstances. As we have seen, the growing popularity of the Soviet Union as a powerful ally in the struggle against fascism sometimes led to negative public perceptions of exiled Poles. But, in addition, the outbreak of open anti-Semitism in the Polish Army in the course of 1944 did the image of the Poles no good at all within the British Government and other circles.[93]

This idea of the complexity of responses can be pushed a stage further. It was not uncommon for a positive virtue to be made out of intolerance. In the month before the outbreak of the war, Walter Oakeshott, then High Master of St. Paul's School, wrote to *The Times* and stated:

> What has caused trouble in Central European countries has been the existence of Jewish minorities as separate entities, unabsorbed by the nations among which they lived. Refugees can and are already making a great contribution to the life of the country. How can we enable them to make it in the next generation, not only . . . as honoured guests but as Englishmen?[94]

In other words, in the last resort, 'I do not accept you for what you are but only when you become like me'. This belief cannot be regarded as unusual. On the contrary, it has constituted a common thread in the thinking of liberal defenders of immigration into Britain during the twentieth century.[95] Such sentiment was certainly present in responses towards Jews during the war. Hence the observation that the strength of British antisemitism during the world conflict lay not in the type of violence that characterised Nazi policy but in the demand echoed by prominent members of the Government that Jews, British-born and refugees alike, must assimilate as a way forward towards a safer future. At the same time as such demands were being placed on these groups, they were being denied equal access to society's scarce resources.[96]

Finally, it should be noted that writers on immigration into Britain have tended to focus on those groups that arrived from 'beyond the oceans'.[97] In this respect the wartime years, characterised chiefly by the entry of European groups, provide a much-needed balancing perspective. Moreover, it further reminds us, taking a broader view, that the majority of people who have arrived in Britain during the twentieth century have been from white ethnic groups.[98] The arrival of such groups during the Second World War followed a long history of immigration from Europe, most notably of the political exiles in the nineteenth century who arrived from many countries and reflected a variety of political opinions, and stretching back to the Huguenots, the French Protestants who fled from persecution in the sixteenth and seventeenth centuries, the Hanseatic merchants who cemented trading links between England and Europe, as well as to the even earlier Lombards and Flemings of the medieval epoch. That sample alone reflects the continual process of European movement.[99] Some of these people eventually returned home, back to their original roots. But for others, particularly refugees, their final resting place lay in what we now call Britain. Hence the poignant observation: 'Many corners of English graveyards are for ever Poland, or Italy or Spain.'[100] In the course of the Second World War it was recognised that some refugees would not return home.[101] Indeed, in the autumn of 1945 the impossibility of complete repatriation was recognised at the highest levels of government.[102] If, then, the wartime experiences need to be located against a larger background of previous European migration, it has also to be recognised that the consequences of the wartime migration of some acute and anticipatory refugees spilled over into the postwar world.[103] For Poles, and German and Austrian Jews, particularly, no quick return to continental Europe took place. Many individuals from such groups, like many earlier European exiles, proceeded to live and die far away from their original roots, bearing witness in their lives to the traumas and upheavals of the twentieth century and underscoring the significance of 'exile', that 'gaunt, harsh word', in Europe's history.[104]

Notes

1. Royal Geographical Society, *Geography and Refugee Policy*, London, 1993, p. 3.
2. D. Joly, et al, *Refugees in Europe – The Hostile New Agenda*, London, 1997, pp. 7–10. See also G. Melander, 'The concept of the term "Refugee"', in *Refugees in the Age of Total War*, ed. A.C. Bramwell, London, 1988, pp. 7–14.
3. Joly, *Refugees in Europe*, p. 3. See also M. Marrus, *The Unwanted*, New York, 1985, p. 365.
4. Royal Geographical Society, *Geography and Refugee Policy*, p. 6.
5. L.P. Moch, *Moving Europeans. Migration in Western Europe since 1850*, Bloomington and Indianapolis, 1992, p. 169.
6. E. Kulischer, *Europe on the Move*, New York, 1948, p. 255. See also M.J. Proudfoot, *European Refugees 1939–52, A Study in Forced Population Movement*, London, 1957, for additional detail. There is later comment in Marrus, *The Unwanted*, pp. 190–295.
7. See W. Wordsworth, 'November 1806', in *The Poetical Works of Wordsworth*, ed. T. Hutchinson, London, 1953, p. 247.
8. G. Orwell, *The Lion and the Unicorn – Socialism and the English Genius*, Harmondsworth, 1982, p. 35 [First published 1941]. For historical works on this period, see L. Thompson, *1940, Year of Legend – Year of History*, London, 1966 and the later studies, C. Ponting, *1940: Myth and Reality*, London, 1990 and R. Collier, *The years of Attrition, 1940–1941*, London, 1995.
9. Orwell, *The Lion and the Unicorn*, p. 79.

10. J. Walvin, *Passage to Britain. Immigration in British History and Politics*, Harmondsworth, 1984, p. 90.
11. W. Sansom, *Westminster at War*, London, 1947, p. 167. For a more general picture of the wartime capital, see P. Ziegler, *London at War 1939–1945*, London, 1995.
12. C. Holmes, 'Cosmopolitan London', in *London, the Promised Land?* ed. A.J. Kershen, Aldershot, 1997, pp. 10–37.
13. Report of the Anglo-American Committee of Inquiry regarding the problems of European Jewry and Palestine, Cmd 6808, London, 1945–46, p. 59.
14. T.W.E. Roche, *The Key in the Lock – A History of Immigration Control in England from 1066 to the Present Day*, London, 1969, p. 129.
15. A. Calder, *The People's War – Britain 1939–1945*, London, 1994 ed., p. 129.
16. *The Times*, 15 and 17 May 1940. The Ministry of Home Intelligence noted some tension regarding the arrival of the Belgians. See PRO INF 1/264, Reports of 3 June 1940, 21 June 1940, 29 June 1940, 7 August 1940. See Part Two of this volume for a comprehensive assessment of the Belgians in Britain during the War. See Part Three, ch. 13 of this volume for D. Barnouw on the Dutch.
17. *The Times*, 16 May 1940.
18. B. Wasserstein, *Britain and the Jews of Europe 1939–1945*, Oxford, 1979, p. 82.
19. T. Kushner, *The Persistence of Prejudice – Antisemitism in British Society during the Second World War*, Manchester, 1979, p. 152.
20. *Parliamentary Debates* (Commons) vol. 388, 1942–43, 7 April 1943, col. 637 (written answers).
21. PRO FO 371/57739/WR 338. My thanks to Sean Kelly for this reference.
22. J. Zubrzycki, *Polish Immigrants in Britain – A Study of Adjustment*, The Hague, 1956; Idem, *Soldiers and Peasants: The Sociology of Polish Migration*, London, 1988, contains later reflections on the Poles in Britain.
23. N. Davies, *God's Playground – A History of Poland in Two Volumes*, vol. 2 – *1795 to the Present*, Oxford 1981, chapter 20. See also J. Bardach and K. Gleeson, *Man is Wolf to Man: Surviving Stalin's Gulag*, Berkeley, 1998 and, more recently, S. Waydenfeld, *The Ice Road*, Edinburgh, 1999.
24. W. Anders, *An Army in Exile*, London, 1949. For more general comment on Poland and Poles during the War, see J. Garlinski, *Poland in the Second World War*, London, 1985.
25. A. Fiedler, *Squadron 303*, London 1943; 303 was the Kosciusko Squadron. The Polish contribution to this 'spitfire summer' was recognised in 'Passage to Britain', Channel 4 TV, 16 May 1984.
26. See R. Hillary, *The Last Enemy*, London, 1942 and S. Faulks, *Fatal Englishmen. Three Short Lives*, London, 1996, pp. 111–208.
27. Fiedler, *Squadron*, chapter 13, 'A Gallant Czech. Sergeant Frantisek'. A permanent recognition of the role of Czech forces in the Allied victory can be found in a plaque in Chester Cathedral. See generally on the Czech military contribution, A. Brown, 'The Czech Armed Forces in Britain', Prt Three, ch. 10 of this volume and also his doctoral thesis, 'The Czechoslovak Air Force in Britain, 1940–1945' (Ph.D. diss., University of Southampton, 1998). There is also an interesting vignette in the *Sunday Telegraph*, 21 February 1999.
28. R. McOwan, 'The Friendly Invasion', *Scots Magazine*, ns (1982), p. 487.
29. *The Times*, 24 September 1984.
30. The serried ranks of crosses at the military cemetery in Newark, the location from which the remains of General Sikorski were recently disinterred and transferred to Poland, serves as a bleak permanent reminder of exiled Polish losses in the Allied cause. *The Times*, 4 March 1999, carried a reminder on Polish

involvement at Monte Cassino. P. Latawski, 'The Polish Armed Forces in
Britain', paper presented at the Conference on European Exile Communities in
Britain 1940–45, at Balliol College, Oxford, 1 October 1998, provided a recent
account of Polish military involvement in the War. For the most recent assess-
ment of the wider Polish experience in exile in Britain see J. Zamojski, Part
Three, ch. 11 of this volume.

31. N. Atkin, 'The French Community in Britain' (Part Three, ch. 12 of this volume), discusses the exiled French community in all its complexity. M.R.D. Foot,
*SOE in France: an account of the Work of the British Special Operations Exec-
utive*, London 1966, contains references to the involvement of exiles. See B.
McLoughlin, 'Proletarian Cadres en route: Austrian NKVD agents in Britain,
1941–43', *Labour History Review*, vol. 62 (1997), pp. 296–317, on Austrian
agents.

32. *The Times*, 15 May 1940.

33. Ibid, 17 May 1940.

34. See the letter from the Marchioness of Reading in ibid, 21 May 1940.

35. F.H. Hinsley, et al, *British Intelligence in the Second World War – Its Influence
on Strategy and Operations*, vol. 1 London, 1979, pp. 487–95, on code breaking.

36. P.K. Hoch, 'The Reception of Central European Refugee Physicists of the
1930s: USSR, UK, USA', *Annals of Science*, vol. 40 (1983), p. 222 and, generally, A.J. Sherman, *Island Refuge: Britain and Refugees from the Third Reich
1933–1939*, London, 1973.

37. W.E. Mosse, et al, *Second Chance. Two Centuries of German-Speaking Jews in
the United Kingdom*, Tübingen, 1991.

38. A.J.P. Taylor, *English History 1914–1945*, Harmondsworth, 1979 ed., p. 598.

39. M. Gowing, *Britain and Atomic Energy 1939–1945*, London, 1965 ed., p. 46.

40. Ibid, pp. 45–46.

41. Ibid, p. 176.

42. Kellner Gyorgy, *Magyar antifasisztak Angliaban 1940–1945*, Budapest, 1983.

43. L. Sponza, unpublished manuscript and A. Briggs, *The War of Words, The History of Broadcasting in the United Kingdom*, vol. 3 Oxford, 1995, pp.
395–401.

44. Briggs, *War of Words*, Section 5, see also M. Balfour, *Propaganda in War,
1939–1945: Organisation, Policies and Publics in Britain*, London, 1979; *Film
and Radio Propaganda in World War II*, ed. K.R.M. Short, London, 1983; J.F.
Slattery, '"Oskar Zuversichtlich" a German Response to British radio propaganda during World War II', *Historical Journal of Film, Radio and Television*
12 (1992): pp. 69–85, which all provide detail.

45. Wasserstein, *Britain and the Jews*, pp. 7 and 81.

46. Ibid, p. 81.

47. *Parliamentary Debates* (Commons), vol. 361, 1939–40, 23 May 1940, col.
298.

48. Ibid, cols 299–300, T.Kushner, 'An Alien Occupation: Jewish Refugees and
Domestic Service in Britain, 1933–1948', in Mosse, *Second Chance*, pp.
553–78, notes the employment of refugees in this capacity in the early twentieth century. With tongue in cheek, Auberon Waugh in the *Sunday Telegraph*, 11
April 1999, noted that women refugees from Kosovo might help to solve the
servant problem in England.

49. A. Weissberg, *Advocate for the Dead: The Story of Joel Brand*, London, 1958.
See also R. Braham, *The Politics of Genocide*, New York, 1981, pp. 921–951.

50. See Braham, *Genocide*, pp. 113–18.

51. Wasserstein, *Britain and the Jews*, p. 8.

52. *Palestine – Statement of Policy*, Cmd 6019, London, 1938–39, p. 1.
53. W. Laqueur, *A History of Zionism*, New York, 1972, p. 35.
54. Wasserstein, *Britain and the Jews*, p. 38.
55. *Parliamentary Debates* (Commons), vol. 361, 1939–40, 13 June 1940, col. 1404, written answers and ibid, vol. 362, 1939–40, 4 July 1940, cols. 978–979.
56. K. Sword et al, *The Formation of the Polish Community in Great Britain 1939–1950*, London, 1989; J.A. Tannahill, *European Volunteer Workers in Britain*, Manchester, 1958; D. Kay and R. Miles, *Refugees or Migrant Workers? European Volunteer Workers in Britain 1946–1951*, London, 1992, and C. Holmes, 'Hungarian Refugees in Britain', unpublished manuscript.
57. C. Pearl, *The Dunera Scandal, The WW2 Injustice Britain and Australia tried to Forget*, London, 1983. 'The Dunera Boys' formed the subject of a television play transmitted on Channel 4 TV on 15 and 16 October 1985.
58. L. Sponza, 'The British Government and the Internment of Aliens', in *The Internment of Aliens in Twentieth Century Britain*, eds D. Cesarani and T. Kushner, London, 1993, pp. 125–144. PRO INF 1/264, Reports of 16 July 1940, 29 July 1940 and 3 August 1940 reflect public disquiet in London over the problems of the Italian minority.
59. See from the growing literature, Wasserstein, *Britain and the Jews*, ch. 3; Kushner, *The Persistence of Prejudice*, pp. 142ff; Sponza, 'The British Government'; F. Lafitte, *The Internment of Aliens*, Harmondsworth, 1940; P. and L. Gillman, *Collar the Lot*, London, 1980; and C. Holmes, *John Bull's Island – Immigration and British Society1871–1971*, London, 1988, ch. 4. For personal reminiscences see A. Perles, *Alien Corn*, London, 1944 and P. Leoni, *I shall die on the carpet*, London, 1966.
60. V. Bevan, *The Development of British Immigration Law*, London, 1986, pp. 72–73.
61. J.C. Bird, *Control of Enemy Alien Civilians in Great Britain 1914–1918*, London, 1981 and P. Panayi, *The Enemy in Our Midst – Germans in Britain during the First World War*, Oxford 1991, focus on the treatment of enemy aliens in the earlier world conflict.
62. P. Panayi, 'Introduction', in *Minorities in Wartime*, ed. P. Panayi, Oxford 1993, p. 18, is therefore too simplistic.
63. C. Holmes, '"British Justice at Work": Internment in the Second World War', in ibid, pp. 150–65. See also *The Times*, 6 August 1998 on MI5's over-zealous approach, on evidence drawn from PRO HO 45/23672.
64. Taylor, *English History*, p. 616.
65. 'Some Notes and Feelings about Russia', 10 March 1943, Tom Harrison Mass-Observation Archive (THMO), University of Sussex, File Report 1623, p. 3. On Mass Observation there is T. Jeffrey, *Mass Observation: a Short History*, Birmingham, 1978.
66. See, for example, PRO INF 1/292, Report of 25 July–1 August 1944 and PRO INF 1/292, Report of 15–22 August 1944. On Home Intelligence, see I. McLaine, *Ministry of Morale – Home Front Morale and the Ministry of Information in World War II*, London, 1979.
67. Sir Frank Roberts, evidence in 'Cold War', BBC 2 Television, 19 September 1998. For other evidence on the warmth of sentiment see F.D. Klingender, *Russia – Britain's Ally 1812–1942*, London, 1942. See also PRO INF 1/292, Weekly Reports, 6–13 October 1941, 26 May–4 June 1942, 1–8 September 1942, 12–19 January 1943 and 26 January-2 February 1943, for example, as well as the later reports (cited in note 66). For a more generally accessible source see P. Lewis, *A People's War* London, 1986, chapter 9.
68. THMO 79 'Public Feeling about Aliens', 25 April 1940, p. 11.

69. THMO 107 'Feeling about Aliens', 14 May 1940, p. 1.
70. *Manchester Guardian*, 13 May 1940; *Jewish Chronicle*, 24 May 1940.
71. Kushner, *The Persistence of Prejudice*, p. 143.
72. Major Gordon Home in *The Times*, 20 May 1940. Home Office papers just released, also dwell on Mussolini's use of Italian cafes as a front for Italian fascism, see PRO HO 144/21079.
73. On the internment of Italians see Leoni, *I shall die*; Sponza, 'The British Government'; *The Collected Essays, Journalism and Letters of George Orwell*, vol. 2, *My Country Right or Left, 1940–1943*, eds. S. Orwell and I. Angus, Harmondsworth, 1980 ed., p. 394, reveals the hostility towards Italians at the entry of Italy into the War.
74. PRO CAB 96/15, Minutes of Cabinet Committee on Refugees, 16 May 1945.
75. *The Times*, 8 December 1981.
76. Z. Najder, *Conrad's Polish Background. Letters to and from Polish Friends*, London, 1964, p. 234, 'It is widely known that I am a Pole . . . It does not seem to me that I have been unfaithful to my country by having proved to the English that a gentleman from the Ukraine can be as good a sailor as they, and has something to tell them in their own language'. [Letter to Józef Korzeniowski, 14 February 1901].
77. All from *The Times*, 8 December 1981.
78. A.W. Chapman, *The Story of a Modern University: A History of The University of Sheffield*, Oxford, 1955, pp. 366–7. See *The Dictionary of National Biography 1981–1985*, eds Lord Blake and C.S. Nicholls, Oxford, 1990, pp. 229–30, for outline details on Krebs, as well as H. Krebs, in collaboration with A. Martin, *Reminiscences and Reflections*, Oxford, 1981 for Krebs' self-assessments of his life. He also features on an Imperial War Museum Tape [IWM Tape 004498/05, in the series 'Britain and the Refugee Crisis 1933–1945'].
79. Krebs to the Czech Refugee Trust Fund, 21 June 1940, Krebs File J333, University of Sheffield Archives.
80. Krebs to the Czech Refugee Trust Fund, 2 July 1940, Krebs File J333, University of Sheffield Archives.
81. Krebs to the Society for the Protection of Science and Learning, 5 September 1940 and Krebs to Alien War Services Department, 18 November 1940, Krebs File J333, University of Sheffield Archives.
82. Krebs to Simpson, 4 November 1940, Krebs File J333, University of Sheffield Archives. On Simpson see the obituary in *The Times*, 30 November 1996 and also R. Cooper, *Refugee Scholars – Conversations with Tess Simpson*, Leeds, 1992.
83. Krebs to Rathbone, 4 December 1940, Krebs File J333, University of Sheffield Archives.
84. Rathbone to Krebs, 8 December 1940, Krebs File J333, University of Sheffield Archives.
85. Chapman, *Modern University*, chapter 32 and Appendix F discuss war work in the University but in anodyne fashion.
86. See *Symposium on Membrane Thought and Metabolism*, eds A. Kleinzeller and A. Kotyk, Prague, 1961. For the correspondence with Krebs see Krebs File J334, University of Sheffield Archives.
87. University of Sheffield Record Card.
88. Holmes, *John Bull's Island*, pp. 98 and 342, Note 63.
89. Panayi, *Minorities in Wartime*, p. 18.
90. A. Smith, 'War and ethnicity: the role of warfare in the formation, self-images and cohesion of ethnic communities', *Ethnic and Racial Studies* 4 (1981): pp. 375–97; Holmes, *John Bull's Island*, Part II, summarises the drift of

developments during the Great War. See PRO INF 1/264, Report of 3 June
1940 on the revival of hostility towards the Belgians. See also MO174
'Refugees . . . Cricklewood', 6 June 1940, p. 2. Belgian experiences in Britain in
the First World War are discussed in P. Cahalan, *Belgian Refugee Relief in England during the Great War*, New York, 1982.

91. Kuczynski served as a Soviet agent. But in 1940 that link had not become
apparent. By contrast, his anti-Nazi credentials remained impeccable. See *The
Times*, 11 August 1997 and *The Independent*, 13 August 1997, for obituaries
of Kuczynski. His internment file has not yet been released. On hapless individuals whose fate turned on arbitrary classification by the British authorities,
see Wasserstein, *Britain and the Jews*, pp. 91–2.

92. R. Benewick, *The Fascist Movement in Britain*, London, 1972, p. 10.

93. See generally, J. Higham, 'Anti-Semitism in the Gilded Age', *Mississippi Valley
Historical Review* 43 (1957): p. 656. See also specifically, THMO 79, 'Public
Feeling about Aliens', 25 April 1940, pp. 3–5 for a recognition of mixed
wartime responses. See also THMO 1669 Q, 'Attitudes to Foreigners', April
1943, p. 2 (comment on the mixed images of Poles); THMO 523B, 'Report on
the October Directive', Question (4), 10 December 1940, pp. 7 and 13 for the
observations on the Czechs and the Dutch, respectively, as well as THMO
1669Q, pp. 4 and 5, on a similar theme; THMO 523B p. 5 notes the different
perceptions according to gender. See also PRO INF 1/292, Home Intelligence
Reports, 25 April–2 May 1944 and 2 May-9 May 1944, on antisemitism in the
Polish armed forces and its influences. On this theme see also H.F. Srebrnik,
London Jews and British Communism 1935–1945, London, 1995, pp. 111–21.
The corollary of all such observations is that we should be wary of celebratory
accounts of the type found in *Fifty Years of the Polish School of Medicine
1941–1991*, ed. W. Tomaszewski, Edinburgh, 1992, a study which omits comment on the antisemitism faced by some students: see Wasserstein, *Britain and
the Jews*, p. 125.

94. *The Times*, 29 August, 1939.

95. See B. Williams, 'The Anti-Semitism of Tolerance: Middle Class Manchester
and the Jews, 1870–1900', in *City, Class and Culture*, eds A.J. Kidd, and K.W.
Roberts, Manchester, 1985, pp. 74–102. See also *Parliamentary Debates* (Commons), vol. 120, 1919, cols 1230–1231, for comments by Josiah Wedgwood, a
leading defender of immigration.

96. Kushner, *The Persistence of Prejudice*, p. 198.

97. V.G. Kiernan, 'Britons Old and New', in *Immigrants and Minorities in British
Society*, ed C. Holmes, London, 1978, p. 54.

98. K. Paul, *Whitewashing Britain: Race and Citizenship in the Postwar Era*,
Ithaca, 1997.

99. Kiernan, 'Britons Old and New', pp. 23–59, for a compact account.

100. Ibid, p. 49.

101. *The Times*, 3 April 1943, 'Men without a Country'. At this stage the Poles were
viewed as 'temporary absentees' from their homeland, who would return home,
along with the Belgians, the Dutch, the French and the Norwegians.

102. *Parliamentary Debates* (Commons), vol. 414, 1945–46, 10 October 1945, cols
225–226. Following the war the government did engage in some deportation.
See K. Sword, '"Their Prospects will not be bright": British Responses to the
Problem of Polish "Recalcitrants" 1946–49', *Journal of Contemporary History*
21 (1986): pp. 367–90. Such deportation paled into insignificance compared
with the forcible return by the Allies of Soviet citizens who had come under
their control in Europe at the end of the War. A fierce and furious debate has
surrounded this episode, which involved Cossacks and other groups.

103. E.F. Kunz, 'The Refugee in Flight: Kinetic Models and Forms of Displacement', *International Migration Review* 7 (1973): pp. 125–46. For academic work which reveals how the issue of refugees hung over the immediate postwar world, see, for example, Kulischer, *Europe on the Move*; Proudfoot, *European Refugees*; J. Vernant, *The Refugee in the Post War World*, London, 1953 and *Flight and Resettlement*, ed. H.B.M. Murphy, Paris, 1955, as well as two articles specifically on refugees in Britain: E. Stadulis, 'The Resettlement of Displaced Persons in the United Kingdom', *Population Studies* 5 (1952): pp. 207–37 and M. Bulbring , 'Post-War Refugees in Great Britain', in ibid 8 (1954): pp. 99–112.

104. The phrase is Andrew Marr's in 'Exile is not some archaic notion', in *The Observer,* 7 March 1999.

2

PRE-WAR BELGIAN ATTITUDES TO BRITAIN: ANGLOPHILIA AND ANGLOPHOBIA*

JEAN STENGERS

Admiration for Britain and for the British takes many forms. When the Belgian government in exile met during the last few years of the war, two great admirers of Cardinal Newman used to sit at the table: the minister Auguste de Schryver (who was born in England during the First World War) and the cabinet secretary, who was also the principal private secretary to the Prime Minister, André de Staercke.[1] This small detail, illustrating the admiration felt by particular exiled Belgians for a famous Englishman, serves to demonstrate the diversity of connections between Britain and Belgium, which it is impossible to include in a contribution of this kind. Similarly, it is not possible to examine, for instance, the famous motion voted by the Oxford Union in 1933 according to which 'This House will not fight for King and country', and which was to some extent echoed by Belgian pacifists with the consequence that three young students from the Université Catholique de Louvain, who had publicly supported it, were very nearly sent down from the University by the Recteur Magnifique. These particular influences, be they intellectual, artistic, religious, political or indeed in any other form, will be omitted from this study, which, taking as its starting-point the turn of the nineteenth and twentieth centuries, will instead concentrate on two levels of reactions to England: the reactions of public opinion, that is of the greater part of the population; and those, on a political level, of the ruling circles of the country. Looking in turn at these two levels, I shall attempt to measure the extent of anglophilia and anglophobia.

In attempting this analysis, it is of course essential to avoid the great peril, which always haunts historians, of anachronism. Nowadays, talking about relationships with Britain, and more generally with the English-speaking world, means talking about a world that many people enter into contact with almost every day, through popular music, through the cinema, or through the media. English still remains a foreign language, but one with which one often tends to feel familiar. This was not the case during the period under examination here. The language barrier was a real obstacle for the majority of the Belgians at that time. Leopold II read *The Times* very attentively every morning, but he was probably the only person to do so in Belgium, whereas bundles of Parisian newspapers were delivered all over the country. At the time of the campaign directed against the abuses in the Congo and conducted by the journalist Morel in England, the Belgian Socialist leader Emile Vandervelde was anxious to warn the latter that, though the journalists from the Socialist newspaper *Le Peuple* were interested in receiving his brochures, they could not use them easily as they could barely read English.[2]

Similarly, at the Ministry of Foreign Affairs, before 1940, several high senior officials could not speak English. When part of the Belgian government left for London in 1940, the Prime Minister, Hubert Pierlot, knew sufficient English, but the Foreign Affairs Minister, Paul-Henri Spaak, could hardly speak a word of it: he was to learn English, albeit with great difficulty, in London itself.[3] In these ways, the language barrier could and no doubt did contribute to a lack of understanding.

As far as public opinion was concerned, one must commence with the wave of anglophobia caused by the Boer War. Sympathy for the brave little Boers as well as hostility towards British imperialism were of course sentiments that permeated many European countries. In Belgium, however, these feelings were particularly intense. In the Chamber of Deputies, where remarks regarding foreign countries were usually moderated by the constraints of diplomatic neutrality, some left-wing members of Parliament denounced 'une guerre criminelle', 'un crime abominable', 'un attentat international', 'une guerre odieuse', and 'l'abominable et criminelle entreprise poursuivie contre les peuples libres de l'Afrique du Sud par l'Angleterre'.[4] The press was even harsher in its attacks. The Flemish were just as moved as the Walloons and the French-speaking community and tended to look upon the Boers as 'racial brothers'. Even after the end of the war, these feelings persisted. The Boer generals were welcomed in Belgium as heroes. Some of the participants in these demonstrations have even told me that they had never shouted as much in their lives as on the day of the celebration in their honour. On the British side, the attacks from the Belgian newspapers were deliberately ignored. Real offence was only caused when journalists or satirical cartoonists vented their spleen – sometimes very rudely – on the venerable Queen Victoria. On such occasions, the ambassador of Great Britain protested vigorously. But what could be done? Offences against foreign sovereigns were punished by the Belgian penal code, but they were a matter for the Assize Court and, given the state of public opinion, if they had been brought to it, triumphant acquittals would have resulted.

The event that caused more anger towards Belgium was an assassination attempt perpetrated on the Prince of Wales, the future monarch Edward VII, in Brussels in April 1900. At the Gare du Nord, a young fanatic, of around fifteen years of age, called Sipido, had got near the *coupé* in which the Prince of Wales was sitting and had fired at him with a revolver, without hitting him.[5] There was violent outrage in Britain, all the more so as this attempted assassination was interpreted as the result of the incitement to violence fostered in Belgium. This was not, however, the end of the scandal. Two further incidents followed. First, in July, Sipido appeared in front of the Assize Court. He was defended by the lawyer Paul Spaak. By one of those remarkable coincidences, Paul Spaak's son, Paul-Henri Spaak, the future Belgian Foreign Minister in the London government, subsequently won fame as a barrister for the first time in the Brussels legal world by defending the perpetrator of another assassination attempt against a crown prince, namely the Italian De Rosa who in 1929, like Sipido, had shot at Prince Umberto of Italy, without actually hitting him. One of the questions that the jury was asked in the Sipido case was whether the defendant had acted 'avec discernement' (It should be remembered that Sipido was in fact aged under sixteen at the time). The answer of the jury was negative. Sipido was therefore acquitted, which provoked a second scandal with headlines in British newspapers such as 'Monstrous decision'. But there was worse to come: in accordance with the ruling of the Assize Court, Sipido was to be handed over to the government, and thus locked up, until he came of age. However, as his defenders introduced an appeal against this judgement, following a judicial muddle, Sipido, who had been acquitted and was now free, was able to take the train safely to Paris. The fact that a young man who had shot at the Prince of Wales could go and live peacefully in France seemed to be the last straw. The newspaper *Punch* published an avenging caricature: *The Stain on the Belgian flag*.[6] To appease Britain, Belgium had to resort to drastic measures.

In October 1900, Leopold II went to Paris. Officially, he was there to visit the Great Exhibition, but in fact his objective was primarily a political one. He visited the President of the Republic and the Président du Conseil, as well as the Minister of Foreign Affairs and the Minister of Justice. Why? To persuade France, with all the weight of his royal authority, to defer to an official request from Belgium to extradite Sipido. 'J'ai plaidé la question sous toutes ses faces avec la plus grande chaleur', he wrote to Queen Victoria after his meeting with the President of the Republic. Finally, his request was granted, because, although the French Government did not allow the extradition of Sipido, it deported him to Belgium.[7]

The crisis caused by the Boer War was soon to be followed by a new one, caused this time by the British campaign launched against the abuse of the regime of Leopold in the Congo. Its nature, however, was very different from the preceding crisis. In the case of the Boer War, severe political judgements – even though their severity was excessive and often unfair – could be justified. When the Congo was at stake, though, for a long time the Belgians showed complete ignorance of the essential nature of the British campaign. When one studies this campaign in detail, one finds that it was in essence one of those great humanitarian campaigns of entirely disinterested moral fervour of which there is a certain tradition in Britain. This was also true of the man who was at the heart of this campaign, the journalist E.D. Morel, whose largely autobiographical *History of the Congo Reform Movement* I edited for Clarendon Press with Roger Louis.[8] When one reads carefully his private papers, the impression that emerges is of an entirely honourable man, and one understands from his correspondence the description given of him by Vandervelde in the latter's *Mémoires*:

> J'ai bien connu E.D. Morel. J'ai été étroitement associé à son effort. On me l'a amèrement reproché. Je ne l'ai jamais regretté. Je m'en vante, au contraire ... Parmi les hommes que j'ai connus et pratiqués, il en est peu qui m'aient, à un tel degré, inspiré de la sympathie, et aussi de l'admiration, pour ses merveilleuses qualités de *fighting man*, pour l'intrépidité sereine avec laquelle il défiait les pires attaques de l'adversaire et – je tiens à y insister – pour la loyauté absolue et le désintéressement total de son action ... Je tiens pour une calomnie atroce d'avoir prétendu, ou de prétendre, comme certains le font encore en Belgique, que Morel ne poursuivait pas des fins désintéressées.[9]

The image that was portrayed in Belgium of Morel and of the British campaign was therefore far from being the truth. The Belgians were left bewildered by the sudden attacks from Britain, the virulence of which stunned them. Had the British really discovered in the Congo some serious abuses? People could hardly believe it, because, although they knew that in the Congo, as in any other colony, there were certain injustices inherent to the nature of colonial rule, nobody had ever heard of any abuse specific to the Independent State. On the other hand, what everybody knew about was the all-consuming nature of British imperialism; people therefore came to the conclusion that it must be this imperialism that lay behind this affair. The reason why Belgian public opinion set its face against the campaign in such a way was first and foremost, of course, because of the very recent and still vivid memory of the Boer War. After attacking the Boers to strip them of their riches, the British were now turning on the Congo: was it not obvious that they were doing so with the same spirit of profit? 'C'est l'histoire du Transvaal qui recommence. Il s'agit de préparer, de justifier une nouvelle annexion', wrote the newspapers. This quasi-instinctive analogy with the Transvaal was the emotional element that, at the beginning, predominated over all others.[10] Right from the outset, people therefore attributed self-interested motives to the English campaign. The great Liberal leader, Paul Janson expressed an almost universal opinion when he exclaimed in a speech in the Chamber in July 1903: 'Je ne puis admettre que l'Etat du Congo soit mis spécialement en suspicion. Je ne puis surtout m'associer à une campagne dont le dernier mot semble être: ôte-toi de là que je m'y mette'. A Liberal newspaper, the *Gazette*, used similarly strong language, expressing 'le sentiment de révolte indignée que nous inspire la campagne anticongolaise menée depuis quelques temps dans un but aussi visible que malhonnête de pure et simple expropriation'. Paul Janson, a man of considerable intelligence, and the *Gazette*, which was an honest and independent newspaper, were to change their minds subsequently when they realised the extent of the abuses in the Congo, but for the vast majority of the public, the simplistic idea of British covetousness, of the 'get out so that I can take it over' motto, remained deeply fixed in their minds for a long time.

To denounce Britain was, of course, easy in private conversations. But, however appalling British imperialism might seem, it was hard to imagine that Britain as a whole, led by its government, might harbour annexationist designs on the Congo. A campaign such as this one must, therefore, have an origin that provided the impulse and the direction for these covetous ambitions. This centre was soon discovered and denounced by most Belgian newspapers: it was the group of the 'marchands de Liverpool'. The Liverpool merchants had evidently sworn to ruin the Congo. Once this apparent explanation had been found, everything became simple. Charles Buls, a former mayor of Brussels and a man of considerable distinction, gave a brief summary to a foreign audience in a lecture in 1904 of what people should think of the 'attaques injustes dont l'Etat indépendant [i.e. the Congo] a été l'objet'. He declared that: 'Elles ont eu pour origine l'envie qu'a excitée sa prospérité chez les marchands de Liverpool, qui ne peuvent admettre qu'un marché colonial puisse ne pas leur appartenir.' The newspapers endlessly reiterated this theme. According to this interpretation, E.D. Morel simply appeared to be the instrument, as well as the spokesman, of these fearsome Liverpool merchants. For most Belgian newspapers, Morel and the 'marchands de Liverpool' became one and the same. The slanderous English campaign against the Congo will not cease, proclaimed the *Indépendance Belge* in its headlines in August 1905; it will continue 'ne fût-ce que pour permettre au Morel des marchands de Liverpool de mener grand tapage et de se poser en sauveur de l'humanité souffrante.'

A small number of enlightened Belgians, however, had recognised, before the First World War, the merits of the British campaign, and those of Morel in particular. Félicien Cattier, in an article written in the *Revue de l'Université de Bruxelles*, spoke of the 'admirable campagne anglaise' while A.J. Wauters, the editor of the *Mouvement Géographique*, and probably the Belgian publicist who was most aware of Congolese affairs, wrote to Morel in 1910 to express his 'admiration' for him: 'Vous avez combattu avec une grande noblesse et une infatigable vaillance en faveur de la cause de la liberté et de l'humanité'. Similarly, at a gathering organised in 1911 in Morel's honour, Emile Vandervelde, who said he was speaking on behalf of Belgium, had thanked him publicly. One last and unexpected element of this affair, however, occurred during the subsequent war. For the Belgians, as the victims of German aggression in 1914, the pacifism highly tinged with Germanophilia that Morel demonstrated during the war was a cause for outrage. The scandal came to the fore when Morel was sentenced to six months in prison. As the judicial system could not prosecute him for expressing his highly unpopular opinions, it punished him harshly for the crime of sending some political brochures through illicit channels to the French writer Romain Rolland in Switzerland. This sentence was perceived by Belgians as a just one punishing a real treason, and the conclusion therefore seemed obvious. As a Belgian journalist wrote: we had believed that Morel was an agent of British imperialism; in fact, he was nothing but a henchman of Germany.

In this way, a legend was born. It was strengthened by the fact that, quite naturally, an analogy was made between Morel's case and that of the Irish nationalist, Roger Casement. As a British Consul in the Congo, Casement had been one of the main accusers of the regime of King Leopold, but then had been sentenced to death and executed by the British in 1916 for what amounted to high treason in favour of Germany. As an Irish patriot, Casement had sided with Germany against Britain with the aim of serving the cause of Ireland. The theme of Morel and Casement was soon to be exploited by some Belgian journalists, and was even supported by official patronage. After the bad memories left by the regime of King Leopold, it was imperative for the Belgian governmental authorities to rehabilitate the Congo in the eyes of international public opinion. They soon realised the possibilities offered by the combined Morel and Casement cases and, as early as 1918, began to exploit this theme. In May 1918, a dispatch from the Minister of Foreign Affairs which had been drafted by the Directeur Général de la Politique himself, the Baron de Bassompierre declared:

> Il est désormais avéré que la campagne contre l'Etat Indépendant du Congo n'était point inspirée par un souci désintéressé du sort des indigènes. N'a-t-on pas appris depuis la guerre que les deux anciens chefs du mouvement anti-congolais étaient deux séides de l'Allemagne et travaillaient dans son intérêt, qui était de nous brouiller avec l'Angleterre et d'entraîner celle-ci à provoquer un remaniement du statut territorial de l'Afrique?[11]

The Morel and Casement theme was still included in propaganda brochures circulated by the Belgian Government during the Second World War, prompting the Belgian ambassador in Ireland to point out respectfully to his superiors that the brochures he was being sent on the subject were rather inappropriate as Casement was considered a national hero in Ireland. Indeed, it can still be found in 1961 in the *Textes et Documents* published by the Ministry of Foreign Affairs.[12] However, it was mainly outside official circles, and especially in the writings of popularising journalists or historians who sought to defend the Congo, that this theme developed after 1918. One could almost call it an epic legend, with all the misrepresentations that are peculiar to legends. Some journalists wrote – and once something has been written, it is soon copied – that Morel and Casement had both been sentenced to death and hanged for treason.[13] As years went by, the idea was gradually forgotten that Germany had pulled the strings in the campaign against the Congo, but what was still denounced was Casement's and Morel's moral unworthiness in the light of which the anti-Congo campaign had to be measured. In the eyes of many, this campaign seemed to have been all the more discredited as Leopold II's posthumous glory rose steadily between the two wars.

The year 1914 represented, of course, an extraordinary turning

point. In Britain, people were filled with admiration, almost to the
point of fanaticism, for heroic and martyred Belgium, and particularly for King Albert, as can be seen in the famous *King Albert's
Book* published with enormous success at Christmas 1914. People
were profoundly moved by the sufferings endured by the Belgian
people. Vera Brittain, for instance, whose wartime letters have
recently been published, wrote to her fiancé, who was fighting at the
front, on 21 May 1915 that: ' I don't think I have ever read anything quite so terrible as the official report on the German outrages
in Belgium . . . their treatment of the women and children is worst
of all . . . I don't know how any man can read it and not enlist'.[14]
Within Belgium, sentiments of military alliance now prevailed. Former suspicions were erased and had given way to feelings inspired
by solidarity in battle. This solidarity was sometimes very close: the
main intelligence service organised in occupied Belgium, the Dame
Blanche, directed by Walthère Dewé, worked directly for Britain
and was the most efficient intelligence service behind the German
lines during the war.[15]

After the war, public opinion and the ruling circles remained
grateful towards Britain. Public opinion and leaders, however, did
not always follow the same course. When it came to affection and
confidence, in the eyes of public opinion, France won by several
lengths over Britain. When both British and French troops took
part in parades together, after the liberation of Belgium, it was the
French who were most acclaimed. In governmental circles, on the
other hand, and especially within the Ministry of Foreign Affairs, it
was Britain that undoubtedly inspired greater confidence. They
were somewhat wary of France and of its ambitions, especially as
regards the issue of the Grand Duchy of Luxembourg, which helped
to explain their keen desire to involve Britain as much as France in
guaranteeing the future defence of Belgium. It was this factor that
the influential Belgian diplomat Fernand Van Langenhove, in his
book entitled *La Belgique en quête de sécurité*, termed 'la quête de
la garantie anglaise'.[16] The Foreign Affairs Minister, Paul Hymans,
made his position clear in a speech made in the Chamber in December 1919. We want, he said, to 'conclure avec les deux Grandes
Puissances occidentales, la France et l'Angleterre, des arrangements
militaires qui assureraient notre défense'. This goal

répond aux intérêts communs des trois pays. La Belgique . . . est le
champ historique des invasions germaniques. Le jour où elle serait
attaquée, la France et l'Angleterre seraient en péril. Il nous paraît
naturel et nécessaire à la stabilité de l'Europe que les trois pays se
concertent et qu'ensemble, d'égal à égal, ils prennent les mesures que
leur commande le souci de leur sécurité.[17]

But, on this issue of military agreements, France and Britain's attitudes to Belgium proved to be profoundly different. France was eager for such an agreement while Belgium postponed its assent until the question of Luxembourg had been settled. In Britain's opinion, on the contrary, it was Belgium that had a vested interest in such an agreement whereas Britain sought to avoid any commitment. Many pressing overtures were made to Britain, as, for instance, in the conversation that Paul Hymans had with the ambassador of Great Britain in Brussels in March 1920. We are turning, he said, 'vers l'Angleterre et la France' and we are asking them

> de nous aider à assurer notre sécurité par des arrangements militaires
> ... La France est toute disposée à s'entendre avec nous à ce sujet. Elle
> en a même le vif désir, mais notre but ... est de réaliser l'entente à
> trois ... Si dans quelques temps, j'étais amené à dire à la Chambre
> que nous avons proposé une entente militaire à la France et à
> l'Angleterre, que la France a accepté et que l'Angleterre a refusé,
> l'effet moral serait déplorable. La Belgique a toujours considéré
> l'Angleterre comme son amie naturelle.[18]

The Belgian ministers, however, failed to shift the British stance. The Prime Minister, Delacroix, in a conversation with Lloyd George at the Spa conference in July 1920, received a very blunt refusal. Delacroix had asked for the British general staff to be allowed to take part in military talks about the possible ways of 'parer à une agression éventuelle de l'Allemagne'[19] (warding off a possible attack by Germany). Lloyd George, according to the Belgian diplomatic documents, answered:

> Lord Curzon [the British Foreign Affairs Minister who – it should be
> noted – was a close friend of King Albert],[20] nous a exposé la situa-
> tion à un récent Conseil des Ministres et il opinait pour l'affirmative;
> mais il a été seul de son avis. Tous les autres membres du Conseil ont
> successivement émis l'opinion qu'il n'était pas opportun actuellement
> de s'engager dans cette voie. Je n'ai même pas eu à me prononcer,
> mais je partageais leur opinion.

In subsequent remarks, Lloyd George went on to reveal the motivations that lay behind this attitude. Britain was already more worried about French policy than about German attitudes. 'Je considère que pendant vingt ans l'Allemagne sera trop faible pour avoir même l'idée d'une nouvelle guerre ou d'une offensive contre les Alliés', he said. On the other hand, he added,

> ce que nous pouvons redouter, c'est que les Alliés, pendant cette
> période, soient amenés, eux, à intervenir en Allemagne, par exemple
> pour y remettre de l'ordre, y réprimer une révolution ou empêcher

l'invasion du bolchévisme, ou bien aussi pour imposer par la contrainte l'exécution du traité de Versailles. Ce sera là une éventualité très dangereuse qui pourrait mettre le feu à toute l'Europe et qui achèverait de la ruiner.[21]

Under those circumstances, it was out of the question for Britain to enter into any form of military agreement that also involved France. Confronted with this impasse, Belgium was, therefore, forced to negotiate with France alone: this was to become, once the problems posed by Luxembourg had been dealt with, the Franco-Belgian military agreement of 7 September 1920. This did not, however, put an end to the 'quête de la garantie anglaise'. Belgium made another attempt at reaching an agreement with Britain in 1922, and a draft-agreement of limited duration was even drawn up in January 1922 once again by Lord Curzon and the new Belgian Foreign Affairs Minister, Henri Jaspar. It did not, however, succeed. The main reason for this failure was the question of the occupation of the Ruhr, in which Belgium chose to side with France against Britain.[22] Belgium however did not abandon hope. In February 1925, Paul Hymans, who was again the Minister of Foreign Affairs, made a last effort to conclude a tripartite pact between Belgium, France and Britain. Hymans did not underestimate how difficult these negotiations would be, but he thought they could be brought to a successful conclusion 'en manœuvrant avec prudence et habileté'. British fears concerning France had to be appeased, he thought, and it must be emphasised that 'il ne s'agissait que de la Belgique, dont les sentiments pacifiques sont connus'.[23]

Alas, his optimism proved to be misplaced. As early as March 1925, in Geneva, Austen Chamberlain, who was at the head of the British Foreign Office, took it upon himself to make Hymans aware of the situation once and for all. 'M. Chamberlain', Hymans wrote, 'm'a déclaré qu'il était impossible au Gouvernement britannique d'envisager l'entrée de l'Angleterre dans un Pacte à trois. Lui-même y est favorable, mais la majorité du Cabinet y est hostile. On rencontrerait l'opposition irréductible du parti travailliste et du parti libéral et de vives résistances dans une fraction importante de la majorité conservatrice'.[24] Beyond the political parties, it was in fact the whole of British public opinion that shared this attitude. As Austen Chamberlain had already pointed out previously to the Belgian ambassador in London, 'le pays a de la répugnance pour des pactes ayant le caractère d'une alliance menaçante contre une autre nation'.[25] In the end, the agreements that were signed were, therefore, inspired by a very different spirit, as they also included Germany: these were the Locarno Agreements of October 1925.

Outside the Belgian Ministry of Foreign Affairs, where the

friendship with Britain mattered a great deal (whereas the military agreement between France and Belgium had brought nothing but problems), members of other Belgian circles who were interested in issues of international affairs were also drawing much closer to some British circles. In particular, there were those who, on both sides of the Channel, shared a common belief in the League of Nations. Henri Rolin in Belgium and Lord Cecil in England were in this respect both men who shared the same idyllic internationalist dreams. Their various actions, however, had hardly any influence on Belgian policy.

Within the Belgian Ministry of Foreign Affairs, on the eve of the Second World War, the traditional trust in Britain proved to be weakened by a new aspect of British policy: appeasement. Belgium did not condemn the general policy of appeasement, but worry and indignation were aroused when the Belgians realised that, for the British, one of the aspects of appeasement was colonial appeasement, and that this might pose a threat to one of Belgium's vital interests, namely its sovereignty over the Congo. In this respect, there were two major crises, each of which caused considerable indignation in Brussels.[26] The first crisis was caused in November 1937 by the visit to Germany of the British Foreign Secretary Lord Halifax, where he met Hitler, among others. The British Foreign Affairs Minister spoke in general terms about the possibility of meeting Germany's colonial claims. He did not mention explicitly the Congo or Rwanda-Burundi, but colonial appeasement was officially on the agenda of Anglo-German conversations and this soon became publicly known. There were some leaks to the press which originated either in Germany or in France. The Labour newspaper *The Daily Herald* published a caricature that infuriated Lord Halifax. It depicted a woman representing Europe, holding out her baby, who represented the colonies, to Hitler and telling the threatening German leader: 'Take my child, but spare, oh spare me'.

Lord Halifax's conversations in November 1937 did not have any direct consequences, other than giving great cause for worry, especially in Brussels and Lisbon, where it was felt that Belgium and Portugal might bear the brunt of any colonial deal. This danger did, however, become more acute when, at the beginning of 1938, Chamberlain personally took the matter in hand. The Prime Minister devised a plan that he thought brilliant, even idealistic – 'based on high ideals' – and which would permit the inauguration of an 'entirely new chapter in the history of colonial development in Africa'. This plan consisted of creating, south of the Sahara, a vast area in which an international agreement would guarantee the protection of indigenous populations, freedom of trade, freedom of communication and – a vital point – demilitarisation. In that zone, Germany could be given 'some territories' to administer. Amongst the colonies that might be part of that area, the Congo and the Portuguese colonies were, for the first time, mentioned explicitly. According to Chamberlain's plan, the Congo should, therefore, form part of a redistribution of the territories of Central Africa.

In March 1938, the ambassador of Great Britain in Berlin, Sir Neville Henderson, was put in charge of informing the Führer of his government's proposals. The Belgian diplomat, Robert Rothschild, summed up the scene in his book *Les chemins de Munich*. Henderson encountered the German leader 'ramassé dans son fauteuil comme un animal prêt à bondir, une grimace féroce lui déformant le visage'. The ambassador 'fit briller sur un globe terrestre l'étendue de la part offerte au Reich dans un bassin du Congo réorganisé', but it was to no avail. Hitler only replied with a 'furieuse diatribe contre la presse, les évêques et les ministres britanniques… Les colonies n'étaient pas pour lui une affaire urgente; l'Europe centrale l'était. Il n'y tolérerait aucune intervention extérieure. Si la Grande-Bretagne devait s'opposer à un juste arrangement, l'Allemagne se battrait'.[27]

A few days later, the annexation of Austria took place and the tentative diplomatic negotiations collapsed.[28] On the Belgian part, however, the harm was done. Once again, there had been many leaks.[29] In Brussels, people felt both alarmed and angry. They were all the more worried as British official statements were anything but reassuring. When the Belgian Foreign Minister Spaak confronted him at the end of January 1938 in Geneva, Anthony Eden merely declared that 'l'Angleterre étudiait la question coloniale' but 'rien ne serait fait sans que nous les Belges soyons prévenus'.[30] This was scarcely adequate reassurance. Moreover, a senior official from the Foreign Office, when he spoke in December 1938 with the counsellor of the Belgian embassy in London, was keen to emphasise that the British guarantee applied to Belgium, but not the Congo.[31] Not only at the Belgian Ministry of Foreign Affairs, but also in Parliament and in the press, there were reactions to what was perceived as a threat. In the Chamber, in November 1938, Count Carton de Wiart stressed that there could be no question of interfering with the Congo, 'qui est le fruit du génie d'un grand roi et des efforts de tous les Belges'.[32]

Paul-Henri Spaak, for his part, kept his cool. On the issue of Belgian sovereignty over the Congo, he was categorically uncompromising. During the debate in the Chamber, following Carton de Wiart's intervention, he declared: 'Le Congo est à nous, notre droit sur le Congo est certain, personne ne peut le contester, et toutes les forces que le gouvernement a seront mises à la disposition de notre colonie'.[33] Likewise, in a memorandum sent in January 1939 to all of Belgium's diplomatic representatives, he wrote: 'Une fois pour toutes, sachez que l'intégrité du Congo belge est un principe fondamental de la politique de la Belgique. Le Congo belge fait partie intégrante de notre Pays. Le Gouvernement n'admet même pas qu'on puisse discuter devant lui d'un projet qui tendrait à nous dépouiller de la moindre parcelle de notre colonie. Il défendra celle-ci, au besoin, par les armes'. This was followed by a laudatory account – undoubtedly written by someone other than Spaak – of the work of the Belgians in Africa, where they had shown 'les plus grandes aptitudes colonisatrices'.[34] But just as he was uncompromising on principles, so Spaak thought it tactless, from a tactical point of view, to raise the problem too often. 'Quand on est sûr de son droit, on ne le discute pas' he said in the Chamber. If one repeats too often that one would like guarantees, one might 'faire naître le doute dans l'esprit des autres'. In a letter he sent to the Minister of the Colonies on 14 November 1938, he stressed the importance of maintaining 'un calme absolu . . . Il importe que nous ne donnions pas au dehors l'impression que nous regardons nos possessions coloniales comme menacées'.[35]

This was at the heart of the major crisis that occurred in January 1940.[36] King Leopold III was very worried about the possible risks for the Congo within the context of what, even after the war had begun, he still considered a possibility and was in fact hoping for, namely a peace settlement between Britain and Germany. As early as December 1939, this preoccupation resulted in a draft letter to King George VI. With the help of his military advisor, General Van Overstraeten, he expressed the wish that guarantees be given to Belgium in a 'déclaration spontanée de la Grande-Bretagne, publique ou privée'. He had not mentioned this draft letter to his Foreign Affairs Minister, but he did consult his secretary, Baron Capelle. The latter respectfully voiced his objections, pointing out that King George VI would probably not be in a position to do anything other than to pass on Leopold's request to his government, which would in turn get in touch with the Belgian government, thereby causing an unavoidable crisis. Faced with these objections, the King resigned himself to informing the Foreign Affairs Minister of his plan. He submitted to Spaak a draft of a 'secret note' containing the demand for guarantees. Spaak was, however, entirely opposed to the idea, and he remained unshakable in his resolve despite the King's efforts to convince him. The Minister considered such a step to be fraught with dangers, as London would almost certainly consult Paris, and this might provide the stimulus for pressure upon Belgium on military matters.

The matter was not immediately taken any further, but hardly three weeks later something new happened. In mid-January 1940, there was the famous incident of Mechelen-sur-Meuse: a German warplane that had lost its way in mist landed on Belgian soil and on it was found a German plan for an invasion of Belgium. The military threat to Belgium appeared to be imminent, provoking complete pandemonium in Brussels. Leopold III immediately returned to his idea of asking Britain for guarantees. He knew that Spaak was resolutely hostile to this initiative. Thus, he decided to take it upon himself to make the decision, and to make it quickly. He summoned Admiral Keyes, an old English friend of the Belgian royal family, to the royal palace at Laeken and, in the presence of Van Overstraeten (Capelle was not consulted this time), he handed him a note (of which an autograph copy has survived) in which he had put down in writing the commitments he would like to see Britain make. Its second point was: 'Garantie de la restauration intégrale du statut politique et territorial de la Belgique ainsi que de sa colonie [the King personally underlined the word 'colonie']'.[37] Keyes was charged with presenting this request directly to the British authorities. In a comment highly typical of Leopold III's personal policy, Keyes was also asked to let them know that the Belgian King wished to conduct these negotiations alone, without going through the intermediary of his government, in order to make 'la solution moins difficile', as he said.

The rest of Keyes' mission has often been described. Following a series of misunderstandings, not only did it turn out to be a complete fiasco, but it put Belgium itself at risk: in London and Paris, the authorities imagined that the message from Brussels amounted practically to a request for a preventive military intervention on the part of France and Britain. For the Belgian government, this proved to be a very difficult time. Leopold III, for his part, had, with considerable difficulty, to confess his personal initiative to Spaak. This incident from January 1940 was highly revealing: it was anchored in the past and, at the same time, it also heralded the future. It was born out of the fears aroused by Britain's attempts at colonial appeasement and yet, by showing the premises of the personal agenda that Leopold III wished to pursue, it also presaged the constitutional crisis between the Belgian King and his government that would take place in May 1940.

Notes

*Translated by Christine Arthur.

1. Cf. A. de Staercke in *Veertig jaar Belgische politiek – Liber Amicorum August De Schryver*, Antwerp, 1968, p. 358.
2. Vandervelde to Morel, undated, London School of Economics, British Library of Political and Economic Science, Morel Papers. Vandervelde wrote in *Le Peuple*

of 10 July 1907: 'Presque tout ce qui se publie sur le Congo est en anglais et, dans la presse démocratique, il n'y a pas beaucoup de rédacteurs qui lisent couramment cette langue.'

3. When the Minister of the Colonies, Albert De Vleeschauwer, met Churchill at the beginning of July 1940 and declared to him, while shaking his hand, that he was 'delivering' the Congo to him, De Vleeschauwer spoke in French, for at that time he still spoke English very imperfectly. Cf. J. Stengers, *Léopold III et le gouvernement – Les deux politiques belges de 1940*, Paris-Gembloux, 1980, pp. 92 and 114.

4. *Annales parlementaires, Chambre*, 1899–1900, pp. 889–92, seance of 5 April 1900.

5. On the attack by Sipido and its consequences, see A. Notebaert in 'La décision politique et judiciaire dans le passé et dans le présent', Archives Générales du Royaume, Brussels, 1975, pp. 215–57, and the notice on Sipido by the same author in *Biographie Nationale*, vol. 42, 1982, col. 661–79.

6. *Punch, or the London Charivari*, 15 August 1900.

7. J. Stengers, *L'action du Roi en Belgique depuis 1831 – Pouvoir et influence*, 2nd ed., Brussels, 1996, p. 277.

8. E.D. Morel's *History of the Congo Reform Movement*, eds R. Louis and J. Stengers, Oxford, 1968.

9. E. Vandervelde, *Souvenirs d'un militant socialiste*, Paris, 1939, pp. 75–6.

10. For all the following material, see the references in J. Stengers, 'Morel and Belgium', in *E.D. Morel's History of the Congo Reform Movement*, pp. 221–51.

11. The Minister of Foreign Affairs to Forthomme, 14 May 1918, Archives du Ministère des Affaires étrangères, Brussels, A F I 26.

12. 'About "Belgian Atrocities"', in *Textes et Documents*, Ministère des Affaires Etrangères, August 1961, p. 3.

13. See, for example, G.H. Dumont, *Histoire des Belges*, vol. 3, Brussels, 1956, p. 160.

14. V. Brittain, *Letters from a Lost Generation*, eds A. Bishop and M. Bostridge, London, 1998, p. 110.

15. Cf. H. Bernard, *Un géant de la Résistance – Walthère Dewé*, Brussels, 1971.

16. F. Van Langenhove, *La Belgique en quête de sécurité, 1920–1940*, Brussels, 1969, pp. 29–40.

17. *Annales parlementaires, Chambre*, 1919–1920, p. 86, seance of 23 December 1919. See also P. Hymans, *Mémoires*, vol. 3, Brussels, 1958, p. 552.

18. *Documents diplomatiques belges, 1920–1940*, vol. 1, eds C. De Visscher and F. Van Langenhove, Brussels, 1964, pp. 346–7. See also Villiers to Curzon, 20 March 1920, in *Documents on British Foreign Policy, 1919–1939*, 1st series, vol. 12, pp. 8–9. Hymans, it should be noted, alluded himself to the divergence between the general attitude of public opinion and that of the government. 'Vous savez', he said to Villiers, 'que l'opinion publique belge, pour diverses raisons, éprouve quelque froideur à l'égard de l'Angleterre': *Documents diplomatiques belges, 1920–1940*, vol. 1, pp. 346–7. Similarly, in another letter to the British ambassador he commented: 'Affinities of language, literature and sentiment, as well as the practical reasons which arise from contiguous territory, induced many to advocate close relations with France alone, but the Government were not prepared to follow a course which might involve a diminution of Belgian independence' (*Documents on British Foreign Policy, 1919–1939*, 1st series, vol. 12, pp. 8–9). Paul Hymans renewed his offensive in April 1920, this time by approaching Lord Curzon directly: cf. *Documents diplomatiques belges*, vol. 1, p. 286, and *British Documents*, 1st series, vol. 9, pp. 432–3.

19. *Documents diplomatiques belges*, vol. 1, p. 398.

20. Cf. Albert I, *Carnets et correspondence de guerre, 1914–1918*, ed. M.R. Thiele-mans, Paris-Louvain-la-Neuve, 1991.
21. *Documents diplomatiques belges*, vol. 1, pp. 398–9.
22. Cf. Van Langenhove, *La Belgique en quête de sécurité*, pp. 35–8.
23. Hymans to Baron de Gaiffier, Belgian ambassador to Paris, 9 February 1925, in *Documents diplomatiques belges*, vol. 2, 1964, pp. 66–7.
24. *Documents diplomatiques belges*, vol. 2, p. 131.
25. Ibid, vol. 2, p. 108.
26. On the following section, see in general terms, K. Hildebrand, *Vom Reich zum Weltreich – Hitler, NSDAP und koloniale Frage, 1919–1945*, Munich, 1969; R. Louis, 'Colonial Appeasement, 1936–1938', in *Revue Belge de Philologie et d'Histoire*, 49 (1971), pp. 1175–91; A.J. Crozier, *Appeasement and Germany's Last Bid for Colonies*, New York, 1988; R.A.C. Parker, *Chamberlain and Appeasement*, New York, 1993; C.S. Pansaerts, 'Anglo-German Conversations on Colonial Appeasement, and the Involvement of the Belgian Congo', in *Cahiers d'histoire de la seconde guerre mondiale*, 16 (1994), pp. 41–80.
27. R. Rothschild, *Les chemins de Munich*, Paris, 1988, p. 282.
28. The Foreign Office did not, however, abandon all hope. In November 1938, William Strang, the head of the Central Department, raised in a note the advan-tages of relaunching the discussion of 'suitable colonial concessions to Germany'; cf. D. Lammers, 'From Whitehall After Munich: The Foreign Office and the Future Course of British Policy', in *Historical Journal*, 16 (1973), pp. 846–7; and Crozier, *Appeasement*, p. 266.
29. Cf. J.L. Vellut, 'L'ombre de la Conférence et de l'Acte de Berlin', in *L'Afrique Noire depuis la Conférence de Berlin*, Paris, 1985, p. 81 n. 25.
30. *Documents diplomatiques belges, 1920–1940*, vol. 5, 1966, p. 48.
31. Ibid, vol. 5, p. 133. That high official was William Strang, whose views we have already mentioned.
32. *Annales parlementaires, Chambre*, extraordinary session of 1938, p. 34.
33. Ibid, p. 44.
34. *Documents diplomatiques belges*, vol. 5, pp. 148–50.
35. Cited in Vellut, 'L'ombre de la Conférence', p. 82.
36. On what follows, see Stengers, *L'action du Roi en Belgique depuis 1831*, 2nd ed., pp. 282–3. The most recent general study of January 1940 is that of G. Janssens, 'België in januari 1940: door Duitsland bedreigd, door Groot-Brit-tanië en Frankrijk onder druk gezet', in *Bijdragen en mededelingen betreffende de geschiedenis der Nederlanden*, 113, 1998, pp. 457–83.
37. Facsimile in J. Vanwelkenhuyzen, *Les avertissements qui venaient de Berlin*, Paris-Gembloux, 1982, p. 201.

PART TWO

THE BELGIAN EXAMPLE

Belgian Society in Exile:
An Attempt at a Synthesis*

Luis Angel Bernardo y Garcia and Matthew Buck

Although a number of academic studies have looked at the small Belgian political community in exile in the smart districts of London,[1] a large part of the history of the most important population of war refugees in Britain has remained untold.[2] In this article we shall attempt to paint a broad picture of it as well as of the different stages of this exile: from the reception of the refugees to their repatriation, via the British structures of help and the administrative structures set up by the Belgian government in London.

In the summer of 1940, around 15,000 Belgians disembarked in Britain. For four years, they were to share the fate of the Belgian Government in exile. Initially, this heterogeneous community consisted of a handful of evacuated Belgian soldiers, and these were progressively joined by those who had chosen to continue to fight alongside Britain, but the overwhelming majority were simple citizens who had been besieged by the German advance on the Belgian and French coasts. Twenty-five years on, they were repeating the experience of exile that around 150,000 of their fellow compatriots had gone through during the First World War.[3]

Since 1939, the British authorities had been actively preparing for the possible arrival of a mass of refugees from Belgium and the Netherlands. These belated plans were prepared without prior consultation of the countries in question. His Majesty's Government feared the arrival of an 'army of poor people' of 200,000 men, women and children strong that would have to be absorbed.[4] Although it agreed to support and house the Allied refugees, it was reluctant to commit itself to any further expenditure. The war effort was to monopolise all the country's available resources. In order to relieve the pressure on the British Treasury, the authorities added most of the burden of welcoming and helping the refugees to the already considerable responsibilities of voluntary organisations, particularly those of the Women's Voluntary Services for Civil Defence.[5] Although they only possessed very meagre resources, these Women's Organisations accomplished a remarkable job.[6] In order to organise and to control this help, around sixty Local War Refugee Committees were set up, headed by a Central Committee for War Refugees from Holland, Belgium and France. Its room for manoeuvre was to be limited. The management, on a day-to-day basis, of these refugees fell upon the local committees composed of the relevant authorities, as well as representatives from the churches and of charitable organisations. This financial disengagement by the British Government did not mean that it had abdicated all responsibility towards the refugees, but it was based on a strict control over the initiatives taken by voluntary organisations and by the Belgian services in charge of social aid which were gradually being set up. The government's main concern was to prevent the war refugees from being granted a 'privileged' status, and to ensure that they were subject to the same measures as those in place for its own needy citizens.

In fact, the influx of war refugees, which was smaller than anticipated, was easily channelled. The official objective was, as far as possible, to separate the arrangements for the reception and settling of the war refugees from those for the evacuation plans in place for British civilians. The speed of the invasion of Belgium, however, drastically disrupted all these plans. Instead of moving to the north and west of Britain, as had initially been anticipated, between 14,000 and 15,000 Belgians were sent towards London and its suburbs, directly under the bombs of the Luftwaffe. Their welcome was somewhat different from that received by the Belgian refugees in the summer of 1914. The first exile had left the British with bad memories. Most of them agreed that Belgians were dirty and lazy. Moreover, Leopold III's capitulation caused unfavourable comment in the press.[7] This unease was, however, soon to be dispelled. The British people were otherwise preoccupied at the time. Confronted with the hardship of rationing and tormented by the evacuation of the children, the threat of invasion and, soon, the staggering blows of the German airforce, they largely accepted the Allied war refugees with indifference.

Although a number of key personalities from politics, business and the unions, who had deliberately opted for exile, could be found at the side of the Belgian Government, most Belgian refugees ended up in Britain only as a chance consequence of their flight from the German invaders. Some of them attempted in vain to be repatriated to their occupied country, and had to resign themselves to endure an exile that they had not chosen. These ordinary refugees came from a wide variety of socio-professional backgrounds: civil servants who had been evacuated on the orders of the government or who were fleeing from the invaders, workers of all trades and fishing communities escaping onboard their own ships. Though the Belgians made up the largest single component of the Allied war refugees, their numbers fell well short of the original official fore-casts.[8] In a census carried out in 1943 by the Belgian authorities, some 14,781 refugees were counted. Women and children repre-sented 63 percent of the population. The average age of men was high and there were few young people old enough to be in the army.[9]

After the large-scale dispersal that took place in the autumn of 1940 as a result of the Blitz, around one third of the refugees stayed in the capital. More than 60 percent of Belgians were to settle in around sixty towns and villages, each of which took in more than fifty Belgian refugees.[10] The others were to spend this period of exile in relative isolation within nearly 700 other towns or villages.[11] We only know a little about the geographical origin in Belgium of the refugees. It appears, however, that the vast majority were Flemish.[12] The fishing community stood out because of its large size and its precise location. For instance, Brixham harbour in south-west Eng-land became the home of up to 1,300 Belgians. Nearly half of the fishing fleet was able to reach Britain, amounting to 217 ships of various tonnages. Fitted with modern equipment, it constituted the most sizeable fleet in exile and was to contribute actively to the pro-vision of fresh fish supplies in Britain.[13] This distinctive community of sea-faring people was also characterised by the conflictual rela-tionships between the Belgian authorities in London and their representatives on the ground.

The other important community in exile was composed of the civil servants and state officials who had been evacuated to France on the order of the government. Their presence in Britain was quite fortuitous. The ships on which they had embarked in Ostend had been re-routed by the Royal Navy. The governmental services around Eaton Square and Eaton Place were to be rebuilt around these fragments of administrative staff and around a number of temporary agents recruited amongst the refugees. The Finance Min-ister, Camille Gutt, talked about a civil service made of 'odds and ends' like his department.[14] This central civil service, working alongside the ministerial cabinets, was to ensure conscientiously the

permanence and continuity of the State in exile, as well as representing it on an international level. The four ministries that were
essential in wartime, namely the Ministry of Colonies, the Finance
Ministry, the Defence Ministry and the Ministry of Foreign Affairs
were rapidly rebuilt. Most of the other ministerial departments were
nothing more than 'empty shells' populated with a few specialists
responsible for preparing for the return to their country. These ministerial departments would grow progressively larger as the
liberation of Belgian national territory drew closer.[15] In May 1941,
some 750 people belonged to the machinery of state.[16] The senior
civil service was composed both of high-ranking civil servants and
of a number of key personalities from the political, trade-union and
business worlds. These elites and their families represented, just like
the fishermen, a group that stood out because of its homogeneity
and its concentration in particular locations. They were also characterised by their intense social life, centred around the Belgian
Institute in London.[17] This was created in 1942 on the initiative of
a Belgian businessman, Armand Dutry, with the help of the British
Council.[18] It was a meeting place for people in exile from Belgium
and Luxembourg, and for their British sympathisers. From then on,
all official receptions held by the Belgian Government would take
place in its function rooms. The Art School division of the Ministry
of National Education, in charge of 'artistic propaganda', was also
to play a part in cultural life in exile. It organised numerous art
exhibitions, concerts,[19] lectures for the Belgian community and also
for some British organisations. This section of the Art School was
also involved in creating a rather colourful national folk group per-
sonified by six Gilles clowns from Binche. They were very successful
and British propagandists made sure they immortalised their per-
formances.

Although the Belgian Government focused its attention throughout its exile on occupied Belgium, it did not neglect the thousands
of fellow citizens who felt somewhat lost in a country whose language and customs were foreign to most of them. Faced with a
large-scale influx of Belgian nationals, the Belgian Embassy in London did not remain idle. However, its reactions gave the impression
that it was acting in an amateurish way and merely taking hasty initiatives. As early as mid-May 1940, it had set up an information
office, organised a collecting centre for clothes and tried to speed up
the formalities required by immigration rules and regulations. In
order to remedy the organisational failures of the British, Belgian
doctors provided medical help. By mid-August, a relief committee
had been created, chaired by the business adviser Charles Bastin,
and it took over the management of private donations in cash and

in kind received from abroad. The Belgian Government, which was being re-formed in London, was to call upon the inevitable Bastin to take charge of a central service, the purpose of which was to coordinate and centralise the disparate activities that had been organised by the embassy. Although he agreed to chair this service, Bastin's agreement was conditional on his having a Flemish assistant to act as his deputy. The agricultural attaché, Louis Borremans, was chosen for this post.

Subsequently, the Belgian Government took over both the structures for the refugees organised by the British authorities and the relief services created by its embassy in London, and sought to assert its authority by rapidly setting up a much more substantial administration to deal with the refugees. A Service Central des Réfugiés (Central Service for Refugees) was created in September 1940.[20] Its tasks covered nearly all the aspects of exile, from material assistance to moral help, including teaching, medical care and employment.[21] By creating a specific ministerial department, and giving it the means and staff it needed, the Belgian Government was, as far as possible, trying to compensate for the lack of care on the British part. As it only had limited powers, it sometimes had to resort to withdrawing material help in order to keep refractory refugees in order. One priority was to provide the refugees with work. This proved to be a slow and difficult task. Those Belgians who found themselves without employment were subjected against their will to a British welfare policy that enabled them at best to lead their lives as paupers. As a result of the severe restrictions imposed by the Ministry of Labour, work permits were only given out sparingly. Priority was given to the one million British unemployed who had not yet been found a job in the war economy. Most of the refugees who were able to find tenuous employment as workmen and technicians. Around one hundred men were singled out to carry out dangerous demolition work in the districts that had been bombed. Women could only find work as domestic staff.[22] Due to their lack of knowledge of the English language, intellectuals found it much more difficult to find jobs.[23]

The massive bombing raids of September 1940 scattered Belgians all over the United Kingdom. This dispersal increased their feeling of isolation and complicated the implementation of British and Belgian help. However, the Service Central des Réfugiés, which was financed by private funds collected in North and Latin America, endeavoured to distribute money, clothes and food as quickly as possible through its network of liaison officers across the country. It still had to overcome the reluctance of the British authorities, who tolerated this help in kind and in cash as long as it was only exceptional. Any regular supplement, if noticed, was followed by a reduction – to the same value – of official assistance allocated to the refugees.[24] British regulations did not take into account the isolation of the Belgians, their lack of knowledge of English and their ignorance about the mysteries of rationing and the black market. Nearly eight months after the exodus, in March 1941, the Service Central des Réfugiés still mentioned the tragic cases of children 'chez qui les effets de la sous-alimentation sont journellement constatés par les médecins attachés au Service Central'.[25] At the time, some 13,000 to 14,000 needy refugees were still dependent upon British authorities.[26] Their idleness only reinforced their feeling of helplessness, which was fuelled by their precarious material situation and the absence of news from those who had stayed on the continent. The Abbé de Voghel, a keen observer of the exile, mentioned the difficulties that the Belgians 'gros mangeurs et gourmets' faced in adapting to 'une cuisine anglaise maigre et sans goût'. He added, 'Les Belges, portés par tempérament à se plaindre, ne manquaient pas de se lamenter, moins cependant que les Français. Mais bien vite les Belges, avec leur facilité de s'assimiler les langues et leur esprit de débrouillardise, surent s'adapter à leur nouvelle situation.'[27]

Indeed, the refugees progressively recreated a social fabric and a network of associations thanks to the benevolent help of local British committees. A large number of Belgian clubs were created and were a great success. Meetings took place in a wide variety of venues: halls of Protestant, Anglican, Methodist and Wesleyan charity organisations, village halls, those of the Salvation Army and of the Labour Party.[28] The moral assistance provided by the Belgian Government included the distribution of national newspapers published in Britain, setting up leisure centres and organising a service for sending letters to the occupied country. This moral assistance was also backed up by the provision of spiritual welfare for the refugees, amongst whom the Catholic Church of Great Britain and the Belgian Prime Minister believed there to be a large proportion of believers. Cardinal Hinsley, the Archbishop of Westminster, and Archbishop Amigo, Bishop of Southwark, immediately devoted their efforts to attending to the spiritual needs of the Allied war refugees. In May 1940, they created the Catholic War Refugees Spiritual Welfare Committee in order to bring religious, moral and also social and material assistance to the refugees. Hubert Pierlot, the Catholic Prime Minister, was soon preoccupied with their religious welfare. The existence of a British Catholic committee that mobilised approximately ten Belgian priests, the extent of its involvement with the refugees, the patronage of Cardinal Hinsley and the active collaboration of the Belgian authorities were not sufficient, it appears, to satisfy Pierlot. The Prime Minister intended to centralise the organisation of refugee priests and ensure in this way a greater cohesion among the exiled Belgians. He considered this cohesion to be essential at a religious and national level. After bitter negotiations with the Catholic hierarchy of England and Wales, he was allowed in January 1941 to set up a central figure of authority, namely Mgr. Myers, Bishop of Lormus. The latter was put in charge of organising the Belgian pastoral ministry. It was a difficult task. Myers only had around twenty priests to deal with nearly 15,000 refugees. Faced with this reality, the Spiritual Committee, first, and Mgr. Myers, later, had to establish priorities. Their effort focused first on the main clusters of refugees and on teaching religion within the schools that were financed by the Belgian Government. The remaining faithful, who were scattered all over the country, had to be content with the all too rare visits of Belgian priests who were practising a 'flying ministry' and with the British clergy.

Belgian services were soon preoccupied with the type of teaching that should be given to the thousands of children of refugees, and they took a census of nearly 2,500 children for whom they were legally obliged to provide an education. As early as the first few months of their exile, a large number of refugee children attended British schools free of charge, and a small group of students was helped to join different universities.[29] With a view to speeding up the integration of young Belgians, it was decided at first not to create any primary schools but to facilitate the enrolment of children in British schools. Extra coaching sessions were to be given in their mother tongue by Belgian primary-school teachers. This solution proved to be not entirely satisfactory. The evacuation complicated matters, and parents struggled to follow their offspring's school results. So the Department of National Education, now restored, decided to teach on a national scale simultaneously in Belgian and British schools. Additionally, it made the teaching of English compulsory from primary school onwards in all Belgian schools. Correspondence courses were organised for children who lived in isolated areas. In order to complete the study cycle introduced during the period of exile, the Department introduced technical and professional teaching and English lessons for adults. During the academic year 1942–1943, 300 pupils attended lessons in eight Belgian primary schools and 464 pupils were grouped in seven mixed-system schools. In addition, 560 pupils attended British schools in which no extra teaching sessions were given.[30]

Secondary school teaching was also organised rapidly. The French Lycée of London, which had been evacuated to Penrith, in

Cumberland, resumed activity teaching young girls and boys in exile. In Derbyshire, a Belgian College was created in Buxton on the initiative of Father Robert Jourdain. The Department of National Education was in favour of sending Belgian pupils to British schools, rather than creating *athénées* or independent Catholic schools with a boarding-school system. This solution would have had the advantage of saving public funds and facilitating the integration of the young refugees. However, as had always been the case in Belgium, the Department chose to respect the free choice of the head of the family by letting him choose between English schools, official Belgian schools and grant-aided private schools.[31] In 1941, the Belgian Institute opened its doors in Kingston in Surrey. A boarding-school *athénée* was created in Braemar not far from the royal residence of Balmoral in Scotland. In 1943, these four schools had some 330 pupils in total.

However, there was insufficient educational and school material and the premises were inadequate. The Department attempted to make up for these shortages with the sympathetic help of the Board of Education, the Ministry of Health and the British Council. Teaching staff were scarce and their numbers were boosted, as well as could be expected, by people recruited within the Belgian administration and among the refugees. Some classes were composed both of Flemish and French-speaking pupils. In others, year groups or different sections were taught together. Another problem was that, while the vast majority of pupils attending Belgian schools were Dutch-speaking, the majority of the teachers in the secondary schools were French-speaking. Consequently, despite the efforts of the Department and the goodwill of the teachers, both qualified and temporary ones, the level of secondary school teaching did not measure up to that of the pre-war period. As stated in an inspection report: '[il] serait vain de le dissimuler, nous avons affaire surtout à un enseignement d'occasion, où l'excellent est uni au médiocre et même douteux.'[32] The Department nevertheless subsequently recognised the diplomas issued in Britain.

Exile entered a second phase during 1941, when the Belgian Government collaborated closely with the British authorities in finding employment for the refugees. The transformation of the government financial organisation that helped needy Belgians into a Caisse Belge de Prêts et d'Epargne set up to collect their savings is typical of how the status of the Belgian population was evolving at that time. This return to work followed the British mobilisation of its citizens and took place in three stages. In April 1941, it was decided that an Anglo-Belgian Employment Exchange should be created. Its task was to undertake the placement of Belgians who were fit to work. In May, the British Government decreed that all Belgians should enrol.[33] In July, a registration record book for work and social welfare was introduced. This enabled the authorities to identify those refugees who were wrongfully benefiting from Belgian welfare or who were trying to avoid returning to work. The Belgian Government did not hesitate to impose sanctions on those guilty of these forms of dishonesty. The level of mobilisation of refugees in the war effort was extraordinarily high. At the end of 1941, 80 percent of men and 30 percent of women had been put to work.[34]

Since 1 April 1942, the Belgian Government had at last been able to take charge of the cost of welfare for needy refugees, which had up until then been borne by the British authorities. But it was not able to establish a regular supplement for the Belgians and the Service Central des Réfugiés merely reimbursed the expenditure of the British local authorities. The number of Belgians who were helped was therefore minimal.[35] By May 1943, nearly 90 percent of men and 40 percent of women had found employment.[36] The mass of paupers of the summer of 1940 had turned into a worthwhile workforce for the British economy in the context of total warfare.

On 8 September 1944, the Belgian Government landed in Brussels amidst complete indifference. The refugees, however, would have to wait before they could return to their country. The main part of the repatriation was to take place in successive phases throughout the summer and autumn of 1945. The last refugees would return to their country in September 1946.[37] For the 15,000 Belgians who experienced it, exile was an exceptional and extraordinary period in their lives, marked by the traumas of the exodus from Belgium, bombardments and separation. The objective of the Belgian Government had always been to include its refugees in the British war effort as quickly as possible in the same way as it had treated its gold, its army and its colonial resources. The restrictions imposed by the British forced it initially to focus on improving the daily lot of the Belgians, but, surprisingly, the large number of documents that have survived never mention the slightest criticism of the shortcomings of the British welfare policy. Undoubtedly, the room to manoeuvre was small and this was the price that had to be paid in order to enjoy British hospitality and to contribute to the war effort.

The Belgian Government was also obsessed with asserting its authority over the population of refugees and ensuring its cohesion. This search for national cohesion was at the root of a cumbersome administrative machinery and of the costly organisation of Belgian teaching. It also explains why the Prime Minister was keen to establish a religious authority over the thousands of refugees; a pre-occupation that was particular to Pierlot and that was not evident in the speeches and the actions of the other ministers. Moreover, in October 1940, before any steps had been taken to organise the refugees, the Prime Minister had granted himself all the ministerial departments and services that were principally concerned with the refugees, namely their welfare, work, education and even conscription. The Finance Minister, Camille Gutt, seemed merely obsessed with the scale and the management of the expenses incurred by the department for the administration of the refugees. The Minister of the Colonies, Albert De Vleeschauwer, and the Minister of Foreign Affairs, Paul-Henri Spaak, who at one point were both in charge of the key ministries concerned with refugees, seemed to have little to do with the daily management of the Belgians in exile.

Beyond the heroic attitude of the British, who showed resistance and solidarity when faced with the Blitz, what can we learn about this exile, which spanned five long years? The impressions are contrasting, but the first must be the absence of generosity on the part of the official British authorities. In the early stages of exile, this was made worse by a series of restrictions concerning travel, work and evacuation from disaster-stricken areas. All these limitations to British hospitality gave the impression that the status of the war refugees was precarious. This reinforced the feeling of alienation and did not favour the Belgians' integration into British society. Their involvement with the war effort was to dispel this initial bad impression and facilitate their integration, albeit into factories.

The period of exile was also characterised by a feeling of isolation among the Belgians. There were few contacts between the different clusters of refugees and still less between the 40 percent of refugees scattered all over the country, and the Belgian soldiers, most of whom were not aware of the scale, if not of the presence, of a population of Belgian refugees. National unity and bonds were expressed through the Belgian press published in Britain and at the main patriotic ceremonies that punctuated this period of exile. But Belgian society in exile did not appear as a homogeneous national group. Instead, it was composed of small, compartmentalised worlds among which we can distinguish the armed forces, politicians, state employees and approximately ten clusters of refugees comprising some 5,000 Belgians. If the pre-war conflicts of opinion among the Belgians still existed in a microscopic way, they probably merely affected the political spheres surrounding the Belgian Government in London. In any case, they did not apply to the vast majority of refugees, who merely lived through exile in anonymity and silence. We cannot really say that the Belgians integrated with

British society, but rather that there was peaceful cohabitation in residential areas and the workplace. The period of exile was marked by fellow countrymen gathering together in the expectation of their return home. This natural tendency towards a withdrawal into oneself was, however, counterbalanced by the openness of the children to British culture, which they encountered in the classroom and in the street. It was these young Belgians who were the principal motor of integration, together with the few fishermen who were to settle permanently in Britain and the military, some of whom married British women.

Notes

* Translated by Christine Arthur.

1. Cf. J. Gerard-Libois and J. Gotovitch, *L'an 40, la Belgique occupée*, Brussels, 1971; J. Stengers, *Léopold III et le gouvernement : les deux politiques belges de 1940*, Paris-Gembloux, 1980; L. Schepens, *De Belgen in Groot-Brittannië 1940–1944: feiten en getuigenissen*, Bruges, 1980; J. Gotovitch and H. Balthazar, *Camille Huysmans. Documenten C. Huysmans in Londen*, Antwerp-Amsterdam, vol. 7, 1978; R. Devleeshouwer, *Henri Rolin 1891 – 1973: Une voie singulière, une voix solitaire*, Brussels, 1994; J. Gotovitch, 'Camille Huysmans et la Seconde Guerre Mondiale', in *Etudes de la personnalité de Camille Huysmans*, Antwerp, 1971, pp. 123–69.
2. In July 1940, the four most important groups were the Poles (with 3,122 refugees over fifteen years of age), the French (1,642), the Dutch (948) and British expatriates (732). Women's Royal Voluntary Service (WRVS) Archive (London), 'The Story of the War Refugees in Great Britain 1940–1947', Appendix, 'Statistics of Foreign War Refugees' in W.V.S. Index up to 1 June 1954.
3. P.-A. Tallier, 'Les réfugiés belges à l'étranger durant la Première Guerre mondiale', in *Les émigrants belges-Réfugiés de guerre, émigrés économiques, réfugiés politiques ayant quitté nos régions du XVIème siècle à nos jours*, ed A. Morelli, Brussels, 1998, p. 20.
4. 'War Refugees from Holland and Belgium – Report by the Aliens Advisory Committee'[draft], Public Record Office (PRO), London, Assistance Board 11/70; 'War Refugees from Holland and Belgium – Report', Aliens Advisory Committee to War Cabinet Civil Defence Committee, PRO CDC (40) 9.
5. The WVS had been set up in June 1938, following the suggestion of the Home Secretary Samuel Hoare, in order to prepare women for the bombing attacks that an impending world war would inevitably bring. With no equivalent among other voluntary organisations, they subsequently grew to have millions of active members spread out over a network covering the whole country.
6. 'Refugees from the Continent in the event of invasion of their countries – Assistance by the Board – Part B', April 1940–July 1940, WRVS Archive, File RFG 25/1, and 'War Refugees and Central Committee for War Refugees – Correspondence & Reports – Part 1', 14 February 1940 – 1 December 1940, both PRO AST 11/71.
7. Cf. J. Vanwelkenhuyzen, *1940 – Le grand exode*, Paris-Gembloux, 1983, p. 299; Abbé J. De Voghel, *La vie religieuse des Réfugiés Belges en Grande Bretagne pendant la guerre 1940–1945*, Bruxelles, 15 September 1945, p. 2, Archief

Aartsbisdom Mechelen, Kardinaal Van Roey 1926–1961; 'Second Report from
Mass Observation on Refugees' 6 June 1940, Tom Harrison Mass-Observation
Archive (THMO), University of Sussex, File Report 174; 'North London
Refugees', 27 May 1940, THMO, File Report 143.

8. In 1941, according to British statistics which do not take into account children
under sixteen years of age, there were 9,853 Belgians amongst the 17,188 allied
war refugees. Among the 238,720 'non-enemy' residents, 5,677 were Belgian citizens.

9. *Travaux statistiques* (employment statistics), London, 15 April 1943, Centre
d'études et de documentation Guerre et Sociétés contemporaines (CEGES), Brussels, Louis Borremans Papers, PB10/15.

10. Ten localities were to accommodate more than a fifth of all Belgian refugees in
Great Britain: senior civil servants were concentrated in Westminster and Kensington (London County Council); refugees from various origins could be found
in Potters Bar, Dewsbury (Yorkshire) and Hornsey (Middlesex), sailors and fishermen and their families were concentrated in Preston (Lancashire), Newlyn
and Penzance (Cornwall), Brixham (Devon), Cardiff and Swansea (Glamorgan).

11. 'Liste statistique des réfugiés par comté', CEGES, PB10/12; 'Répartition des
Réfugiés par localités Anglaises et par Comtés', undated, CEGES, PB10/12.

12. Abbé J. De Voghel, *La vie religieuse*, p. 1; 'A la mémoire de M. Charles Bastin',
in *Bulletin des Anciens de l'Institut Supérieur du Commerce de l'Etat à Anvers*,
1966, p. 3, CEGES, PB10/1; letter from the Prime Minister to the Belgian
Ambassador to the Vatican, London, 6 December 1940, Archives Générales du
Royaume (AGR), Brussels, Premier Ministre de Londres (PML), 58. In 1942, the
parliamentarian Werner Koelman put pressure on the Belgian government 'pour
que l'on veille à ce que, à la Croix-Rouge, les réfugiés, dont la majorité sont
d'expression flamande, puissent trouver des médecins comprenant leur langue
maternelle'. Procès-verbal of meeting of 3 March 1942, Conseil Consultatif
auprès du Gouvernement Belge en Grande-Bretagne, London, no.12, p. 5, AGR,
PML, 115.

13. 'Bateaux de pêche belges en Angleterre pendant la guerre 1940–1945', AGR,
Administration de la Marine, I 215/9985.

14. State employees in France were sent back to Belgium after the collapse of France.

15. Apart from its daily work of preserving and defending Belgian interests throughout the world, mobilising all the forces on the free territory and developing the
war effort in Congo, as the end of the war and the liberation of its national territory seemed to be getting ever closer, the machinery of state had to spend an
ever increasing part of its time in dealing with the essential problems associated
with re-occupying its own country, such as repressing collaboration, providing
fresh supplies, helping with the return of transferred people or dealing with civil
matters. R. Motz, *Angleterre et Belgique*, London, 1944, p. 84.

16. Apart from the vast majority of *fuyards*, there were some 700 civil servants who
had been evacuated on order on 17 May from Ostend to Dieppe and had been
re-routed to Britain. Altogether, some 3,000 civil servants and State officials
were present in Britain. Most of them were not employed in the Belgian administration in London but shared the fate of their compatriots, who were first
helped and later put to work: PRO FO 371/26 430; F. De Kerckhove D'Exaerde,
'Quelques questions en droit international public relatives aux fondements
juridiques de la présence et de l'activité du gouvernement belge en exil à Londres. Octobre 1940 – Septembre 1944' (mémoire de licence, Brussels University,
ULB, 1988), p. 51.

17. *Activité du Département de l'Instruction Publique belge en Grande-Bretagne*
(juin 1940 à octobre 1943), undated, 64 ff. in AGR, PML, 255.

18. It was set up in Belgrave Square not far from the governmental services and from the embassy, and inaugurated in May 1942 in the presence of many personalities, including the Grand Duchess of Luxembourg and the Duke of Kent. Two 'Belgian style' restaurants were opened, as well as a bar, a library and large meeting rooms. After the war, the Institute became the Anglo-Belgian Club: A. Dutry, *Mémoires résumés* (Abridged version), no date or place, pp. 8 and ff, Tinou C. Dutry Private papers, Brussels.

19. The famous Belgian string quartet of London (Léonard Ardenois, Marcel Gazelle, Maurice Raskin and Rodolphe Soiron).

20. Décisions prises par le Gouvernement concernant les services chargés des réfugiés belges en Angleterre, London, 21 September 1940, AGR, PML, 199.

21. Subsequently, once the ministerial departments were re-established, they regained control of their respective activities.

22. For women's experience of exile see F. Raes, 'Femmes belges réfugiées en Angleterre pendant la Seconde Guerre mondiale. – Une histoire orale' (mémoire de licence, University of Liège, ULg, 1995).

23. L'activité de l'Office Parlementaire Belge de Londres (Rapport de M. Armand Dutry, Secrétaire), undated, AGR, PML, 177. The Belgian Parliamentary Office was created on 22 July 1940 under the Presidency of Camille Huysmans, socialist *bourgmestre* of Antwerp. The Office was intended to reunite the exiled parliamentarians and to help the refugees.

24. G.G. Kulmann to Baron Ruzette, London, 18 December 1940, AGR, PML, 199.

25. Notes on the Service Central des Réfugiés Belges, 25 March 1941, p. 3, AGR, PML, 199.

26. C. Bastin, 'Pour nos vingt mille réfugiés. L'activité du Service Central', *La Belgique Indépendante*, 24 April 1941.

27. Abbé J. De Voghel, *La vie religieuse*, p. 3.

28. Ibid.

29. Rapport général sur l'activité du Service Central des Réfugiés, 20 June 1943, CEGES, PB10/1.

30. *Activité du Département de l'Instruction Publique belge en Grande-Bretagne*, p. 32.

31. Ibid.

32. H. Van Daele, *Camille Huysmans en het onderwijs*, Antwerp, 1976, p. 142.

33. All men between the ages of sixteen and sixty-five and women between the ages of sixteen and fifty.

34. Out of 5,720 men registered, 4,638 were sent to work. The number of women sent to work was smaller due to numerous exemptions, which were granted in particular to housewives. It amounted to 1,569 out of the 5,105 who were registered: Rapport général sur l'activité en Angleterre du Ministère du Travail et de la Prévoyance Sociale, undated, 1943, AGR, PML, 199.

35. It was brought back down to 600 people living under the scheme of all meals provided and 1,750 people entitled to subsistence allowance as well as housing benefit. In 1944, these numbers only amounted to 130 and 1,360 refugees respectively.

36. The figures reached 5,306 out of 5,983 men and 2,547 out of 5,527 women, respectively.

37. M.-P. Herremans, *Personnes déplacées (rapatriés, disparus, réfugiés)*, Ruisbroeck-Brussels, 1948.

4

FEMALE BELGIAN REFUGEES IN BRITAIN DURING THE SECOND WORLD WAR: AN ORAL HISTORY*

FRANÇOISE RAES

Half of the Belgian refugees in Britain were women. It is this simple fact that formed the starting point of this work. If the records of the whole Belgian community exiled in Britain remain extremely limited, they are non-existent when we consider women. The history of daily life dissolves in the incidental and the ephemeral; it is composed of trivial actions that, because of their repetitive and unchanging character, seem never to constitute part of history.

Research, census work and the transcription and analysis of the accounts given by the people who lived during this troubled period remain the only possible way of understanding this reality. It is therefore easy to understand our choice to use oral sources to carry out our research, not to say our necessity of doing so. We traced and contacted fifty-seven women. Around thirty of them responded positively. Out of our various meetings with them, we selected twenty-six interviews, on the basis of the sound quality and contents, which represented more than six hundred pages. All the women interviewed were French speaking. A study of Flemish-speaking women (a large number of whom were present in Britain) would be necessary to present a complete picture of Belgian women's experience of the war in Britain. Trying to piece together these women's experience of the period of exile has a two-fold interest for us. First, by studying their daily lives we can cast a distinctive perspective on the war period and the difficulties experienced in exile. Second, Belgian women, with their cultural characteristics (most of them being Catholic and non-working) had to fit into a

British society in which because of the enforced conscription of women – whether they be British or not – war seemed to have drastically changed the traditional division of gender roles.

The people we encountered can be categorised into two age groups: in 1940, two thirds of them were between fourteen and twenty-four years old; the remaining third were between twenty-five and thirty-four. Nearly three quarters of them were single. Belgian women who were forced to work in Britain represented 69 percent of our sample. The remaining population in the sample was composed of 8 percent of young women who were starting or continuing University studies in Britain, while housewives represented 23 percent. Among those in paid employment, 44 percent had been nurses, 22 percent had enrolled in the women's contingent of the Royal Air Force while 17 percent had worked in war factories. The remaining 17 percent were made up of women working in the service sector, such as domestic staff, teachers and civil servants.

Britain: A Destination Between Choice and Contingency

The British authorities were preparing to greet a flood of refugees from the Netherlands and Belgium as early as January 1940. The experience of the First World War, when nearly one hundred thousand Belgians had found refuge in Britain, offered a good model for the Ministry of Health, which was in charge of co-ordinating the arrival of displaced persons. So, as early as the beginning of 1940, when the Belgian Government, torn between optimism and neutrality, was not contemplating any measures to evacuate its population, the British Minister of Health took care of organising assistance for the Belgian refugees. The structure of this assistance for the foreign evacuees fitted in with the evacuation plan set up for British citizens, the Prevention and Relief of Distress Scheme (P.R.D.).[1]

From 1939, Great Britain decided to evacuate school-age children and infants accompanied by their mothers from the industrial suburbs of large cities, taking them to the country where they would be protected from the bombing. Following the principle of communicating vessels, the areas that had been 'emptied' – such as London and its suburbs – would be repopulated by the refugees coming from Belgium and Holland. The Home Office quoted the provisional figure of 200,000 Belgians who, once their country had been invaded by the Germans, would land on British soil. The inhabitants of the Belgian coast, the sailors and their families amounted to 40,000 of them.[2] These figures proved to be highly exaggerated: the

Belgian community in Britain during the Second World War in fact never reached more than 15,000 people altogether.[3]

In most cases, the women we met did not take any deliberate decision to leave Belgium for Britain. They left for France with the intention of following their husbands (or fathers) who were members of the administrative services of the Belgian government and in order to prevent their younger sons (or brothers) from being captured by the occupying forces:

> Mon frère avait dix-huit ans [. . .] On entendait constamment, à la radio, des appels du Gouvernement qui disaient: Les jeunes gens, partez de Belgique parce que les Allemands vont vous rappeler, vous mettre au travail. Tous les jeunes gens devaient partir. Mon oncle était ingénieur sur la malle Prins Albert, il nous a dit: partez avec nous, nous allons en France. On a pris un tout petit peu de bagages, fermé la porte, donné la clé au voisin et on est parti . . . C'est d'avoir un fils de cet âge là qui a décidé mes parents à partir.[4]

Others left to follow the rest of the refugee column, haunted by their memories of the Great War and the fear of bombings: 'Mes parents, mes grands-parents surtout, ont décidé de partir, de s'évacuer. Parce que ma marraine attendait un bébé pour bientôt. Ma grand-mère ayant connu les atrocités à la guerre de 14–18 avait peur et voulait partir. Alors nous sommes partis.'[5] A small number deliberately chose to go to Britain. They were Jewish, leftist militants, nurses or patriotic members of the Resistance. Denise Herrera, a nurse working for the army Medical Corps, decided, after France had capitulated, to carry on with her journey as far as England, as her charge nurse, who had served at the Ocean Hospital during the Great War, had persuaded her that she would meet up again with a large number of the Belgian armed forces.[6] Many of the refugees who arrived directly from Flanders were families of civil servants sailing from Ostend to meet up with the heads of the family in Le Havre. As the ships found that the French ports had been bombed by the Germans, they had to change course and to land on the English coast. Other Belgian families had fled to the North of France. Once there, some chose or were obliged to embark on British ships bound for England. A third route was through the Pyrenees to Lisbon and then England. After enduring several months of a long and dangerous journey, these people finally managed to arrive in Britain.

When the refugees arrived in the English ports, the British authorities took them to reception camps. Each person was interrogated by the police and had to undergo a medical examination. The refugees were fed and given basic accommodation. Within twenty-four hours, trains or buses were taking them towards London, where people without any income were placed in host families:

Arrivés à Plymouth, on nous a logés trois jours dans un cinéma . . . à
notre arrivée, on nous a donné des scones et du thé. De là, nous
avons été à Londres dans une famille d'accueil, chez des Anglais. Je
n'étais pas avec mes parents parce qu'ils ne savaient pas prendre trois
personnes. Mais nous habitions le même quartier. J'ai été bien
accueillie, on mangeait bien.[7]

The women we interviewed felt relief during their first few days in
England. As soon as they had arrived, they felt safe. But, being
physically and emotionally exhausted, the police interrogations
were a painful experience for them. During the first few weeks, they
became aware of their status as refugees. The price to be paid for
the British welcome was limitations on their freedom: no unautho-
rised trips, no bicycles, no radio and no cars or cameras.[8]

The War Years

Between the appeals of the British Government to mobilize the population and the restricted freedom they were given, Belgian women
lived, until 1941 – when all those between the ages of nineteen and
forty had to register with the Labour Exchange – in a state of partial
and often involuntary idleness, which drove them to devote all of
their energy to coping with daily life. Their daily routine, as was the
case for British civilians, was punctuated by bombings, the black-out
and rationing. But their feeling of exhaustion was compounded by
anguish as they waited for some news from their home country.
Despite the rationing of foodstuffs and the queues, preparing a good
meal was their way of rediscovering the scents from home, which
served as a means of identification in their otherwise completely disrupted environment.[9] For some of them the only time when they
could get out of the house and meet other women was when they
went shopping. At the market or in shops they had to speak English,
check their change, fend for themselves and, above all, be patient.
Older women often sent out the younger ones, who were more
resourceful, to do the shopping. Although they sometimes had some
difficulties with the English language, Belgian housewives kept a
clear head when it came to their wallets: 'Quand on était une bonne
cliente, qu'on achetait des fruits, des légumes, de tout, on vous don-
nait parfois des choses en-dessous du comptoir, comme on disait.'[10]

These women, who were gathered in the London conurbation
and were unable to leave freely, suffered enormously under the aerial barrage:

Pendant les alertes, nous protégions le bébé. On le mettait dans le
masque à gaz en carton . . . On descendait les quatre marches à la

cave. Et l'enfant était couché là, sur le petit matelas, et moi sur le béton à côté. On était vraiment mal mis et cela a duré longtemps, toutes les nuits. Quand il y avait du brouillard, on descendait quelquefois à cinq heures jusqu'au lendemain matin. Heureusement que je le nourrissais, il ne fallait pas remonter faire des biberons.[11]

They retain a mythic memory of the stoical behaviour of the Londoners caught in the middle of the Blitz. But when they recount their own experience of the bombardments, they recall times of fear, endless sleepless nights and the absence of safe shelters. In this way, their memory was split into two parallel and contrasting fields: their own experience of the Blitz and their perception of the behaviour of the British. In contrast, four years later, when the V1 and V2 missile attacks on Belgium started, the Belgian Government attempted, as far as possible, to evacuate young mothers and pregnant women to the country.

The exile was experienced very differently by women from one generation to another. The young Belgian mothers in Britain who were separated from their husbands, had to take on – often for the first time in their lives – the role of head of the family. During the absence of their husbands, the young women would tell their children about them. The fathers retained their symbolic place and their status as the head of the family as a result of the presence of photographs and what the mothers said about them. For the older mothers aged fifty to sixty, the experience of exile was a very painful one indeed. For the first time in their lives, they had to manage on their own, without the support of a man. Having never really adapted to British society, these women lived cut off from the world. They went out to the market and knitted frantically for the Belgian Red Cross in London:

Ma mère ne cherchait pas de travail. Elle aurait été bien incapable de trouver du travail là. C'était une ménagère. Elle n'avait pas de qualifications, elle ne connaissait pas l'anglais ... Ma mère était une enfant unique qui a toujours fait ce que son père et sa mère lui ont dit de faire. Jusqu'au jour où elle s'est mariée. Et là, elle a fait ce que son mari lui disait de faire.[12]

Compulsory Conscription: Women at Work

Great Britain was the only country in the world to use feminine conscription to increase the labour force in wartime. The women from Allied countries who had found refuge in Britain were subjected to the same obligations as the British nationals. The mobilisation of the female labour force was carried through gradually. Between

1939 and 1943, the number of women employed increased by 30 percent. It reached a peak in 1943, when 7,250,000 women were at work in industry, the armed forces or civil defence; 8,770,000 remained full-time housewives.[13] From September 1939 to May 1940, the British government took no initiative whatsoever to integrate women in the workforce. It merely conducted a laissez-faire policy, in the hope that the people needed by industry would flood in to meet the demand. On 3 September 1939, the Service Armed Forces Act organised the conscription of men between eighteen and forty-one years old. During this period, many qualified women were hoping to be enlisted and offered their services as volunteers. But their job offers were not considered. In May 1940, the Government speeded up the procedures for voluntary enlistment by concentrating the work in the war industry. Exchanging workers between the war industry sector and other ones was not, however, a straightforward process. The output of the so-called secondary industries (ready-to-wear clothes, shoes, textiles, perfumes, etc.) declined and they consequently laid off workers. The available female workforce resulting from these cuts found it difficult to find new employment, and the number of unemployed people remained greater than the number of people employed by the war industry.[14] The propaganda of the Ministry of Information during this period expressed ambiguous and contradictory messages for women. A film made by the Ministry of Information, *They Also Serve*, released in 1940, presented a celebration of housewives. Domestic tasks and the education of children had become a patriotic duty for women in wartime; that was why men were fighting on the front. On the other hand, however, the propaganda stressed the necessity for women to enlist as volunteers in the war effort, with the emphasis placed on working in the women's services and in nursing. The authorities still failed to promote factory work. Nursing jobs were presented as the model of female employment, in which women's qualities of devotion and sacrifice came into their own. The nurse, like the man who was fighting, found her identity in her work.[15]

In the course of 1941, the government gradually moved towards compulsory work for women, although at each stage of this process it strove to preserve the spirit of voluntary enlistment. The compulsory enrolment of all women aged between nineteen and forty at the local labour exchange constituted the first stage of this evolution (in the autumn of 1942, this measure was to be extended to forty-five year old women and, eventually, to fifty-year-old women by 1943). This measure, however, did not bring about the results that had been expected and the authorities had to take the policy of conscription even further, because the number of women in war factories was not increasing sufficiently quickly. In December 1941, the National Service Number 2 Act sought to recruit more women into the women's services, but still left women the option of enlisting in the armed services, in civil defence or in industry instead. In January 1942, single young women aged twenty and twenty-one were called up. The Employment of Women Order became law on 16 February 1942 and marked the final stage towards the conscription of women. Apart from a few exceptions, women aged between twenty and thirty years could only be employed through the Labour Exchange and were sent where their labour was needed. This law, which was extended to forty year old women in 1943, also enabled women to secure a part-time job.[16]

Domestic responsibilities remained the most important barrier to voluntary enlistment. Older women often looked after very young children, while families often considered young women to be responsible for the domestic chores. Women themselves perceived it as essential to wait patiently in the queues when everything was rationed and to prepare meals to feed the other members of the family. Women would have more willingly enlisted if the British Government had offered the possibility of part-time work, as well as other incentives, such as childminding facilities and set shopping hours. Moreover, the men in the family (husbands or fathers) were often opposed to allowing their wives or daughters go out to work, sometimes far away from home. Quite a few government ministers also shared the view that women's first duty in wartime was to look after the house.

The propaganda messages did not affect women greatly. The Ministry of Information based its slogans on feelings of patriotism and national unity, and such speeches proved to have little effect on a feminine audience. The propaganda was predominantly addressed to women who were not working and called on them to become involved in a job that was essential to the war. But all these women considered their domestic tasks as essential. Besides, such propaganda could only work if it was supported by policies designed to create good working conditions. Yet during the first few years of the war, the authorities asked women to join the labour force before creating the material conditions necessary to integrate them into it.[17]

Factory work was perceived in negative terms by British women: it appeared simple, repetitive, boring and monotonous. The war factories were still associated with working-class women, who tended to be considered to be immoral. Though the propaganda put forward an image of great social diversity within the factories, where young women from aristocratic and working-class backgrounds

mixed, the statistical and documentary evidence contradicted this
myth and demonstrated the persistence of class segregation within
them. The prejudices of employers against a female workforce also
slowed down the process of mobilisation. Manufacturers considered
women to be unsuitable for factory work and sometimes believed
them to be immoral. In addition, the trade unions were strongly
opposed to allowing women to enter traditionally male sectors, for
fear that they might not find vacancies for the male workforce after
the war.[18]

Belgian women entered the world of female employment with
their specific cultural values. Compared with British women, their
position and their autonomy in pre-war society remained defined
and limited by a conservative political and economic context.
Therefore they entered the work force in very different circumstances from British women, who, after their participation in the
First World War, had won the right to vote and become full citizens.
During the First World War, Belgian women had suffered the German occupation of their country. Deprived of the right to vote, they
remained second-class citizens during the inter-war years.[19] Subordinated and subjected to the same regulations as British women,
female Belgian refugees had to comply with the progressive mobilisation of women in war production. During the first few months,
however, the issue of employment was as serious a problem for Belgian men as for women. A proper structure for the employment of
both male and female Belgian refugees had to await the arrival of
the Belgian Government in London at the end of 1940, as well as a
change in the British Government's initially distrustful attitude
towards them. The Ministry of Health had initially intended to
employ the Belgian refugees, who were considered to be competent
skilled workers, as quickly as possible,[20] but this confidence in the
flexibility of the labour market appeared to be undermined by the
inability of the British Ministry of Labour to curb unemployment
among the local population. To alleviate its expenses, the Ministry
of Health hastened to organise the conscription of refugees into
work, while the Ministry of Labour, for its part, prevented foreign
refugees from being taken on, in order to give priority to unemployed British nationals.

For both male and female refugees, working was first and foremost a question of pragmatism: working meant improving one's
standard of living without having to depend on British public welfare. For several months, both men and women found it difficult to
find work. British regulations did not allow foreigners to be
employed for posts that British nationals could have occupied,
while the British authorities required a special permit to work in

arms factories. However, women of all nationalities who had found refuge in Britain had a more flexible approach.[21] Belgian women found work more easily than their male companions. They managed to cope by taking on menial tasks, such as cleaning and cooking for the wealthy.[22]

In January 1941, Belgian men who had a good command of English and had been granted authorisation by the Aliens War Service Department were allowed to join training centres set up to prepare people for work in war factories. Women were also able to receive such training from June 1941. In January of the same year, the Belgian authorities had also created an Anglo-Belgian Labour Exchange to improve communication between both governments. From this period onwards, the 'Situations Vacant' column in the official Belgian government newspaper *La Belgique Indépendante* offered job opportunities for both men and women.[23] Two months after the compulsory enrolment of British citizens in their local labour exchange, male and female Belgian refugees also had to register with the labour exchange of the local authority in which they were resident. The age brackets involved, for men, were sixteen to sixty-five and for women were sixteen to fifty.[24] Over the subsequent months, more and more Belgian women registered. Already, before the decision of the British government to pass the National Service Number 2 Act, the Belgian authorities had been encouraging women to volunteer to work in a sector in which they had an interest, rather than be simply allotted a job. The principal options open to them were to work in a factory, to enrol in the women's services of the Royal Air Force (WAAF) or of the Army (ATS), or to be trained in the ambulance courses of the Belgian Red Cross prior to working for the organisation.[25] For the overwhelming majority of the participants whom we interviewed, this constituted an unprecedented experience.

In contrast, women of modest origin rapidly sought employment on their arrival in Britain. They were forced to find a job in order to improve their living standards. As they worked as domestic servants or in factories, the subsequent conscription of women in industry or the army had little real significance for them. For these Belgian women, working always remained primarily a necessity, rather than an act of patriotism or of support for the Allied cause.

Working conditions in factories were uncertain because of long working hours and repetitive tasks requiring stamina and sustained attention, as well as the repeated bombings. On the other hand, salaries could be quite high. For most people, however, factory work continued to be perceived as men's work. Wearing overalls, with their nails blackened by the grease from the machines, female factory workers radically changed the definitions of male and female spheres, and established new relationships between the sexes. On the one hand, the Allied soldiers were fighting for the status quo of the moral and social values of the pre-war years, and, on the other, this fight required radical changes in women's economic and social situation. This contradiction, which proved difficult to accept for both sexes, was also blurred by the ambiguous propaganda messages:

> A leur type, j'ai tout de suite reconnu debout, devant leur machine, quelques femmes de chez nous, de belles Flamandes aux yeux clairs, les joues pleines, le teint frais ... J'y ai vu des réfugiées en salopettes mais coquettes en diable, la permanente en plis, le dessin des sourcils et des lèvres ravivés d'un coup de crayon de fard, travaillant comme des hommes aux tours de revolvers ... Elles paraissaient tellement heureuses dans leur travail libérateur.[26]

In the factories, the young Belgian women used to strike up friendships with their British companions. These new social links helped to make the harsh working conditions more bearable and enabled the Belgian women to sail more easily through the hardships of exile, even if this only meant an education in the ways of resourcefulness, or even of the black market. Similarly, this complete immersion in the British culture forced them to learn the English language.

In wartime, working as a nurse seemed to be the ultimate female profession, in which the qualities of dedication and of self-sacrifice, associated at that time with the female gender, acquired their full significance and conferred a certain dignity. Many of the women whom we encountered during our research had chosen this profession during the war. Coming from middle-class backgrounds, they opted for nursing as result of their social position and their moral values. Working as a nurse challenged neither their female identity nor their role in society. The fear of having to work in factories and mixing with other social classes also encouraged these women towards an occupation better suited to their education. The Belgian Red Cross in London, an improvised medical organisation, appears to have attracted a good deal of goodwill but perhaps rather less medical competence. Nevertheless, it trained its young female recruits as ambulance assistants. The young women employed in the medical sector lived a strict and austere life. While this work experience might have been a novelty for them, their professional activity was anything but liberating.

The young women who enrolled in the women's contingent of the RAF (the WAAF), were also drawn from the more privileged strata of society. The enrolment of a father, a brother or a cousin in the British or Belgian armies prompted a number of young women to sign up in the women's services of the British armed forces. Driven by a heightened sense of patriotism, they were eager to participate in the war effort. All of the women whom we interviewed had been volunteers who had been attracted by the uniform and the spirit of adventure of this enterprise. Despite the efforts of British propaganda, they had no wish to work in factories, as this occupation was deemed to be degrading and of ill repute.

These young women were obliged to leave their families or loved ones for months on end. During their training, they experienced the difficulties of the hierarchical and collective lifestyle of the armed forces: thrown together for the first time in a collective life with other women, they discovered the loss of modesty as well as camaraderie and cultural and social diversity. Frequently allocated to office jobs, their lives in the WAAF were dominated by the rhythms of leave days and new postings. These young women found the hardships of a double separation difficult to cope with: far away from their families, they found it difficult to get used to transfers to new positions. At the same time, however, the women experienced a hitherto unknown closeness to the male soldiers. Mixed army life made it easier to establish friendships or love relationships between men and women.[27] For all those who joined the RAF, this enrolment remained the big adventure of their life:

> Les WAAF venaient de classes sociales excessivement différentes. Et c'est, je crois, ce dont mon père avait peur. J'ai fait des amitiés. C'est à ce moment que j'ai réalisé: ce n'est pas le travail que l'on fait qui compte, mais qui l'on est. Si votre père est éboueur, ça m'est tout à fait égal, mais vous, vous êtes une personne pour qui j'ai de l'estime. Il y a une espèce de nivellement si vous voulez. J'ai ouvert les yeux sur toutes ces classes sociales.[28]

For some young women who lived in London, leisure-time activities were of paramount importance. With the daily violence of bombings as a background, the cinemas, dance-halls and night clubs provided everyone with moments of light-heartedness and escape.

Memories and the Manipulated Memory

The Belgian women who lived in Britain during the Second World War remember the country as a friendly and generous one. These women's opinions of British people vary considerably, depending on whether they are evoking their own experience of daily life with the British or whether they are referring to the British people as a whole. Overall, the Belgian refugees tend to forget the hardships of the war which were shared by both communities, and to remember only the heroic qualities of the British. This process of idealisation might be seen as a way for these women to express their gratitude towards the country that had welcomed them, and, at the same time, as giving a more meaningful sense to their own experience of exile. After five years spent in exile, returning to Belgium was not easy. War experiences had been quite different on either side of the Channel. These women, whose youth had been put on hold for five years in Britain, now found their friends married or engaged, which dislocated their relationships and caused a mutual lack of understanding. Many of the exiled families came back to find their houses in ruins or looted, while the difficulties faced by the women who had joined the army when returning to their country were compounded by their need to adapt to civilian life once more.

For the women we interviewed, this wartime experience was not expressed in terms of female liberation or any new demands. Though they say that they felt more confident, more mature and more independent when they came back from Britain, none of them ever questioned their role within the family or society. Decision-making, whether in the family or in politics, remained the domain of men. Today, they still have very vivid memories of their experiences. They have retained special relationships with Britain, whether it be through friendships or tourism. The nurses from the Belgian Red Cross in London and the veterans of the WAAF still meet up, some fifty years later, to relive together their experience in Britain. But they are reluctant to speak about their memories with their families, other than to recall a humorous anecdote. Some of them do not even mention the war at all, as they feel their story is not worth telling.

Conclusion

Why has this modest, yet revealing element of Belgian history during the Second World War previously been ignored? First of all, the Belgian community in Britain amounted to some 15,000 people. Representing only a trivial percentage of the population, the story of this small community of refugees may seem anecdotal compared to that of occupied Belgium, which the vast majority of the population experienced. Moreover, Belgian women came back to their country strengthened by their participation in total warfare and imbued with the messages of British propaganda. They found it difficult to tell the story of their exile when confronted with the experience of occupied Belgium. Their British experience seemed to make them feel more guilty than heroic. Although they had not deliberately chosen to head for Britain, they regarded exile as a fortunate option when compared with the situation they would have experienced in occupied Belgium. Also, their participation in the British war-effort was belittled compared with tales of the Resistance and deportations. Finally, Belgian society in the post-war period only took into consideration the participation of men in liberating the country, thereby overshadowing Belgian women's experience and their role in the war.

Upon their return, they found a country that, despite the sufferings caused by German occupation of the territory, had not experienced fundamental changes in social or economic relationships between the sexes, unlike the United States or Britain. The Law of 19 February 1948, giving women the right to vote, was more the result of the Catholic Party's strategy to win an absolute majority, rather than a determined claim by Belgian women to participate in the political life of the country. The reintegration of the wartime exiles into Belgian society after the war took a traditional form, therefore. For those from bourgeois backgrounds, marriage (and the cessation of all employment as a consequence) served as an integrating force. For their part, the women from the working classes recovered their place in Belgian society by returning naturally and immediately to their work in factories. Wartime exile had thus enabled social differences to be maintained. Belgian women from good families working in factories alongside workers from the East End of London seems more than ever to have been a myth: the Belgian community had exported the social relations of the pre-war era. Women who worked in British factories had already done this type of work before their exile. For young women from the bourgeois classes, the novelty of having a job wore off because of their choice of so-called 'female' jobs. For them, the only way of breaking away from the conservatism of that period was to join the British armed forces.

Politics hardly ever features in the stories of the women we interviewed. Voluntary enrolment in the war effort was more often than not the result of a Belgian patriotic reflex rather than motivated by antifascist ideologies. The traditional role of women – particularly in ensuring the survival of the family unit – remained the major preoccupation for this Belgian community, which had been integrated into a society whose ideas on women's liberation were more progressive than its own. These women did not try to profit from their participation in the war effort in order to gain greater economic and legal equality. For Belgian women, exile reinforced the feeling of insecurity caused by total warfare. We can therefore assume that this conservative attitude – both during and after the war – enabled them to find reassuring points of reference in a situation that was chaotic and alien to them. So, for Belgian women in Britain, who often found themselves obliged to participate in the war effort, this experience remains an important episode in their lives. Exile did not, however, modify their perception of their role in society. Their participation in the public world remained acceptable because it was perceived as only temporary and justified by the necessity of winning the war.

Notes

* Translated by Christine Arthur.

1. Treasury Chambers, 24 February 1940, Public Record Office (PRO), London, AST 11/70.
2. Home Office, 13 February 1940, PRO AST 11/70.
3. Central register of aliens, Census figures (1943–45), PRO HO 213/588.
4. Interview with Josette Bens.
5. Interview with Alberte Leconte. Also interviews with Aline Delwarte, Evelyne Prilor and Renée Snoek.
6. Interview with Denise Errera.
7. Interview with Lucienne Bourguignon.
8. J. Vanwelkenhuysen and J. Dumont, *1940: Le grand exode*, Paris-Gembloux, 1983.
9. Interviews with Mariette Goffin and Aline Delwarte.
10. Interview with Léa Karny.
11. Interview with Aline Delwarte.
12. Interview with Madeleine Van Eeteveld.
13. M. Pugh, *Women and the Women's Movement in Britain, 1914–1949*, London, 1992.
14. P. Summerfield, *Women Workers in the Second World War: Production and Patriarchy in Conflict*, London, 1984, pp. 29–67.
15. S.L. Carruthers, '"Manning the factory": Propaganda policy on the employment of women, 1939–1947' in *History* 75 (1990): pp. 232–56.
16. Summerfield, *Women Workers in the Second World War*.
17. Carruthers, '"Manning the factory"'.
18. Summerfield, *Women Workers in the Second World War*.
19. M.L. Pirotte-Bourgeois, 'Episodes marquant dans la lutte des femmes belges pour leur droit au travail', in *Femmes, liberté, laïcité*, Brussels, 1989; F. Thebaud, 'La grande guerre: Le triomphe de la division sexuelle', in *Histoire des femmes en Occident*, vol. 5, eds G. Duby and M. Perrot, Paris, 1992.
20. Draft circular from the Ministry of Health to local authorities, 25 February 1940, PRO AST 11/70.
21. C. Lloyd, 'Les réfugiés', in *Londres 1939–1945: Riches et pauvres dans le même élan patriotique: derrière la légende*, ed. F. Poirier, Paris, 1995.
22. See, for example, *Richmond Herald*, 24 August 1940, PRO AST 11/72.
23. *La Belgique Indépendante*, 9 January 1941, p. 3; 12 June 1941, p. 3; 23 January 1941, p. 1.
24. *La Belgique Indépendante*, 26 May 1941, p. 3.
25. *La Belgique Indépendante*, 8 September 1941, p. 4.
26. *La Belgique Indépendante*, 25 February 1943, p. 4.
27. P. Summerfield, 'Sex, love and marriage', in *Out of the Cage: Women's Experiences in Two World Wars*, eds G. Braybon and P. Summerfield, London, 1987.
28. Interview with Christine Dumont.

5

THE RECONSTRUCTION OF BELGIAN MILITARY FORCES IN BRITAIN, 1940–1945*

Luc De Vos

On 28 May 1940, King Leopold III capitulated at the head of the Belgian army while his government, which had fled to France, maintained that the fight should continue. The question therefore arose immediately as to whether the capitulation applied to all the soldiers or only to the field army that was encircled. A few weeks later, after the French capitulated in June, the situation became very bleak indeed and all hope appeared to be lost. It was thus something of a miracle that in August 1944, a very modern military unit, displaying the Belgian flag, took part in the liberation of the national territory. What had happened in the meantime to make this possible?

Tenby: The Beginning

By 28 May, a number of Belgian soldiers had already reached Britain. Lieutenant-General Victor van Strydonck de Burkel, who had been called back out of his retirement, had arrived on 15 May 1940, at the head of a commission, with a view to buying horses in the country. When the catastrophe loomed in Belgium, the British Government sent him, together with those other Belgians eligible for military service, to Haverfordwest. When the Dutch soldiers arrived there too, the Belgians were moved to Tenby, on the south coast of Wales, on 24 May. Even those Belgian wounded who were in Britain on convalescent leave were sent to the Atlantic Hotel there.

The news of the capitulation had a devastating effect on the Belgian troops in the field. On the day it happened, a regular officer, Lieutenant Richard Smekens, from the 25th Engineer battalion, declared during a ceremony to the sound of the bugle in Klemskerke, that he would not abandon the struggle. Twenty men from his company decided to follow him. Later, a further eleven Belgian soldiers joined this group, among whom were a number of officers and even a Dutch corporal. On 29 May at 9 pm, this small unit, which also contained First Sergeant-Major Pierre Harboort was amalgamated with the 1st company of the 92nd Engineer Battalion of the 2nd North African Infantry Division of the French army. On 30 May, three further Belgian soldiers joined the troop. The unit was heavily involved during the evacuation of Dunkirk, and a few men were severely wounded during this operation. On the evening of 30 May, the Belgian sailed onboard a ship, the *Saint-Hélier*. On 31 May, they reached Folkestone. There, to their amazement, the Belgians were disarmed – but, after all, had Belgium not capitulated? – and later transferred to the military camp on Perham Downs near Salisbury. On 3 June, the group of Belgians was sent to Tenby. Soon after, around twenty Chasseurs Ardennais, under the command of a regular officer, Major Emile Cambier, and of Warrant Officer Monneau, also joined them in Tenby.

A few other individuals, most of them reserve officers, also fled on 28 May. In most cases, they attempted to join the French and British units that were being evacuated from one of the many beaches on the Belgian coast. Others left from the ports of Ostende and Nieuwpoort. One of them was the Socialist member of parliament from Liège, reserve First Lieutenant Georges Truffaut, who embarked at Nieuwpoort on 30 May with reserve Lieutenant Dieu, while Lieutenant Georges Danloy, the future founder of the commandos, embarked at Ostend. On 2 June, a considerable number of Belgian wounded soldiers were also taken to England onboard hospital ships. At the same time, a small number of Belgian soldiers, totalling some 550 men, including sixty officers, were sent back to France from Britain, via Brest, to resume the fight. In the meantime, however, the military situation had worsened considerably in France and the collapse of the country seemed unavoidable. When the French opened negotiations with the Germans with the intention of signing an armistice, the Belgian Government thought, not for the first time, about emigrating to London. Around 600 ministers and officials needed to be transferred from Poitiers to Britain, but the British offered to transport merely twelve or eighteen of them at most. Meanwhile, the idea of sailing to Britain from Bordeaux on board the ship the *Baudouinville* came to nothing because the Compagnie Maritime Belge was not prepared to take such a risk. The majority of the members of the cabinet therefore decided to offer the King their resignation, so that a new team might be able to negotiate with the victors. Thereupon, the Minister for Public Health, the francophone Liberal Marcel-Henri Jaspar, who was married to a Jewish woman, emigrated to London, where, on 23 June, he made a radio address calling on all Belgians to continue the war effort.

Jaspar's initiative was not, however, approved by his colleagues in France. On 20 June, Lieutenant General Albert Wibier, as the commander of Belgian troops in France, had sent a letter in which, on behalf of the Minister of National Defence, he announced that the attitude of the Belgian Government and of its military forces would mirror that of France – on 18 June, France has asked Germany to give it peace terms. On 27 June, the Belgian Prime Minister, Hubert Pierlot, announced that the issue of the return of all Belgian people, civilians and military, to Belgium should be settled in France. The troops stationed in France at that time were composed of the remaining soldiers from the 7th Infantry Division, namely around 3,600 men (in Brittany), as well as various training centres, among which were the officer cadets from the École d'Application of the École Royale Militaire, elements of the navy and the gendarmerie, most of the airforce and a number of other organisations as well as the CRABs (Centres de Recrutement de l'Armée Belge), which had been hastily established in France after the withdrawal from Belgium. A number of these soldiers were demobilised. Others presented themselves at the demarcation line and 25,000 of them were sent to Germany as prisoners of war. The huge quantity of Belgian war *matériel* would eventually fall into German hands and would later be given to the Romanians on the Eastern front.

Not all Belgians, however, seemed prepared to indulge the whims of the enemy. To opt for Britain in the summer of 1940 supposed a good deal of courage, clear-sightedness or naivety. To cite only a few examples among many: Jacques Wanty, the son of the general and writer Emile Wanty, has given a rather watered-down description of the escape of a group of his fellow junior officers in the artillery. When it became clear that France would cease the fight, Jacques Wanty and a few of his friends decided to emigrate to Britain to continue the military struggle, aware, more than their senior officers, that there would be no place for them in the new European order. A group of six of them set out in a taxi, wearing their uniforms. They had forged marching orders sending them to Bayonne as a group of quartering officers. With these papers, they succeeded in crossing twelve road blocks without being unmasked. It was with the same spirit of self-confidence that these young officers boarded a ship, the *Léopold II*, which they found moored in Bayonne harbour. The ship had arrived from Argentina with a consignment of wheat. On board there were already a few Belgian socialist intellectuals, artists and politicians. Some of them had merely fled in fear of their lives, while others had a stronger will to continue the fight. Eventually 400 people climbed on board, among whom there were three further Belgian officers: Captain Baron René Lunden and Lieutenant de Buyl, who were both pilots; and a young reserve first lieutenant, the journalist Léon Terlinden. For the latter, however, this was not his first escape from France. He had already escaped from the Dunkirk pocket to England on 29 May before returning to France to continue the fight. On Sunday 23 June, the *Léopold II* reached Falmouth, in south-west Cornwall, and three days later the nine Belgian soldiers finally arrived in Tenby. They were not the only ones among their year group to 'jump the wall'. Twenty-four hours earlier, André Marchal and Adolphe Meny had also reached Tenby. They had left Limoux on a motorcycle and headed for Bordeaux, where they had embarked on board ship.

Other Belgians reached Britain via Sète and Gibraltar. For instance, on 29 June, the doctor Albert Guérisse and the officers Paul Nicod and Frédéric Gréban de Saint-Germain embarked on the ship, the *Rhin*. On board already was also another recidivist, Georges Danloy. The socialist deputy from Liège, Georges Truffaut, had already escaped from Dunkirk before returning to France, and he arrived in England for a second time on 17 July. The Flemish reserve officer and future socialist minister Pierre Vermeylen also disembarked at Tenby, where he shared a room with the rich diamond merchant from Antwerp, Léon Maiersdorf. In the end, some 163 Belgian soldiers arrived in Britain during this period. Did they all, however, wish to continue the fight? Lieutenant Lemaire handed a petition, signed by twenty-seven officers, to Minister Jaspar, with a view to creating a military unit in order to continue the fight from Britain. At that time, the majority of the Flemish soldiers wished to continue the military struggle, but this fact could not disguise the reality that only a minority of the total number of Belgian soldiers in Tenby were actually prepared to fight. At the beginning of August, all the soldiers who were in Tenby were assembled to choose what to do. In the end, only 124 men out of some 300 chose to continue to fight.

All the Belgian soldiers in Tenby had, however, taken part in the military parade for the national commemoration day on 21 July, and they received, two days later, their first battledress. On 10 August, the UCB (Unité Combattante Belge) was founded; this unit was composed of the hundred or so soldiers who really wished to continue the fight. The first commander was Major Edmond De Paepe, a notorious alcoholic. The real driving forces behind it, however, were Lieutenant Smekens, the second in command, and his Company Sergeant Major, Harboort. The enthusiastic officer cadets formed the core of the platoons. To swell the ranks, Lieutenant-Colonel Louis Wouters, the Belgian military attaché, opened a recruiting office in London on 12 August 1940. After consulting the Belgian Ambassador, Emile Cartier de Marchienne, Jaspar ordered a general mobilisation of all Belgian men aged between nineteen and forty-five who were in the free world.

The development of the Belgian force was, however, severely disrupted by the arrival of new figures, some of whom had been in Belgium at the time of the capitulation, and all of whom fully supported King Leopold III in his decision to abandon the military struggle. Their propaganda within the ranks of the UCB resulted in the drafting of a manifesto on 10 November, which was hostile to the government and supportive of the King. To put an end to the dispute, Camille Gutt, who had arrived recently with a number of other ministers from France and had assumed the post of Minister of Defence in addition to his responsibilities as Minister of Finance, appointed the leader of the troublemakers, Louis Legrand, as his chef de cabinet in November 1940. This able officer became the driving force behind the creation of a small army. In August 1941, after the Syrian campaign, he recruited many soldiers of Belgian origin among the units of the French Légion étrangère that were stationed in Syria. In 1943, he joined the British army and in 1944 he was reported missing in Normandy as an officer in the 7th British Armoured Division, the so-called Desert Rats.

Belgians in Action

From August 1940 onwards, small numbers of new recruits, some of whom had escaped from occupied Belgium, continued to join the UCB, and by the end of September 1940 two Belgian companies were deployed to guard the Welsh coast. Nevertheless, the creation of a small Belgian Army was to remain a long and painful process. However, other Belgians were already taking part in the conflict, though in different ways. The German attacks of May 1940 had annihilated almost all of the Belgian Airforce. Its staff had, however, re-formed in Montauban in France and at the flying school at Oujda in Morocco. In June, the British offered to provide some *matériel* to the Belgian pilots, on the condition that they should come to

Britain, but this offer was rejected by the government. Then, on 28 June, some pilots and pilot-cadets took the initiative of crossing the Channel and by 5 August 124 of them had arrived in Britain. Many of them were tried in absentia for desertion by a Belgian war council sitting in France, but this act of 'disobedience' meant that they became the first Belgians to resume the fight. The Battle of Britain was beginning, and no form of co-operation was to be despised. So, experienced Belgian pilots as well as air gunners and observers were immediately enrolled either in Fighter Command or in Coastal Command. By the end of the Battle of Britain, Belgian pilots had shot down twenty-one German planes, but ten of them had lost their lives in the process.

On 11 February 1942, the 350th air squadron – composed entirely of Belgian soldiers – was created. It boasted no fewer than 110 pilots and took part in the raid on Dieppe in August 1942. In November, a second Belgian squadron – the 349th – was commissioned. Many other Belgians remained scattered throughout a large number of British airforce units, principally in the 609th squadron. The strength increased to 1,200 men, half of whom were flying personnel, and, from 1942 onwards, they were carefully trained in Canada, before being actively engaged in operations. Belgian airmen took part in the protection of the landing beaches in Normandy from D-Day onwards. They also took part in Operation Market Garden at Arnhem and won fame in the hunt for the flying bombs that the Nazis, in their last desperate gesture, were showering over London and Antwerp. Belgian airmen also took part in combat in the Mediterranean and in Africa, and even in the distant campaign in Burma. At the end of the war, the global record of the achievements of the Belgian aviators was more than laudable: 161 confirmed victories, but at the cost of around 300 deaths.

Belgians were also quickly enrolled in the British Navy. Around 350 Belgian seamen were in Britain in July 1940. By the end of the year, the British Admiralty had allowed many of them to serve in the Royal Navy, a Belgian section of which had been created at Devonport by Lieutenant Victor Billet, a former naval officer who had joined the merchant navy in 1919. So, as early as 1941, two corvettes, the *Godetia* and the *Buttercup*, took part in escorting convoys through the Atlantic. The 118th flotilla of minesweepers, the crews of which were entirely Belgian, were brought together for the landing in Normandy. After the D-Day landing, it was given the tricky task of clearing mines that were blocking access to Antwerp harbour, so that it could be used by the Allies. There, the Belgians acquired solid experience and a reputation in dealing with mines that has lasted until the present day. Moreover, 4,000 Belgian sailors onboard some hundred ships served in the Allied merchant navy. These ships were chartered by the central British organisation that oversaw the whole of Allied transport. In this way, Belgians took part in the convoys in the Atlantic, the Mediterranean and the Indian Ocean. Although these sailors were not actually military personnel in the strict sense of the term, their courage, their devotion and the severe losses that they incurred more than entitle them to be mentioned alongside those who fought.

On 8 October 1940, the first Belgian battalion of the UCB was created in Britain and two days later, Major Charles Cumont, the deputy to the military attaché, was appointed as the commander of this battalion. In September, the Belgians had been given helmets, light weapons and some vehicles, and in December, the first three Bren-Carriers arrived as a Christmas present. During that same month, the first mortars and anti-aircraft machine-guns followed. By the end of 1940, Charles Cumont's battalion was already 823 men strong. On 15 February 1941, in Tenby, Gutt attended a ceremony at which he presented the battalion with a Belgian flag in the presence of the Prime Minister, Pierlot, and the Foreign Minister, Spaak. A few days later, on 20 February, the battalion moved to Carmarthen, in West Wales, while an artillery-battery was created at Crickhowell in mid-Wales.

In the meantime, on 31 October 1940, the government had mobilised all Belgian able-bodied men eligible for conscription between 1935 and 1941 who lived in countries with which Belgium had diplomatic relations. At the same time, the battalion of pioneers composed of soldiers who did not wish to participate in the armed conflict was abolished. On 3 December, the conscription measures were extended to those eligible for conscription between 1925 and 1934. These measures, however, did not significantly boost the numbers in the armed forces. Some 15,000 Belgians lived in Britain, of whom around 7,000 were employed in British industry. There were also around 2,300 school-age children. Of course, some Belgians also lived in Canada, in the United States (1,000) or in South America. But these populations only provided on average approximately 100 new recruits annually during the remainder of the war.

On 23 February 1941, the Belgians created a second battalion. A shipowner from Antwerp, Reserve Major William Grisar, became the commander of this battalion and was assisted by Reserve Captain Jean Bloch, who was of Jewish origin. The unit was stationed in Malvern. In June, some 200 Belgians from North America, under the command of Eddy Blondeel, joined the troop, having received their basic training in Canada, and formed the initial core of the new battalion. These Belgians from across the Atlantic were a real hotch-potch: Flemish, Walloons and Belgians who spoke only English or sometimes even Spanish. At the same time, the Belgians also set up a reconnaissance unit equipped with armoured vehicles, of which Captain Lechat was the commander and Roger Dewandre became the platoon leader. By the end of July, the unit was already 60 men strong. Meanwhile, Great Malvern became the garrison town for the staff of Belgian military forces in Britain, now termed the Belgian Independent Infantry Group.

On 21 July 1941, during the celebration of Belgian National Day, a military ceremony was held in Westminster Abbey. Two companies paraded, providing a solemn setting for the award of military decorations to Belgian fighter pilots. Shortly afterwards, General Raoul Daufresne de la Chevalerie, who had been promoted to the grade of lieutenant general, was appointed commander-in-chief of the Belgian national military forces. The original commander, General van Strydonck, was 'promoted' to the rank of army inspector. With this appointment, it appeared that the 'royalists' within the Belgian armed forces had gained the upper hand, and these political tensions further exacerbated an already tense atmosphere. In January 1942, the Belgian Infantry battalion was stationed in Hereford, and, while Camille Gutt was giving a speech to it on 2 February, a young officer, Albert Deton, lost his temper and shouted out: 'Donnez-nous un champ de bataille, nom de Dieu'. The Belgians were now trained and armed and were impatient to be deployed in battle. In May 1942, during a grenade-launching training session, Reserve Captain Georges Truffaut, the fiery-natured socialist deputy from Liège, lost his life. Garrison life was clearly becoming unbearable for the Belgian soldiers. The British were being sent everywhere, so why were the Belgians no fighting too? In addition, the Flemish did not greatly appreciate the fact that Camille Gutt only spoke French.

However, two timely events intervened to ease the internal pressure: the creation of both a commando unit and a formation of paratroopers. In the early spring of 1940, the British had created small assault units, which were capable of carrying out raids on the enemy coasts and thus obliging the Germans to remain constantly on the alert. Between 1940 and 1942, these commando units developed and started to specialise in carrying out raids that enabled them to gain more experience and great fame. At that time, the British were considering using the many foreign nationals who were living on their territory to facilitate raids on the Continent. These men, most of whom were scattered among British units or already gathered within national troops, could increase the chances of success of the raids through their knowledge of both the country and the language. In the event, an international unit was created, Commando No. 10, comprising a British general staff and eight troops, each around one hundred men strong. The creation of such a unit came at just the right time to rescue the most volatile Belgian volunteers from the monotony of the training garrisons. Thus, the 4th Belgian Troop was born in August 1942; at the time, it was composed of seven officers and eighty-five volunteers, drawn from all the Belgian units in Britain. Captain Georges Danloy, a graduate in economics from Brussels University and a reserve artillery officer, was put in charge of it. The Belgian troop trained intensively for a year at Abersoch in Wales. It also stayed several times in Portsmouth and Plymouth, where the commandos familiarised themselves with landing techniques.

During September 1943, the Belgian commandos, accompanied by their Polish equivalents, were selected to take part in operations in the Mediterranean. They arrived in Algiers on 22 September and had to undergo further training for six weeks at the camp at Bir-Kadem. Eventually, on 29 November, Troop No. 4 sailed on the *Ville d'Oran* to its first battlefield, where its mission consisted essentially of patrols and hit-and-run raids. In very difficult weather, the Belgians fulfilled their missions successfully, but also incurred their first losses. In January 1944, the troop was sent to the front of the Fifth American Army with a view to taking part in the operations to cross the River Garigliano, opposite the German defensive line, the Gustav Line. Thanks to their outstanding conduct during these operations, the Belgians were mentioned in dispatches: the Belgian commando troop 'proudly carried our colours on the battlefields of Italy where, thanks to its enthusiasm, it received the highest praise from the officers under whose command it demonstrated the value of our weapons, in particular ... through its outstanding participation in the attack against the Gustav Line'. On 4 February, the troop was brought back from the front line and was able to enjoy a brief period of rest near Naples. Between March and May 1944, it was sent to the island of Vis to take part in the defence of what was the only island on the Dalmatian coast occupied by the Allies. The Belgians also supported operations to help partisans land on neighbouring islands and set up boarding teams to attack enemy ships. A month later, the mission of the Belgian commandos on Vis came to an end. On 14 May, they returned to Naples and sailed to Liverpool. On 3 June, they set up camp in Eastbourne.

Until the end of September 1944, the troop was re-equipped and maintained ready for combat before being sent to seize the island of Yeu, off the west coast of France, only to discover on carrying out a reconnaissance mission that the Germans had already left the island. After another short period of rest in Bruges, the Belgian commandos were in action once again. It was already October, and the Allies were experiencing considerable logistical difficulties. After the lightning advance through France and Belgium, the offensive marked time. The principal reason was that, although the port of Antwerp had been captured intact thanks to the Resistance, it remained unusable. The Germans blocked access to the port by occupying Flemish Zealand as well as the islands in the estuary of the Scheldt. After the Canadians had conquered Zealand, the islands needed to be brought under Allied control. At that time, the Belgian troop was placed under the command of the 4th Commando Brigade and prepared to take part in an important amphibian assault against the extremely well-fortified island of Walcheren. The Belgian commandos attacked on 1 November 1944; they landed in Westkapelle and Domburg and secured their objective at the cost of losing a quarter of their soldiers. After returning briefly to Belgium, they returned to occupy Walcheren and stayed there until the end of January 1945. The troop then went back to Britain to train and integrate reinforcements, and subsequently moved to Neustadt, in Germany, in April 1945.

In a decree dated 27 July 1945, the Prince Regent of Belgium, Prince Charles, mentioned the commandos in the dispatches of the army and allowed them to inscribe on their flag the names 'Italy, Yugoslavia, Walcheren'. The troop of Belgian commandos was the first unit among the land forces to resume the fight after the capitulation in May 1940. It was also the only Belgian unit that was involved in the battles in the Mediterranean theatre. Moreover, through its action on Walcheren, it made a direct and important contribution to the opening of the Scheldt and of Antwerp harbour.

Paratroopers were a completely new weapon at the beginning of the Second World War, but it only took them a short time to establish their considerable reputation. Towards the end of 1941, the Belgian forces in Britain decided to create a contingent of paratroopers. From January 1942, twenty Belgian volunteers were sent every month to the training school at Ringway to receive special training and to practise their first jumps. On 8 May 1942, the Compagnie Indépendante Belge de Parachutistes was created in Malvern. This unit underwent intensive training before being recognised as operational in January 1943. Subsequently, the total number of its paratroopers reached 210 men, and at the beginning of 1944 it was joined to the SAS brigade (Special Air Service), which was composed of two British regiments, two French battalions and a Belgian squadron. Shortly before the Normandy landings, plans had been made for the Belgian SAS Squadron to be parachuted into the

Belgian Ardennes, while the French SAS would operate in Brittany. But, to their great disappointment, the Belgians' mission was cancelled at the last minute. It was not until 27 July that the first three Belgian groups went into action. They were parachuted into Normandy, in the hills of the Perche region, a long way behind the German front line. They took part in harassing the enemy, attacked German columns and sought to speed up the German retreat. Once the Allied advance had caught up with them, they were taken back to their initial base, a transit camp in the south of England. Later, on 16 August, 120 men were dropped at night in the Falaise pocket to reconnoitre the retreat routes of the enemy forces encircled in the trap and to increase their confusion by harassing them.

A few days later, a group of soldiers under the command of Lieutenant Kirschen was parachuted into German-occupied France with the mission of sending reports on the volume of German traffic along the routes between Paris and Compiègne and Soissons. Due to a technical error, they landed some ten kilometres away from the target area, but succeeded in getting hold of a German document of the utmost importance: the enemy's complete battle orders for the front on the Somme. Meanwhile, on 15 August, a reconnaissance group had been parachuted into the French Ardennes with a mission to cross over into Belgium and prepare for the arrival of new contingents. From 27 August, all the groups who had taken part in the French operations and that had been overtaken by the Allied advance were once more parachuted behind the lines in successive waves in southern and eastern Belgium. They remained there until the arrival of the Allies. In the context of these operations, the Belgians became the first Allied troops to cross the *Westwall* (the 'Siegfried Line' of Allied propaganda), albeit by mistake. The team of Captain Vanderheyden (a future lieutenant-general) was dropped so far behind the lines that it landed on the territory of the Reich. Hiding during the day and walking at night, it eventually managed to cross the *Westwall* in order to rejoin the other Belgian units.

On 13 September 1944, the various groups from the SAS were gathered in Brussels, which had been liberated ten days earlier, and transferred to England prior to being parachuted north of Arnhem, as part of the Market-Garden operation. When this operation turned into a disaster, two groups of Belgian SAS found themselves isolated in the province of Utrecht. They stayed there for nearly six months, hiding in every possible place, helped some survivors to escape from Arnhem and also radioed some valuable target locations to the Allied bombers.

Having been re-organised in November 1944 as a land reconnaissance squadron and equipped with armoured jeeps, the Belgian paratroopers returned to combat. During the Von Rundstedt offensive of December 1944 in the Belgian Ardennes, they were thrown into the Saint-Hubert breach and carried out many combat patrols. At the end of the offensive in the Ardennes, the unit was reinforced. In April 1945, it left for the front in Holland and was given the mission to scout the route to the north for the advance of the Polish Armoured Division. This marshy country was the scene of incessant engagements, leading to heavy casualties. The Belgian paratroopers eventually reached the sea at Edem, on 15 April, and then accompanied the Canadian armoured units to Wilhelmshaven. On 5 May 1945, the order came for a cease-fire.

On 19 February 1942, the socialist senator and professor at Brussels University, Henri Rolin, had been appointed under-secretary to the Minister of Defence. However, he found it very difficult to adapt to the small world of idealists, defeatists and disappointed and frustrated people that comprised the Belgian land forces in Britain. This was particularly the case for the ex-soldiers of the Légion étrangère and for those who had fled Belgium during 1941, whose presence added to the existing atmosphere of frustration and frayed tempers. Moreover, Rolin exacerbated matters by lending an ear to all who wished to complain, with the consequence that the last semblance of discipline began to disappear. The head of the Belgian Independent Group, Daufresne, appointed in 1941, had, in the meantime, made himself unbearable, and, as soon as it became known that he had frolicked with a pretty red-haired girl in the chaplain's ambulance, he was replaced in August 1942 by the insignificant figure of Colonel Lecomte, jokingly referred to as the 'comte à dormir debout'.

However, this change in leadership did not bring peace. In November 1942, fourteen Belgian soldiers rebelled: their principal demand was for the Belgians to be deployed in battle. Perhaps without being aware of it, they also had the support of a communist organisation that advocated the opening of a second front. Most of its members were students from privileged backgrounds, including an engineer and a priest. In a manifesto they reproached the government for betraying democracy. Immediately, a noisy court martial was held which produced a large number of revelations that shocked the British press. On 2 October 1942, Henri Rolin was forced to resign and the Prime Minister, Hubert Pierlot, took over the post of Minister of National Defence himself. On 12 December 1942, Cumont, too, was forced to leave and was replaced by BEM Major Jean-Baptiste Piron. At that time, the Belgian military forces were approximately 2,300 men strong including a few deserters; there were around 100 commandos and 150 paratroopers under British command.

Who served in the Belgian land forces in Britain? The Centre de Documentation Historique des Forces Armées contains 1,021 identification forms of Belgian soldiers in Britain. The most striking group among them was that of the Belgians from the diaspora: notably from the United States and Canada, but also from Turkey, Egypt, Iran, the Dutch East Indies, Hong Kong and Shanghai. They accounted for 15 percent of the forms. Thanks to General de Gaulle, Belgium was able to recruit its own nationals and those from Luxembourg, who were serving within the Légion étrangère units that had fought in the Allied task force in Norway in April and May, notably at Narvik, as well as those soldiers who had been liberated by the reversal of the situation in Syria (August 1941), in Madagascar and in North Africa (November 1942). Among them, a little more than a half, or 10 percent of the total number, had belonged to the Legion before 1940. Just under half of them, that is around 9 percent of the total, had been arrested by the Vichy police either for attempting to escape to Spain or for simple vagrancy and had been presented with a stark choice: prison or the Foreign Legion.

A large proportion of the Belgian soldiers in Britain had fled to the country during the war. Among them, three quarters had spent some time in the Miranda camp in Spain, a detention camp operated by the Francoist regime. There were also fugitives who arrived via Sweden and Switzerland. Among them were a good many Belgian Jews (representing more than half of the total) as well as members of the Resistance whose lives had been endangered. When studying the soldiers' geographical origins within Belgium, we can see that 2 percent were from the Luxembourg, 2 percent from the Limburg, 5 percent from East Flanders, 6 percent from the Hainaut, 13 percent from Liège and around 33 percent from Brabant (which included Brussels). For various reasons, however, these figures give a misleading impression of the francophone character of the Belgian military in Britain. In fact, the majority of the initial core of the UCB in 1940 was largely Flemish, but no records have survived of these first recruits. No reference to the occupational background of the soldiers was made on 39 percent of the forms, but 20 percent of the soldiers were workers, 15 percent were career soldiers, 13.5 percent were employees and 12.5 percent were students.

The Piron Period

The morale and mood of the Belgian troops in Britain changed very quickly after the appointment of Piron. Jean-Baptiste Piron, soon nicknamed 'the lion', or sometimes 'the pasha', was a military leader in the strictest sense of the term. Among other changes, he gave the command of the various sub-units to men with a born ability to lead. Under his direction, the Belgians took part in a variety of major manoeuvres alongside British, Dutch and Czech soldiers. During one such exercise against the Polish armoured division, the Belgians were forced to use their rocket-launching guns to contain the overly aggressive Poles. Above all, it became ever clearer that the Belgians in Britain had chosen the victors' camp. Consequently, the anti-Leopoldists gained the upper hand among the Belgian troops.

In addition, the Belgian Government, thanks to its considerable financial resources, was increasingly able to obtain the necessary *matériel* for the war, with the consequence that the military began to feel that their interests were being taken into account. On 22 January 1943, the First Belgian Independent Group was created and placed under the command of Lieutenant-Colonel Piron. The garrison was stationed in barracks at Clacton-on-Sea, in Essex. For the first time, therefore, the west coast was abandoned in favour of the east coast. However, this certainly did not mean that all the earlier problems had been solved. In a report dated 7 July 1943, Major BEM Henri Bernard noted the lack of Flemish officers. Only one language was spoken in individual platoons, either French or Dutch, while the Belgian paratroop unit chose to use English. In fact, all three languages were used to issue orders. There was, however, a marked superfluity of officers, with the consequence that many of them tried to obtain postings to military units through intrigues or through their acquaintances. Many, however, had to be content with minor posts as liaison officers, which meant they had practically nothing to do. Some of them even resorted to trying to join the British Army, but the Belgian Government agreed to this only very rarely.

In March 1944, the Belgian group practised landing techniques on a beach in the Dover area, and later moved to Great Yarmouth in April 1944. On 6 June 1944, however, the Belgians learned that the landings in Normandy had begun and were surprised and disappointed not to be part of them. Would their role merely be to serve as a praetorian guard upon the return of the government to Belgium? The Belgian Government and the British military staff had, of course, been very wise not to engage this small unit in combat too soon; the symbol of the Belgian military presence in the Allied ranks could not be allowed to be destroyed. On 3 August 1944, however, the vanguard of the Piron brigade finally left Newhaven, and most of the troops left Tilbury a day later onboard four Liberty ships. The infantry landed at Courseulles in Normandy. The Belgian unit, composed of 1,800 or 2,200 men, depending on which calculations one chooses to believe, was engaged alongside a few commando units and the Dutch 'Princess Irene' brigade, which had a strength of 1,800 men. Their task was to support the Sixth British Airborne Division, which was on the River Orne. The airborne division was able to make considerable use of the mobility and the fire power of the Belgian unit. The Belgians liberated many towns and villages on the coast of Normandy, including the fashionable resort of Deauville, where there is still a 'Pont des Belges' to commemorate the event. The 235 men and the eighty-two vehicles of the armoured squadron worked mainly as a reconnaissance troop in Pont-Audemer, amongst other places. The Belgians also encountered their first civilian compatriots, farmers who had settled in Normandy and some pro-German collaborators. On 28 August, the Belgians were placed under the direction of the commander of the 49th British Infantry Division in order to take part in the mopping up of the Seine estuary and in the siege of Le Havre. Meanwhile, some Belgians were killed and others, among whom was a son of the President of the Chamber of Deputies, Frans van Cauwelaert, were wounded.

In the meantime, the British Guards Division had begun its rapid march towards Belgium. On 1 September, Piron received the order to be ready for a major deployment, and on the following day the order was issued to follow the Guards Division toward Brussels. The Belgian reconnaissance troop tried to keep up with British advance but had to stop just beyond Amiens due to a lack of fuel. On 3 September at 4.30 p.m., the Belgians finally crossed the border at Rongy; in the evening, they reached Enghien. In the meantime, the Guards Division had arrived in Brussels. On 4 September, the *groupement* was finally able to take part in a victory parade. This was a memorable day, both for the liberators and for those who had been liberated. During the course of the following days, the Belgian reconnaissance unit acted as a guide for the British troops and tried to help the Resistance during skirmishes with the departing Germans. The Belgians also took part in mine-clearing operations at the Evere and Melsbroek airports. On 11 September, the Belgians were thrown into battle at the bridgehead over the Albert canal. The garrison town of Leopoldsburg was conquered the same day, resulting in the liberation of 900 political prisoners. In the Campine region of eastern Belgium, the Belgian unit fought alongside the Dutch Princess Irene brigade against the SS, German paratroopers and the Dutch SS Landsturm.

During the Market-Garden Operation, the Belgians were thrown into the battle on the right flank of the 30th British corps. Later they joined forces with the Americans of the First Army. On 25 September, the Belgians reached the Wessem canal; sporadic fighting ensued and this reached a peak on 11 November. On 17 November, the *groupe-ment* was withdrawn from the front line. Thanks to the arrival of new recruits, it was re-organised into a real brigade for the first time at Leuven, and on 3 April 1945 it was engaged in battle again in the Nijmegen area. The last Belgian soldier to die fell on 27 April 1945. On 28 April, the armistice was implemented in the Netherlands. In May, the Belgians entered Germany. In December, the Brigade, which had been the only unit to be under Belgian command during the war, was disbanded. It survived, however, within the First Brigade as a battalion, the Bevrijding (Liberation) battalion, which subsequently merged with the 5th Regiment of the Line.

Conclusion

It was thanks to the First Belgian Independent Group that Belgium was officially present in Allied ranks. There were, of course, many other Belgians in the Allied armies. The sons of Camille Gutt, the Minister of Finance, even served in the British armed forces. It was, however, the First Belgian Independent Group that made Belgium's most important contribution to the Allied war effort. Among its various commanders, it was, moreover, indisputably Piron who played the major role in transforming the unit into a well-oiled military machine.

The fact that they were exiled in Britain also explains clearly enough why a number of future Belgian military commanders, including Pierre Roman, married British young women. The veterans of the brigade also propagated the English language in their own country. In the final reckoning, five officers and eighty-five non-commissioned officers of the Piron brigade were killed, while twenty-four paratroopers and commandos died while serving under the British flag. The Belgian section of the RAF mourned the deaths of 207 men and the Belgian section of the Royal Navy lost twenty men. Losses were heaviest in percentage terms among agents sent into occupied Europe, with 120 agents killed. The heaviest losses in absolute numbers, however, were suffered in the Merchant Navy, in which 587 men were killed. In addition, sixty Belgians also perished in various British, American and French units. Sixty Belgian soldiers also succumbed in Britain to the after-effects of bombings, illnesses and accidents. Nor should one forget the approximately 17,000 members of the Belgian Resistance who lost their lives during the war. In total, therefore, some 8,000 Belgians fought for the Allied cause between 1940 and 1945; a figure that must be compared with that of approximately 20,000 of their compatriots who fought on the German side.

Note

* Translated by Christine Arthur.

References

J.-L. Charles, *Les forces armées belges. Au cours de la Deuxième Guerre Mondiale 1940–1945*, Brussels, 1965.

L. De Vos, *La Libération. De la Normandie aux Ardennes*, Eupen, 1994.

L. De Vos, *Veldslagen in de Lage Landen*, Leuven, 1995.

L. De Vos, 'De taaltoestanden bij de Belgische strijdkrachten in Groot-Brittannië tijdens W.O. II' in *Wetenschappelijke Tijdingen* XLVIII, no. 4 (1989) pp. 239–51.

L. De Vos, 'La reconstruction des forces militaires belges en Grande-Bretagne, 1940–1945' in *La Première Division Blindée du Général MACZEK dans le cadre de la Libération de la Belgique en 1944*, Zagan, 1994.

L. De Vos, 'De Belgische krijgsmacht tijdens de Tweede Wereldoorlog' in *Kultuurleven* LXII, no. 3 (1995): pp. 90–3.

L. De Vos, *De Joodse deelname aan de Belgische strijdkrachten in Groot-Brittannië, 1940–45*, Antwerp, 1995.

R. Dewandre, *Au galop de nos blindés. Les opérations du 1er escadron belge d'autos blindés*, Louvain-la-Neuve, 1981.

R. Didisheim, *Au-delà de la Légende. L'histoire de la Brigade Piron*, Brussels, 1946.

E. Genot, *Bérets rouges, bérets verts ... 50.000 Para-Commandos, historique des Para-Commandos belges*, Brussels, 1986.

J. Gotovitch, *L'armée belge de Grande-Bretagne. Remous 1940–1942*, Brussels, 1978.

C. Gutt, *La Belgique au carrefour 1940–1944*, Paris, 1971.

C. Messenger, *The Commandos 1940–1946*, London, 1985.

E. Michael, *Carnet de campagne. La Brigade Piron en Normandie*, Ostende, 1946.

R. Motz, *Angleterre et Belgique*, London, 1944.

J. Piron, *Souvenirs 1913–1945*, Brussels, 1969.

L. Schepens, *De Belgen in Groot-Brittannië 1940–1944. Feiten en getuigenissen*, Bruges, 1980.

C. Segers, *Donnez-nous un champ de bataille!*, Brussels, 1969.

P-H. Spaak, *Combats inachevés*, 2 vols., Paris, 1969.

J. Wanty, *Combattre avec la Brigade Piron*, Brussels, 1985.

G. Weber, *Des hommes oubliés. Histoire et histoires de la Brigade Piron*, Brussels, 1978.

In addition, this article is based on the documentary material preserved in the archives of the *Centre de Documentation Historique* of the Belgian Ministry of National Defence, Evere (Brussels).

6

BELGIAN MILITARY PLANS FOR THE POST-WAR PERIOD

PASCAL DELOGE

Security policy can be defined as the series of diplomatic, military or other measures taken by a country in order to avoid war and to protect its territorial integrity.[1] In the field of national defence in particular, plans and instruments are necessary in order to be able to face any eventuality. In 1940, the policy of neutrality had failed Belgium for the second time in twenty-five years. Consequently, a new policy was gradually defined and the terms and implications of this new policy were discussed amongst the Belgian community in London during the years throughout which their national territory was occupied. In September 1944, the plans that form the subject of this paper began to be put into effect. The immediate concern was to rebuild the military; in addition, the enemy and its capacity to strike again were to be monitored carefully, mainly by means of the occupation of its territory. In addition, the Belgian Government, rejecting its former neutrality, now attempted to work with its neighbours.

The debate over future security

The Belgian exiles first had to defend the right of small states[2] to exist at all; some people, in the United Kingdom and elsewhere,[3] had a tendency to accuse them of being responsible for the war due to their inability to defend themselves, or of being an obstacle to Europe organising itself in the aftermath of the war.[4] In the face of those who disparaged the small countries and who felt badly let down by the capitulation of 28 May 1940 and by the sudden political volte-faces of the pre-war period, the Belgian Government and a few other members of the Belgian community, looking to the post-war era, began to make their views known. For example, Professor Cammaerts[5] became one of these zealous advocates and propagandists. He published numerous books,[6] magazine articles[7] and press articles while giving lectures,[8] in all of which Belgium was restored to its status as a victim of German aggression.

In addition, newspapers controlled by the Ministry of Information tried to raise the reputation of the Belgian Army in Britain and thereby contributed to reinforcing the unity of the Belgian community in exile.[9] *La Belgique Indépendante*[10] was published weekly from 5 December 1940, and, amongst the endless justifications for the capitulation of 28 May and the in-depth descriptions of Belgian participation in the war effort and of the country's resistance to German occupation, it published a column in English, 'To our British Friends'. In this, various ideas about security plans were expressed for the benefit of Belgian and British readers. The monthly magazine *Message*,[11] written almost exclusively in English, was started in November 1941 on the initiative of Paul Weyemberg and Pierre Vermeylen. Its purpose was to 'mieux faire connaître la Belgique' to the British; and politicians and members of the Belgian Parliament published their ideas, sometimes freely, in it. Apart from the famous broadcasts from Radio-Belgique on the airwaves of the BBC, other types of media also existed in London and were aimed, for example, at sailors (*Marine*), Belgian students (*Bulletin de l'Association des Etudiants Belges*) or expressed the opinion of more specific groups such as the Chamber of Commerce (*Anglo-Belgian Trade Journal*) or Belgian soldiers stationed in Britain (*Vers l'Avenir*). Imitations of these journals were also launched in the United States (*Free Europe*). Finally, Belgian lecturers, ministers and parliamentarians also made use of the liking of the British for clubs and associations[12] to put forward their views and a *Belgian Institute* was established that offered a further forum for those thinking about the post-war era.[13]

The debate about future security also took place through diplomatic correspondence. The Belgian ambassador in London, Cartier de Marchienne,[14] an experienced member of the diplomatic service, carried out important missions in China and the United States on behalf of the Belgian Government; it had only been the outbreak of the war in 1939 that had prevented him leaving London after twenty years' residence there. When the war broke out, his influence enabled him to 'rallier son gouvernement dans la voie commandée par l'intérêt national' (F. Van Langenhove). Once the Minister of Foreign Affairs, Paul-Henri Spaak, and the Prime Minister, Hubert

Pierlot, were in London, Cartier, thanks to his connections, was able to retaliate against the attacks that were made against Belgium, enabling this monarchist ambassador to reconcile his defence of King Leopold III and his Anglophilia. Within the small community of the Belgian exiles in London, the ambassador held a special position. By virtue of his duties he had been permanently in exile, and as a consequence of the circumstances of wartime he met his fellow countrymen in exile[15] among whom were the members of a government that depended a great deal on him[16] as well as coming into frequent contact with the other communities in exile.[17] Cartier, moreover, was never lost for words: he did not hesitate to give his opinion, sometimes leaving to others the cold and objective analyses that usually play such a prominent part in diplomatic correspondence.[18]

The question of security was also briefly raised at the Commission pour l'Etude des Problèmes d'Après-Guerre (CEPAG). The commission members, however, preferred to concentrate on socio-economic and internal political issues. International politics, of which security was only one element, only represented 15 percent of the issues discussed during the debates, which were restricted to discussing general points.[19] The military experts at the Ministry of Defence, in accordance with democratic conventions,[20] did not express their views openly; they merely provided technical answers to the questions asked by the Minister to whom they were responsible or by the Foreign Affairs Minister[21] about concrete commitments, such as the conditions that should be imposed on Germany in the eventuality of an armistice.[22] They did not take part in the meetings organised by CEPAG.[23]

The need for a Belgian army

On 4 June 1942, the British Foreign Affairs Minister Anthony Eden and Paul-Henri Spaak agreed that a Belgian brigade should be created. Equipped and trained by the British, it also mirrored British forms of organisation in order that it could take part in military operations at their side and blend in with their divisions and army corps without facing any problems with repairs, supplies, and so on.[24] On 2 January 1942,[25] the Defence Minister, Camille Gutt, ordered the Inspector of the Belgian Forces, General Delvoie, to study the possibility of re-forming a Belgian army. Five days later, work started on this project.[26] It was anticipated that units would probably need to be created as soon as the landings in Europe had taken place before recruiting classes of conscripts in order to rebuild

a modern military machinery[27] with the help of the British War
Office and the collaboration of the military decision-makers who
had stayed in Belgium. Subsequently, in June 1943, Pierlot, by then
both the Prime Minister and Defence Minister,[28] contacted Lieutenant General Grassett, the British chief liaison officer with the
Allied contingents.[29] His reasons for doing so arose out of the
report commissioned from General Delvoie and concerned a number of general issues.[30] The first of these was that the image
projected by Belgium to its principal Allies had been tarnished by
the pre-war policy of independence and the capitulation of May
1940. The great powers would not, therefore, understand the reasons for continued Belgian inaction. The Belgians' military effort
should therefore be aimed at ending the present conflict and preparing for the post-war period. Moreover, by fighting they would
acquire the right to defend their own interests once the peace had
returned. Second, the Belgian politicians and diplomats in London
also recognised Britain's need for extra troops in order to finish off
the war with Germany and subsequently to occupy German territory. Belgian forces would reduce the demands on the British
military and would be welcome assistants if they could be ready in
time.

In addition, the Belgian planners recognised that, once in Belgium, the government would have to assert its authority and obtain
the support of the population. Patriotic fervour would be increased
by the participation in the defeat of Germany, and, by investing the
Belgian units with an air of prestige,[31] post-war recruitment into the
armed forces would be encouraged. The 'moral and material' dividends reaped thanks to this effort would give Belgium the right to
occupy Germany and so to drain the German economy of the
resources necessary to rebuild production and restore the Belgian
standard of living. Recruiting volunteers would also have the dual
advantage of alleviating the unemployment crisis and of making it
unnecessary to use foreign units – at the state's expense – to maintain law and order and to protect the lines of communication,
which would have been both humiliating and disastrous on a political level.[32]

None of these reasons was at heart military. The only purpose of
Belgian forces would only be to occupy Germany and guarantee the
interests of Belgium. From the outset, their organisation, stemming
from the circumstances of the war, did not correspond to any global
defence plan. This led to serious problems after the war, as a parliamentary commission noted in the spring of 1948. The Pierlot plan
consisted of two phases. First, to pursue the war alongside the Allies
by means of troops levied by the Ministry of Defence in Belgium as

soon as the country was freed: the plan envisaged six infantry battalions, six fusilier battalions, and six battalions of auxiliary engineering troops (pioneers). This project was approved by the War Office, on 17 January 1944, and then by the Supreme Headquarters Allied Expeditionary Forces, on 25 May 1944. This programme was modest, realistic and useful; but the second stage, however, involved equipping Belgium with a new military force in the form of an infantry division. This might have been a reasonable goal, but it was one that was difficult to achieve in practice. Initially, it was hoped that the necessary weapons could be recovered from the defeated Germans.[33] When this idea was abandoned, it was proposed to start buying material from the British authorities during the war and to stockpile it, but this suggestion appears to have been ignored (and with good reason) by the War Office.[34] Nor was recruiting new troops an easy task either. The measures taken by the enemy within occupied Belgium towards the male population would determine the number of soldiers who would be available and would affect the teaching and training of the newly-recruited units. Four hypotheses were therefore envisaged: first, all the male population would have been evacuated by the Germans; second, all the people formerly in the armed forces would have been evacuated; third, only the regular soldiers would have been evacuated; and, fourth, the regular soldiers and the conscripts would still be present in Belgium. In order to set up the six infantry battalions required for the first phase, 6,000 men[35] would need to be recruited in liberated Belgium. The division envisaged under the second phase represented 17,000 men[36] and 800 officers as well as 3,500 vehicles, 1,200 motorbikes, 11,000 rifles, 1,020 light and medium-size machine guns, 3,700 Tommy guns, 360 mortars, seventy-two field guns, 114 anti-tank guns and 183 anti-aircraft defence guns. The officer corps would be provided by the core of Belgian officers present in Britain. The cost of buying the *matériel* from the British was estimated to be £6,000,000, making allowance for the existing Belgian stocks of ammunition.[37]

Why should the United Kingdom have supported such an initiative? The available resources were needed in Britain for the current war. Besides, the War Office was sceptical about the value of the armed units that Belgium might be able to provide and about its prospects of levying additional ones. Finally, the Belgians lacked an officer corps with the appropriate experience of weaponry, techniques and tactics in the present conflict, and also lacked men of suitable age to serve in the armed forces.[38] Therefore, if the War Office had already promised to supply the police force with weapons and equipment 'sans contrepartie financière',[39] it was essentially only to maintain law and order at the rear of the front.[40]

In fact, the real motivation of the British was that they wished to
see the Belgians enter their sphere of influence, as a result of the co-
operation that had been initiated during the war and the financial
and material dependence that would follow from their need for military equipment.[41] In 1944, the decision-makers at the Foreign
Office intended to reap the dividends of the United Kingdom's effort
and to maintain its status as a great power. As far as Belgium was
concerned, it wished for its part to obtain rights for the country
within the international community that had been emerging since
1942 and to assert its rights after the German defeat. The military
possibilities, in both quantitative and qualitative terms,[42] left no
doubt as to this intention. As a result, the initial plan – to be enacted
as soon as the country was liberated – was to recruit in Belgium to
increase the strength of the exile Piron brigade sufficiently to enable
the establishment of a first Belgian division with the help of the War
Office, but this was subsequently postponed until the end of the
war. Yet the almost exclusively political motivations that underlay
this plan would harm both the quality of the result and prejudice
any effective collaboration with the War Office.[43]

For the whole of the post-war period, the co-operation between
the Belgian Defence Ministry and the British War Office was therefore essentially a two-speed one: a fast track as regards the units
that needed to be set up to ensure peace behind the front and
Twenty-first Army Group; and a slow track as regarded setting up
the first infantry division dear to the Belgian politicians, diplomats
and the military. In fact the assistance memorandum signed by Eden
and Spaak in November 1944 would not be carried out to its conclusion, as the War Office began to try to pull out as soon as the war
was over.

What should be done with Germany once it had been defeated?

In a circular of 2 March 1943, Spaak asserted his confidence in the
victory over Germany and the Belgians' persisting resentment
towards Germany.[44] But success was not yet guaranteed, and speculation continued to be based on hypotheses about the course of
future military operations.[45] Moreover, the Belgian community in
London was not united about what the fate of a defeated Germany
should be.

The Belgian Ambassador, like many others, pointed clearly to
Germany as the principal country of which to be suspicious after
the war. It had to be punished for what it had done and prevented

from forever restoring its military power. Besides, Cartier distrusted the intentions of the major states that would settle this question. He repeatedly recommended creating an association of small states in order to suppress every 'doute possible sur la politique qu'il est essentiel de suivre . . . dans le cas où, par un mouvement d'opinion, l'Angleterre serait de nouveau encline à la mansuétude si l'Allemagne s'enveloppait d'un manteau pacifique, comme en 1918'.[46] Probably sympathetic to Vansittart's views on post-war Germany, Cartier became worried, at the end of the conflict, that Hitler might be overthrown by a putsch that might convince the victors to be lenient towards the rebels who had just taken power.[47] That harsh treatment be inflicted on a defeated Germany was, in his eyes, an essential part of the policy to be carried out in order to prevent Germany from remilitarising. Germany had to be occupied, and Belgium should participate in this retaliation and control measure: 'nous nous devons à nous-mêmes et nous devons à nos alliés de participer, dans la mesure la plus large possible, à toutes les dispositions que nos grands alliés croiraient devoir prendre pour mettre définitivement la nation allemande dans l'incapacité totale de recommencer une nouvelle guerre dont nous serions encore les victimes'.[48]

Others recommended that the spirit of revenge and the pursuit of economic benefits should be avoided.[49] Though he did not lack determination towards the aggressor, the Liberal politician Victor de Laveleye showed some moderation: no cash reparations, no annexation against the wishes of the population, but help for the German people.[50] After the war, this divergence of opinions persisted, and when Spaak aligned himself with Britain's policy on Germany, which was based on restoring the economy and later the political system of the former enemy, the Catholic opposition fought violently against him in Parliament and in *La Libre Belgique*, and then defeated him in the 1949 elections against the background of the controversy surrounding the status of the King.

For the Belgian government in exile, occupying Germany alongside the Allies meant to 'éviter de laisser l'impression aux Anglais et aux Américains que la guerre est finie pour nous du moment où notre territoire est libéré',[51] – in other words to prevent them from believing that Belgium intended to return to its pre-war policy of independence. As early as June 1942,[52] General Delvoie was asked by Kaekenbeeck, the Belgian delegate to an inter-Allied Committee for the study of an Armistice,[53] to study the military aspects of the sanctions to be imposed on Germany. Relying on the lessons of 1919, and copying the measures taken by Hitler against the Czechs, the Belgians and then the French, his aim was to render the defeated country incapable of resuming hostilities. In order to achieve this goal, all the enemy's weapons had to be handed over intact to Belgium in the same quantities as the weapons seized by the Germans in May 1940.[54] In this way, the future Belgian forces would be equipped, though distrust of the Belgians' intentions, however, led the committee subsequently to abandon this proposal.[55] The former Reich should then be completely[56] occupied.[57] This presence would make its defeat effective and permit control of its disarmament and factories. It would only cease with the advent of a new generation[58] that would be less bellicose than the previous one. The German Army had to be abolished, with the occupying powers monitoring the borders with the help of a weakly-equipped German police force. Courts of law would also need to be set up to punish those who opposed this decision.

Finally, Belgium had to participate in this occupation of Germany and to claim the territory bounded by its borders, the Moselle and Rhine rivers, up to a line stretching through Neuss and München-Gladbach.[59] In order for Germany to be weak and for the Belgian border to be strong, Belgium had to protect itself behind the Rhine. But, since this natural obstacle itself had to be defended, General Delvoie advised that the right bank of the river should be occupied, as had not happened in 1919. In 1945, this was indeed the region that the Belgian Government wanted to be occupied by the First Belgian Division which was being set up at the time.[60] Belgium still wished to see the German nation-state dismantled, that is to say 'la création d'un état rhénan désarmé et d'une Bavière indépendante'.[61] Delvoie strongly wished for a permanent British presence in 'le Schleswig, le canal de Kiel, les îles d'Heligoland et cette région maritime',[62] because he anticipated the departure of the Americans, though he felt that only a limited presence in terms of British troops would be required thanks to the international character of the occupation.

Belgium must not be alone

In 1944, the Belgian leaders and the other Belgian exiles in London came back to their country, apparently united on the fundamental point that Belgium had to collaborate with its neighbours under the leadership of Britain. The emigres in London, however, did not always share the same perception of this collaboration. As early as March 1941, Belgian 'Londoners' got together in a Commission d'Etude des problèmes d'Après-Guerre (CEPAG).[63] Working in collaboration with Belgians resident in the United States, for example

Hervé de Gruben,[64] and others who had stayed in Belgium during the occupation, in particular Charles Snoy[65] and other members of the Resistance movement,[66] this commission worked, among other things, on the role of small nations within the Europe of the future. Its judgements were hardly based on sound realities, and some dismissed it as a 'Committee of illusions'.[67] Indeed, Jef Rens, its General Secretary, in publishing the results of the commission and attempting to legitimate its work, even felt obliged to mention this objection in order to defuse it.[68] Security issues naturally formed a part of these studies,[69] but the solutions that were considered remained global ones.[70] The introductory report of the commission linked the security of small states with disarmament, with the establishment of an international military force and restrictions on weapon production. Though the existence of the national State was not questioned, unspecified restrictions on Belgium's sovereignty were expected with a view to organising a common security policy, imposed by the failure of neutrality and by technical progress, with its industrial and budgetary corollaries.[71] Although Germany remained the biggest threat,[72] as the phoenix could easily rise again from its ashes, the solution to Belgium's problem lay in a Western Europe under British leadership.[73]

De Laveleye, as a member of the CEPAG, demanded a permanent alliance with Great Britain, collaboration between the general staffs and even, extraordinarily, British participation in the Belgian defence budget, as well as British troops stationed in Belgium.[74] Such ideas did not mean that the Belgian community in Britain was unanimous on this question. Some Belgian officers in the Belgian forces in Britain strongly criticised their host because of its position over the emerging dispute surrounding the wartime actions of Leopold III.[75] For the socialist Max Buset, leadership was synonymous with 'protectorate' and subordination[76] to Britain, following the example of its policy in the colonies.[77] He advocated building a European military power that would be composed of national contingents. On 12 June 1941, the Prime Minister, Hubert Pierlot declared, 'la Belgique apportera son concours à l'organisation de la sécurité commune dont la Grande-Bretagne prendra l'initiative'.[78] He and the members of his government considered that in order to guarantee its strength, this alliance should be based as much on economics and politics as on military bonds.

Spaak vigorously defended with the ardour of a new convert the idea of a Western Europe under British leadership. If Britain remained strong and took an active interest in Europe, it could achieve supremacy itself rather than merely preventing another power from doing so, he said to Mrs. Ward, a Conservative MP.

Otherwise, it would lose the benefit of all of its war efforts. The geopolitical position of the United Kingdom in relation to the Continent, Spaak argued, indisputably granted it the status of an arbiter. Belgium's ambition was not to be on an equal footing with the major powers; it was only interested in security and prosperity for Western Europe. So its desire for a western union was based not only on military factors but also on political and economic ones.[79] Cordial relations between the great powers were also essential for a small country that traditionally relied on its exports and was dependent on the international situation as a result of its geographical location.[80] In a note of 2 July 1941 concerning 'les conditions dont dépendent la conclusion et le fonctionnement d'une union douanière hollando-belge', Fernand Van Langenhove, the influential Secretary-General to the Belgian Foreign Office,[81] thought that American-British supremacy was the best guarantee for the security of the small states after VE Day. In his eyes, the common conduct of the war was uniting the United States and Britain ever more closely; but, once the conflict was over, new reasons would have to be found to unite to consolidate the peace.[82]

The more Atlanticist approach advocated by the Dutch Foreign Minister, E.N. Van Kleffens, as early as the winter of 1941/42[83] was responded to half-heartedly by Spaak, who considered that the United States was too far away for Europe to expect it to help in a concerted manner.[84] Others, however, in the Belgian community in London voiced similar opinions to those of Van Kleffens. For the Catholic politician Frans Van Cauwelaert, for example, Europe could only be unified under the leadership of one country only, and the only possible one was Germany. The European project was therefore unrealistic and would lead to the small states being subordinated to the larger ones, he believed. The only hope for safety lay on the other side of the Atlantic.[85]

In a conversation at the British Foreign Office, however, Van Langenhove stressed again the divergence of 'intérêts politiques, culturels, historiques et économiques' between the Americans and the Europeans. The preference of the Belgian government for Britain was therefore quite clear.[86] In a 'note sommaire sur l'orientation' of Britain 'à propos des projets de fédération européenne',[87] the Secretary-General to the Foreign Office reflected this choice, ranking the United Kingdom at the head of the 'puissances auxquelles la Belgique est unie par une communauté durable d'intérêts et d'aspirations'. Being brought together by a 'longue tradition', by their democratic and institutional principles and by their economic relations, the two countries must collaborate in the future, albeit within the scope of ongoing collaboration between the USA and Britain.

At the end of December 1943, Van Langenhove saw in 'la coopération entre la Grande-Bretagne et les petites démocraties de l'Europe occidentale'[88] a possibility of reinforcing Britain against the great powers, to the ranks of which it no longer belonged. So, although he did not accept the idea of Belgium joining the British Commonwealth, as some people had suggested, fearing that it would subordinate Brussels to London, he developed the concept of a Western Europe grouped around Britain by means of direct and regular contacts. This presupposed more profound relations than the war-time consultations during which the Americans and British had largely made decisions without consulting the occupied democracies, merely collecting the opinions of the exile governments if they chose to express them. Three months later, Van Langenhove described the famous 'trois niveaux' of international life after the war: the United Nations, a continental organisation, and a regional one.[89] On 29 April 1944, this led him to propose a 'programme de négociations avec nos alliés'[90] in which he argued that there were good reasons on grounds of foreign security for entering into negotiations on a series of issues: military co-operation with London and The Hague, particularly on the question of the occupation of Germany; German disarmament; and, finally, the status of the territories in the Rhine-Westphalia basin.

In the summer of 1944, this plan changed into 'principes directeurs à suivre dans les pourparlers avec les Etats d'Europe occidentale'.[91] The latter would be composed by right of three elements: the Benelux countries, France and Britain. A close co-operation between Belgium and The Netherlands represented, according to Van Langenhove, the minimum threshold below which one should not fall, and the starting point of a co-operation that then needed to be extended to France and Britain. In terms of defence, this plan entailed a standardisation of weapons and materiel, the co-ordination of the plans of the various armed forces, the unification of tactical rules and the exchange of information and training of army officers. In addition, a whole host of other measures were envisaged, including common organisation of manufactured goods connected to defence, the creation of depots and facilities for the Belgian troops in Britain, such as bases for the airforce and a permanent committee of the Joint Chiefs of Staff. Politically, the proposals put forward in November 1944 were supposed to open the door to a peaceful settlement of points of conflict and a concerted organisation of governmental action in general, as well as, more particularly, common decision-making about the obligations to be imposed on Germany, the measures to be taken to ensure their enforcement and the future political regime of Western Germany.[92]

As far as the post-war period was concerned, the Belgian ambassador in London, Cartier de Marchienne, relentlessly recommended that the small powers should form an alliance, and, after Germany's defeat, should be ready to collaborate with other nations. But, he added, 'elles voudront rester ce qu'elles sont'.[93] His principal fear was that the great powers might decide matters without consulting the small European states. During the preparations for the San Francisco conference in 1945, for example, he expressed his worries: 'les grandes puissances sont à l'apogée de leur puissance et les petits états au minimum de leur influence'.[94] In addition, Cartier was deeply annoyed, like a number of other people, by grandiose projects for the post-war era.[95] In 1941, he enthusiastically adopted the words of the British Secretary of State Arthur Greenwood, about the aims of the peace and of the organisation that would arise out of their definition: 'franchement, je trouve oiseux d'épiloguer longuement à l'avance sur des conditions qui peuvent fort bien ne jamais se réaliser et perdre son temps à des discussions qui rappellent les querelles théologiques qui divisaient les Byzantins la veille même de la prise de Constantinople'.[96]

But his opposition to such planning seems to have waned a little. Won over to the views of his government on the role of Britain, and a great admirer of the leaders of that country – and even Anglophile in his attitudes – he did not dismiss all speculation about the nature of the post-war order.[97] He sometimes regretted the vagueness of the declarations made by the principal British political leaders, and, occasionally, even criticised their lack of interest in the future,[98] prompting him to welcome a debate about the post-war period in the House of Lords.[99] He was also concerned to see the United Kingdom assume its share of responsibilities in post-war Europe and emerge from its insular isolation.[100] He therefore seized enthusiastically upon even the slightest hint of a wish for future co-operation with Europe among the British leaders.[101] He also wished for the recovery of France,[102] and for its participation in European security through the co-operation of its government with the British.[103] In his opinion, this Franco-British alliance was a precondition for Britain to be a powerful nation in the future,[104] and he hoped that a regional European association could be created under British leadership on the basis of their co-operation.

The existence of such a regional association would not, however, exclude the existence of a world-wide organisation. The latter was sometimes mentioned by the Belgians in exile in London when they tackled the problems of security, but their pronouncements on the subject often remained general and vague. Their attitudes concerning such projects also varied. Some people, like the socialists Louis de Brouckère[105] and Max Buset,[106] considered that the quest for world-wide security should be recommenced as long as it took into account the teachings of the past. They therefore believed that an international force should be created and that the United States should take part in it.[107] But, more often than not, the views expressed about this project by the Belgian exiles merely consisted in listing its difficulties. Once the danger was over, it was argued, would the Allies not go back to their isolation, with the more powerful ones leading the way?[108] In any case, it would be better not to 'trop présumer de la bonne volonté de tous'.[109] On the whole, plans for a world-wide security structure were denounced as an unrealistic abstract idea in order to stress all the more emphatically the value of smaller but more concrete groupings.[110]

For example, in his initial study commissioned in 1942, General Delvoie considered the occupying forces in Germany to be 'la première réalisation concrète d'une force armée pour la future société des vainqueurs qui pourra peut-être un jour mais bien plus tard et après de solides preuves d'amendement des Allemands, Japonais, Italiens et Bulgares, devenir une société des nations'.[111] In subsequent reports, it was suggested that the occupying forces might form part of the United Nations.[112] The newspaper *Vers l'avenir*, the mouthpiece of the Belgian forces in Britain, also pronounced itself in favour of a regional solution.[113] Britain had to come out of its isolation and the state of under-armament that it had been in before the war, in order to bring to Europe a 'Pax Britannica', whose tool would be a European association capable of organising a first-class military force, with the necessary number of divisions, planes and ships being contributed by its members. Once this had been created, the size and budget of the Belgian army could be smaller than before the war and the country would be able to devote itself to rebuilding its economy. Each country in this association would have to manufacture its own weapons or would buy them from its more industrialised neighbours 'au prix le plus juste'. National armies would exchange their officers and open the doors of their military schools. Joint exercises would take place in the border areas and in the occupied zone: 'Un système militaire de ce genre, tout en sauvegardant l'indépendance des nations, assurerait à moindre frais et d'une façon équitable la sécurité de l'Ouest européen.'[114]

What about the Russians?

Throughout the war years, Germany was generally considered the enemy to be watched after the victory over Nazism. From 1942, the

USSR was an ally – and a mighty one indeed – in the joint fight; yet traces of anti-communism were noticeable among the Belgian community in exile in London. In October 1942, General Delvoie was particularly frank: 'dans le demi-siècle à venir, la Russie, avec ses buts sociaux, sera probablement aussi un danger pour la paix'.[115] As part of his new thinking about the post-war period, he wrote: 'si une vague communiste les jetait vers les Russes,' the Germans would be 'un sérieux appoint pour ceux-ci contre nous'.[116] According to the same military expert, a complete occupation of Germany would be disadvantageous, since it would enable the Russians to participate: 'Ils communiseraient leur zone d'occupation. Leur rapprochement des autres pays de l'Ouest européen n'est pas souhaitable.'

Such assertions subsequently disappeared from the documents of the Ministry of National Defence in London. Other people, however, showed little inclination to like the USSR. Thus, for example, Ambassador Cartier de Marchienne attacked those writers who had no scruples about sacrificing 'le principe d'indépendance nationale à l'autorité d'une fédération socialiste sous l'égide des Soviets ... Ces bons juges s'inquiètent de voir poindre certaines prétentions telle que la réalisation d'un rêve séculaire des Moscovites de posséder les Dardanelles, telle aussi que l'acquisition d'un port libre de glace sur l'Atlantique'.[117] With the end of the war drawing near, his views did not change: a Soviet 'threat' in Central Europe existed, although this word was not actually employed.[118] In 1943, for example, he found evidence for his concern in Soviet policy towards Poland.[119] Once again, he took advantage of this example to expose the Communist ally's craving for territory, but also to worry about British attitudes on this issue: 'si la politique anglaise devait être, aux yeux des petits peuples de l'Europe, complice d'une organisation de la sécurité par des moyens aussi radicaux, l'Angleterre ne perdrait-elle pas le prestige qu'elle s'est acquis dans son rôle de défenseur des petits peuples?'[120]

Conclusions

The debate in London about the future security of Belgium was more open than would appear from the analysis provided by Fernand Van Langenhove in his classic work *La Sécurité de la Belgique*: different ideas were in direct opposition concerning issues such as the future of Germany, regional and world-wide associations and British leadership.

Sometimes, these conflicts continued after the war. In 1949, the attacks of *La Libre Belgique* and the Catholic party, the PSC, against the German policy of Spaak – which was thought to be too moderate – were particularly violent. In Germany, the Belgian military often held similar views. Belgian-British co-operation did, however, emerge at the end of the exile period, and the will to create a regional association in Western Europe became a permanent feature of Belgian diplomatic policy in the immediate post-war era. Yet, some obstacles, such as the mistrust shown by the British War Office towards the Belgian military, had begun to act like sand in the cogs of the machinery of this co-ordination as early as the war period, while more long-term difficulties, such as the loss of sovereignty and danger of subordination, were noted by the more clear-sighted observers. Some also understood the Soviet peril and forecast a scenario in which Eastern Europe became subject to Communist rule. Therefore, the reproaches of a lack of realism frequently levelled at the plans of the CEPAG should not be extended to include all the plans devised during the period of exile.

The debate on security matters often remained rather vague and general in nature. Nevertheless, the military was questioned about two specific points: the fate of Germany and the rebuilding of the armed forces. As a consequence, it worked out hypotheses and drew up plans that were put into practice after the Liberation. Yet it never succeeded in developing a global and systematic vision of Belgium's national security in the future. The Belgian armed forces born of the war soon turned out to be badly organised and lacked any military mission. Between 1942 and 1943, when the various studies were commissioned from the Belgian military authorities, the future was uncertain and the traditional supremacy of politics over the army in Belgium resurfaced. Moreover, even if the military planners had been asked to carry out a fundamental review of post-war needs, one must doubt whether they would have had at their disposal a civil service and headquarters sufficiently developed to bring this task to a successful conclusion. Even so, it is worth noting that some decision-makers (notably Defraiteur, De Soomer and Gierst, among others) of the war period kept their jobs after the war and as a result were able to give a pro-British orientation to the policy of national defence for some time.

Notes

1. 'Sicherheits politik', in *Brockhaus Enzyklopädie*, Mannheim, 1993, vol. 20, p. 231; J. Doise and M. Vaïsse, *Politique étrangère de la France – Diplomatie et outil militaire*, Paris, 1992, p. 6; L. Freedman, 'The concept of security', in *Encyclopaedia of Governments and Politics*, eds M. Hawkesworth and M.

Kogan, London-New York, 1992, pp. 730–1; K. Ritter, 'Sicherheitspolitik', in *Staatslexikon*, vol. 4, Freibourg etc, pp. 1173–7; F. Van Langenhove, *Documents diplomatiques belges, 1920–1940 – Politique de sécurité extérieure*, vol.1, Brussels, 1964.

2. Cartier to Spaak, 26 March 1942, Archives des Affaires Etrangères (AAE), Brussels, no. 11575. Cartier expressed the 'inquiétude que j'éprouve de voir ces groupes d'intellectuels anglais ... partagée par de nombreux représentants diplomatiques de moyennes ou de petites puissances actuellement occupées'. See V. Gollancz and G.D.H. Cole, *Shall Our Children Live or Die – Europe, Russia and the Future*, London, 1942. For example, the Minister of Foreign Affairs of Luxembourg, J. Bech, reacted in a similar manner, declaring in a speech: 'it would be a strange new world if the small nations must be sacrificed to prevent them being devoured by beasts of prey'. Cartier to Spaak, 23 March 1942, AAE 11575. On this subject, see T. Grosbois, 'Les projets des petites nations de Bénélux pour l'après-guerre', in *Plans des temps de guerre pour l'Europe d'après-guerre, 1940–1947*, ed. M. Dumoulin, Brussels etc, 1995, pp. 105–15.

3. J.Gerard-Libois and R. Lewin, 'Roosevelt et la flamingie', in *La Belgique entre dans la guerre froide et l'Europe, 1947–1953*, Brussels, 1992, p. 35.

4. Cartier to Spaak, 7 October 1942, AAE 11575. An article in *Time and Tide* refers to 'ces faiseurs de plans d'après – guerre' according to whom 'les petits états seraient un obstacle à la création d'un système économique et politique rationnel en Europe'.

5. Cartier to Spaak, 4 May 1942, AAE 11575.

6. *Message*, no. 4 (February 1942) p. 34 provides an account of his actions since the beginning of the war.

7. Cartier noted with satisfaction the reactions in the *Contemporary review*, the *Spectator* and *Message*, writing 'depuis plusieurs semaines, je n'ai plus relevé aucune attaque dans ce sens'. Cartier to Spaak, 3 June 1942, AAE, 11575.

8. Cartier to Spaak, 11 January 1945, AAE, 10958 bis. Cartier wrote, 'Rappelant les paroles de Léopold Ier suivant lesquelles l'existence des petites nations dépend de la bonne volonté des grandes puissances, il a montré que la faillite de la SDN n'était pas due comme certains le pensent à l'étroitesse d'esprit des petits Etats...'.

9. Delfosse to MDN, 31 March 1944, Centre de Documentation Historique des Forces Armées (CDH) Evère, London, 1101/71. Delfosse explains the tasks of the ministry and the manner in which they should be carried out. In the same dossier, see also the complaints or observations of the relevant ministers about articles either when they were published or prior to their publication. See also Weyemberg to Gutt, 25 November 1941, CDH 15; Motz to Rolin, 20 April 1942, CDH 23; Spaak to Gutt, 30 April 1942, CDH 38.

10. *La Belgique Indépendante (BI)*, 5 December 1940, no. 1, p. 1; I. De Hertogh, 'Persstudie – Onafhankelijk België (1940–1944): De tweede wereldoorlog bekeken door de Belgen in Londen' (mémoire de licence, University of Leuven KUL, 1982).

11. *Message*, no. 1 (November 1941) p. 1.

12. Professor Cammaerts, for example, gave a lecture at Chatham House on 30 May 1940 and to the Association of Woman Journalists. See *Message*, no. 4 (February 1942) p. 34.

13. They were published in the press: *Message*, no. 6 (April 1942) pp. 30–1.

14. L. Claeys-Bouuart, 'Le baron E. de Cartier de Marchienne. Missions diplomatiques en Chine et aux Etats-Unis (1898–1922)' (mémoire de licence, University of Louvain, UCL, 1977), pp. 7–11.

15. See Cartier to Spaak, 4 May 1942, AAE 11575 on the activities of Professor Cammaerts in Britain; Cartier to Spaak, 22 May 1944, AAE 11575 regarding the Belgian press in Britain; or Cartier to Spaak, 27 April 1944, AAE 11575 concerning his speech to the Anglo-Belgian Union and that of A. de Staercke to the Anglo-Belgian Northern Association.

16. See, for example, AAE 11639, 15924, 15925, 17951, 18299 and others.

17. See, for example, Cartier to Spaak, 12 November 1941, AAE 11575, on an article by Benes in the *Daily Telegraph* on the question of post-war European reconstruction and also Cartier to Spaak, 19 November 1941, AAE 11575, on an article by Trygve Lie in *The Times* entitled 'The Bankruptcy of Neutrality'; also Cartier to Spaak, 25 March 1943, AAE 11575, on a letter by Van Kleffens to *The Times* on the lesser powers and their role.

18. Cartier to Spaak, 2 April 1941, AAE 11575: 'ces remarques de M. Greenwood me paraissent frappées au coin du bon sens . . .'; Cartier to Spaak, 9 May 1942, AAE 11575: 'Ces idées, ainsi que vous le voyez, Monsieur le Ministre, demeurent dans le domaine des généralités . . .' and 'Personnellement, je suis très heureux que M. Eden soit allé à Washington car son clair bon sens, sa maîtrise en politique internationale et sa bonne grâce souriante contribueront grandement à dissiper les nuages qui sans cesse reparaissent à l'horizon . . .'.

19. D. De Bellefroid, 'La Commission d'Etude des Problèmes d'Après-Guerre, 1941–1944' (mémoire de licence, University of Louvain, UCL, 1987) pp. 212–14 (appendices 4 and 5 on documents and themes) and p. 139 (on the work of the international section).

20. These remained unchanged after the war. See P. Deloge, 'Enthousiasme ou réticence? Analyse de la conscience européenne des décideurs militaires belges durant la négociation de la CED (1950–1954)', in *Revue Belge d'Histoire Militaire (RBHM)*, vol. 31, nos 7–8 (1996) p. 173.

21. Major-General Delvoie to the Under-Secretary of State for Defence, 16 July 1942, CDH 1241: 'copie d'une lettre que j'envoie à Monsieur Van Langenhove'; Major-General Delvoie to the Minister of National Defence, 23 June 1942: 'copie d'une lettre que j'adresse à Monsieur Kaekenbeeck'.

22. Inter-Allied Committee for the Study of the Armistice, CDH 1241/3.

23. They did not submit any reports to it. See J. Rens and P. van Zeeland to Spaak, 18 October 1944, AAE 11780, and general reports of the CEPAG. Certain military officers did attend CEPAG meetings, but they were reserve officers who attended in their civil capacity relating to the work of the economic section: D. De Bellefroid, 'La Commission d'Etude des Problèmes d'Après-Guerre, 1941–1944', pp. 150–1.

24. J.M. Sterkendries, 'Les répercussions de la politique internationale sur la politique militaire belge de 1944 à 1949' (mémoire de licence, Brussels University, ULB, 1988), p. 31.

25. The Minister of National Defence to Lieutenant-General van Strijdonck de Burkel, Inspector of the Belgian Forces, 2 January 1942, CDH 1241/6.

26. With a request for personnel: van Strijdonck de Burkel to the Cabinet of the Minister of Defence, 17 January 1943, CDH 1241/6.

27. Without necessarily having any illusions as to its size: 'après cette guerre, pour des raisons d'économie, nous devons avoir le plus petit appareil militaire possible'. General Delvoie to Van Langenhove, 15 July 1942, CDH 1241/3. See also *Vers l'Avenir*, 17 December 1942, p. 5. Even the military, it seems, envisaged the future army reduced to its strict minimum.

28. R. Defraiteur, *Les accords militaires conclus avec les alliés depuis 1943*, typescript, March 1946, p. 3, Centre d'études et de documentation Guerre et Sociétés Contemporaines (CEGES), Brussels.

29. J.L. Charles, *Les forces armées belges au cours de la seconde guerre mondiale, 1940–1945*, Brussels, 1970.
30. 'La reconstitution d'une armée sur le territoire national', pp. 1–21, CDH CAMP. 40–45/MDN, 1ère division, undated. The study of the General Inspectorate was the first military and technical consequence of the political analysis cited below. The process concluded eventually in the formulation of a note dated 23 March 1944 by the General Director of the Ministry of National Defence.
31. 'Note au sujet de la reconstruction d'une armée lors de la libération du territoire belge', CDH CAMP. 40–45/MDN, 1ère division, undated. While the note was written anonymously, its content was essentially political.
32. The use of symbols relating to individuals and units was, in effect, used after the war to encourage efforts at military reconstruction. See P. Deloge, 'La défense commune dans l'opinion militaire belge: Europe et interdépendance, 1945–1955', in *RBHM* vol. 30 no. 8 (December 1994) pp. 613–36.
33. See later in this chapter for the armistice conditions to be imposed on Germany.
34. R. Defraiteur, *Les accords militaires conclus avec les alliés depuis 1943*, pp. 4–5. The *matériel* was urgently needed for the war. To buy or sell it and then stockpile it in a corner while awaiting the formation of a hypothetical Belgian division therefore made no sense at all.
35. Note for the Minister, 23 December 1943, p. 1, CDH CAMP. 40–45/MDN 1ère division.
36. 9,000 infantrymen, 5,000 artillerymen, engineers and signals staff and 3,000 maintenance staff. An armoured division is much more difficult to create because of the greater level of technical expertise it requires. 6,000 men from six infantry batallions made up one part of the personnel of the first Infantry Division. 'Note for the Minister', 23 December 1943, p. 4, CDH CAMP. 40–45/MDN 1ère division.
37. 'Note relative à la reconstitution d'unités militaires belges en territoire libéré', pp. 2–3, CDH CAMP. 40–45/MDN 1ère division, 23 March 1944.
38. R. Defraiteur, *Les accords militaires conclus avec les alliés depuis 1943*, p. 3.
39. 'Note relative . . .', p. 4, CDH CAMP. 40–45/MDN 1ère division, 23 March 1944.
40. 7,000 rifles and 1,000 sten guns with ammunition, 8,000 gas masks, 8,000 pairs of boots, 1,000 bicycles, 74 trucks of 4 tonnes, 24 two-seater cars, 40 motorcycles and, for the police, 10,000 pistols with ammunition. 'Note pour M. le Ministre', 20 August 1943, pp. 2–3, CDH CAMP. 40–45/ MDN 1ère Division. This was intended for the 'formation d'unités belges et l'organisation de la gendarmerie en territoires libérés'. We will not consider the issue of the Gendarmerie here as it concerns the internal security of Belgium and the measures to be taken to ensure civil peace behind the lines in Belgium after liberation.
41. R. Defraiteur, *Les accords militaires conclus avec les alliés depuis 1943*, pp. 1–3.
42. Quantitatively, because the number of units provided to the Allies remained small in comparison with the British and American contributions; qualitatively, because the conditions of their training prevented any sophisticated development. As a quantitative comparison, five British divisions, a Canadian division and two American divisions (some 156,000 men) landed in Normandy on 6 June 1944. On 15 June, the Allies had three army groups in the area: C.M. Schulten, J. Schulten and H.L. Zwitzer, '1944–1945: D-Day au V-Day', in *J'avais vingt ans en 1945 – La Belgique et la deuxième guerre mondiale – Livre de l'exposition*, eds L. De Vos, P. Lefevre and R. Boijen, Brussels, 1995, pp.

89–91. Belgium at this time possessed only one brigade, which was not used in the landings.

43. P. Deloge, 'A star felt in the Belgian sky: La coopération belgo-britannique de sécurité au début de la guerre froide, novembre 1944–décembre 1951' (Ph.D. diss., University of Louvain, UCL, 1998).

44. Information circular no. 12 on Belgian Foreign Affairs, 2 March 1943, AAE 15925.

45. General Delvoie to F. Vanlangenhove, 15 July 1942 and General Delvoie to the Under-Secretary of State for National Defence, 19 September 1942: CDH 1241/3: 'si au contraire nous étions déjà en territoire allemand au moment de l'armistice, le texte proposé devrait être modifié'.

46. On debate in the House of Lords, Cartier to Spaak, 27 May 1942, AAE 11575. This opinion is repeated in a letter of 2 June 1942. He feared the influence of those he terms 'les milieux d'extrême gauche qui soutiennent en dépit du précédent de 1919 qu'une Allemagne républicaine et socialiste serait une bonne Allemagne': Discussion on Lord Vansittart, Cartier to Spaak, 18 June 1942, AAE 11575. He returned to this theme at the end of the war: see note above. See also how he feared the danger of fraternisation when British and American troops arrived in Germany: Cartier to Spaak, 21 and 27 September 1944, AAE 11575.

47. Cartier to Spaak, 25 July 1944, AAE 11575, in which he underlined once again the nature of English opinion 'toujours trop accessibles aux sentiments de pitié et de douceur'.

48. Télégramme par courrier, Cartier to Spa, 27 September 1944, AAE 11575.

49. For example, the well-known case of Baron de Gruben: see T. Grosbois, *Les plans*, p. 110. See also the ideas circulating in the CEPAG from December 1942: J. Hoste, 'Note relative à l'occupation de l'Allemagne', December 1942, AAE 11781.

50. Memorandum on war aims, 5 January 1941, Schreiber papers, CEGES PS11.

51. Ibid.

52. Major-General Delvoie to Kaekenbeeck, 23 June 1942, CDH, London Archive, 1241/3.

53. Inter-Allied Committee for the Study of an Armistice, Minutes of meetings. Documents, part 2, London, 1943–44, CDH, London Archives. This group was comprised of Belgian exiles, French, Greeks, Dutch, Norwegians, Poles, Czechs and Yugoslavs. Meetings took place from 1942 to the end of the war presided over by F. Van Langenhove. These experts worked for a committee composed of Allied Ministers of Foreign Affairs chaired by Spaak.

54. This was the position defended by Kaekenbeeck in meetings. See ibid, seventh meeting of the sub-committee of financial experts, 23 March 1943. His position was probably based on the preliminary report submitted on 19 September 1942 by General Delvoie.

55. Major Kerstens to the Under-Secretary of State for National Defence, 10 September 1943, CDH 1241/6.

56. If this was not the case, the German police would maintain order in the territory which remained free and 'ce qui s'est produit de 1806 à 1813 et 1918 à 1939 se reproduira. L'action des commissions de contrôle sera bien entendu illusoire': General Delvoie to Van Langenhove, ibid, 1241/3.

57. 'Avant-projet', ibid, 19 September 1942.

58. He added elsewhere: 'je doute, si l'on est d'accord à l'armistice pour imposer à l'Allemagne une occupation de 25 ans, que celle-ci dure ce temps': Delvoie to Van Langenhove, 15 July 1942, ibid.

59. Delvoie to Kaekenbeeck, 23 June 1942, ibid.

60. 'Note sur la participation de la Belgique à l'occupation militaire de l'Allemagne', early August 1945, AAE 11839.

61. Delvoie to Van Langenhove, 15 July 1942, CDH 1241/3.

62. Ibid. This maritime region comprised Russia, Poland, Czechoslovakia, the Netherlands, Belgium and France. Delvoie hoped they would also formulate proposals to divide German territory.

63. T. Grosbois, *Les projets*, pp. 95–125. This is the most recent work on the subject. See also D. De Bellefroid, 'La Commission d'Etude des Problèmes d'Après-Guerre, 1941–1944'; J. Gotovitch, 'Views of Belgian Exile on the Postwar Order', in *Documents on the history of European Integration*, vol. 2: *Plans for European Union in Great Britain and in Exile, 1939–1945*, ed. W. Lipgens, Berlin-New York, 1986, pp. 215–43 and 414–50; and B. Henau, 'Shaping a new Belgium: the CEPAG, 1941–1944', in *Making the new Europe. European unity and the Second World War*, eds M.L. Smith and P.M.R. Stirk, London-New York, 1990, pp. 112–32.

64. J. Gotovitch, *Archives du baron Hervé de Gruben*, Brussels, 1982, pp. 3–5 and T. Grosbois, *Les projets*, pp. 107–10.

65. T. Grosbois, 'Portrait de Jean-Charles Snoy et d'Oppuers', in *Regards sur le Bénélux. 50 ans de coopération*, Tielt, 1994, p. 168; and T. Grosbois, 'L'Europe vécue, pensée et en action du comte Jean-Charles Snoy et d'Oppuers avant 1945', in *Lettre d'information des historiens de l'Europe contemporaine*, vol. 4, nos 3–4 (December 1989), pp. 161–4.

66. J. Gotovitch, 'Perspectives européennes dans la résistance et à Londres durant la guerre', in *La Belgique et les débuts de la construction européenne*, ed. M. Dumoulin, Louvain-la-Neuve, 1987, pp. 39–50.

67. C. Wiebes and B. Zeeman, *Belgium, Netherlands and the Alliances*, Leiden, 1993, p. 34.

68. *BI*, 16 February 1943, p. 4.

69. J. Gerard-Libois and R. Lewin, *La Belgique entre dans la guerre froide et l'Europe*, Brussels, 1992, p. 26.

70. C. Wiebes and B. Zeeman, *Belgium*, p. 38.

71. Rapport liminaire sur les travaux de la CEPAG, July 1941, AAE 12647.

72. See above for further details.

73. R. Coolsaet, *Histoire de la politique étrangère de la Belgique*, Brussels, 1988, pp. 81– 91. In a circular sent to Belgian embassies, Spaak affirmed: 'c'est la Grande-Bretagne qui devrait avoir nos préférences' because of the identity of the two nations' political ideals, Britain's security interests on Belgian territory and the commercial opportunities for Belgian businesses within the Commonwealth: Circulaire d'information no. 12, 2 March 1943, AAE 15925.

74. 'Note sur la politique extérieure de la Belgique', April 1941, CEGES PS11 (Schreiber papers).

75. See the various writings of Professor F. Balace.

76. 'Subordination' became a key term in Belgian-British security collaboration after 1945. It was particularly evident in Germany in relations between the Belgian forces and the British Army of the Rhine. The Belgians tried in vain to extricate themselves from this situation in December 1949.

77. 'La sécurité de la Belgique', June 1941, CEGES PS11 (Schreiber papers).

78. F. Van Langenhove, *La sécurité de la Belgique – Contribution à l'histoire de la période 1940–1950*, Brussels, 1971, p. 30.

79. P.F. Smets, *La pensée européenne et atlantique de PH. Spaak, 1942–1972*, vol. 1, Brussels, 1980, pp. 3–4.

80. C. Wiebes and B. Zeeman, *Belgium*, pp. 34 and 38.

81. Ibid, p. 37.

82. Ibid, p. 43.

83. A.E. Kersten, 'Nederland en België in Londen, 1940–1944 – Werken aan de naoorlogse betrekkingen', in *Colloquium over de geschiedenis van de Belgisch – Nederlandsche betrekkingen tussen 1815 en 1945*, Gent, 1982, p. 501.

84. P.F. Smets, *La pensée européenne et atlantique de PH. Spaak, 1942–1972*, vol. 1, p. 19; C. Wiebes and B. Zeeman, *Belgium*, p. 43. Spaak subsequently came round to these Atlanticist views in 1948 when he sought American assistance and guarantees.

85. *Message*, no. 17 (March 1943), pp.17–18. After the war, the same doctrine could be identified among influential military decision-makers. See P. Deloge, 'Enseignement militaire belge et interdépendance en Europe après 1945', in *Lettre d'Information des Historiens de l'Europe Contemporaine*, vol. 5, nos 3–4 (December 1990), pp. 214–22.

86. C. Wiebes and B. Zeeman, *Belgium*, p. 43.

87. F. Van Langenhove, *La sécurité*, pp. 83–4.

88. Ibid, pp. 86–9.

89. R. Coolsaet, *Histoire de la politique étrangère de la Belgique*, p. 87.

90. F. Van Langenhove, *La sécurité*, p. 118.

91. Ibid, pp. 120–2.

92. See 'Suggestions relatives à l'organisation de la coopération entre la Grande-Bretagne et la Belgique dans le cadre d'une entente régionale de l'Europe occidental', AAE, no. 1575, 8 November 1944. This document was written by F. Van Langenhove.

93. On the small powers' role in post-war plans see Cartier to Spaak, 7 October 1942, AAE 11575. On the post-war reconstruction of Europe as liberation approached, see Cartier to Spaak, 31 August 1944, AAE 12647.

94. On the San Francisco conference, see Cartier to Spaak, 17 March 1945, AAE 10958bis.

95. F. Van Cauwelaert, for example. See T. Grosbois, *Les plans*, p. 106.

96. On his conversation with Greenwood see Cartier to Spaak, 2 April 1941, AAE 11575.

97. Speech of Clement Attlee to the Labour Party Annual Conference, Cartier to Spaak, 4 June 1941, AAE 11575: 'La partie la plus intéressante à été celle où M. Attlee a défini en termes généraux les intentions du parti dans la réorganisation de la paix.'

98. Speech of Anthony Eden at Edinburgh: Cartier to Spaak, 9 May and 29 September 1942, AAE 11575: 'le seul reproche que l'on pourrait faire au discours de M. Eden ... est qu'il ne présente pas une vue claire du but final ... les buts proposés ... demeurent vagues'. See also Cartier to Spaak, 31 May 1944, on the debate on foreign policy in parliament.

99. On the parliamentary debate on the post-war period see Cartier to Spaak, 4 June 1942, AAE 11575.

100. Speech of Anthony Eden, Cartier to Spaak, 29 September 1942, AAE 11575.

101. See, for example, Cartier to Spaak on Eden's speech on organisation of the peace, 31 May 1941, AAE 11575.

102. On Franco-British relations, see Cartier to Spaak, 29 August 1944, AAE 11575. Without, however, having any illusions about the post-war situation of France. See, on the post-war period and occupation of the Rhineland, Cartier to Spaak, 3 February 1945, AAE, 10958bis.

103. On Eden's speech to the House of Commons and Franco-British relations, see Cartier to Spaak, 9 December 1942 and 29 August 1944 respectively, AAE 11575.

104. On Franco-British relations, see Cartier to Spaak, 29 August 1944, AAE 11575.

At this time, many Belgian diplomats wanted to see in Franco-British collaboration the means for Britain to remain a major power in the post-war world. On the San Francisco conference, see Cartier to Spaak, 17 March 1945, AAE 10958bis.

105. *BI*, 27 February 1941, p. 4.
106. 'La sécurité de la Belgique', June 1941, CEGES PS11 (Schreiber papers), p. 12 . Further, see V. de Laveleye, 'Mémorandum sur les buts de guerre', 5 January 1941, CEGES PS11.
107. *BI*, 30 December 1943, p. 4.
108. *BI*, 27 May 1943, p. 1.
109. *BI*, 22 January 1942, p. 7.
110. *BI*, 2 February 1941, p. 3.
111. Delvoie to Kaekenbeeck, 23 June 1942, CDH 1241/3.
112. Avant-projet, 19 September 1942, ibid.
113. *Vers l'avenir*, 22 March 1941, p. 1.
114. Ibid, 17 December 1942, pp. 5 and 7.
115. 'Avant-projet de justification des moyens à envisager pour empêcher l'Allemagne de provoquer une nouvelle guerre', 1 October 1942, CDH 1241/3.
116. This phrase is underlined in the text: 'Justification de l'avant projet', 17 October 1942, CDH 1241/3.
117. Cartier to Spaak, 23 March 1942, AAE 11575. Two months later he returned to this theme: 'il n'y a pas si longtemps, beaucoup de bons esprits ici craignaient que la Russie ne s'effondre à l'instar de la France mais, en ces derniers mois, il semble acquis que le patriotisme russe renaît de ses cendres': Cartier to Spaak, 28 May 1942, ibid. Further, the USSR 'fatalement, a repris à son compte les ambitions territoriales de l'empire des tsars': Cartier to Spaak, 13 June 1942, ibid.
118. On the Russo-Polish frontier, see Cartier to Spaak, 21 January 1944, AAE 11575: 'la Russie, qui se sent le vent en poupe, trouve l'occasion bonne pour faire son "pré carré" en Pologne et peut-être aussi dans les Balkans'. See also Cartier to Spaak on Russian politics, AAE 10958bis: 'le maréchal Staline qui a beaucoup de suite dans les idées, s'apprête apparemment à étendre à la Tchécoslovaquie la politique soviétique du droit de regard dans les affaires intérieures de ses voisins'.
119. On rectification of the Russo-Polish border see Cartier to Spaak, 3 March 1943, AAE 11575.
120. On a *Times* article on security in Europe see Cartier to Spaak, AAE 11575, 10 March 1943.

7

THE COMMISSION POUR L'ETUDE DES PROBLÈMES D'APRÈS-GUERRE (CEPAG) 1941–1944[*]

DIANE DE BELLEFROID

The Commission pour l'Etude des Problèmes d'Après-Guerre or CEPAG, created at the beginning of 1941, was an institution that had been created in the orbit of the Belgian Government in exile in London and was composed of a large number of Belgian intellectuals who had found refuge in Britain. The purpose of this article is to try to study the organisation of this institution and the people involved in it. It also provides an account of the work carried out by this commission to try and assess the influence on it of the plans drawn up before the war and to show the imprint they made on the reorganisation of Belgian society after the conflict, thereby demonstrating the continuity that can be traced from prewar to postwar politics. This overview must, by its very nature, be incomplete, given the diversity of the problems studied by the commission and the scope of the reforms carried out after the war. Studying CEPAG, however, enables us to escape from viewing the war as a rupture, and that is why I shall focus on the creation of CEPAG more closely, as well as the role of a few key figures and the influence of their ideas, both upon the commission's work and its method of working.

This article, is based on an unpublished thesis written in 1987,[1] which was based essentially on volumes of primary material and unpublished sources. These came mainly from three archives: the Ministry of Foreign Affairs, the CEGES-SOMA in Brussels and the Archives Générales du Royaume. The official archives of the commission could only be consulted at the Ministry of Foreign Affairs and at the CEGES-SOMA, but the study of this collection yielded very few interesting documents. At the time, it was not possible to consult all of the CEPAG collection, which is stored in the Archives Générales du Royaume. Fortunately, we were able to make use of the personal papers belonging to Jef Rens, the General Secretary of the Commission, whose archives, kept in two collections at the Archives Générales du Royaume and at CEGES-SOMA, were the main source of documentation for this article. Jef Rens, who was very methodical and well organised, left behind some very interesting archives. All the reports from CEPAG, the minutes of the meetings of the departments and of the central committee, the correspondence with the American division in New York and his personal correspondence were the main areas examined in Rens' papers. These official archives are silent on the personal relationships between the members of CEPAG, as well as on its relations with the government. However, we were fortunate enough to be able to consult Paul van Zeeland's personal papers, which were, at the time, kept in the Archives Générales du Royaume but are now in the possession of Professor Michel Dumoulin at the Université Catholique de Louvain.[2] Although these archives are very interesting, some areas still remain unexplored, notably the atmosphere that prevailed within the Commission.

The Origin and Creation of CEPAG

As soon as the Belgian Government had arrived and settled in London, it thought about creating a commission to study postwar problems.[3] Though he was convinced that the Allies would eventually be victorious, the Prime Minister, Hubert Pierlot, believed that the conflict would last a long time. The government should therefore make the best possible use of the number of Belgians in London by directing their energies to preparing for the aftermath of the war, especially as Allied circles were emphatic that there would not be any peace conference.[4] It was therefore essential for Belgium to position itself in the framework of international relations. Moreover, the position of the government was fragile and it was looking for measures it could take within the spirit of the constitution, which would enable it to secure a solid foundation for itself and to give it greater authority when it eventually returned to Belgium. All of these various motives undoubtedly played a role in the decision to create CEPAG.

In January 1941, a few days after his arrival in London, the socialist trade-union official Jef Rens met Pierlot, who straightaway offered to put him in charge of 'la direction du plan de reconstruction de la Belgique après la guerre'.[5] Pierlot was probably well informed about the numerous encounters that Rens had had in the United States with Belgian and American diplomats, during which he had expressed his concern about the need to prepare for the postwar period. Jef Rens was therefore put in charge of 'une liste des moyens' necessary for the implementation of this task.[6] At the same time, two other Belgian socialist exiles, Max Buset and Louis de Brouckère, who were probably also acting on the government's orders, wrote a note advocating the creation of a similar study committee. These notes were dated 4 and 9 January 1941 respectively.[7] It proved to be Rens' note, however, that attracted the Prime Minister's attention, and, on 15 January 1941, Rens was appointed advisor to the government.[8] From then on, he devoted himself to the establishment of the commission, and subsequently became its Secretary General.

CEPAG, however, only acquired official status in 1942 as a result of a royal decree of 4 June. This defined it as a study organisation in charge of: first, studying the problems connected with the reforms that needed to be carried out in the political, economic and social domains; second, examining and preparing, together with the relevant departments or sections of the government, measures that it would be necessary to take at the time of the liberation of the territory, with a view to ensuring that life would resume normally in Belgium; and third, keeping close contact with the British and Allied groups, both official and private, that were engaged in similar activities, with a view to informing the government about the trends that emerged among these organisations concerning postwar problems.[9]

So CEPAG's work would focus on a complete overhaul of postwar Belgian society, both from a domestic standpoint and in its international relationships. The Belgians in London were aware of the necessity of not repeating, at any cost, the mistake committed after the First World War, which had been to seek to return to the prewar system.[10] The latter had clearly shown weaknesses, and it was imperative to build a new world if a third world conflict was to be avoided. The task of CEPAG was therefore essentially one of research. Of course the urgent problems caused by the liberation of the territory would need to be analysed, but what needed to be done was to make a methodical and exhaustive assessment of all the issues and the reforms that would be made at the end of the war. In addition, its role was also to collect as much documentation as possible. Finally, it drew up reports that were intended to enable the government to take rapid decisions at the opportune moment. So, though the commission was required to carry out detailed studies, issues of execution did not form part of its competence and remained the responsibility of the ministerial departments.

Organisation, composition and methods of work

How did CEPAG function and what links did it have with the government that created it? A central committee headed the commission. This co-ordinated the work according to the principles of 'planning' in vogue on the eve of the conflict: it assessed the problems and looked for associates able to provide a detailed note about each question that arose; it shared out the tasks between the departments; and it made an abstract of its studies in a report presented to the government. To accomplish this mission in an effective manner it had the right to recommend both appointments and the establishment of new departments to the government. As early as January 1941, it was decided that the central committee of the commission would be composed of five people: the Catholic former Prime Minister Paul van Zeeland presided over it. He was chosen on the basis of his prestige in international circles – and particularly in English-speaking ones – which would help to compensate for the weak relations between the British Government and the Belgian Government in exile.[11] Van Zeeland's advocacy of a regime of political and economic liberty, directed by an economic council and regulated by a structure of corporatist professional organisations was also close to the socialist ideas that were favoured in London. Van Zeeland initially insisted on remaining in the United States, but accepted "de collaborer avec la Commission que le Gouvernement a souhaité voir se constituer ... à New York".[12] He aspired to be appointed a minister, but the government refused to make the appointment because of his alleged support for King Leopold III. The government had also made it a point of honour not to go beyond its constitutional role by appointing new ministers. Nevertheless, van Zeeland might have been appointed instead as a Secretary of State, but his involvement in the scandal concerning the Banque Nationale de Belgique only dated from two or three years earlier, and the government, already fragile, could not run the risk of appointing somebody whose reputation had been weakened in occupied Belgium.[13] Moreover, and significantly, there was personal and political rivalry between the Minister of Finance, Camille Gutt, and van Zeeland that went hand in hand with their conflicting ideas on economic doctrines. Despite these problems, however, CEPAG had to justify its existence by the presence at its head of someone who was well-regarded in Allied circles. Meanwhile, as he could not obtain a ministerial post, van Zeeland had decided to settle in the United States, for it was there, according to him, that everything was being decided. The Foreign Affairs Minister, Paul-Henri Spaak, was therefore asked by the government to win him round. A great number of letters were subsequently exchanged between the two men, and van Zeeland finally agreed to head CEPAG, hoping by doing so to be able to exert influence over the government, on the condition that he could continue his overseas missions. His arrival marked the real start of the commission's work and he devoted much time and energy to what he considered to be his war service.[14] He left his imprint on the work of CEPAG, writing its general reports himself; and we can recognise his own ideas about economic and social issues in them.[15]

If van Zeeland was able to limit his activities to overseeing the work of the commission, it was thanks to the professionalism of Jef Rens, Secretary General of CEPAG, and so a member of the central committee. A well-known trade-unionist in the political world, he had been Spaak's friend and immediate associate in the Ministry of Foreign Affairs,[16] and it was probably because of this connection that he met Hubert Pierlot when he returned from the United States. Before the war, he had attended the lectures by the future President of the Belgian Socialist Party (POB), Henri de Man, in Germany and he became a follower of his ideas during the pre-war international conferences about *planisme*. Rens, who combined his duties in CEPAG with those he had in the Centre Syndical Belge in London, tried to apply the principles of *planisme* in the ideas as well as in the working methods of the commission. As van Zeeland was often absent, it was in effect the secretary general who was in charge of its daily operation, and his organisational qualities and drive were utilised to the full.[17] Paul Lévy, a technical advisor with CEPAG, described Rens as the 'king pin' of the organisation, which seems to sum up his character rather well.[18]

Louis de Brouckère, Raoul Richard and Julius Hoste were vice-chairmen of CEPAG. The veteran socialist politician de Brouckère was still a very dynamic man, in spite of being seventy: he held the record of attendance at the various meetings of the commission. His participation was not, however, always constructive, judging by the number of minority dissenting reports that he wrote. Raoul Richard was the representative of the business world in CEPAG.[19] He was, however, familiar with public service, because he had been a member of the government before the war. He appeared at CEPAG only occasionally because he was – like van Zeeland – based in New York, where he proved to be very valuable in resolving problems about food supplies. He also acted as a representative of CEPAG and of the Ministry of Economic Affairs on the Leith-Ross Committee, which was an inter-Allied committee in charge of food supplies and provisioning for the countries invaded by Germany. It was with this goal in mind that the government appointed him Under Secretary of State for the Supply and Restocking of Belgium. Finally, Julius Hoste was 'la voix flamande et libérale' in CEPAG.[20] A regular attender at the meetings of the central committee, and also those of the Foreign Affairs Department, he was a fervent advocate of the idea of European integration.

The central committee also benefited from the participation of two official members (appointed by ministerial decree): the manager of the Belgian weapons factory, the Fabrique Nationale, in Herstal, Gustave Joassart, who was able to share his experience regarding professional organisations and *commissions paritaires*, as well as the Socialist trade-union representative Joseph Bondas from the Confédération Générale du Travail de Belgique. Professor Bigwood, a medical doctor and Professor of Nutrition at the University of Brussels (ULB), was summoned to attend many meetings of the central committee to advise its members about food supplies. Baron Ruzette, a diplomat and a man of letters, was also an active, though unofficial, member of the central committee. The composition of this committee revealed a good deal about the general direction of its work. Three of its members (van Zeeland, Richard and Hoste) used to belong to the van Zeeland Government before the war. If one includes Rens, who was sympathetic to Henri de Man's theories and was one of Spaak's former associates, it is easy to understand the atmosphere that prevailed at the meetings of the central committee.

The other members of the committee broadened its horizons in order to enable it to meet effectively the objective of CEPAG, namely to reorganise postwar Belgium in all aspects of its social life. It should be noted, however, that most members were concerned primarily with social and economic issues and believed firmly that the society of the future would be ruled by economics. The central committee oversaw seven departments (foreign policy, reform of the state, teaching, economy, social affairs, reconstruction and colonies), the main role of which was to discuss issues that came within their remit and to submit reports to the central committee. It would be beyond the scope of this article to provide an account of all the studies carried out by the different departments; we shall nevertheless endeavour to present a synthesis of them, after describing first the social composition of the CEPAG.

CEPAG managed to secure the participation of seventy-six members (those who had worked for the American division in New York are not included in this total). Among them, the most important were the permanent employees, appointed by the government. These were the secretaries, technical advisors, heads of departments and some members of the central committee. The other participants were unpaid volunteers and were recruited among Belgian intellectuals living in London. They had other jobs in Britain but were pleased to be able to serve the national cause. Some of them worked regularly for CEPAG; others only helped out occasionally, for example by writing a study on a specific technical question. In order to persuade them to participate in CEPAG's work, Rens sent them the preliminary note that he had written himself, so that they could gauge the objectives of the commission.

Who were the members of CEPAG? They were almost exclusively male (there were only two women!)[21] and were aged on average fifty at the beginning of the war. The majority were political figures (twenty),[22] or economists and industrialists (seventeen). But there were also civil servants (nine), diplomats (eight), jurists (six), scientists (five) and representatives of the trade unions (four) as well as journalists (two). It is evident that the central committee cast its net wide in its recruitment, always with the objective of not neglecting any area of society. But among the political figures what is striking is the number of socialists (fifteen representatives out of twenty-seven, plus four union officials), reflecting the reality that they constituted the largest, the most closely-knit and the best-organised group in London.[23] Yet, in general, a consensus of opinion proved possible about the general direction of the commission's work, as if there was a will to unite in adversity. So, CEPAG was in many respects a representative sample of the Belgian intelligentsia in London, which also explains why the detractors of the commission's work also saw it as existing only to provide an alibi for these intellectuals' failure to engage personally in the war effort.

A synthesis of the work of CEPAG

The commission considered that its raison d'être forced it to 'se placer nettement au point de vue des intérêts nationaux belges',[24] but its members realised that the situation of Belgium made it closely dependent on the international political and economic order. Hence they always approached their work with an awareness of this international dimension and were very active, either in a private capacity, or on behalf of the commission or the government, within international organisations and conferences concerned with addressing postwar issues.

In accordance with the mission assigned to it by the royal decree, CEPAG made a clear distinction between two types of issue. The first category was concerned with the transitional period that would extend from the end of the hostilities to the return to a normal life:

this involved issues such as food supplies, the restocking of industries, the fight against inflation, war damages and the punishment of acts of collaboration. In order to avoid conflicts of responsibilities with the various ministerial departments, CEPAG created enactment committees, the role of which was to liaise between the different sections of the commission and the departments concerned, in close collaboration with the government, in order to advance as far as possible in the preparation of the enforcement of these immediate measures. These committees only dealt with the problems of the transitional period, and, although in practice they depended on the government, they were inspired by the studies of CEPAG. They even drafted decree-laws, believing that, if they did so, the measures were more likely to be implemented. The Gutt Plan for postwar financial stability, for instance, was not drafted by CEPAG as such: Gutt asked CEPAG for a note about the principles of monetary policy and was then inspired by it, although he always subsequently sought to deny its influence on his plans. CEPAG devoted a third of its studies to transitional problems of this type but they were accorded priority and had to be considered in conditions of great secrecy.[25]

The second category of issues concerned long-term reforms, which were based on a common philosophy developed within the central committee, notably by van Zeeland.[26] This was based around a simple slogan: 'le bien-être pour tous' (welfare for all). What they aimed to achieve was the establishment of a political and social democracy by means of a reform of the economic system. Starting from the analysis of the prewar economic situation, the members of the central committee realised that total economic freedom led to anarchy. Thus, whereas a maximum of individual liberty would be retained, the State would be obliged to intervene as a regulator of economic activity. The economic policy should be pursued according to a 'plan d'action'[27] to be developed by the State in association with the various social groups. A higher council of the national economy would represent the professional organisations, the employers' associations and the *commissions paritaires*, as well as consumers' groups. The role of this body would be to co-ordinate economic activity and decree rules of professional activity as well as advising about laws and decrees. This advisory capacity in the field of laws would be complemented by a right of initiative. This proposal was not a novel one. Under van Zeeland's second government in the 1930s, an organisation of a similar kind, OREC (Office for Economic Recovery), had already been created at the initiative of the Socialist minister Henri de Man.

Welfare for all could only be achieved by the establishment of a social security system ensuring a minimum standard of living for every citizen. Everybody would be entitled to social security that would cover 'les risques que l'homme subit au cours de sa vie, de façon à lui assurer stabilité et sécurité' and would particularly apply to unemployment, health, diseases, disability, industrial injury, occupational diseases, funeral costs, premature death, old-age pensions, family allowances, maternity benefits and wedding and birth allowances.[28] To ensure the effective operation of the system, a national office 'doté de la personnalité juridique et jouissant d'une complète autonomie administrative et financière' would be created. The professional associations would have representatives in it, as well as in a social council that 'à l'instar du Conseil Supérieur de l'E-conomie Nationale a le droit d'avis et le droit d'initiative dans des conditions analogues'.[29] All of these principles owed an evident debt to the report presented in 1942 by Sir William Beveridge at the British Government's request, commonly known as the Beveridge report. The secretary of the social section, Jean Leroy, analysed the Beveridge report and it was used as a source of reference for its work.[30]

These ideas were not in essence original; they had been clearly expressed by a number of different economic and political prewar thinkers, who had argued that democracy could only be achieved when economic and social equality existed. In Belgium, Henri de Man had played an important part in disseminating such ideas. De Man was a member of the prewar Van Zeeland Government and there were numerous members of CEPAG – and particularly those of the central committee – who were followers of his system of planning. But these projects were also closely akin to Keynesian economic philosophy, which was based on the postulate that full employment depends on the volume of demand. To increase consumption, the income of the workers should be improved by granting them social benefits. These theories featured prominently in the work of the reconstruction section.

Through the impetus given by the central committee, the section for the reform of the state tried to revivify the democratic system so that it might be 'plus conforme à son essence même'.[31] With this aim in mind, auxiliary councils should be created in order to participate in the exercise of governmental power with the goal, so the CEPAG report stated, of coordinating and systematising the many institutions that had emerged out of private initiatives and that gave voice to the aspirations of the nation on social and economic issues. In this way, these auxiliary councils would harness the energies of the 'forces vives' of the nation to support the national political authority.[32] The new role given to professional organisations and the *commissions paritaires* implied the creation of a Conseil d'Etat that would oversee the smooth running of the system. The section for the reform of the state was also aware of the 'importance capitale' of the linguistic problem in Belgium. It was allowed only, however, to do no more than raise this problem as the government urged it not to carry out studies in this highly sensitive area.[33]

A similar logic of state planning underlay the studies by the section of international policy,[34] presided over by Paul-Henri Spaak: 'De cruelles expériences ont démontré que la solution des problèmes posés par les mouvements des cycles économiques ne pourraient être laissés à l'initiative arbitraire des Etats travaillant en ordre dispersé'.[35] On this basis, the members of the section advocated the idea of international collaboration through the reduction of obstacles to international trade. They imagined a three-tiered international society, with the national state as its basis, but with limits on its sovereignty within areas such as access to raw materials, monetary policy and means of transport. Between the national and the world level, there would be regional groups, the function of which would be essentially economic, with the purpose of increasing the opportunities for trade by suppressing tariff barriers. A more political goal was also evident in the plans for the creation of a European union in order to achieve a regime of international security.

This brief overview of the plans by CEPAG demonstrates that the prewar projects and experiments in Belgium already contained the seeds of all of these ideas. Limited intervention by the state, be it from a political, cultural or economic standpoint, was considered to be an inescapable means of creating a more democratic and egalitarian society.

Conclusion

What came of the work of CEPAG? It is difficult to reach a general conclusion because each of the reforms launched after the war needs to be assessed on a case-by-case basis. Generally speaking, however, CEPAG could not claim the exclusive responsibility for any of the postwar reforms, which were largely the result of a dialogue between the different social groups that had articulated plans for the postwar era. The most striking such example was the *Pacte Social* concluded by employers and trade-union leaders in occupied Belgium in the spring of 1944, which – as its very name indicates – was the result of a dialogue. Indeed, the Belgians in London generally, and those in CEPAG especially, had recognised from an early stage that they should withdraw their projects and let the ones planned by those who had stayed in occupied Belgium proceed.

The real influence of CEPAG should therefore be traced in terms of personal history, as all the members of the commission returned to Belgium with their own files, containing the reports that might be of value to advance measures within their own areas of competence during the postwar era. Thus, van Zeeland in the Repatriation Commission, the Finance Minister Gutt and his famous recovery package for the franc, or Roger Roch as the *chef de cabinet* of the postwar Socialist Prime Minister Achille van Acker in his proposals for the creation of a Conseil d'Etat, all drew on ideas initially proposed by CEPAG. The work of CEPAG therefore influenced the postwar era in a more diffuse and more insidious way, and we should also bear in mind the long-term ideological effects of the commission, such as, for example, Europeanist ideas which were widely spread in political and intellectual Belgian circles after the war, through the impetus given to them by Paul-Henri Spaak, among others.

Therefore, generally speaking, it must be acknowledged that the structure of society set up in the days following the Liberation was that which had been drafted by CEPAG, which in itself was modelled on prewar currents of thought and experiments. The former members of CEPAG did not, however, constitute a pressure-group campaigning for the enactment of their programme. In effect, a small group of people existed before the war (van Zeeland, Spaak, Rens, de Brouckère, Hoste and Richard), all of whom had participated in the van Zeeland governments, and between whom there existed political as well as ideological bonds. In 1984, the Flemish newspaper *De Nieuwe Gazet* characterised CEPAG as a 'Commission des Illusions' whose members wasted their time in order to give themselves a good conscience.[36] This harsh assessment is not completely justified in as much as all the members committed themselves to serving their own country and were driven by the ideal of building a more just society. However, they were aware that they would have to hand over to those who had continued the struggle in occupied Belgium and who had devised their own plans for the postwar order. What is certain is that a consensus of opinion was reached within CEPAG about the society that people hoped to develop in Belgium after the conflict, and that this must have left traces. One can at least say that this collaborative work had the merit, for all who participated in it, of serving to highlight the principles that should predominate after the war and thereby ensure the continuity between the prewar and the postwar eras.

Notes

* Translated by Christine Arthur.

1. D. de Bellefroid, *La Commission pour l'Etude des Problèmes d'Après-Guerre (CEPAG) 1941–44*, Louvain-la-Neuve, 1987.
2. The numbering used in this article corresponds to that of the *Archives Générales du Royaume* (AGR), Brussels; thus it needs to be updated according to Michel Dumoulin's classification. Professor Dumoulin consulted this collection frequently for the biography of Paul van Zeeland that he wrote with Vincent Dujardin. See V. Dujardin and M. Dumoulin, *Paul van Zeeland 1893–1973*, Brussels, 1997.
3. Spaak to van Zeeland, 18 November 1940, AGR, Paul van Zeeland papers, no. 532.
4. J. Rens, *Ontmoetingen 1930–1942*, Antwerp-Amsterdam, 1984; Fonck to Rens, 23 April 1942, Jef Rens papers, Centre d'Etude Guerre et Sociétés Contemporaines (CEGES), Brussels, PR5–205 American division, correspondence, no. 17.
5. J. Rens, *Ontmoetingen*.
6. Ibid.
7. M. Buset, 'Note sur la constitution d'un Comité d'Etudes Nationales', 4 January 1941, AGR, Fonds Rens-CEPAG, no. 16; L. De Brouckère, 'Commission pour l'étude des problèmes relatifs à la reconstruction nationale', AGR, Rens-CEPAG collection, no. 16.
8. Organisation and plan of action for the Commission pour l'étude des problèmes d'après-guerre, August 1941, AGR, van Zeeland papers, no. 712.
9. *Moniteur Belge de Londres, année 1942*, London, 1942, p. 268.
10. Rapports de la Commission d'Etude des Problèmes d'Après-Guerre (CEPAG), (1941–1944), [London, 1944] p. 4.
11. B. Henau, 'Shaping a new Belgium: the CEPAG – the Belgian Commission for the Study of Post-War Problems, 1941–1944', in *Making the New Europe: European Unity and the Second World War*, eds M.L. Smith and P. Stirk, London-New York, 1990, p. 113.
12. Van Zeeland to Spaak, 31 January 1941, AGR, van Zeeland papers, no. 532.
13. Interview with Paul Lévy, 1 December 1986.
14. Ibid.
15. Correspondence, notes and preparatory work for the fourth CEPAG report, AGR, van Zeeland papers, no. 716. This file contains the manuscript of the fourth report of the CEPAG, written in Van Zeeland's own handwriting. Also see the minutes of the central committee meeting of 7 April 1942 where van Zeeland 'expose ses conceptions en matière économique'. AGR, Rens-CEPAG collection, no. 7(2), Comité Central. The manner in which this meeting proceeded demonstrated clearly the way in which van Zeeland assumed a leadership role and succeeded in winning over the other members of the committee to his views.
16. J. Gotovitch, *Archives de guerre de Jef Rens*, Brussels, 1986, p. 2.
17. Ibid.
18. Interview with Paul Lévy, 1 December 1986.
19. On this subject, see P. De Boeck and F. Van Langenhove, 'Baron Raoul Richard', in *Biographie Nationale*, vol. XL, Brussels, 1977–78, col. 721–30; A. Dantoing, *Archives Baron Raoul Richard*, Brussels, 1982, pp. 1–2.
20. J. Hoste, *Een Vlaamsche stem in de oorlogstijd*, London, 1944.
21. Isabelle Blume and Madame Schreiber, presumably the wife of Max Schreiber.
22. For example, Paul-Henri Spaak, Max Buset, Victor de Laveleye, Camille

Huysmans, Fernand Van Langenhove, Hubert Pierlot, Henri Rolin, Roger Taymans, Charles and Paul Tschoffen, André van Campenhout, Pierre Vermeylen, Werner Koelman, Roger Motz, Arthur Wauters and Isabelle Blume.

23. J. Gotovitch, 'Views of Belgian Exiles on the Postwar Order in Europe', in *Documents on the History of European Integration*, vol. 2: *Plans for the European Union in Great Britain and in Exile, 1939–1945*, ed. W. Lipgens, Berlin-New York, 1986, p. 415.

24. Rapports de la Commission d'Etude des Problèmes d'Après-Guerre (CEPAG), (1941–1944), [London, 1944] p. 4.

25. Ibid, p. 5.

26. During the twenty-third meeting of the Central Committee, on 7 April 1942, Paul van Zeeland 'a fait un bref exposé de ses vues en matière économique'. These views were almost exactly word for word those expressed subsequently in the reports. Apart from Louis de Brouckère, all the members were won over to his opinion. Rens, however, would have liked to expand these ideas even further, but was afraid that bureaucratisation might take over. Minutes of the meeting of the Central Committee on 7 April 1942, AGR, Rens-CEPAG collection, no. 7(2), Central Committee.

27. It is interesting to notice how the reports avoided speaking of 'planisme' directly. They rather used the words 'plan d'action' or 'programme économique', probably because of Henri de Man's pro-German activities within occupied Belgium! Reports by the CEPAG, p. 45.

28. Ibid, pp. 95 and 100–1.

29. Ibid, pp. 102–3.

30. W. Beveridge, *Social Insurances and Allied Services*, London, 1942; J. Leroy, *Analyse du Rapport Beveridge*, January 1943, Archives du Ministère des Affaires Etrangères de Belgique (AMAEB), Brussels, no. 4542.

31. Reports by CEPAG, pp. 38 and 76.

32. Ibid.

33. Van Zeeland to Delfosse, 30 March 1944, AGR, van Zeeland papers, no. 826.

34. For more detail on the work of this section, see D. De Bellefroid, 'Les projets d'union européenne élaborés par la Commission pour l'Etude des Problèmes d'Après-Guerre', in *Lettre d'Information des Historiens de l'Europe contemporaine* or *Contemporary Historians Newsletter*, June 1987, pp. 57–61.

35. The reports of CEPAG officially mentioned as the source of inspiration of the work of the section the report already submitted to the French and the British governments in 1938. Reports by the CEPAG, pp. 6–7.

36. *De Nieuwe Gazet*, 30 July 1984.

8

THE STAFF OF THE HIGH COMMISSARIAT FOR NATIONAL SECURITY: A SOCIO-PROFESSIONAL PROFILE

ERIC LAUREYS

The High Commissariat for National Security, or HCNS (*Hoog Commissariaat voor 's Lands Veiligheid – Haut Commissariat pour la Sécurité de l'Etat*) was set up in London in July 1943 by the Belgian Government in exile. The organisation's purpose was to oversee the control and co-ordination of the institutions that were charged with the maintenance of law and order after liberation of the national territory. Law and order was an important pre-condition if the power vacuum left after the departure of the occupying forces was to be quickly filled. To achieve this, the disarmament and the channelling of the armed resistance as well as the re-arming and the purging of the armed forces were of vital importance. This sensitive task was entrusted to Advocate General Walter Ganshof van der Meersch, a tough magistrate who was put in charge of the High Commissariat.

In this contribution I will limit myself to an analysis of the officials whom Ganshof recruited at various times. The archives of the HCNS enable some light to be shed on the people with whom Ganshof chose to work, and the intention of this contribution is to make the information contained in these archives more widely available in the hope that it can be compared with that from other sources within the framework of future research. The assumption on which this article is based is that a better knowledge of the people to whom the High Commissioner entrusted his representation in the field will serve to shed some light on the motives that drove the government in matters of law and order and in the restoration of 'legality'. With this aim in mind, an overview will be provided of the recruitment criteria and their evolution, but first and foremost of the social and professional profiles of the officials.

The Establishment of HCNS

As the moment of Belgium's liberation drew nearer, the London-based Pierlot Government paid increasing attention to the problem of the restoration of normal public life and the maintenance of law and order in the country. The forces of order were weakened, divided and rather inefficient, and there were fears of an unchecked wave of repression against the occupying forces and collaborators. Co-ordination under governmental control was thus necessary. Furthermore, the Allied command demanded guarantees about the way in which the government would maintain law, order and military justice. In the eyes of the Belgian authorities, national sovereignty was to some extent at stake: they believed that an Allied military occupation would have catastrophic consequences for both the government and the country. For this reason it was desirable to appoint an official who was able to exercise powerful, legitimate and credible authority over the various services to which the maintenance of law and order were entrusted. Right from the outset of the project, the overriding belief was that this task should be the preserve of the military judiciary. Under the powers invested in him in a war situation, Ganshof already exercised control over the agents of the State Security Service for the performance of judicial police duties. Moreover, this top magistrate enjoyed a substantial reputation and was well regarded in Resistance circles. He was, for this reason, approached by the Prime Minister.

The job of High Commissioner for National Security was created by the decree of 29 July 1943, under which the government could appoint a magistrate to enforce law and order and entrust him with the control of all organisations that were responsible for state security and the maintenance of law and order.[1] Ganshof was appointed to the post by the decree of 4 August 1943. At the insistence of the Prime Minister, and with the aim of reinforcing his links with the governmental structure, Ganshof was given, over and above his job as Advocate General, the title of High Commissioner for National Security, a formula that permitted him to act as an advisor to the government. According to the agreement with the Allies of 14 May 1944, HCNS was made part of the third section of the Belgian Military Mission (BMM), which was entirely under Ganshof's command. This third section was, in particular, responsible for the repression of attacks against the security of the state and the Allied armies in Belgium.

In the execution of his duties the High Commissioner was, to a large extent, reliant on the military authorities. His representatives therefore had to be convincing in their dealings with Allied officers, and the Allied Supreme Command demanded in fact that Belgians taking part in these discussions be army officers. For this reason the officials of the HCNS were commissioned as Civil Affairs Officers (CAO). This cadre of officers had been established within the BMM at Allied Supreme Command as a consequence of the decree of 3 February 1944.[2] The inspiration for it can clearly be found in the similar bodies which the Allies had already set up precisely to address problems relating to the liberation of occupied countries, such as provisioning, public and economic life and relationships between the local population, the government and the Allies. I will not, at this point, explore further the prerogatives of HCNS. They are explicitly described in the report that Ganshof himself drew up in November 1945.[3] The main aims of the body have, however, already been made clear: the restoration of public life and the maintenance of law and order through centralised control and co-ordination.

Recruitment Criteria for HCNS

In December 1943 Ganshof had already started to request permission to recruit competent members of staff from other public services that were established in London. He preferred staff to be reserve officers and law graduates with sufficient knowledge of administrative affairs.[4] In April 1944 the Supreme Headquarters of Allied Expeditionary Forces (SHAEF) let it be known that it expected the officers of the Belgian Military Mission (BMM) to have a high degree of knowledge of matters such as espionage, police affairs, security, port protection, collaborationist activities and refugee control.[5] Candidates would also preferably speak English and Flemish, in that order of preference. Knowledge of French was apparently presumed and was not specifically required.[6] Officially no account was to be taken of the political inclinations of the candidates. The typical candidate was preferably to be distinguished, cultured, energetic, decisive, helpful, sharp-witted, sensible, dynamic and strong-willed. As if this was not enough, there was also the specification that he must leave a 'good impression'.[7] This was important, because the High Commissioner's representative had to have a high standing among the local population and dignitaries.[8]

In July 1944 the organisational framework of HCNS and that of the entire BMM began to take shape, and the recruitment criteria were somewhat more concretely formulated in the examination that the candidates for CAO were obliged to sit. It stands out that the list of criteria always started with physical qualities. Staff members had to be fit and in good health. The second requirement was for professional criteria, such as a knowledge of administrative law (particularly that relating to provincial and local council institutions), judicial organisation, the structure and role of the state and local police, war and occupation legislation, the laws decreed in London with respect to the responsibilities of HCNS and, finally, the collaborationist groups. The importance of legislation regulating public order is immediately obvious, but a good knowledge of who exercised what authority at a local level was also important. Finally, and here one touches on a more subtly expressed criterion, the contribution that the candidates could make to the information that had been collected in London about the collaborationist groups was also considered. Later in this study it will be shown that various members of Ganshof's staff were former members of the Resistance and had information about pro-German collaboration that the early 'Londoners' lacked. However, it should be added that these members of staff had mostly been in France, Switzerland or Portugal for a long time before they managed to reach Britain, and had doubts themselves about the validity of their reports, which were months or years out of date.[9]

The third factor taken into consideration was a knowledge of languages. The most important criterion for recruitment was a sufficient knowledge of English. The close relationship that the HCNS rapidly established with the Allied armies is most striking. Obviously, therefore, knowledge of English was a serious consideration in the recruitment of the Civil Affairs Officers. In addition, perfect fluency in the language of the region in which the member of staff would eventually be stationed was also required, as well as an excellent knowledge of that region.[10] What was more surprising was the last criterion, which demanded that, should he not already do so, the candidate should learn to ride a motor cycle.[11] Telephones, the road network and means of transport were all badly damaged at the time that HCNS became operational, and presumably this criterion indicated the difficult communications that were anticipated in the liberated region.

Ganshof was personally responsible for the recruitment of his immediate staff and his administrative personnel.[12] This produced a few problems in the London of 1943–44. Potential candidates were often working in the London offices of Belgian multi-national companies who were not too willing to give up their staff.[13] The other public services, including Civil Affairs,[14] were, moreover, already monopolising the personnel who were eligible for recruitment. Initially, in December 1943, Ganshof asked the Minister of Defence for nine officers or capable officials.[15] He was only given three: Cambier, Lapierre and Watteeuw. Only the last of these held a degree in law and was a lawyer. The other two were lower-ranking civil servants who were apparently transferred by Ganshof from the Military Justice administration to HCNS.[16] A competent deputy seemed impossible to find. This situation was not pleasing to Ganshof who between December 1943 and September 1944 repeatedly expressed his dissatisfaction.[17] Competent and reliable personnel were scarce in London; and after arriving in liberated Belgium in September 1944, the huge increase in the range of duties that were entrusted to HCNS emphasised this scarcity of competent staff.[18]

After the liberation of Belgium, the recruitment criteria were once again refined. Attention was paid to the attitude of the candidate during the occupation. This criterion is symptomatic of the fact that from then on recruitment took place in Belgium and no longer in London, where all Belgians who were active in the war machine had already been vetted by the British. Consequently, there was suddenly a need to assess the morality of the candidate.[19] This difference in emphasis was also perhaps because of a change in the person carrying out the recruiting. These latest criteria were no longer drawn up by Ganshof but by François Cattoir, his right-hand man, who was entrusted with the actual command of HCNS in Belgium.

How Staffing Levels Evolved

Are the difficulties that were experienced in the recruitment of personnel apparent from the study of how HCNS's staff evolved? If so, this would confirm the findings of the previous section but such a study would also provide a picture of the relative presence and thus the power of the HCNS during the entire period under discussion. Some caution is, however, necessary, since it is still uncertain who was a staff member of the HCNS and for what period, as well as who was a volunteer, a commissioned officer, an adjunct registrar, a driver or a clerk – to cite just a few examples. There is also some vagueness concerning a number of staff members because it is not clear to which section of the Belgian Military Mission they belonged. They were transferred several times by Ganshof from one section to another for short periods.

Based on a thorough analysis of the available personal and related files, it has, however, proved possible to establish with some certainty that, irrespective of the level of responsibility or the period of employment of the persons concerned, over the entire period a total of 182 persons worked for HCNS, sixty-nine of whom were military and militarised personnel, seventy-five were civilians and thirty-eight were of unknown origin. Sixty-five of the 182 staff members were mentioned in Ganshof's final report on the activities of HCNS. The members of this group, which is referred to as the 'core' on the graph *below*, were better educated and were considered sufficiently important by Ganshof to be mentioned in his report. Of these sixty-five people, forty-nine were officers. This distribution allows us to isolate the remaining staff members of HCNS, who were mainly lower-ranking personnel such as administrative employees, drivers and motor cyclists.

How can these figures be distributed over the period during which HCNS existed? Based on our own statistics, a curve can be drawn representing monthly staffing levels. Though it would be unwise to rely on the specific figures, the shape of the curve is, however, probably broadly correct, and it enables us to establish when the HCNS underwent expansions and reductions. Some corrections to the curve can also be made on the basis of a report from Major Jules Lerot, a Regional Officer who was entrusted with the dissolution of HCNS between November 1945 and May 1946, and which in broad terms confirms the evolution of the active personnel between December 1944 and January 1946.[20] From the graph, it can be seen that recruitment between July 1943 and July 1944 proved extremely difficult. It is evident that between July and September 1943 almost no one was recruited, and really significant growth only occurred from September 1944. As approximately

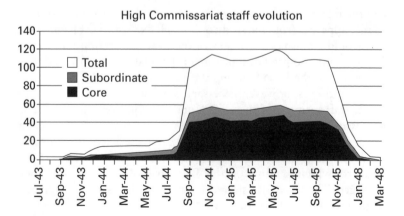

High Commissariat staff evolution

fifty-five members of staff left London for Belgium when it had been liberated, it can reasonably certainly be concluded that this additional recruitment took place on Belgian soil rather than in London. Although it would be wrong to ascribe the spectacular growth of HCNS exclusively to this factor, it is nevertheless not unrealistic to assume that the pool of candidates in Belgium was much larger than in London. In addition to the sharp increase in September 1944, there was a further slight increase in May 1945. What is noteworthy is that this further increase coincided once again with a specific event, namely the return of numerous Belgians from the German prisoner-of-war and work camps. This was followed by a marked decrease from October 1945 (through the laying-off of civilian personnel) until January 1946. It is also clear that after the dissolution of HCNS on 1 November 1945 there was no sudden lay-off. A possible reason for this was the change in function of a number of the remaining officers, who from then onwards carried out liaison missions with Allied units. Major Lerot, for example, finally left on 31 May 1946.[21] Finally it is worth noting that the curves of the core personnel and that of the lower-ranking personnel run in parallel. Therefore there seems to have been no excessive bureaucratisation of HCNS.

Profiles of Regional Officers

This section analyses the social and professional profiles of the group of regional officers. This consisted of the delegated (provincial) officers, their deputies, the co-ordination officers who represented HCNS in the harbours, the subordinate officers attached to the central sections and the liaison officers seconded to the Allied armies. Over the entire working period of HCNS it totalled 44 men. In analysing this group an attempt will be made to establish what differences, if any, existed between the staff members who were recruited in London, those who were recruited in liberated Belgium from September 1944 and those who remained active after HCNS was officially disbanded. It is also important to compare the profiles with the recruitment criteria already studied, in order to ascertain whether they in fact coincided. Any differences might either suggest that Ganshof relied on certain circles to carry out his recruitment or that he had a personal connection with some of his staff. So in these various ways it may be possible to detect both Ganshof's and the government's motives, as well as the prevalent ideology the officers of HCNS.

Prior to carrying out this analysis, however, it is worthwhile to provide a brief overview of the administrative personnel of HCNS, which numbered about 138 members of staff including thirty-one women (22.5 percent). Only one of these women, Lucienne Bricman, a translator seconded to Germany in the summer of 1945, was an officer. The other female staff members were secretaries, typists or shorthand writers, who in some instances were given the rank of non-commissioned officer. Five of them had had a higher non-university education in economics, commerce, shorthand, secretarial work or English. Among the male staff members, in addition to numerous drivers and motor cyclists, there were also eighteen law graduates, whose responsibilities included the car pool, the weapon depot and the press section. Twenty-six of these staff were already present in London when they joined HCNS, and of them six had a university degree. The administrative personnel worked both in the central section of HCNS and in the provincial sections. Although the available documents do not provide sufficient information to generalise about its members' Resistance activities or the role of language and secondary education in their selection, the administrative personnel is however known to have included some excellent bi- and trilingual employees. Some of them, like Renée Scaillet, were already present in London and remained in service under the direction of Major Lerot until the last few months of activity.

The main tasks of the staff of HCNS in London were essentially administrative in nature. Before leaving for Belgium, a great deal of information had to be gathered and officers had to attend a special training course. Most of the staff who were recruited early worked in the documentation section headed by Captain Cattoir and Secretary Captain-Commandant Van de Vloet. Here, links with the Belgian Resistance enabled the establishment of lists of public servants, such as mayors, aldermen and state and local policemen, with notes about whether the official concerned was suspected of collaboration. In addition, the clandestine Belgian press was analysed. This exceptionally detailed and complete information subsequently proved to be of inestimable value in establishing the authority of the regional representatives of the High Commissariat over local administrations and the forces of law and order.

The officers were also given training courses on war legislation, German and collaborationist organisations and the political situation in Belgium. There was no need to emphasise the importance of a legal education. As we have already seen, law graduates were favoured. The question, however, remains as to whether these ideal candidates were available in London. In fact, the relative success of HCNS and the words of praise of Ganshof for his staff would suggest that this did prove to be the case. It is self-evident that only individuals who were financially well-heeled and who had the necessary international contacts were able to escape to Britain at the outbreak of the war; and this was even more true during the war. We are therefore dealing with a relatively limited elite group, and Ganshof could therefore draw on a small but qualitatively high reserve to swell his ranks. Nevertheless recruitment remained very difficult. As the earlier graph demonstrates, recruitment only really took off on the eve of the liberation of Belgium.

Ganshof was also interested in candidates who had particular links with the forces of law and order. It should not be forgotten that, once in liberated Belgium, the local and state police assumed responsibility for operations concerning its maintenance. The task of HCNS was one only of coordination and information. The concerns that arose from this arrangement were demonstrated in the particular interest that Ganshof showed in the possible candidature of Colonel Bernier of the Namur Gendarmerie to assist him in his duties. Bernier, a former Resistance comrade of Ganshof, was not, in the end, appointed as an assistant to Ganshof but continued to inform him of certain developments within the police corps.[22] The presence of Police Commissioner Jean Crèvecoeur at HCNS provided further confirmation of the importance that was attached to good connections with the police.[23]

The choice of deputy to the High Commissioner finally resulted in the appointment of François Cattoir, who has already been mentioned. This French-speaking Brussels lawyer born in 1908, a reserve officer with the prestigious cavalry unit of the 1st Guides and son of a Lieutenant-General, stood out because of his great efficiency, his striking personality and also his excellent grasp of English. He was, after all, married to an Englishwoman and had studied economics at the renowned Princeton University in the USA. This knowledge of English, which was stressed in the recruitment policy of HCNS, was one of the reasons why Cattoir was given responsibility for the relations between the HCNS and the highest Allied authorities. It has already been mentioned that he led the documentation section, and it emerges from the archives that, once in Belgium, he took on the effective leadership of HCNS on behalf of Ganshof. Cattoir had fled from Belgium on 14 July 1942 and arrived in Britain on 24 September 1943. On 8 October he was employed by HCNS as assistant to the High Commissioner, a responsibility that he combined with acting as the Regional Officer for Brabant until he was replaced by Major Lerot, who would subsequently be responsible for the abolition of HCNS.

In addition to Cattoir a further twenty-eight members of staff were recruited who later belonged to the elite corps of regional officers, and, though it is not possible in this article to give individual biographies for all of the officers of HCNS, a number of general characteristics can be demonstrated. In 1943 the average age of the regional officers recruited in London was thirty-seven. They had often occupied high office in both the private sector (Deswarte and Périer were respectively managers of Innovation and SABENA, while Fraikin was a vice-president of Pieux Franki) or the public sector (Drapier was an alderman in Anderlecht, de Groote was the Mayor of Houthulst while Ganshof himself was a professor at the Free University of Brussels and Watteeuw was an ambassador). After their time at HCNS a number of them went on to enjoy prestigious careers. Nieuwenhuys became a member of the Royal Household, while Deswarte became principal private secretary to the socialist politician and future prime minister Camille Huysmans. Their fathers, too, occupied important positions, being surgeons, judges, generals, an ex-minister, senators and members of parliament.

The aristocracy was not represented in this group, although some of its members had relatives with connections to it. Another factor that might indicate a high social profile was that some members had foreign links. A number of the regional officers had lived, or had been, abroad for a while or had studied abroad. For example, Deswarte studied in Amsterdam, Soudan was born in Egypt, Merckx had family in New York and Watteeuw's mother was Australian. Though clearly not all of the London staff of High Commissioner Ganshof had these links, the fact that so many existed confirms the generally high social standing of the officers. A more striking characteristic was probably how many officers had a university education. With one exception (Crèvecoeur) all of the regional officers had university degrees. Twelve of them held law degrees, seven of whom were barristers. Most of them, especially the lawyers, had studied at Brussels University (ULB). Three had studied at Leuven University, two in the Facultés Notre Dame de Namur and two at the Solvay Institute. What is noticeable, however, is that four officers had graduated abroad (Oxford, Cambridge, Princeton and MIT), all from English-speaking institutions.

As far as the regional origin of the regional officers was concerned, the distinctly 'Brussels' nature of HCNS is striking. Only three officers came from Flanders and only one from the Walloon provinces. Nineteen came from Brussels and its suburbs (eight from Ixelles), and two originated abroad. Of twenty-nine officers, only three could be confirmed to have Dutch as their mother tongue. These were Willem Deswarte, Hugo Van de Perre and Joseph Van

Dorpe. The last of these was also the only one who did not study at a French-speaking university but at one in Britain (he did, however, give his children French names). In the personal dossiers that were drawn up by HCNS, it was always stipulated whether the person concerned spoke Dutch, English, German, Italian or Spanish. Not a word was said about their abilities in French. We can deduce from this that the marked French-language bias of the corps was regarded as natural. The quasi-exclusive use of French in reports and correspondence also points in this direction.

There are only sporadic and vague indications concerning the political tendencies of the staff. Clear information exists for only four members: Soudan and Drapier were socialists, Devèze and Périer liberals, while according to some reports Van Dorpe had once had links with the Flemish New Order leader, Joris Van Severen. Ganshof himself was a Protestant, and this may help to explain the relative absence of Catholics. The sources frequently refer to the strong patriotism of these officers, and we have not been able to find any indications that would cast doubt on their patriotic loyalties, whatever the nature of their political affiliation or convictions. One factor that certainly aided a candidature was participation in the Resistance. The knowledge of the terrain and the situation in occupied Belgium that participation in the Resistance gave was a not inconsiderable advantage in the eyes of HCNS. Only eight of the fifty-five can be said to have been active in the Resistance with any certainty prior to arriving in Britain, of whom six were regional officers. On the whole, it is not known to which Resistance group they had belonged. Further biographical investigation is needed here. However, what is significant is that of the entire staff of HCNS (182 people) only twelve Resistance members are known, of whom eight joined HCNS in London. This would suggest that the 'Londoners' formed the core of future HCNS personnel. This thesis can be demonstrated in various ways. First of all, the majority (forty-four out of a total of fifty-five, or 80 percent) of the London staff members were active in HCNS until at least 1 November 1945. So there was no replacement of a first generation by a second. It comes as no surprise, therefore, that twenty-nine of them became regional officers. Only fifteen new regional officers joined this group after the liberation. So there was a clear difference between the support personnel, who were mainly recruited in Belgium, and the regional officers, of whom the majority were already active in London.

It is not yet clear whether Ganshof knew his staff prior to their recruitment. We have already noted that Colonel Bernier belonged to Ganshof's circle of friends. Auguste Gérard was also a friend and Michel Devèze shared his wartime imprisonment by the Germans in the citadel of Huy with Ganshof. It is noticeable in the documents studied that they spoke to each other in familiar terms (employing 'tu' instead of 'vous' in French), although this does not necessarily indicate a prior friendship. What is significant is their collaboration in the Resistance before being captured. Whether more of Ganshof's staff shared similar links with him is not clear. It is certainly noticeable how many law graduates completed their studies at Brussels University, where Ganshof taught.

The same analysis can also be carried out oo the staff who were recruited in Belgium after the country was liberated. In particular, it is worth investigating any subtle distinctions that might indicate an evolution in the recruitment criteria used, resulting in changes to the social profile. Certainly the job description for an officer in HCNS in Belgium differed greatly from that of London. Regional officers were now sent to the various corners of the liberated country to represent the High Commissioner in a fairly autonomous manner. In the provincial capitals, a provincial representative was appointed, flanked by one or more assistants. In the port cities of Ostende, Gent and Antwerp port co-ordinators were appointed from 20 July 1945 (Majors Limpens, Van Leirberge and Erkes), while others had liaison positions with the various Allied units.

The average age of the new recruits was higher than that of the 'Londoners'. In 1944 it rose to forty-one. One of the reasons for this was the recruitment of two additional majors to carry out co-ordination in the ports of Gent and Ostende. Clearly, candidates with the necessary maturity and experience were sought. Another factor was the recruitment of High Commissioner Ganshof's brother, François (aged forty-nine), a professor of history at the State University of Gent and provincial representative for the province of East Flanders. There is also evidence that the recruits were of slightly higher professional standing. More than among the 'Londoners', lawyers featured prominently in this second generation. Nine of the ten known graduates were law graduates, and they included two judges and four barristers. The documents do not provide sufficient information about the origins of their qualifications (apart from the fact that one was from Brussels University) but two lecturers from the State University of Gent were also recruited. Other recruits came from banking and employers' organisations. Three officers continued their careers with the army after completing their duties with HCNS. Major Limpens left to join the General Staff, Georges Fontaine went to the Ministry of Defence and Jean Gevers went to the 4th section of the BMM as a specialist in maritime matters. Less is known about the social background of these staff. We only know that the father of Gevers was a stockbroker.

There seem to have been no members of the nobility among the Belgian staff members, and links with abroad were less conspicuous than among the 'Londoners', denoting a lower social standing. Only Gevers had been an intern in Great Britain.

What is most noticeable is that more of the recruits came from provincial backgrounds. Of the fifteen in this group only four were from Brussels (including one from Ixelles), but five were from Antwerp and three from Wallonia. All of these officers, including those from Antwerp, spoke French. Even so, it would seem that the rules of HCNS concerning the appointment of native speakers of each language were only partly observed. A number of officers who, according to their personal dossiers, did not speak perfect Dutch were appointed in Flanders. This was the case with Gevers (Antwerp), Van Leckwijck (Antwerp and Limburg), Crèvecoeur (Flemish-Brabant) and Cattoir (Brabant). The political loyalties of these officers could not be identified, the exception being Maurice Anspach, who, as a Resistance member, had maintained connections with the Catholic *Libre Belgique* group. The Resistance, however, is a constant factor. It is known that four out of the fifteen (two as members of the Secret Army organisation) were involved in the Resistance. Less obvious are the signs that could indicate that the new staff members had close or friendly connections with High Commissioner Ganshof. None of them appear to have shared resistance activities or any time in captivity with him. Just as with the 'Londoners', the question remains open as to whether the legal circles connected to Brussels University were, more than others, a recruiting base for him.

An answer to the question of whether the recruitment criteria evolved can only be attempted with great caution. The scarcity of the material available does not permit complete statistical analyses to be undertaken. Nevertheless, certain differences in the profile of the two groups can be detected. The 'Londoners' seem to have belonged to a higher social class, as is partly demonstrated by the very fact that they were in London. Their more prestigious careers, the professional activities of their fathers and their foreign contacts also support this impression. The later members of staff were also clearly older. Several reasons for this change have already been mentioned, but it should also be noted that it was probably more difficult for older persons to escape from occupied Belgium. Of course, a number of mature persons made it to Britain prior to or during the German invasion, but it seems that younger people would have been more likely to have tried to escape from Belgium. However, it is undeniable that the proportion of lawyers among the regional officers who were recruited in Belgium was high. Ganshof clearly wanted to recruit law graduates, and had perhaps been forced by the scarcity in London of the available personnel to relax his criteria somewhat. Just as clear is the Brussels origins of the 'Londoners' in comparison to those recruited in Belgium. Ganshof consequently experienced difficulty in consistently carrying through the policy of putting recruits to work in their own regions as far as possible. By contrast, a systematic comparison of the place of birth, place of residence and place of employment of the regional officers clearly demonstrates that this policy was carried through with greater consistency after the return to Belgium.

Conclusion

In the course of the summer of 1943, the government in exile entrusted the establishment of the High Commissariat for National Security to the Advocate General, Walter Ganshof van der Meersch. HCNS would control the maintenance of law and order in liberated Belgium and should facilitate a rapid transfer of power. Ganshof was particularly well suited for this job. As Advocate General he could act with authority on both the military and the civilian levels. Moreover, he had a good reputation in Resistance circles. The fear felt by the London government regarding its limited popularity and legitimacy in liberated Belgium perhaps partly explained the decision to create HCNS. Military justice, which was one of Ganshof's prerogatives, was to play the principal role in the restoration of public life and the maintenance of law and order. To retain the link with the government structure, which was a particular concern of the Prime Minister, Ganshof was also given, in addition to his job as Advocate General, the title of High Commissioner for National Security, which permitted him to act as an advisor to the government.

To assist him in his task, Ganshof painstakingly searched for competent staff. Command of the English language and a thorough knowledge of Belgian legislation were the most important criteria. Personal relationships, participation in the Resistance, special links with the local police or the state police were desirable, but a respectable appearance nevertheless proved to be just as important. However, people of this calibre were scarce in London. Moreover, they were already employed in private companies and other state organisations that were rather reluctant to give up their valuable staff. Ganshof searched, in particular, for qualified law graduates. Most HCNS recruits had studied at Brussels University, where Ganshof had taught, which leads us to suspect that less official factors also played a role in recruitment. The pronounced French-speaking character of the staff is clear however and no account was taken of the legal requirement for parity between the linguistic communities in governmental organisations. HCNS diverged from the original recruitment criteria, which clearly specified that the regional officer should be fluent in the language of the region to which he was appointed.

The regional officers had to represent the High Commissioner in the country and therefore needed to have a dignified appearance. 'Well-bred' candidates were therefore particularly welcome. The almost complete absence of the nobility among the ranks of HCNS is also striking. It is not clear whether the political sympathies of the candidates were taken into account when they were recruited. According to François Cattoir, this emphatically was not the case. The fact that lawyers who had studied at Brussels University were present in large numbers, and that the only four regional officers whose political sympathies are known belonged to the non-Catholic camp leads one, however, to suspect that socialists and liberals were in the majority. This might also help to explain the absence of the nobility. After the liberation in September 1944 HCNS moved to Belgium in various phases. Here recruitment was noticeably easier. The elitist nature of the new staff members, who did not to any significant extent replace the old ones but supplemented them, was much less obvious. These later staff members were older, more specialised and originated from the regions in which they were to represent the High Commissioner. The rules in force were thus applied more consistently in Belgium than they had been in London.

At the present stage in this research, the study of the available sources does not permit me to draw any definitive conclusions concerning any targeted recruitment policy. Rather, it would seem that within the relatively elitist Belgian milieu an unwritten consensus prevailed about the measures that had to be taken, firstly to outmanoeuvre the Communist danger, and secondly to purge the state apparatus of unpatriotic elements. Rather than speaking of a conscious policy of targeted recruitment, it would therefore be more accurate to report an unconscious tendency to recruit staff whose attitudes reflected the values current in London, and most especially held dear by Ganshof. These values were patriotic and favoured the establishment of what they regarded as the only legitimate administration in liberated Belgium: that of the government in London. The profile of the staff of HCNS, as described in this study, reflected that goal.

Notes

1. Projet de fascicule relatif à l'organisation judiciaire et au maintien de l'ordre à l'intention des officiers de liaison, CEGES-SOMA Brussels, Haut Commissariat à la Sécurité de l'Etat Archive (HCSE), 345.
2. 'Arrêté-loi instituant le cadre des officiers conseillers d'affaires civiles', 3 February 1944, *Moniteur belge*, 28 February 1944, 4, pp. 91–2.
3. W. Ganshof van der Meersch, *Rapport sur l'activité du Haut Commissariat à la Sécurité de l'Etat, 29 July 1943 – 1 November 1945*, Brussels, 1946.
4. Ganshof to Ministry of Defence (MD), 'Personnel du Haut Commissariat. Recrutement du personnel parmi les éléments faisant partie des administrations civiles belges', 15 December 1943, p. 3, HCSE, 21.
5. Lieutenant Colonel Sheen, SHAEF, to Strydonck van Burkel, Mission Militaire Belge, 'Formation des officiers', 5 April 1944, HCSE, 3.
6. Ganshof to Marissal (MD), 'Candidats d'officiers de liaison à faire venir', HCSE, 96.
7. 'Note: Dispositions en vue de rapatriement de fonctionnaires d'autres départements, mis provisoirement à la disposition du HCSE', 19 April 1944. HCSE, 21d.
8. Note from Ganshof, 'Formation des officiers', 28 June 1944, HCSE, 3.
9. Interview with F. Cattoir, 9 October 1996.
10. Ganshof to MD, 'Officiers-Généralités', 28 Sept 1944, Document No. 182, HCSE, A1.
11. Ganshof to Ministry of Justice (MJ), 'Formation des officiers', 5 July 1944, HCSE, 3.
12. Directive from MJ about the application of the decree of 29 July 1943, 'Statut du Haut Commissariat', HCSE, 16.
13. Boereboom, Director-General of the Cabinet of Prime Minister (PM) Pierlot to Delfosse, MJ, 'Recrutement du Personnel Permanent – Formalités à remplir', 23 August 1943, HCSE, 1L.
14. Ganshof to MJ, 'Militarisation des membres du Haut Commissariat', 1 August 1944, HCSE, 24.
15. Ganshof to MJ, 'Personnel du Haut Commissariat. Recrutement du personnel parmi les éléments faisant partie des administrations civiles belges', 15 December 1943, HCSE, 21.
16. Ganshof to PM Pierlot, 'Personnel en fonction', 5 January 1944, HCSE, 21a.
17. Ganshof to MJ, 'Recrutement', 7 July 1944, Document No. 2144/2193, HCSE, 867.
18. Ganshof to MD, 'Officiers-Généralités', 28 September 1944, Document No. 182, HCSE, A1.
19. Cattoir to Mouraux, 'Recrutement', 6 March 1945, Document No. 650/4093, HCSE, 867.
20. Lerot to PM Pierlot, 'Liquidation', 7 January 1946, HCSE, 880.
21. Cattoir to Procureur du Roi, Première Instance, Brussels, 'Liquidation', HCSE, 880.
22. Bernier to Ganshof, 'Projets de réorganisation et d'épuration', July 1942 and August 1944, HCSE, 627.
23. Ganshof to MJ, 'Recrutement', 7 July 1944, Document No. 2144/2193, HCSE, 867.

PART THREE

THE EUROPEAN DIMENSION

THE NORWEGIAN ARMED FORCES IN BRITAIN

CHRIS MANN

This contribution examines the experience of the armed forces of the Norwegian Government-in-Exile and their relationship with the British political and military authorities. During the war the small number of defeated Norwegians who escaped to Britain in June 1940 were equipped and expanded into a force that could contribute usefully to the Allied cause and participate fully in Norway's liberation in May 1945. Given the dire condition of what remained of Norway's military resources in the summer of 1940, this was a turnaround of considerable proportions. It owed its success in no small part to the pragmatic approach the Norwegians took to their great power partner, Britain.

Norway and Britain's military relationship had not, however, started particularly well. Germany invaded Norway on 9 April 1940 and Britain pledged military assistance that day. Unfortunately British military intervention proved ill-prepared, poorly organised and wholly inadequate. Disastrous defeat puts a strain on any partnership and this one was not helped by the British and their French allies proving somewhat reticent in informing the Norwegians of their plans, particularly with regard to their intention to withdraw.[1] Although the Allies met with some limited success around the northern Norwegian port of Narvik, the opening of the German offensive in France on 10 May distracted Anglo-French attention from Norway. As the situation in France worsened, the British and French decided to end their commitment to Norway and evacuate their troops. The Norwegian Government, knowing that defeat was inevitable, decided to move into exile. So King

Haakon VII, his government and elements of the Norwegian military left Norway aboard the British cruiser HMS *Devonshire* on 7 June 1940. The remaining Norwegian forces in the Narvik area surrendered the following day.

The dejected Norwegian Government that arrived in Britain had some cause to resent its hosts, therefore. Also the very real possibility of British defeat – which appeared apparent to everyone but the British – led elements of the Norwegian Government, particularly Foreign Minister Halvdan Koht, to urge caution in establishing formal ties with Britain. While Koht advocated considerable practical co-operation, he warned against making commitments that might damage the Norwegian position in a compromise peace with Germany.[2] Those in the cabinet advocating full partnership with Britain and a reversal of Norway's long held traditional policy of neutrality were much strengthened by the position taken by the King. On 8 July 1940, King Haakon rejected a request to abdicate from parliamentary leaders remaining in Norway. He stated that his government had received its mandate to continue the struggle in the last free parliament held on 9 April 1940. Free was something that the source of this proposal was most certainly not.[3] Two days later the Norwegian Ministry of Defence sent an aide-mémoire to its British counterpart stating that: 'It is the intention of the Norwegian Government to continue the fight outside Norway in collaboration with our allies and so far as our means will permit until final victory'.[4] In the formal treaty, eventually signed on 28 May 1941, the British and Norwegian Governments pledged to re-establish 'the freedom and independence of Norway' and to that end agreed that:

> The Norwegian Armed Forces in the United Kingdom . . . shall be employed either for the defence of the United Kingdom or for the purpose of regaining Norway. They shall be organised and employed under British command, in its character as the Allied High Command, as the Armed Forces of the Kingdom of Norway allied with the United Kingdom.[5]

The armed forces, however, at the disposal of 'the kingdom of Norway' in the summer of 1940 were somewhat limited. The navy was easily in the best position of the Norwegian services. Thirteen ships, including two destroyers, and some 400 men escaped to Britain. These were soon joined by two motor torpedo boats (MTB) that the Norwegians had ordered from the British shipyards in 1939. The hard-pressed Royal Navy put most of these vessels into service at once, providing immediate operational experience for the fledgling exile navy.[6]

The situation for the army and the naval and army air sections was far grimmer. Although the British might have been able to embark a substantial proportion of the Norwegian Army from Narvik at the end of the campaign, they happily left them behind as a covering force for the evacuation. Furthermore, politically, the Norwegian Government felt that it could not order conscripts to leave Norway for exile.[7] They did, however, instruct a few professional officers to accompany them to Britain. These men formed the basis of the Norwegian staff in London. Major-General Carl Fleischer was appointed Commander-in-Chief of Norwegian Forces. The former C-in-C, General Otto Ruge, the only senior Norwegian officer to come out of the campaign with any credit, had elected to stay behind and surrender with his troops. Fleischer established a training camp in Scotland and by July 1940 could muster just over a thousand men from various sources. The position of the two air arms was no better: the army had thirty-five pilots available and the navy thirteen. The only aircraft were four navy Heinkel He 115 float planes that the British refused to allow the Norwegians to operate, postponing their intention of returning straight to combat.[8]

A small number of Norwegian troops, however, went into action earlier than most of their compatriots, and were certainly the first members of the Norwegian armed forces to set foot on Norwegian soil again. Special Operations Executive (SOE), the British organisation formed to support Europe's resistance movements, approached the Norwegian Army with a view to forming a unit of Norwegian volunteers, and this subsequently took part in a raid on the Lofoten Islands in March 1941. Although British documents imply that the Norwegian military and Koht's replacement as Foreign Minister, Trygve Lie, had been consulted and proved enthusiastic, Lie claimed that 'the Norwegian Government was unacquainted with the preparations and execution of the raid'.[9] Therefore, he and the rest of the government were angered by the use of their men on Norwegian territory without their sanction. This anger deepened when news of German reprisals against the Lofoten islanders filtered back to London. The unit, however, expanded and was named Norwegian Independent Company 1 (Kompani Linge after its Norwegian founder, Captain Martin Linge, to its Norwegian members). The Norwegian Government's annoyance did not inhibit the British from using the company again in December 1941 in two simultaneous raids against Vågsøy on the Norwegian west coast and the Lofoten Islands once more. These raids brought to a head the Norwegian authorities' irritation at their exclusion from the decision-making process regarding operations in Norway. Lie ordered his Foreign Ministry to make it clear to the British that 'the Norwegian Government was one step away from publicly taking a stand against the British action'.[10] This would have caused a politically disastrous rift and been an excellent propaganda victory for the Germans and the puppet Quisling administration in Norway.

The issue caused a crisis of confidence in Kompani Linge. Much of the bitterness of their government had been directed at them and they were left feeling isolated and resentful at the way in which they had been used by the British. This was not helped by news of another round of German reprisals. On top of this, Martin Linge was killed at Vågsøy, further shaking the Company's morale. As the SOE Norwegian Section history recalled 'the Linge Company was full of dissatisfaction and its founder and leader was not there to put matters right'.[11] The discontent was manifested by twelve members who refused to continue without the assurance of the Norwegian Government's approval for their activities, claiming that they felt 'almost like mercenaries'.[12]

Sir Charles Hambro, Deputy Director of SOE, approached the new Norwegian Defence Minister Oscar Torp to arrange some form of compromise because, as Hambro succinctly noted, the British could not operate in Norway without the Norwegians and the Norwegians needed British equipment, facilities and expertise.[13] Torp said that he hoped to maintain and improve the good relations between the Norwegian authorities and SOE but in return he made it clear, as Hambro reported, that 'he personally expected to be taken into our confidence absolutely'. Hambro had anticipated the problem before the December raids and, fearing the loss of SOE's Norwegian troops, he had pressed the British military authorities to agree to some level of co-ordination with the Norwegian authorities, at the very least with Lie or Torp, in whom he had 'absolute confidence'. He met considerable resistance. The opinion of much of the British military establishment was well summed up by an internal SOE memo that believed that 'of the races on earth there is surely none so indiscreet as the Norwegians'.[14] However, the refusal of Winston Churchill's Chief of Staff, General Hastings Ismay, is more telling. He felt that involving the Norwegian authorities, quite apart from anything else, would be a dangerous precedent that 'would inevitably lead to the Dutch, the Belgians, the Free French – and possibly the Poles and Czechs – demanding a similar privilege when their territories are concerned'.[15]

A crisis point, however, in the relationship had developed and Hambro had to find a solution. He proposed to Torp that an 'Anglo-Norwegian Collaboration Committee' be set up and promised that SOE 'will not initiate any expedition to or against

Norway without the knowledge and consent of the Norwegian members of the committee who will, of course, be at liberty to report direct to you'. Although he could not make a similar commitment for the services, any request for use of SOE's specially-trained troops by other departments – and operations in Norway would be impossible without them – would be submitted to the committee for the Norwegian members' and consequently Torp's approval. In return, Torp appointed a successor to Linge and visited the company to steady its morale and reassure the commandos of their Government's approval. The committee worked remarkably well, ensuring no repetition of the December 1941 incident, giving the Norwegians a hand in SOE's policy towards Norway and cementing a remarkably successful relationship between SOE, the Norwegian High Command and the Norwegian Resistance.

As part of a Norwegian desire to have a wider influence on military issues relating to Norway, Torp also reformed the Norwegian command system by establishing a unified Norwegian High Command. Quite apart from the military logic, creating a centralised military organisation made sense, given the limited number of staff officers at Torp's disposal. Although establishing a working relationship with the British took time, the High Command eventually assumed an integral role in the planning for Norway's liberation. General Fleischer disagreed with the reform that did not envisage him in the role of supreme commander and he therefore resigned. Fleischer was sent to Canada, where he subsequently committed suicide.

The Norwegian Government was fortunate that its financial needs were met by its most important resource, the Norwegian merchant fleet, which was the fourth largest in the world, granting them a considerable degree of fiscal independence. The British were willing to provide equipment and places on training courses at no charge, dependent on availability. Norwegians, meanwhile, met the running costs of their establishments and paid and maintained their own men. However, finding those men was far more problematic. In expanding Norwegian forces, the main difficulty, experienced by most governments-in-exile, was the provision of manpower. A handful of the Norwegian military had left Norway with the government and in the first year of the occupation many Norwegians escaped across the North Sea to Britain. This was not sufficient, and the conscription of Norwegians in Britain began at the end of 1940.

The allocation of Norwegian military personnel demonstrated the government's belief about where the most useful contribution to the Allied cause could be made. Keeping the Atlantic supply line open was probably the most important commitment that Britain faced, certainly in terms of mere survival. The Norwegian Government concurred and gave precedence to the Norwegian Navy. The Navy expanded rapidly, having the priority with regard to manpower, even drawing on the 30–35,000 sailors of the merchant fleet and the recruits transferring from the army. The Admiralty gratefully provided the Norwegians with as many ships as they could man. The Chief of the Navy Staff, Admiral Sir Dudley Pound, claimed that this afforded 'very welcome relief to our manning problems'.[16] The British also willingly put through the Royal Naval training establishment at Skegness as many recruits as the Norwegian Government could provide while officer cadets attended the Royal Naval College. This training was supplemented by special Norwegian-run courses.[17]

Therefore, considering the importance given to the Atlantic convoys by both the British and Norwegian governments, the main Norwegian contribution lay in the crewing of numerous corvettes and destroyers in escort and anti-submarine duties. The quality of these vessels varied. Such was the need for ships even the ageing destroyer *Draug,* which was rather mildly described by the Norwegians as 'rather old', having been commissioned in the Norwegian Navy in 1908, saw extensive escort service in English coastal waters and the Channel.[18] However, the vast majority of the navy's vessels were British or American built ships. In total six corvettes were manned by Norwegian crews at various times, as were ten destroyers of varying vintages from the old ex-U.S. town class to modern British Hunt and S-class vessels.

The Norwegians also operated a motor torpedo boat (MTB) flotilla out of Shetland against shipping along the Norwegian coast. The British had long taken an interest in disrupting German coastal traffic off Norway that transported Swedish iron ore southwards and supplies to the large German forces in the north. The shipping was difficult to attack as it sheltered in the Leads, the series of channels well protected from the open seas by numerous islands and reefs. The Norwegian MTBs, however, were able to operate effectively in these waters, often laying up overnight on the Norwegian coast. In conjunction with small complements of British and Norwegian commandos that they carried on board, they made a considerable nuisance of themselves and gained successes, although minor, out of proportion to the resources employed and the losses that the Norwegians suffered. They were particularly effective in the raiding season of late 1944 to early 1945, by which time most of Germany's merchant shipping was to be found operating along the Norwegian coast.

Indeed, the skilful nature of their attacks led Captain Sayer of the Admiralty Directorate of Tactics, Torpedoes and Staff Duties to note that 'the success of these Norwegian manned MTBs are sufficiently remarkable to be worthy of comment'. He estimated that they achieved a percentage of hits in their torpedo attacks three times higher than their English counterparts.[19] In conjunction with Coastal Command aircraft of 18 Group (*see below*) they did much to undermine the German position in Norway and their combined attrition of such an important asset as German shipping was a useful strategic goal. Admiral Ciliax, the German Naval C-in-C in Norway, believed that these two methods of attack caused him the greatest anxiety and losses.[20]

The Royal Norwegian Navy operated under the control of the British Admiralty and senior British naval commanders. The Norwegian ships generally formed part of larger British formations, although they also worked with Canadian and occasionally American vessels. Thus the Norwegians served in almost every theatre in which the Royal Navy operated, from the Arctic Sea, where the destroyer *Stord*, operating with the Home Fleet, was involved in the sinking of the German battle-cruiser *Scharnhorst*, through to the Normandy Landings, where the destroyer *Svenner* was lost, to the Persian Gulf but most importantly in the Atlantic. A suitable example of Norwegian naval deployment is provided by the Norwegian ships engaged in the Battle of the Atlantic at the turn of 1942–3. One destroyer, four corvettes and three smaller patrol/escort vessels formed part of Liverpool Escort Forces under the command of Max Horton, C-in-C Western Approaches. At times the Norwegian contribution to the Liverpool Escort Forces had been as large as five destroyers, but losses and the decommissioning of elderly ships had taken its toll.[21] It was a useful and arguably vital contribution, because, at times during the finely balanced Battle of the Atlantic, the British needed every escort vessel they could put to sea.

The Norwegian Air Force came next in the Government's priorities. During the Norwegian campaign, a small staff of Norwegian Army Air Force officers led by Captain Bjarne Øen was sent to the United Kingdom to rebuild the shattered Norwegian air arm with whatever assistance the British or French could afford. The German victory in Norway made these plans irrelevant, and Øen was forced to look to the establishment of a Norwegian Air Force in Britain. The RAF could offer the Norwegians no independently run training facilities, although they allowed Norwegian pilots to join British units. Those Norwegian airmen who had escaped to Britain were quite happy with this suggestion and were eager to return to action. Øen felt otherwise and was determined to raise identifiable Norwegian units, and was supported in this by the Norwegian Government.

By August 1940 it had been decided to combine the naval and army arms and establish a training camp in Canada to train airmen for service with the RAF in Europe. This would temporarily deprive the RAF of a potential source of aircrew. Indeed, the RAF was in the midst of the Battle of Britain and was desperate for pilots, putting every Dutch, Belgian, Czech and Polish airman in a Spitfire or Hurricane as quickly as it could. To quote Wilhelm Mohr, a wartime Norwegian air force pilot, 'It is fair to assume that the Norwegian proposal was not accepted by the British without reluctance'.[22] Presumably counting on a good future return on the Norwegian investment, the Air Ministry agreed. The camp located near Toronto, known as 'Little Norway', was up and running by early November 1940, providing courses from pilot training to the various ground trades. Such was the demand that 'Little Norway' moved to a larger site at Muskoka in April 1943. They used a hundred or so American Fairchild elementary trainers and Curtiss and Northrop fighters purchased by the Norwegian Government. Indeed, the whole enterprise was Norwegian funded and run and 'quite independent of the Empire and RAF training schemes in Canada'.[23]

The Canadian enterprise first bore fruit in April 1941, when the Norwegians were able to form their first squadron in RAF Coastal Command. Using seaplanes, No. 330 operated throughout the Battle of the Atlantic, initially from Iceland and then from 1943 from Scotland. No. 330 was joined at Coastal Command in mid-1943 by a second squadron, No. 333, which operated a flight of Catalina seaplanes in anti-U-boat operations and a second flight of Mosquitoes. There were some early teething problems as the conversion of Norwegian air crew to Mosquitoes was evidently undertaken too quickly. Norwegian over-confidence and eagerness to operate such a modern and potent aircraft, coupled with British overconfidence, led to unacceptable loses.[24] Coastal Command was forced to suspend operations temporarily and go through an extensive training programme. The flight returned to undertake anti-shipping operations off the Norwegian coast as part of Coastal Command's 18 Group. Its chief function was to act as 'outrider' reconnaissance by flying ahead of an 18 Group strike force. On finding suitable shipping, the Norwegian 'outriders' would alert the strike aircraft following and provide the location and dispositions of the target. Their knowledge of the Norwegian coastline proved invaluable, and by the end of 1944 about half the shipping attacked in northern waters had been located by Norwegian aircrew.[25]

The first Norwegian fighter squadron, No. 331, equipped with Hurricanes, was formed at Catterick in July 1941 and subsequently moved to the Orkneys. It was a bleak posting. Skaebrae was a difficult airfield, particularly for single-engined aircraft, and operations were constantly hampered by poor weather. Conditions on the ground were somewhat spartan and it came as a relief when the squadron was transferred south to North Weald in May 1942. A second fighter squadron, No. 332, was formed in January 1942 and joined No. 331 at North Weald in June 1942. Both squadrons, operating Spitfires (No. 331 had been re-equipped in November 1941), were involved in the increasingly aggressive Fighter Command operations over the Channel and occupied France undertaken that summer. Both fought with particular distinction over the disastrous raid on Dieppe on 19 August 1942.

These operations evidently fell outside the terms of the May 1941 Anglo-Norwegian Military Agreement, which stated that the Norwegian forces would only be used 'either for the defence of the United Kingdom or for the purpose of regaining Norway'. This became particularly relevant when Fighter Command shifted from 'a largely static' defensive role to an 'offensive strategy', which 'called for increased flexibility'. To this end, the RAF proposed to transfer the two squadrons into 2nd Tactical Air Force. The RAF hoped the Norwegian Air Force Commander, Admiral Riiser-Larsen, 'would welcome the change' as it would 'enable your units to take their place alongside our own squadrons and uphold the reputation they have so well deserved when fighting with the RAF'.[26] Moral pressure aside, this would involve No. 331 and No. 332 Squadrons in operations in support of the Normandy Landings and give them a continuing role in the subsequent fighting in France and beyond. The British Air Ministry reckoned pilot losses in the invasion and afterwards would rise to levels much higher than those experienced so far. The 750 or so Norwegian ground crew would also be at considerable risk once the squadrons began to operate from airfields in liberated Europe.

The Norwegian High Command was well aware of the paucity of British resources available for the liberation of Norway once Operation Overlord began. The lack of RAF units was no exception. Therefore, the Norwegian authorities were eager to husband their own limited resources, particularly such valuable ones as aircrew. They preferred that the fighter squadrons remain in Britain and be conserved for the return home.[27] However, Colonel Motzfeldt of the Norwegian Air Force Command regarded the situation positively, and he told Øen that the Tactical Air Force ought 'to be able to divert a self-supporting smaller air force to a

secondary theatre' such as Norway. Motzfeldt reckoned that 'personally . . . the development is for our advantage'.[28] Presumably
basing their decision on such thinking, the Norwegian authorities
agreed without protest to the transfer, no doubt also feeling that
involvement in such an important undertaking could only enhance
Norway's standing.

Thus Nos. 331 and 332 squadrons with the addition of British
No. 66 Squadron, formed No. 132 (N) Airfield, later No. 132 (N)
Wing, of 84 Group in November 1943. British signal and intelligence
staffs were added and two RAF Regiment squadrons joined to provide point air and ground defence once the move to the Continent
became imminent. The wing moved to France in August 1944 and
from January 1945 flew from forward airfields in the Netherlands.
The Norwegians maintained the excellent levels of serviceability and
formidable combat record that they had established at North Weald.
According to the commander of 84 Group, Air Vice Marshal Huddleston, they 'established a reputation for courage, skill, loyalty and
determination of the very highest order'. He also noted that 'we were
all glad they were able to remain here long enough to see the final
defeat of the enemy'.[29] No doubt the members of Nos. 331 and 332
squadrons concurred. These two squadrons were the only significant
Norwegian contribution to the north-west European campaign.

With the navy and air force taking priority, particularly in manpower, the Army proved to be something of a Cinderella service
with regard to both personnel and equipment. Indeed, it often func-
tioned as an emergency pool of manpower that was raided from
time to time by the other two services and SOE's Kompani Linge.
The greater part of the Norwegian Army, which reached roughly
brigade group size in 1943, was stationed in Scotland as part of 52
Division, Britain's only mountain warfare formation, training for
the return to Norway. However, despite Winston Churchill's advocacy of such a project, the British military had considered and
rejected the launching of an invasion of German-occupied Norway.
This was despite examining the possibility on numerous occasions
from mid-1941 onwards until the invasion of France was finally
accepted as future British-American strategy at the Quebec Conference in August 1943. As Lieutenant General Morgan, responsible
for the plan Operation Overlord, accepted at Quebec, said 'We
went to Normandy or we stayed at home'.[30]

Therefore, the army spent the greater part of the war in Scotland.
Only their liaison officers accompanied the mountain-trained 52
Division when it was sent into the Netherlands in October 1944,
where they proved remarkably useful as they were able to understand and speak with the local population.[31] The Norwegian Army

was a resource, unlike the navy and air force, that could only be committed once. The Norwegians did not have the manpower to create another one, and therefore the bulk of the army had to be saved for operations on Norwegian soil, though elements garrisoned various Norwegian possessions in the Arctic, such as Jan Mayen and Spitzbergen. A contingent of Norwegian troops was based in Iceland, where it trained British and later American troops in Arctic warfare techniques. The Norwegians also formed No. 5 troop of No. 10 (Inter Allied) Commando, which operated with the Norwegian MTB flotilla along the Norwegian coast in the autumn and winter of 1942–43 and took part in the assault on Walcheren Island on 1 November 1944.

In October 1944 the Red Army entered the northernmost Norwegian province of Finnmark in the pursuit of the retreating Germans. The Norwegian Army could at last make a contribution. The Norwegian High Command had been heavily involved in British planning for Norway's liberation, but the entry of the Soviet forces into Norway caused a serious reconsideration of the situation. There was no question of British troops entering a Soviet zone of operations, but the Norwegian High Command managed to gain both British and Soviet approval for their proposal to send a token force of a mountain company of the Norwegian Brigade, roughly 200 men, into Finnmark. Churchill felt this was an inadequate response as this was 'their chance to go back to their country'.[32] However, this was about a third of Norwegian first-line infantry strength and the remainder had to be retained in Britain in sufficient force to carry out the role established under the contingency plans for Norway's liberation. The mountain company entered Norway on 10 November 1944. Its commander, Colonel Dahl, soon discovered that the Russians had halted their advance and that the Germans were continuing to withdraw while carrying out a scorched earth policy. He pushed his limited force forward into the no-man's land in the wake of the withdrawing Germans and wondered what to do with the local population that remained in the area. The Norwegian High Command proposed sending an expanded Norwegian naval and air expedition to Finnmark to facilitate the relief of the civilian population. Ironically, considering Churchill's opinion, the proposal was turned down by the British because the Norwegian naval resources and the Coastal Command squadron requested were deemed too vital to the overall Allied war effort. It took the direct intervention of Norwegian C-in-C Crown Prince Olav at the highest levels in Washington to have the decision reversed, but by then the war was almost over and preparations for the liberation of Norway in the wake of the German surrender had begun.

The smooth and bloodless liberation of Norway, which was garrisoned by almost 400,000 Germans, was a fitting and satisfactory
conclusion to the war for the Norwegian armed forces. Norwegian
paratroops were the first substantive Allied force to enter Oslo, on
9 May 1945. There can be no doubting the tactical skills of the Norwegian armed forces. The air force and navy had formidable
combat records, and in the little fighting that the Army saw –
Colonel Dahl's troops in Finnmark and the Norwegian commandos
on Walcheren Island – they acquitted themselves well. Given such
limited forces at their disposal, it was hardly surprising that the
Norwegian military concentrated its manpower in front-line roles
and devoted particular energy to acquiring tactical expertise. This
led to a neglect of the more mundane administrative and organisational skills so vital to modern warfare. This problem manifested
itself during the liberation, when command, control and logistics
collapsed in the northern sector around Tromsø, which was the
responsibility of the Norwegian Brigade. General Sir Andrew
Thorne, who commanded the Allied forces that reoccupied Norway,
was forced to replace the Norwegian zone commander with a
British officer because of what one of Thorne's staff described as
'the chaos that occurs in Norwegian administration through lack of
trained officers'.[33] While this was partially the fault of the British for
so willingly undertaking so much of the support functions of Norwegian units, it did not bode well for the long-term success of any
independent Norwegian operations.

A few minor difficulties aside, the Norwegian armed forces co-
operated smoothly with their British counterparts and proved to be
a popular and supportive ally. It appears that the admiration was
mutual. So much so that there was talk in Norwegian naval circles
of the two being 'completely integrated' after the war.[34] This idea, of
course, came to nothing and the British influence over the army
waned rapidly when the Norwegians returned home. Indeed, almost
at once, many of the officers who had trained in Britain were side-
lined, and most of the senior posts went to ageing career officers
who had spent the war in German prison camps or in Sweden.[35]
Nonetheless a letter from Admiral Moore, C-in-C Home Fleet, to
Admiral Danielsen of the Norwegian Navy, concerning the crew of
the *Stord*, provides a suitably positive summary of the whole Norwegian war effort: 'Their efficiency and fine fighting spirit have been
the admiration of us all and ... we are glad they now should be reap-
ing the reward of their great contribution to the liberation of
Europe'.[36]

So the Norwegian Government-in-Exile and its forces returned
home to Norway as victors. Yet they had been a very minor part of

the great coalition and largely subordinated their efforts to those of their great power partners, particularly Britain. The Norwegians accepted that they were very much a junior partner and could have very little influence on the overall direction of Allied strategy. In general, the British used Norwegian ships and squadrons as they would any other unit, without reference to the government-in-exile. The government decided that its national interests could best be served by whole hearted and pragmatic military co-operation with Britain and were rewarded with a satisfactory and close relationship that did much to protect Norwegian national interests.

Notes

1. For example, Colonel Getz, commanding Norwegian forces in the vicinity of Namsos, only discovered that his allies were evacuating the port on 2 May, five days after the order to withdraw had been given and hours after the bulk of British and French forces had embarked, see F. Kersaudy, *Norway: 1940*, London, 1990, pp. 179–81.
2. O. Riste, 'Relations between the Norwegian government in exile and the British government' in *Britain and Norway in the Second World War*, ed. P. Salmon, London, 1995, pp. 40–1.
3. J. Andenæs, O. Riste and M. Skodvin, *Norway and the Second World War*, Oslo, 1966, pp. 96–7.
4. Aide-Mémoire from the Royal Norwegian Ministry of Defence, 10 July 1940, Public Record Office (PRO), London, FO 371/24838, No. 297.
5. Riksarkivet (RA – Norwegian National Archives), Oslo, SOK 291, Mappe:70.1 Regjeringen Avtaler, SOK 704,0/TP/EP, *Agreement of the 28 May 1941 between the Government of the United Kingdom and the Royal Norwegian Government concerning the organisation and employment of the Norwegian Armed Forces in the United Kingdom*, 7 April 1942.
6. Aide-Mémoire, 10 July 1940, PRO, FO 371/24838, No. 297; Colban to Halifax, 2 July 1940, PRO, No. 269/1940; B. Helle, 'The Build-up and Operations of the Royal Norwegian Navy in the Period 1940–5' in *Britain and Norway*, ed. Salmon, pp. 75–6.
7. D. Thompson, 'Controversial Aspects of Norwegian Military History', (unpublished 1995) p. 20. A much revised version of this article appeared as 'Norwegian Military Policy, 1905–1940: A Critical Appraisal and Review of the Literature', *Journal of Military History* 61, no. 7. (1997): pp. 503–20.
8. Aide-Mémoire, 10 July 1940, PRO, FO 371/24838, No. 297.
9. *Tip and Run Raids on Fishing Ports in the Lofoten Islands*, 2 January 1941, PRO, DEFE 2/141; T. Lie, *Kampen for Norges Frihet 1940–45*, Oslo, 1958, p. 220.
10. Lie, *Kampen*, p. 253.
11. J.S. Wilson, *Norwegian Section History 1940–45*, Norges Hjemmefrontmuseum (NHM – Norwegian Resistance Museum), 1945, p. 17.
12. Diary of Birger Fjelstad (NHM) cited by A. Moland, 'Milorg and SOE' in *Britain and Norway*, ed. Salmon, p. 144.
13. *Anglo-Norwegian Collaboration Regarding the Military Organisation in Norway*, 24 November 1941, enclosure to CH/88, Hambro to Torp, 25 November 1941, PRO, HS 2/127.

14. *Operation Claymore*, 3 February 1941, PRO, HS 2/224.
15. Ismay to Hambro, 8 December 1941, PRO, HS 2/127.
16. Pound to Corneliussen, 14 April 1941, RA, Marineattasjeen i London, Mappe: MA 418.0.
17. Andre Legasjoner og Konsulater, SOK Jnr12923/7130/RKA/DN, *Foresporsel fra den mexikanske marineattasje*, London, Corneliussen to Defence Department, 20 September 1944 and reply, 13 October 1944, RA, SOK 291, Mappe: 713.0.
18. Helle, 'Build-up and Operations', in *Britain and Norway*, ed. Salmon, p. 75; Aide-Mémoire, 10 July 1940, PRO, FO 371/24838, No. 297.
19. Minute by Captain Sayer (DDTTSD), 12 March 1945, PRO, ADM 199/270. Sayer noted that 52 Norwegian MTB Flotilla hit 67.8 percent of the time as compared to 22.5 percent for all Royal Navy MTB attacks.
20. S. Roskill, *The War at Sea 1939–45*, vol. 3, part 2, London, 1961, note p. 167.
21. *Military Activity of Norwegian Forces, 1941–45*, compiled by Historical Section, 6 January 1953, PRO, CAB 106/318; and Helle in *Britain and Norway*, ed. Salmon, pp. 5–82.
22. W. Mohr, 'The Contribution of the Norwegian Air Forces' in *Britain and Norway*, ed. Salmon, p. 85.
23. *Military Activity of Norwegian Forces*, 6 January 1953, PRO, CAB 106/318.
24. Mohr, 'Contribution', in *Britain and Norway*, ed. Salmon, p. 93.
25. C. Goulter, *A Forgotten Offensive*, London, 1995, pp. 136 and 238.
26. Gp/Capt Dore to Riiser-Larsen, 12 August 1943, RA, Fly-attasjeen London 15, Mappe: 184 Tactical Air Force No. 132 (N) Wing HQ, CS1981/DDAFL/671.
27. Mohr, 'Contribution', in *Britain and Norway*, ed. Salmon, p. 91.
28. Motzfeldt to Øen, 28 July 1943, RA, Fly-attasjeen London 15, Mappe: 184 Tactical Air Force No 132 (N) Wing HQ, 2348/43 AA.
29. Huddleston to Riiser-Larsen, 9 May 1945, Ibid, 84G/ACO/DO.
30. Sir F. Morgan, *Peace and War*, London, 1961, p. 175.
31. Report on study period for the Norwegian Operational Liaison Officer January 1945, Lt Col Pran, Liaison Inspector, 31 January 1945, RA, SOK 291, Mappe H 722.3 Admralstaben krigsoppsetnings planer.
32. Churchill to Ismay for COS, 26 October 1944, PRO, PREM 3/328/8.
33. Col Garner Smith to Col Stockdale, 26 May 1945, PRO, WO 106/1985, GON 111/1.
34. Annex II, *Report on Visit to Norway*, signed Brig Fosbery and Capt Ellison, 10 July 1945, PRO, WO 106/1983, E/2/1.
35. Thorne to Brooke, 14 October 1945, PRO, WO 106/1984, GON 73.
36. Helle, 'Build-up and Operations', in *Britain and Norway*, ed. Salmon, p. 82.

10

THE CZECHOSLOVAK ARMED FORCES IN BRITAIN, 1940–1945

ALAN BROWN

From the beginning, the Czechoslovak army and air contingents that served in Britain suffered from significant disadvantages when compared to other European allies from the occupied states. Militarily, they were much inferior in numbers to the Poles and the French; and, politically, they were answerable to a regime that had few friends in British diplomatic circles, whose attitudes ranged from cold tolerance to blunt hostility. But this is not to suggest that the officers and men of the Czechoslovak armed forces were influenced directly by these factors; rather, the evidence clearly demonstrates that very few Czechoslovak personnel had any accurate knowledge of the military and political difficulties that overshadowed their service in Britain. The object of this paper, therefore, is to throw light upon these two problems in an attempt to portray the émigré experience in its full context.

The soldiers and airmen of Czechoslovakia arrived in Britain in the summer of 1940, the great majority of them having been caught up in the headlong flight from the continent that preceded the collapse of France. The naval operations Aerial and Cycle seldom receive a mention in the histories of that year – most of the limelight being reserved for the earlier Dunkirk evacuations and the later Battle of Britain – yet both accounted for the rescue of enormous numbers of men from the embattled beaches across the Channel.[1] Unlike Dunkirk, which mainly involved British and French troops, Aerial and Cycle rescued the remaining British personnel plus the numerous allied contingents which had fought the rearguard action against the Germans. Various ships under allied flags, operating under the command of the Admiralty, collected groups of men from ports all along the French coast, and among them were 4,000 or so Czechoslovaks.

Yet even while these dramatic events were unfolding, British politicians were expressing concern over this indiscriminate policy of evacuation. In his capacity as Secretary of State for War, Anthony Eden said in the War Cabinet of 19 June that, although he was prepared 'to take off any Czechoslovak troops who wished to leave', he would 'much prefer to embark Polish troops'.[2] These comments bear close examination, for to a considerable extent they reflected the attitudes towards the Czechoslovaks mentioned above. In the first place, Eden spoke of those Czechoslovaks 'who wished to leave', which begs the question, why should they not? In fact, Eden was well aware that a substantial number of the personnel in France had chosen voluntary demobilisation into the hands of the occupying power. Fully two-thirds of the 12,000 men, many of whom were Slovaks with families and jobs in France, accepted French and German offers of peaceful surrender. Many more took advantage of promises of safe conduct back to the Protectorate on condition that they spread defeatist propaganda.[3] Of those who decided to rejoin the fight in Britain, by far the largest proportion consisted of officers and regular service personnel who had escaped from the Protectorate after March 1939. In the eyes of the War Cabinet, however, too many stayed on the Continent, thereby confirming the popular view that the Czechoslovak forces were not wholly dedicated to the common cause.

Two uncomfortable precedents also added weight to the arguments of those who cast doubt on the quality of the incoming forces. In January 1940, the Home Office and the Foreign Office agreed to lend support to a recruitment drive aimed at Czechoslovak citizens who were then refugees in Britain. Opinions were aired to the effect that too many of those eligible for military service had 'subversive tendencies', and a spokesman for the Home Office declared that his department was 'anxious to get rid of as many Czech and Slovak refugees as possible'.[4] The subsequent series of recruitment rallies failed to produce results that even the most optimistic observer could have construed as demonstrating the will to prevail, for little more than 10 percent of the entire group actually sailed for France. Furthermore, a later report strongly suggested that many of the potential volunteers had been approached by agitators, 'a great many of whom seemed definitely opposed to the allied war effort'.[5]

Also, in May 1940, representations to the Air Ministry were made by the Czechoslovak Air Attaché in London, Josef Kalla. He proposed that a specialist Czechoslovak bomber unit be formed in Britain from crews then standing idle in France, emphasising their excellent knowledge of home geography and the advantages this would bring when raids were targeted at enemy locations in the Protectorate. The idea was rejected immediately by the Director of Intelligence, Archibald Boyle. Responding to the suggestion, he wrote: 'I doubt very much if this is worth pursuing. We don't know (1) if there are any pilots worthy of the name and if they are available; (2) their integrity (I am doubtful of many Czechs).'[6] After some hurried attempts to assure him of the integrity of the men, and an impassioned plea by a former British Air Attaché to Prague, Boyle eventually passed the matter to his superiors. Before a decision could be taken, however, the French collapse had begun and the Czechoslovak troops began to arrive in Britain, uninvited and – at some senior levels – unwelcome also.

Eden's other point, that he would give priority to Polish personnel, also bears upon the situation in which the Czechoslovaks found themselves. The Poles were full allies by official treaty, whereas the Czechs were not (and never would be).[7] Even so, this Polish 'alliance', though it existed on paper, was not necessarily an alliance of spirit. Two thousand Polish air personnel had been stationed in Britain shortly after the war began, but the defeat of France meant that many thousands more would soon arrive. These men received glorious public tributes from the professional politicians, but again, deep in the closeted world of the Air Ministry, few words of praise were forthcoming.

A new directorate to co-ordinate the allied air forces had been established under the leadership of Air Commodore Sir Charles Medhurst, but in July 1940 he wrote to the Deputy Chief of the Air Staff and complained bitterly about the Polish influx: 'I have been reliably informed that [the senior Polish Air Force officers] are completely useless and are only out to line their pockets filling cushy jobs'.[8] Medhurst had been warned that the Poles would seek to establish a completely independent air arm, and this he was determined to avoid if he possibly could. He was destined to fail, but in the short term at least he managed to limit new squadron formation to ensure that 'the unskilled and inferior material' did not find its way into the RAF. Thus both the Poles and the Czechoslovaks had bitter critics at the level of command and control, and even Dowding at the height of the Battle of Britain was prepared to roll up British fighter squadrons if necessary to avoid replacing losses with Czech or Polish pilots.[9]

Thus the atmosphere which greeted the Slav air crews, the Czechoslovaks in particular, was not as cordial as the image-makers would have had everyone believe. To be sure, the public feted both as heroes and gallant allies, which they most certainly were, but in private there were serious doubts as to the military spirit and proficiency of the incoming servicemen from East and Central Europe. Furthermore, serious disturbances within the Czechoslovak Army served to reinforce the prejudices of those who saw it as infested with makeweights and communist agitators. The troubles at Cholmondeley Park are well documented elsewhere, and though the matter was considered at the level of the War Cabinet, less sanitised observations were passed across military desks.[10] One especially thorough report, produced by an MI5 officer known only as 'Lieutenant X', was sent to the Foreign Office rather excitedly by Medhurst. The impression given was that the Czechoslovak Army as reconstituted in England was 'full of sedition . . . a rabble . . . rotten to the core'. The post-disorder 'weeding out' of the dangerous influences had restored a degree of uniformity of outlook, but by no means should the force be left unwatched, either by the Czechoslovak authorities themselves or indeed by the British security services.[11] Much of this report was rejected by the Foreign Office – J.G. Ward was of the opinion that the writer was 'violently prejudiced' – whereas Frank Roberts, of the Central Department of the Foreign Office, accepted the general observation but condemned the interpretation that the Czechoslovak Army was intrinsically rotten. He argued in return that both the air and land forces each had their fair share of malcontents, but this had less to do with lack of moral fibre than a simple dislike of the political establishment that they were expected to serve.[12]

Either way, by the end of 1940 the overall impression of the exiled Czechoslovak armed forces was, in the eyes of some senior British officers at least, one of a deeply flawed force riddled with intrigue, insubordination, dissatisfaction and dangerous politics. It mattered little to the critics that 310 and 312 Czechoslovak fighter squadrons had distinguished themselves in the Battle of Britain, and had sustained fatalities in this fight for the common cause. Both the Air Ministry and the War Office contented themselves in the knowledge that they had fulfilled the instructions of the Prime Minister, for it was Churchill who had swept all discrimination aside and demanded that the service personnel rescued in the summer, of whatever nationality, be swiftly formed into fighting units. In mid-July, he had written to the Chiefs of Staff and made them aware of his wishes:

> Mere questions of administrative convenience must not be allowed to stand in the way of this policy of the State. It is most necessary to give to the war which Great Britain is waging single-handed the broad international character which will add greatly to our strength and prestige.

To this Churchill added: 'I hope I may receive assurances that this policy is being wholeheartedly pursued'.[13]

Obviously enough, Churchill was fishing for American support, for he knew that most of the incoming nationalities were well represented in the United States. As propaganda tools, all of the exiled forces were worth the trouble to accommodate and equip, even if most of the land forces stationed in Britain were not going to be active for quite some time. He also demanded weekly reports on the progress of the contingents, and although these were later downgraded to monthly, then quarterly intervals, he made sure that the service departments knew he was watching them closely.

The assimilation of each contingent threw up its own peculiar difficulties, both political and military, but the problem with the Czechoslovaks was the question of political leadership and responsibility for their actions. The British had already secured total operational control of all the foreign contingents, and the smaller air units, such as the Czechoslovaks and the Belgians, had been forcibly incorporated into the Royal Air Force Volunteer Reserve (RAFVR). The argument for this policy rested upon the British insistence that their numbers were too small to form fully independent air units, and in itself this argument was entirely sustainable. A hidden benefit, however, was that this fragmentation of the smaller contingents allowed the British to put them into RAF uniform under RAF commanding officers, and have them serve under RAF military law, thereby weakening the political ties with the governments-in-exile. Members of certain groups, the Poles and the French for example, had initially been drafted into the RAFVR and then released upon the formation of independent national forces, but it remained the firm policy of the Air Ministry whenever possible to avoid granting independence throughout the entire war.

The reason for this intransigence lay in the desire of the British to steer clear of political entanglements that might result from supporting independent forces of high profile, particularly the air forces. By granting independent status, the British felt they were tacitly supporting not only the right of the national group concerned to liberate its homeland, but also whatever political programme its representatives might choose to disseminate abroad. This caused considerable problems when it came to the Free French and the Poles. Their desires to have their own independent forces were rather forced upon the British, but no such pressure would be tolerated from the Czechoslovaks. The army contingent was named the 'Independent Czechoslovak Brigade' not because it enjoyed genuine independence, but because this name satisfied certain aspirations within the political community to which it owed its

allegiance. But the brigade did little but prepare for action; there
was no land war in which it could be deployed until Operation
Overlord in 1944, and even then its activities were restricted.[14] This
gesture of 'independence' for the army therefore cost the British
nothing, but the air force was another matter. For here was a *fighting* unit in every sense of the word, and it featured high on the list
of positive propaganda items broadcast to the occupied territories.
Czechoslovak politics were complicated indeed, and it did not suit
the British to have themselves too closely associated with the programme of Dr. Edvard Benes, the pre-war president and political
leader in exile.

Thus it was the intention of the British to limit the degree of military freedom if it lay within their power to do so. In the case of the
Czechoslovaks, the reason was intimately connected with the political relations between the two countries. Ever since the collapse of
the old republic and the resignation of Benes after Munich, the
British had fought shy of giving him any political legitimacy. Certainly the French did not want to do so, and the British followed the
lead of their ally. The spirit of appeasement cast a long shadow
indeed, well into 1940. The British had recognised a Czechoslovak
National Committee, then based in France, as early as 20 December
1939. This chimed with Neville Chamberlain's declaration that one
of the British war aims would be to see 'the Czechoslovak *people*
freed from foreign domination.'[15] In the desperately pedantic world
of Czechoslovak politics of the time, the lack of the plural could
have implied British commitment to a unified liberation, and this
was swiftly noticed by the men of the Foreign Office who ensured
that the 's' was added to 'people' in all future correspondence. The
reason was that the British did not want to align themselves with a
policy which might be unworkable. As Frank Roberts expressed it:
'We are not at all sure that when the time comes the Czechs and Slovaks will necessarily wish to be reunited in a single State'.[16] So it can
be appreciated why the British were uneasy about political and military connections that might involve them in such delicate issues.

Matters were therefore complicated in 1939, and they grew more
complicated still when the first wave of evacuees arrived in the summer of 1940. Benes had been angling for the creation of a
provisional Czechoslovak government with himself at its head, but
the British had steadfastly refused, raising all manner of obstacles,
the most intractable of which focused upon the apparent inability of
Benes to secure political unity between the various factions squabbling within and without his National Committee. Unless such
unity could be guaranteed, the British argued, there could be no
representative government of any kind. In fact, the recognition of

the National Committee in the first place stemmed from a British desire 'to resist pressure to recognise a provisional government'.[17] The British therefore had no intention of going one inch further than they needed to go, but the arrival of the troops and airmen changed all that.

In the War Cabinet of 3 July 1940, the Foreign Secretary presented a revised assessment of the Czechoslovak position.[18] With admirable dexterity, Lord Halifax massaged the previous arguments against recognition out of existence, claiming, with some justification, that the countries who might have objected to any suggestion that Czechoslovakia might be reconstituted after the war were either moving closer to the Axis camp or had been knocked out of the war. This meant that the sensibilities of Poland, France and Hungary need not be regarded. The issue of unity was now to be ignored; it would be impossible to play host to such a volatile group of politicians and expect them to settle their differences before any representation could take place, and any future attempts by the British to secure unity would be confined to urging Benes to reach some kind of workable accord with his political opponents.

But the key to the new circumstances, and, indeed, Halifax's altered stance on the entire question, lay in the unavoidable fact that several thousand members of the Czechoslovak armed forces had now arrived in England. As Halifax made clear, these personnel would have to be looked after 'whether or not' His Majesty's Government granted recognition to Benes and his committee. As far as the military aspects were concerned – the accommodating, arming, training and deployment of the men – all of them would automatically be the concerns of the British service departments. But general discipline and political authority were more problematic, and it would be greatly in HMG's favour if such thorny issues could be delivered to the door of Doctor Benes. Besides, as Halifax concluded, if Britain chose not to support the exiles, 'the possibility exists that . . . the Czechs and Slovaks may look solely to the USSR for salvation'.[19] Halifax recommended granting the Benes 'Government' provisional status only, with further recognition dependent upon the demonstration of political unity. So the British did no favours for the Czechoslovaks, and certainly did not grant them political legitimacy – albeit in temporary form – because they appreciated the merits of Benes as a national leader, or even because of the abilities of his colleagues to administer Czechoslovak affairs efficiently, but simply because the prevailing circumstances made the decision much less onerous than before and it was infinitely better to have him within the allied sphere of influence than without.

This illustrates that Benes was not seen as a 'friend' of the British Government, but more as a tolerated associate.[20]

But this is not to suggest that the British were prepared to devolve anything more than the bare minimum of authority in regard to the Czechoslovak forces. Matters such as military discipline remained firmly in British hands. Concern had been expressed in Parliament and in the various service departments about the differing military codes that the exiles had brought with them, and in the broad sweep of things each exiled contingent would be subject to the relevant British codes unless special considerations applied. Furthermore, severe punishments could not be administered if a similar offence would attract a lesser penalty under British law, and even then only with the concurrence of the home authorities. This might first appear to be unwarranted interference in the exiles' affairs, but in fact such a policy acted as a protective screen for the individual serviceman. In the case of the Czechoslovaks, there were several instances when the Air Ministry intervened to protest at disciplinary decisions against individuals, and on one occasion a senior air officer accused the Czechoslovak military authorities of 'Gestapo tactics; that is, tactics against which Great Britain is fighting'.[21] The point at issue was not whether the Czechoslovaks were entitled to discipline their men as they saw fit, but whether the offender had committed a genuine military crime and not a political one. Many of the men who served with the army and air contingents through the war had no great love of Benes or his politics, and though they were prepared to accept him as the de facto leader for the duration of the conflict, disputes between rival factions were common. A direct result of this was the tendency of some Czechoslovak officers to interpret any dissent whatsoever as a threat to the stability of the entire group; stability which was, as we have seen, tenuous to begin with. Such were the pressures on Benes to present a united face both to the British and the Resistance at home that his officers and representatives often became heavy-handed, humiliating men before their peers for relatively minor transgressions. By maintaining a watchful eye on the disciplinary affairs of the Czechoslovaks, the British were therefore acting as guardians of the right of the individual to fair treatment.[22]

All of these difficulties, however, remained invisible to the general public. Indeed, with the exception of the near-mutiny in the air force and the temporary disturbances within the army contingent, the problems were unknown to the vast majority of the officers and men in the ranks. It should be kept firmly in mind that the various criticisms directed at the Czechoslovak military forces and its political representatives were never reduced to the level of criticising the individuals who served bravely and steadfastly for the cause in which they believed. Both the War Office and the Air Ministry held the Czechoslovak soldier and airman in high regard; and, though they sometimes had cause to doubt the political motives of some senior officers, such doubts were expressed at some time or another about commanders within all of the allied contingents. By 1942, when the invasion scare was over and Churchill's much sought after 'Grand Alliance' was in place, the officers and other ranks of the Czechoslovak military settled down to take their places in the allied order of battle, purged of unsuitable elements and, in the case of the air force, having collected an admirable array of medals for valour and distinguished service.

It is easy to forget that there was always a human dimension to the exile experience, away from the flags pinned to campaign maps and the stenographed minutes of interminable meetings. Hardly any of the five thousand or so men of the Czechoslovak forces had ever been to Britain, and though they were given food and pocket money upon their arrival in 1940, provision for their general welfare was slow to be established. For example, an absolute tenet of the assimilation policy was that all of the men should learn English, and the burden fell wholly upon the British Council to ensure that the programme was delivered effectively and economically. The service departments had agreed to bear the cost of language training, but on more than one occasion it was necessary for the Council to chase after money it was owed, and to meet some costs from its own funds.[23]

Both the War Office and the Air Ministry had their own agenda in regard to the English language training. The former had issued instructions to the British Council, informing them that 'any cultural or educational work amongst the allied armies' was not required 'on anything more than a trivial scale'.[24] This caused anxiety and despair within the army group, and it effectively condemned the men to learn what English they could through contact with British officers or the general public. The Air Ministry saw things differently, for it required the aircrews to be brought up to a standard of operational English as soon as possible, because without the ability to communicate in the air, the contingent was never likely to reach maximum efficiency. To this end, the Ministry produced its own training manual complete with essential phrases that every allied airman should know, including 'PBI' (Poor Bloody Infantry), 'FA' (Football Association), 'in the drink' and 'out for a duck'.[25]

Overall, the British Council laboured against numerous obstacles to make life in exile at least a tolerable experience, but its efforts to

teach the men English were only partially successful, as a result, perhaps, of the limitations placed upon its expenditure by the service
departments. By January 1942, the average level of English language proficiency within the Czechoslovak air contingent stood at
58 percent (roughly equivalent to intermediate level today).[26] In the
main, an allied serviceman learned most of his English through contact with native speakers, and the British Council advised all of the
allied governments to urge each man to seize every opportunity to
practise his English, especially when on leave or when stationed
near British towns and villages. In short, with regard to education
and social provision, the service departments did something for the
allied forces, but not much. Furthermore, it fell upon the Council to
assist with the organisation of the various clubs and associations
that offered 'a taste of home' for each allied nationality. More often
than not, this assistance extended to subsidising the clubs, and, in
the cases of the Poles and the Czechoslovaks, this support
accounted for virtually all of the running costs, neither government
contributing more than 'odd amounts only'.[27]

By 1942, most of the allied personnel who had arrived in Britain
during the hectic summer of 1940 had become accustomed to life in
exile. A few had married British women; many more had forged
permanent friendships. The Czechoslovaks found their welcome
extended throughout the war; indeed, their popularity actually
increased, whereas the Poles found the British hospitality wearing
thin by 1945.[28] Yet behind the apparent stability of the Czechoslovak position in Britain the political intrigues continued unabated,
both in their complexity and in the impact which they made upon
the ruling echelon in the British military. One of the most harmful
was the renewed question of independence raised by Benes and his
senior commanders in 1942. By promoting a policy that they could
not hope to bring to fruition, they irritated the Air Ministry and
gave rise to ugly sentiments which, had they become common
knowledge, would have irreparably damaged the Anglo-Czechoslo-
vak relationship.

We have seen earlier how the British were determined to keep the
Czechoslovak air contingent firmly within the RAFVR 'for reasons
of administrative convenience', though in practice this meant keeping at arm's length any political entanglements which might prove
embarrassing at the war's end.[29] Karel Janousek, the Inspector of
the Air Force, was liked and trusted by his British colleagues, and
was more than anyone else best placed to know what could be
achieved in terms of reorganisation, future operations, and the general administration of the small air contingent. Yet in 1942 he found
himself arguing desperately against the proposal of independence,

which he knew would not work, and, in doing so, he made political enemies that – very possibly – led to him subsequently serving eleven years in a Communist prison as 'an enemy of the people'.

To understand why the air force occupied such a pivotal position in the political calculations of the Czechoslovaks, one must embrace the military context of the time. First, the army, though well trained and loyal, was also relatively inactive at this stage in the war. It was being prepared for combat, but no one knew when and where the moment would arrive. Second, the air force had secured for itself a fine reputation as a fighting force and played a major part in the propaganda broadcasts to the occupied territory. As a result, it had a political significance all of its own. If Benes could persuade the British Government to grant his air force independent status with its own high command, this would signal to the homeland that the Czechoslovaks were on a par with the Poles and could treat with them equally as fully-fledged allies. This would automatically enhance Benes' prestige and increase his chances of a smooth restoration of power at the moment of liberation.

What triggered this resurgence of an old idea is difficult to ascertain. It could have been the involvement of the Czechoslovak squadrons in the Dieppe Raid of 1942, perhaps inspiring a determination to achieve greater prestige and recognition, or it could have been part of Benes' political programme, by this time turning east towards the Soviet Union. Also, Reinhard Heydrich had been assassinated in June 1942 by British-trained operatives, and the Munich Agreement had been repudiated in the House of Commons by Anthony Eden in August, so perhaps Benes and his commanders felt more confident of success at this time than they had done in 1940. But whatever the reason, Benes informed his Foreign Minister Jan Masaryk in October 1942 of his decision to press the British to grant independence to the air force. To that end, he and his senior officers drafted a new agreement that embodied the concept, and this was submitted to the British.

The files in the Prague archives show Janousek fighting against every clause, slowly pulling the project to pieces, emphasising that nothing had changed since 1940 and that it was an impossible task to change the British attitude.[30] Time and again he was overruled, and by early 1943 the Air Ministry had received the proposals. Each clause, each article, was ruthlessly dismantled and rejected, exactly as Janousek had predicted. But the most revealing result of the exercise – and it should come as no surprise to learn that the Czechs came away with nothing to show for their efforts – was the caustic reaction it provoked from the Air Ministry. In an addendum to the critique of the independence proposals, the Air Ministry saw fit to describe the

Czechoslovak Air Force as 'a political necessity [and a] military lux-
ury'. While drawing attention to the complete absurdity of granting
such a small force any form of independent status, it laid bare opinions that were clearly held by senior RAF commanders, accusing the
Czechoslovaks of suffering from 'a very exaggerated inferiority complex', and stating that though the air contingent had been treated
'sympathetically and generously' by the RAF, it had obviously not
been enough to satisfy the political representatives in London. The
Air Ministry drew a blunt conclusion that the whole exercise had
been politically motivated, adding 'Perhaps we have been too kind to
the Czechs, but then we have had Munich thrown in our face'.[31]

This document has subsequently caused much ill-feeling within
the veterans' community, but it is there to be read. It would also seem
to have been ignored by some Czech and Slovak historians working
with other material from the same file. Even so, we catch here the
merest glimpse of the British-Czechoslovak military relationship at a
senior level, and there can be no doubt that similar opinions were
held by some British officials right through to the end of the war. As
late as November 1944, when the Czechoslovak Government asked
for permission to transfer the air units to the east in support of the
Slovak rising, the Air Ministry was sorely tempted 'to be rid of the
commitment' by handing over the force in toto to the Russians. In the
event, the request for transfer was refused, partly because of the
impossible position regarding supply and maintenance had the
squadrons flown east, and partly because combat on the Eastern
front would have been potentially disastrous for such a small group.[32]

If all of the history of British-Czechoslovak military relations
seems to be nothing but a catalogue of distrust and contempt, the
greatest irony of all was reserved for the time when the squadrons
returned home. The Independent Brigade was already there, having
seen action on the Continent and entered Czechoslovakia as liberators with Patton's U.S. Third Army. For the air force, though, events
were not to be so clear-cut or glorious. Requests from Benes to
transfer them to the homeland began almost as soon as the war in
Europe ceased, but from the outset the British were obsessed with
obtaining Soviet permission. Throughout the midsummer of 1945,
they persistently harangued Benes to supply them with conclusive
Russian agreement to the move, seemingly oblivious to the fact that
for Benes to make such a request to Red Army commanders would
have signalled his weakness at a time when he was most in need of
strong allies in the West.

Various indications of Soviet agreement trickled into Whitehall
through June and July, while simultaneously the British received
ever-darker reports of communist activity within the Czechoslovak

forces. Very soon, they became aware that the Czechoslovak Army was being overwhelmed by Soviet influence, and they became frantic that the air force would also succumb, thereby depriving them of a foothold in the East. Arrangements were made to supply the air force with new equipment and RAF technical staff, but it became increasingly clear that the new order in Eastern Europe was wrenching control of the plucky little air contingent from the Western grasp. Oddly, when Soviet permission for the transfer did materialise, the British refused to believe it, but by then it was too late anyway. The files in London show how the British laboured to secure a new military agreement against impossible odds, as one by one the pro-Western commanders were removed from power – Janousek was amongst their number – and were replaced by officers who had long declared their sympathies for communism. In the end, after a half-hearted mission to London failed to re-forge the bonds, the Czechoslovak Air Force slipped away from the West, followed by the whole country in the coup of 1948.[33]

The story of the Czechoslovak forces in Britain was always one of two dimensions: the public face, which almost without exception was warm and welcoming towards men who fought for their country with a courage unsurpassed by any other nation; and the private, cloistered view in Whitehall and the service departments, who for reasons rooted in prejudice and ignorance extended their political vendetta with Edvard Benes to include, unfairly, the officers and men under his nominal command. For the British, the Czechoslovak forces were in large part an exercise in international propaganda, a way of signalling to the world that the Munich disgrace had been renounced, as well as the hope that such an act of diplomatic vandalism could be obscured by keeping a Czechoslovak national force on British soil and permitting it a share of the war. For the Czechoslovak officers and other ranks, this opportunity was seized with no bitterness, for nearly all of them relished the chance to hit back against the invaders of their country. For Benes, however, it was a chance to regain his prestige and his presidency, and he manipulated both his army and his air force to serve these aims, treating neither with the genuine respect they deserved. There were three agendas, and not one of them was satisfied in whole.

Notes

1. The total number of people rescued has been calculated as 163,225. M. Gilbert, *Second World War*, London 1990, p. 106. An Admiralty report on Operations *Aerial* and *Cycle* appears in the Public Record Office (PRO), London, ADM 1/10481.

2. 19 June 1940, PRO CAB 65/7.

3. See J. Nemec, 'The Crisis of the Czechoslovak Army in England in the Second Half of 1940' and Z. Kordina, 'Those Months in France', in *On All Fronts: Czechoslovaks in World War II*, vol. 1, ed. L.M. White, Boulder, 1991, pp. 83–94 and 23–40; 'Report on the conditions in France' and 'Summary of Czechoslovak Action in France' in the Vojensky Historicky Archiv (VHA), Prague, MNO 5/810/1940 and MNO 5/931/1940.

4. E.N. Cooper at the Inter-Departmental Meeting of 26 January 1940, PRO FO 371/24365.

5. E.N. Cooper, reporting the evidence of Sir Malcolm Delevingne, 11 June 1940, PRO FO/371/2436.

6. Boyle to Wing Commander C. Porri, 2 June 1940, PRO AIR 2/5153.

7. This fact caused a few problems within the Foreign Office. Since no formal alliance existed, it became necessary to find a phrase that satisfied all the diplomatic criteria without committing the British to treating the Czechs as a legal allied entity. The phrase chosen after some deliberation was 'allied to the cause of His Majesty'.

8. Medhurst to Sholto-Douglas, 3 July 1940, PRO AIR 2/5153. Medhurst was later highly decorated by both the Polish and Czechoslovak authorities.

9. Air Ministry Conference, 14 July 1940, PRO AIR 8/370; Sholto-Douglas to AM Sir Richard Peirse, 28 July 1940; DCAS to VCAS, 29 July 1940; ERPC Conference, 3 August 1940, PRO AIR 2/5196. It should be noted that Dowding specified Polish and Czechoslovak pilots, offering no objection to the replacement of wastage with French, Belgian or Dutch pilots.

10. Briefly stated, in July 1940 several hundred men from the Czechoslovak army contingent were held responsible for 'certain disorders' at the holding camp in Cheshire. Ultimately, these individuals were transferred to the Pioneer Corps. Various interpretations of the events may be found, ranging from the defence of genuine protests against army anti-Semitism to charges of deliberate political agitation by communist veterans of the Spanish Civil War. See War Cabinet, 26 July 1940, PRO CAB 65/7; War Diaries of Military Mission to Czechoslovak Land Forces, 22 August 1940, PRO WO 178/21. Also J. Nemec, 'The Crisis', pp. 86–9; M. Liskutín, *Challenge in the Air*, London, 1985, pp. 66–9; E. Kulka: 'Jews in the Czechoslovak Armed Forces During World War II', in *The Jews of Czechoslovakia*, eds A. Dagan *et al*, New York and Philadelphia, 1984, pp. 371–6. Most of those self-professed communists who were detained applied for re-enlistment after the German attack on the Soviet Union in 1941.

11. Report on the French and Czechoslovak Forces in the UK, circa mid-September 1940, PRO C8512/1419/62.

12. Ibid. It is worth noting in passing that the Czechoslovak Air Force also faced a near-mutiny in the autumn of 1940, forcing Edward Benes to dismiss several officers to placate the rebels.

13. Prime Minister to Chiefs-of-Staff via General Ismay, 12 July 1940, PRO AIR 8/370.

14. This is not to deprecate the action of the Middle East contingent that fought in the defence of Tobruk. These men were later withdrawn from that theatre of operations and relocated to Britain to bring the British-based contingent up to strength.

15. 6 December 1939, PRO FO 371/24287(70); PRO FO 371/24288(60).

16. Ibid. Frank Roberts (1907–1998) worked under William Strang in the Central Department of the Foreign Office from 1940 to 1943, thereafter becoming Chargé d'Affaires to the Czechoslovak Government. We must also remember

that Slovakia, in theory at any rate, had become an independent state in 1939 and placed itself within the Axis.

17. Minute from Alexander Cadogan to the Central Dept, 29 June 1940, PRO FO 371/24288.

18. PRO CAB 67/7, WP(G)40(168).

19. Ibid.

20. Provisional status also greatly exercised the Czechoslovak Foreign Minister Jan Masaryk's wry humour. He often signed his personal letters 'Provisionally yours', and had been known to ask if the airmen killed in the Battle of Britain were 'provisionally dead.' Z. Zeman, *The Masaryks*, London, 1976, p. 183.

21. AVM Alfred Collier to Lt.Col. Josef Kalla, 9 January 1941, VHA, MNO 13/67/1941. The dispute centred around an individual who refused to fly with 311 Bomber Squadron over occupied territory, although he had volunteered to transfer to fighter duties. Given that a front-line fighter pilot's life expectancy at this stage of the war was a little over two weeks, this seems to indicate that the man was no coward. Even so, he was convicted of this offence and sentenced to be stripped of rank, dressed in khaki and not RAF blue, and confined to menial labouring duties. The British complained bitterly, adding that it was not RAF practice 'to conduct demotions in such a theatrical manner'.

22. Ironically, in the face of mass dissent, Benes was forced to capitulate. In July and August 1940, 450 officers and men of the air contingent tabled a list of complaints that centred on the recent action in France and the new conditions in England. Within a few days, senior Czechoslovak officers were warning of a 'complete collapse of discipline' if certain named officers – one of them the Commander-in-Chief and Inspector General of the Air Force – were not removed from their commands. Benes complied to save his Air Force from complete disintegration as a viable unit. The officer removed, Brigadier-General Slezák, was later restored to power by the communists in 1945. A. Brown, 'The Czechoslovak Air Force in Britain, 1940–1945' (Ph.D. diss., University of Southampton, 1998), pp. 68–76.

23. One example concerns the initial bill presented before the Air Ministry for teaching fees accrued between September 1940 and December of that year. After repeated letters and invoices, the British Council eventually received the sum of £2,110 a year later. Put into context, that amount represents the approximate annual salary of an Air Vice-Marshal. Internal correspondence, British Council, PRO BW/2/231.

24. Internal correspondence, 28 January 1941, PRO BW/2/229. It was admitted by the Council that this attitude was causing no little resentment amongst the allied governments, but since they would otherwise be expected to foot the bill, the Council had no choice but to comply.

25. For readers unfamiliar with these terms, 'in the drink' meant to crash or ditch into the sea, while 'out for a duck' roughly translated in Air Force slang to 'to have crashed or been captured having had no successes against the enemy'.

26. Results of examinations conducted by the Czechoslovak Air Inspectorate, VHA, CsL VB 131/CI-3/1/76. The full range of scores varied from 5 percent to 95 percent, and prompted complaints to the Air Ministry that not enough was being done to maximise language efficiency.

27. Estimates of expenditure, 17 November 1942, PRO BW/108/1.

28. See A. Zamoyski's excellent work *The Forgotten Few*, London, 1995, for examples.

29. Internal Air Ministry memorandum, 21 July 1940, PRO AIR 2/5162.

30. For a complete examination of this incident, see A. Brown, 'The Czechoslovak Air Force in Britain, 1940–1945', pp. 124–47.

31. Air Ministry circular, circa June 1943, PRO AIR 2/5162.
32. See A. Brown, 'The Czechoslovak Air Force in Britain, 1940–1945', pp. 149–58.
33. For a full account of this episode, see A. Brown, 'The Czechoslovak Air Force in Britain, 1940–1945', pp. 159–75 and 182–94.

11

The Social History of Polish Exile (1939–1945).
The Exile State and the Clandestine State: Society, Problems and Reflections*

Jan E. Zamojski

Before I begin my analysis, I think it is appropriate that I make a few general remarks. First, I must admit that I found the topic of this paper somewhat disconcerting when it was originally suggested to me by the organisers of the conference. I had to ask myself the following basic questions: How does one define the 'social history of Polish exile'? Can the usual rules of social history be applied to the Polish exile of the years 1939–1945? How can it be dissociated from political history, given that exile is a profoundly political phenomenon and that of the Poles was, one could argue, highly politicised? Moreover, how can the Polish exile be dissociated from military questions when the main reason for it was Poland's involvement in the war, particularly on a military level, and the restoration – by force – of the Polish State? This raison d'être meant that the army, with its various misadventures, was omnipresent and more importantly that the major social groupings, notably the peasants, workers, and the middle classes, while organising on a *political* basis also attempted to organise on a *military* one. The final question I asked myself was how to define the topic. Who were the people in exile? Were they only those who fled Poland after 1939 – in other words the refugees? If so, how should one describe those who were deported or taken prisoner, the workers who were

forcibly sent everywhere from the Atlantic Wall to Vladivostok and
those 'who were enrolled against their will' in the Wehrmacht and
the Red Army? And what about the workers from the mines and the
iron and steel industry of Silesia seized in 1945 as 'spoils of war'
and sent to rebuild the mines and the factories in the Donbas industrial region and elsewhere in the Soviet Union?

The answers to these questions are not easy ones. Polish historical studies on the period from 1939 to 1945 have focussed mainly
on its political aspects, both in domestic as well as foreign affairs
and particularly on the often strained relationships between Poland
and the Soviet Union and the relationships with the British and
American Allies, and on its military aspects, such as the killings,
that were once attributed to the Germans and are now regarded as
the work of the NKVD. These issues have been studied to the detriment of problems of a truly social nature, which only figure in those
studies as partial topics and not as topics in their own right. Indeed,
when discussing this issue with colleagues who work on the history
of the government-in-exile, they agreed with some embarrassment
that the social aspect of the topic has been greatly neglected.

With these observations as my starting-point, I therefore had to
choose a few topics within the subject that I considered to be important, but without being certain that I had made the right choice and
without pretending that I could give a thorough and chronological
account of events. It is clearly impossible to talk about a specific Polish exile in England; it formed part of a much larger scale and
many-sided phenomenon, within which exile in England was a main
axis, a focal point, a place where decisions were made and a point of
reference, because the Polish Government-in-Exile was based there.
The 'social' element, in this case, was everything that was not strictly
military: notably, the political and state structures, the relationships
between London and occupied Poland, the cultural activities, the
behaviour and the fate of some social groups in exile, social welfare
and the fragmentation of the Polish exile community after the war.
In order to delineate more effectively the specificity of the topic, it
seems appropriate to mention as well the two reflexes that history
had imprinted on the national conscience of generations of Poles
prior to the war. If somewhat crude terminology may be excused,
one of these reflexes may be called the 'conspiratorial-insurrec-
tionary mode', and the other one the 'exile mode' or 'emigration
mode'. The first of these urged the people, once their country had
been occupied, to organise themselves secretly to prepare successive
insurrections. The second reflex was the consequence of the disasters
that had been caused by the first. Political, military, social and cultural exile has been an omnipresent phenomenon, indeed even an

integral part of Polish history over the last two centuries: it gave refuge to insurrectionists, provided the base for the political and military activities of the 'independentists', formed the safe haven in which Polish culture could flourish[1] and became the sanctuary for the opponents to the Sanacja regime, the so-called 'Colonels' Regime' which ruled Poland before 1939 as well as, after 1945, the basis for the alternative structures to People's Poland.

As has been mentioned, the social history of Polish exile cannot be limited to a study of the Polish community in the British Isles. There are three reasons for this, the first of which is that in 1939 large groups of Polish immigrants lived in the United States, Latin America (notably Brazil and Argentina), France, Belgium and the Netherlands. They were very politicised, especially in the U.S.A. and in France, with strong currents of opposition against the prewar regime composed, broadly speaking, of right-wing groups in the U.S.A. and left-wing groups in France. After September 1939 and June 1940, the arrival of Polish refugees, military figures, intellectuals and, above all, politicians, as well as the installation in several countries of institutions, local offices of the ministries and of governmental organisations, added new elements to this situation and blurred the distinctions between immigrants and refugees. In this way, the relationships between Polish diasporas and the exile state served – in many respects – as a substitute for the relationship between government and society, especially in the case of the Polish diaspora in France.

The second reason that a social history of Polish exile between 1939 and 1945 cannot be limited to the study of Poles in Britain is that several hundreds of thousands (the figures remain somewhat inaccurate[2]) of Polish citizens – I stress Polish citizens rather than Poles – arrived on the territory of the USSR. These citizens had been deported, imprisoned, mobilised in the Red Army and, after June 1941, evacuated. The third reason that a social history of Polish exiles in Britain is only a partial history is related to a phenomenon that only became fully apparent after the war, especially in Germany and after people were freed from the concentration camps: Poles constituted a significant proportion of the prisoners of war in Germany and of those who had been deported and forced into 'voluntary work' in the Reich, as well as of many other categories of deported people, amounting in total to more than one and a half million people.

Finally, there is also the history of how relations between London and Poland evolved, which, I shall argue, constituted the most important part of the social history of Polish exiles in Britain. I shall try to present the chronology of this evolution.

The Polish government-in-exile

The Polish Government-in-Exile must be considered as the main
influence on the social history of the years between 1939 and 1945,
and even for a period after this date. All reflections on the events of
this era must, therefore, be concerned with this government which,
up until its dissolution in 1945, represented the continuity and the
sovereignty of the Polish State. The Polish Government-in-Exile was
created in Paris towards the end of September 1939, after Poland
had been invaded by the Germans and the Soviet troops. The Polish
Government in existence until then, the so-called Sanacja Government, and the President of the Republic had been interned by the
Romanians, despite the right of passage that had previously been
granted to them. This change of government was based on the 1935
Constitution that gave the President of the Republic a great deal of
power, including that of naming his successor in certain circumstances, and which he chose to exercise under the pressure of the
situation.[3] It is one of the paradoxes of history that this constitution, which had been criticised by the opposition for being
antidemocratic, manipulable and illegal, was used to gain power
and to provide a legal basis for establishing the legitimacy of the
new regime. Moreover, the Polish exiles remained fiercely loyal to it
until the end of the war and even for many years afterwards. However, this constitutional manœuvre in 1939 also had consequences
for some of the subsequent internal political crises in the Government-in-Exile, when attempts were made to get rid of Sikorski, and
it was also invoked later as a means of disputing the legality of the
government.

  This government was based on the representatives of four political parties (the so-called quadruple alliance), namely the Peasant
Party (PSL), the Polish Socialist Party (PPS), the National Party (SN)
and the Workers Party (SP).[4] Despite the animosity against the men
of the Sanacja, the government could not manage without their contribution in the governmental structures (notably by the President
and his entourage, the diplomatic staff, the special services etc.), and
above all in the army where, even after a purge (the more refractory
members were expelled in France, while in England they were simply interned on the Isle of Bute, also known as the 'Isle of Snakes'),
the senior officers tended to support 'the old regime'. The role of
representing the political forces was given to the National Council,
a quasi-parliament in exile, which had only an advisory capacity,
and in which – apart from some representatives of the four governmental parties – representatives of Polish immigrants and of
national minorities were also invited to participate. However, this

only proved possible in the case of the Jews; within the other minorities, notably the Ukrainians, it proved impossible to find individuals of sufficient authority who were prepared to join the council, and therefore in effect to collaborate with the government.

Britain proved to be the main 'island' of the archipelago of Polish exile, and it was to there, after the French disaster, that the military (both in units and in disorganised groups), governmental institutions, politicians, the highly specialised technical officials and sailors from the merchant navy, together with members of their families, and small numbers of civilians were evacuated. The Poles were, in numerical terms, the second largest national group of exiled people in Britain after the Belgians. Yet, they differed from the others in respect of their social composition. Out of 24,352 Poles who had been evacuated from France and registered as such by the British services, 15,248 were soldiers from the Army, 6,429 were from the air force and 1,505 from the navy, making a total of 23,182 forces personnel and only 1,170 civilians of all categories, including some employees of the auxiliary services of the army and of state institutions. Subsequent arrivals of Poles did not result in any significant changes. The Poles in exile in Britain were, therefore, overwhelmingly people from the forces and from the government and its services. It is worth noting that, from the outset, the relationships between the British population and the Poles were very positive, and in Scotland they were particularly warm and welcoming. This Polish-Scottish empathy is worth underlining because of its emotional dimension, which is rather difficult to explain. Poles were welcomed everywhere in Scotland, in castles as well as in ordinary families. Closer relationships were not uncommon, including marriages, and this idyll was to leave traces in many people's memories.

The government was at the centre of all Polish activity in the British Isles. The relationships with the British Government, and those with other governments-in-exile who had settled in England are beyond the scope of this article. It is worth noting, however, that in the days of General Sikorski, the Polish Government attempted to be the spokesperson for all of the exiled governments, if not the *primus inter pares*. Nor should it be forgotten that relations between General Sikorski and General de Gaulle were not particularly warm. Polish social life, in its different aspects, could not have existed without the approval and the political and, more importantly, financial support of the government. The leaderships of the governmental parties were re-formed in the shadow of the governmental institutions. The opposition groups, those of the conservative right and of the Sanacja, recreated their own structures, including the press. Among the political parties, only one leadership, that of the Peasants' Party

(PSL) could boast that its authority was recognised by its clandestine organisation in occupied Poland. The others were only considered to be the representatives abroad of the parties in question, which gave rise to plenty of opportunities for political and personal conflicts, splits and obstructions, and procrastination in their relations with the government.

The trade-union movement, which was unfortunately fairly weak at the time, established its official representation abroad in London with a branch in the United States, but little is known about its activity or its links with trade-union groups in Poland. In any case, the latter were rather weak because they had been decimated at the beginning of the German occupation, as a consequence of their attempts to strike and German massacres and were largely smothered in the clandestine underground by political and military resistance movements. The first, and possibly the only, trade union to be re-formed in England was the union of sailors in the merchant navy, which also had a branch in New York. After the war, it pronounced itself in favour of recognising the Polish government in Warsaw. In 1940, the journalists recreated their Journalists' Association of the Polish Republic. A year later, they were followed by teachers, who organised themselves in a Union of Polish Primary School Teachers Abroad. This union still exists in Britain. There were also associations of secondary-school teachers, of technicians, doctors, economists and the like, but they were all purely professional organisations, and, with the exception of the sailors union, not trade unions in the strict sense of the word.

London and the country

The relationships between London and 'the country' – that is to say between the government-in-exile and the clandestine structures in occupied Poland – went through several different stages. This evolution could be defined as a process towards autonomy and progressive emancipation of the country; a shift from subordination to partnership, culminating in the success of the principle that it was the country that had the final say. In this sense, 'the country' meant all of the administrative, political, military and cultural organisations that are often described in Poland as the 'clandestine state'. Of course, some clandestine organisations, both political and military (quite often the distinctions between the two were almost imperceptible) existed outside the structures of this state, as they more or less belonged to the extreme right, to the former Sanacja or to the Communist or Communist-inclined left-wing parties.

During its period of exile in France, the government tried to bring the various organisations in occupied Poland under its control, by creating the Committee of Ministers for Internal Affairs (KSK) and by appointing delegates of the government for the territories that had been annexed to the Reich as well as for the Government General (GG)[5] and for the zone occupied by the Soviet Union. In the spring of 1940, they even succeeded in organising a secret conference in Belgrade of representatives of the country and of government envoys to discuss the problems of clandestine work in Poland and its co-ordination by the services in France. The collapse of France wrecked these plans. It was much more difficult to maintain links with Britain; instead, it was necessary to adapt to the realities of war and of a lengthy period of occupation by preparing to go underground for a long time. Direct control of political, administrative and military matters was therefore handed over to the people of the occupied country who created the clandestine state.

Given the short duration of the period in France, this contribution will concentrate on the British period, that of the London government. It would be impossible to give all the complicated and extraordinary details about the construction of this clandestine state and the various institutions that acted as the instruments of the social policy of the government. It only really took shape in 1942, and was based on three main pillars: an administrative one, with the general delegate of the government and his machinery (the departments that paralleled the exile ministries; the special services concerned with financial links, the press, security and justice etc as well as the regional and local delegations); a political one, with the Political Liaison Committee (PKP), a replica of the National Council that acted as the representative of the four governmental parties; and a military one, composed of the Home Army (AK) with its senior command (SG), which also doubled up as the Staff headquarters, and a few para-military organisations, the tasks of which were more security orientated.

The relationships between London and clandestine Poland were not easy. The need for permanent two-way links, providing channels for mutual information, consultations and, of course, for all kinds of instructions issued by the government, was considered to be extremely important. A surprisingly large number of documents, sometimes amounting to dozens of pages, were exchanged via the various available means of communication between London and Warsaw. Despite the great vulnerability of the radio, because of the Nazi Funkabwehr and its methods of Funkspiele, radio contacts were the main means of communication between London and

Poland, and, despite heavy losses, they fulfilled their mission remarkably well.[6] Air links were limited, due to the long distance between Poland and the Allied bases (this became easier after their establishment in Bari in Italy) and due to the German air defence systems. On the whole, they limited themselves therefore to parachuting people (mainly officers who had been trained in diversionary manoeuvres and partisan struggle), weapons (though too few!), money and medicines. So-called 'pick-up missions' were limited to three (they had to use larger planes that required appropriate air-fields), but during one of them, the underground sent the Allies the essential elements of the German 'V' missiles. Special missions, ordered by the government on the one hand and by the delegation of the leadership of the AK on the other, as well as by – it should be stressed – some political parties, were entrusted to agents who crossed the whole of occupied Europe through specially-prepared routes in both directions.[7] This access of political parties to secret links was important, because the co-ordination of the positions of the various organisations of these parties, both within the country and abroad, played a very significant part in influencing the policy of the government as well as how it was implemented by the delegation of the clandestine state back in occupied Poland.

The government retained control of the broad lines of Polish policy; its directives to the occupied country had the force of law and its opinions about the evolution of the war and about Polish affairs were the main source of all decisions and consequently of the actions of the clandestine state. Almost the very existence and activity of the clandestine State were dependent on financial support from London, which was provided in various currencies.[8] It was only towards the end of the period of occupation that armed hold-ups were carried out by the clandestine authorities, albeit rarely, though they brought in a good deal of booty. The extraordinary phenomenon of the Warsaw insurrection also played a major part in the evolution of relations between the government and occupied Poland, but it represents too large and multi-faceted a consideration to be treated here satisfactorily. One of the consequences of this disaster, however, was the irreparable lessening – in the eyes of Polish public opinion – of the authority of the Polish Government-in-Exile in London, and, inevitably given the new situation (the presence of the Red Army in Poland, the establishment of the Committee of National Liberation in Lublin and later in Warsaw and the division of General Berling's army into several Polish armies), the dissolution of the AK and the end of the Delegation at the beginning of 1945. The leaders of the latter were arrested and tried by the Soviet authorities, without provoking any reaction on the part of the Allies.

The exile and the diaspora

Reference has already been made to the rather specific situation of the Polish diaspora after the creation of the government-in-exile that relied heavily on the support of Polish immigrant communities. The largest of these, the diaspora in the United States (4.5 to 5 million), did not, contrary to expectations, answer the appeals issued to it as had been done during the First World War, when several tens of thousands of Polish immigrants enlisted in General J. Haller's 'Blue Army' and had played a significant part in securing Poland's victory in the wars of 1919–1920 against the Ukrainians and the Soviet Union. The nature of their experiences, notably the subsequent refusal of both Poland and the United States to recognise them as war veterans, did not encourage any repetition[9] and two visits by General Sikorski to the United States failed to move them. The Poles in the United States succeeded in creating their own social structures and they lived according to their own rules. Their most representative organisations supported the government in London, but their support was more directed at 'Poland's cause' than at the government as such; they also gave their support to charities and put political pressure on the American authorities, but that was the extent of their involvement. The general political tendency of the American Polish community, due in part to its social structure, did not match that of the government. Among the Polish refugees who settled in the United States after 1940 were some of General Sikorski's and his government's fiercest opponents, including former members of the Sanacja. They even set up the Józef Pilsudski Institute which still exists today. In short, London did not succeed in imposing its authority, even in a limited way, on the United States Polish diaspora, nor on the Polish communities in Canada and Latin America.

The nearly half-a-million strong Polish diaspora in France was the most striking example of the phenomenon of the inter-penetration of immigrants and refugees. Before the war it was considered to be the 'iron ration' of the Polish nation in Europe, and its Polish identity was reinforced through consular services and patriotic and para-military organisations. But this only affected some of the Poles, because the others, who had been the most disadvantaged socially in both Poland and in France (the majority were miners and factory workers, especially in heavy metallurgy),[10] were under the influence of the French Communist Party (the PCF) and of the left-wing trade unions. It is worth remembering that out of the 5,000 Poles who volunteered for the International Brigades in Spain, 3,000 came from France. The pre-war regime that prevailed in the Polish army in France was unbearable for these men, who were already accustomed to more democratic forms of behaviour and felt demoralised by the French social and political entourage. The fate of this army, which was in total disorder and chaos in 1940, did not improve their relations with the Polish Government. This was particularly evident during the period of German occupation, when all the rather substantial Polish activity that took place in France was divided between pro-London and pro-Communist tendencies. The government set up a semi-clandestine Delegation in France, which was tolerated by the Vichy government but eliminated by the Gestapo towards the end of 1942. Under the cover of the Groupes de Travail Etranger (GTE), composed of demobilised soldiers, a strong Polish military organisation continued to operate that was commanded by officers who had remained in France but was essentially made up of immigrant-soldiers who, for various reasons, were unable to return home. The plans of the Polish General Staff, devised in consultation with the French generals and British services, had anticipated calling upon this 'Polish army corps' if Vichy France had chosen to rejoin the war against Germany. The myth that this would happen was finally exploded in November 1942.

The Polish Red Cross changed its status to an Association d'Assistance aux Polonais en France (TOPF), which carried out real social work (homes for the disabled, for women, children and elderly people, hospitals, schools, grant systems for students and all kinds of other benefits) while providing a cover for the clandestine work carried out by the Organisation Polonaise de Lutte pour l'Indépendance (POWN), which took over the functions of the Delegation and was active in both the political and military spheres. The leadership of the British Special Operations Executive (SOE) took a keen interest in the potential of the Poles in France, and created a special section (EU/P) intended to use the Polish miners from the Nord-Pas-de-Calais coalfield, as well as Polish workers in the Reich, with a view to mounting a vast diversionary operation to be called 'Dunstable'. The Polish Government, which was also under pressure from Poland itself, was categorically opposed to this operation, as it feared that the Poles would be massacred. After all of France was occupied in 1942, the illusion of fighting alongside the French against the Germans vanished; Polish clandestine organisations isolated themselves strictly from the French Resistance and any action undertaken by POWN used its own manpower resources, with the principal aim of supporting by every possible means the Polish Government when the time of the liberation came. This they did indeed do, through military actions during the Warsaw Uprising as well as through political action. Within the scope of this political action, POWN also launched as its own (and therefore also that of the government) the Programme for a People's Poland of the Socialist Party (PPS), in the hope that, thanks to its very 'social' character, it would have greater success among the Polish workers.

The left-wing tendency within the Polish community in France was integrated within the actions inspired by the PCF (notably the branch of the Main d'Œuvre Immigrée), be they military (the Polish FTP/MOI) or political and social (the women's organisations, youth movements, trade unions, cultural organisations, etc.) in nature. Polish workers also played an active part in the strikes of the spring of 1941 and 1943. In 1942, the Polish communists attempted to lay the basis for co-operation with the 'Londoniens', but the experience was not a success. By 1943, and more emphatically by the summer of 1944, all these structures were turning against the London government, and, later, under the leadership of the Comité Polonais de Libération Nationale en France, they subordinated themselves to the Polish authorities in Warsaw. After the liberation of France in the summer of 1944, the Polish FTP/MOI created the Polish battalions of the First French Army, which returned to Poland in November 1945. Some tens of thousands of Polish miners were to follow them between 1946 and 1947 to help rebuild their homeland.

During the war, therefore, the Polish diaspora in France suffered from both the consequences of internal splits and the pressures of their joint experiences with the French. As a consequence, some, notably the young, chose the path of naturalisation and assimilation; others departed for Poland; while still others opted for an ever more marked retreat into a Polish identity.

Culture, education and the press

At the outset of this article, we noted the two fundamental legacies of Poland's modern history of conspiracy and of exile. To these we should add a third one that dates back to the nineteenth century, namely the conviction that 'our fatherland is our language and our culture'. In this way, the notion of the homeland becomes an immaterial concept, and exists within the Poles' consciousness of their national soul. This attitude was not without its negative side: the values it embraced and the pitfalls and dangers to which it could give rise became evident on occasions in recent years in influencing the opposition to the realities of the socialist era. The benefit of this attitude, however, as far as the phenomenon of exile is concerned, was the importance accorded to issues of culture, education, the press and book publishing. This could be observed in the initiatives taken by the government, by professional circles, and also by social and cultural organisations (especially the Polish Red Cross/PCK, the Polish YMCA and the White Cross, which was an organisation in charge of social and cultural activities in the army) and private individuals, everywhere where Polish communities were established. There had already been attempts to create a university in exile in France, but the fall of France did not allow sufficient time for it to come into existence. However, with financial support from the government and with the help of its delegate and of the TOPF, it was possible to establish a Polish *lycée*[11] at Villars de Lans (Isère) and organise a grant system for students and Sunday schools for children, as well as encourage the Polish scouts' activities. The 2e Division des Chasseurs à Pied (DSP), which, in order to avoid the capitulation of the French army in June 1940, managed to reach the Swiss border during the fighting, was interned; but during this internment it transformed itself into a real teaching centre, catering for different levels, including higher education at the University of Freiburg, even up to Ph.D. level.

It was in Britain that the conditions were best for education and cultural activity to flourish, with government subsidies and grants and benevolence on the part of British authorities and institutions. Special attention was paid to higher education, in view of the tragic losses suffered by the Polish intelligentsia and of the expected necessities of the post-war period. The University of Edinburgh proved to be the most hospitable host institution, as it enabled the creation of three Polish departments: a medical school (1941), a veterinary department and a teacher training department (1943). In Oxford, a law department was opened in 1944, while future architects were trained in Liverpool. Clusters of Polish grant-holders, who included officers on study leave, could also be found in several other university centres in England. The exceptional interest shown by the Poles in technical subjects encouraged the Polish authorities to create a special Committee for Higher Technical Studies, which looked after students' placements and results. It was mainly after the end of the war and the arrival of Polish armed forces from Italy, the Middle East, Germany, as well as the arrival of the re-mobilised soldiers from France and of thousands of civilian refugees that a massive influx of students – nearly 3,000 in 1947 – occurred, though numbers later decreased.

As was customary at the time, culture was mainly expressed through literature, since it was simultaneously a bearer of language, history, national values and traditions. Before the war, a small publishing company, Minerve, already existed in England, serving as a bridge between Polish and English literature, thanks to translated texts. After 1940, many others were created. Some furnished military libraries (which were operated by a special service in the Ministry of Defence) and published a selection of educational books, while others had more general goals. Among the latter were two private publishers: Ksiaznica Polska (The Polish Bookshop), run by Mrs. Jadwiga Harasowska in Glasgow (1940–1948) in collaboration with the Polish-Scottish Society, which had a wide range of publications, books in English and musical works; and Skladnica Ksiegarska (Polish Book Depot) in Edinburgh (1942–1946), which was more interested in 'classical' Polish literature. After 1944, the market was dominated by the subsidised publisher Orbis.

The British Minister of Information, Brendan Bracken, is reported to have said: 'if you ever come across a Pole, you will also find a Polish newspaper'. The press, both legal and illegal, became a real Polish speciality during the war. Researchers have itemised nearly 2,500 titles published between 1939 and 1945, and are still finding new titles, which were hitherto unknown. The number found in Britain is quite considerable: 270 titles for the war years; 280 for the period of demobilisation of the army; and 350 during the period from 1951 to 1993. The first Polish newspaper to appear in Britain was published by the sailors' union and was titled *Praca na morzu* (Work on the sea). The Polish press was concentrated in London (40 percent), but it was also prolific in Scotland (Edinburgh, Glasgow, Perth) and was generally subsidised by the government. There were also some opposition newspapers that were very critical of the government and had to struggle both against its pressures and the interference of British censorship (for instance by refusing them paper!). The newspapers, both the official ones such as *Dziennik Polski* (Polish newspaper) and those of political parties, generally stuck to an uncompromising line of intransigence concerning the principal issue of Polish politics, namely the relationship between Poland and the Soviet Union. Discussions on other issues, such as the nature of post-war Poland, were of secondary importance even when held between the political parties in the government.

The wealth of newspapers produced during the Polish exile is illustrated by figures for titles published in other countries: in France, 120 titles were published, among which around 50 appeared during the war years (the majority of which were clandestine); in Hungary,

50 titles; in Romania, 30 titles. In short, between 1939 and 1945, the Polish press outside Poland published around 800 titles, 434 of which were based in Europe. Analysis of their editorial trends and contents is beyond the scope of this article, but they were sometimes of a very high standard, both as regards professional journalistic standards and literature. The subjects that constantly recurred, apart from those always dear to publishers and readers, can be reduced to two: how to behave abroad in a dignified way; and, above all, how and with what to return to Poland?

A special case was that of the Polish Army of the East (APW), which operated alongside General Anders' army after the latter had been evacuated from the USSR to Iran in 1942, and subsequently to Palestine and Egypt via Iraq. With a fairly large population of civilians and semi-civilians, the so-called 'cadet schools' for boys and girls, several cultural institutions, book publishers and newspaper editors, among which the bulletin *Orzel Bialy* (The White Eagle), always kept its distance from a government that it considered to be too soft, it soon became 'a little Poland on wheels'. Its Office for Culture and Press created a publishing centre in Palestine, which published classical Polish literature, the works of scientific authors and scientists helpful to the APW and school books, and stimulated artistic activity. The resources of this office were later used in Italy as the basis for various political and cultural initiatives, such as the Polish cultural foundation, which survived the end of the war, the demobilisation of the army and the elimination of several other Polish institutions. This is also where the Parisian magazine *Kultura* (Culture), which still takes pride of place in Polish cultural and political life nowadays, had its roots.

Rescuing and helping to survive

Because of the situation in which Poland found itself during the war, it was imperative that the biological resources of the nation should be safeguarded (I use the term nation in the French rather than the Polish sense) everywhere where it was necessary and by all possible means. These measures constituted perhaps the most obviously social aspects of the social history of the war years. It would, however, be impossible to describe all of them, and I shall therefore restrict myself to describing the more important ones.

Within the government, these problems generally fell into the orbit of the Ministry of Social Protection, led by a socialist. The agencies and delegates of this ministry were implanted everywhere where Polish communities existed, in small or large numbers, near the camps of the civilians in Africa, in India, Iran and the Middle East, as well as in those locations where help for social welfare was organised in the form of collections of money, goods and medicines (for example, in New York, San Francisco, Calcutta and Teheran). Budgetary expenses of different kinds for social welfare purposes consumed 25–30 percent of the resources available: subsidies to refugees, parcels for prisoners of war, the activities of the Red Cross – which, in France, was termed the TOPF – and subsidies to people involved in cultural activities.[12] In the annual budgets of the government's Delegation in occupied Poland, direct social aid had the largest share (30 percent), but other expenses also had a social purpose, as in the case of those provided for social organisations, youth movements and the like (20 percent) and for clandestine teaching (18 percent). The latter was a unique phenomenon in occupied Europe, comprising all levels of teaching, from primary schools to academic higher education departments, including medicine, sciences and technology. The Government-in-Exile was therefore in the exceptional position of supplying funds for achieving some of the goals of social policy within the country.

One very specific problem was the fate of Polish citizens who had been deported to 'distant regions' (this was the official term for them) within the USSR. The government had been searching for ways and means of helping them since 1940, when the first information about mass deportations from the eastern regions of Poland reached them.[13] The government tried, without much success, to use the U.S.A. as a mediator, as well as the Japanese and the Red Cross. It was only thanks to the Sikorski-Mayski agreement of 30 July 1941 that access was finally possible to these people, who had been deprived of all of their rights.[14]

As a consequence of this agreement, an amnesty returned their freedoms, albeit relative ones, to those who had been deported, captured as prisoners of war or jailed. It was also possible – though such an event would have at one time been absolutely unthinkable in the USSR – to organise a network of delegates from the Polish embassy in Moscow and of 'trusted men', of warehouses for goods coming from abroad and of a distribution system for money and goods bought in different countries or received as donations. The 265,000 people who benefited from this aid received, on average, 1,043 roubles and 12.5 kg of goods (foodstuffs, clothes and shoes) per head.[15] For many, this assistance only just arrived in time.[16] But there was also another side to this aid: an immaterial, moral side, which was invaluable for people who, up until then, had been condemned to oblivion and were now taken under the protective wing of the state. Special attention was paid to children and the young.

The services of the embassy succeeded in setting up 175 nursery schools, 83 orphanages and 43 primary schools, which unfortunately catered for only for 10–11 percent of children and young people. Homes for the disabled, canteens, hospitals and dispensaries helped to the most needy.

This favourable situation did not last long, however. In 1942, with the evacuation of the Anders army, relations between the Polish government and the Soviet Union worsened. The Delegations of the embassy were closed down and several members of staff arrested, but most of the 'trusted men' were retained, which the Poles interpreted as a sign of the temporary nature of the situation in which they found themselves. In the spring of 1943, through a special decree, the Poles were deprived of their citizenship and once again turned into Soviet citizens. After the rupture in relations between the Polish Government and the Soviet authorities in April 1943, the whole system of so-called 'embassy aid' was taken over by the Association of Polish Patriots (ZPP) and by the mixed organisation which operated within the Soviet administration, the Management Committee for Polish Children in the USSR. This committee deserves to be remembered for all it did for Polish children in this difficult period, at least for those who found themselves under its protection.

After the war, in particular from 1946 onwards, it was usually the ZPP that organised the repatriation of the Poles from the 'distant regions' of the USSR. The activity of the ZPP goes beyond the scope of our story, but I shall, nevertheless, allow myself a few personal reflections on the matter. The nature and the activity of this organisation were based on a mixture of Soviet inspiration and of many initiatives from the Poles who found themselves on Soviet territory, notably regarding cultural issues. The head office of the ZPP published a number of titles from classical Polish literature. To this extent, the parallel with the Polish centres in the West was obvious, but in these local groups in the Soviet Union cultural life operated in very different ways. There is now a tendency among historians to remain silent about the ZPP or to condemn it on the basis of its initial Soviet origins. However, as with all historical phenomena, it is necessary to take into account both the historical context, especially the situation in which, at the time, the Polish Government in general and the Poles in particular in the USSR found themselves, and the role of the ZPP as a factor in the USSR's Polish policy. In addition, in my opinion, one has to recognise that the primary issues for those hundreds of thousands of people who had experienced deportation were their survival and their return to Poland. The military aspects of the ZPP's activities, notably the role of the First Polish Army, which was created under the patronage of the ZPP in the USSR, are outside the domain of this article. Nevertheless, it is perhaps worth underlining the fact that its advent and its contribution to the fighting on the Eastern Front had a very beneficial influence on the legal, moral and material situation of the Polish population in the USSR, which had become very difficult after the departure of the Anders Army in 1942.[17]

Regarding the issue of citizenship, it should be mentioned that the Soviet authorities refused to grant Polish citizenship to Jews, Ukrainians and Belorussians, which caused – among other consequences – serious incidents during the evacuation of the Anders army to Iran.[18] After the breakdown in relations between the Polish Government and the Soviet Union, Jews became Poles again from the perspective of the Soviet authorities, but this was not the case for Ukrainians. What we might term the legal situation of the Poles in the USSR had been, up until the first repatriation of 1945–1948, fairly ambiguous: they were, so to speak, 'Polish citizens in suspension' or even 'half and half citizens'. A few tens of thousands nevertheless remained in the USSR after the war, either because they had been prevented from leaving by the Soviet public services, or for personal reasons (health, mixed marriages, a tolerable material situation, etc.).

During the evacuation of the Anders army, more than 40,000 civilians left the USSR. Quite a few of them remained with the army until the departure of the fighting units for Italy. The majority, especially women, children and invalids, stayed for a while in camps that had been set up in Iran, from where they were transported to other camps, this time in India (more than 22,000 people were transferred to Janagar, not far from Karachi) and later to Africa (where there were 16,000 in February 1944) where they settled in Tanganyika, Uganda, Rhodesia, Kenya and in the case of a few hundred children, in South Africa. A fairly large number also found themselves in Algeria. The U.S.A. refused to take any refugees, but in 1943 Mexico agreed to welcome more than 1,450 children, together with accompanying adults. They were all placed in Santa Rosa (Leon), a cross between a holiday camp and a school, of which these children retained fond memories. All of these refugees found themselves under the supervision of the Ministry for Social Welfare, which supported them financially, until they were transferred to Britain in 1946.[19] No in-depth studies have been carried out concerning the experience of these thousands of Poles in such extraordinary geographical, ethnic and cultural conditions. However, from the quite substantial archival material available, the impression that emerges is of a secluded life, with all the consequences inherent in it that are

well-known to socio-psychologists, of a life on the fringe of everything that was happening in the world. Those affected developed the
characteristics typical of people dependent on aid, a syndrome that
proved to be very destructive for the social, psychological and moral
values of these people, the majority of whom were women. Their
cultural and social activities in the artistic, intellectual and educational spheres were always at odds with the tendency to remain
passive and indifferent, or all too often, unfortunately, to lead a friv-
olous life. Devoid of obligations and responsibilities, they led lives
that were on hold, merely surviving from day to day. This social and
psychological experience deserves further investigation.

Poland, but which one. . . ?

For two centuries, this haunting question has been ever-present in
Polish history. War, the occupation and the change in the ruling
political forces brought it once again to the centre of Polish political life. Everyone shared the belief that radical reforms in the social
and economic order were necessary and unavoidable. The progressive radicalisation of the opinions of the Polish population,
especially those of peasants, called for clear answers, that were com-
patible with their desires and their expectations. There was a
general mood of anticipation, and it was the government's task to
prepare and present a programme for the Poland of the future. But,
the Polish Government-in-Exile, with the Prime Minister as its
spokesman, expressed very moderate opinions on these problems
and contented itself with generalities about republicanism, democracy and the equality of all citizens. The leaders of the Polish
Resistance urged the government to go further, particularly after the
advent of the Polish Workers' Party (PPR) in January 1942 and the
popularity of its radical slogans, especially among the poorest peasants. But they were told that the government did not want to outbid
the PPR, and all of these constitutional questions were referred to
the decisions of the Constituent Assembly that had been summoned
to meet after the liberation of the country. Nevertheless, some effort
was made to respond to the demands for political and social
change. Unfortunately, however, the draft legislation that was prepared by the Committee for Reform of the Political System (KSU),
specially created for this purpose within the National Council in
London, was very conservative and avoided even excluding the possibility of a monarchical restoration in Poland.[20] This bill was
heavily criticised, especially by the socialists, and was rejected and
replaced with a simple and fairly superficial declaration by the

government on 24 February 1942. This second declaration nevertheless stood out from the initial bill by its promise of an agrarian reform, the most pressing socio-economic problem, even if it predicated Christian values as the spiritual basis for the State and defined Catholicism as the favoured religion. After the KSU had been disbanded, constitutional issues were entrusted to the Ministry of Justice, but until the end of the war no progress was made in this area.

The political parties did not share the hesitations of the government. Nearly all of them developed their own programmes, which shared similar opinions on issues such as republicanism and democracy, but were deeply divided on economic and social questions. For the socialists, peasants and trade unionists, the principal priorities were agrarian reform to eliminate the relics of feudalism, the division of the estates of the local gentry, the fight against unemployment and equal rights for all citizens without distinction. In addition, they called for the nationalisation, communalisation and co-operativisation of large sectors of the economy, a greater role for state intervention and planning in economic life, local and regional autonomy and the right for the state and the district council to control private enterprises as well as establishing work as the basis of all the socio-economic structure and ensuring social aid for all sectors of the population. Special importance was accorded to education, which was to become free and accessible to all with a system of financial assistance for the young of less-favoured families. These programmes also highlighted 'Europeanist' ideas and voiced the aspiration that Poland should become a member of 'the association of free peoples in Europe'. The programme of the peasants, which was, of course, very agrarian in character, laid great stress on the measures that were to stimulate the development of education and thereby favour cultural life in the countryside, overcome backwardness and favour its own success in this sector.

The Political Liaison Committee, the PKP, established on 15 August 1943 and, subsequently, the Council of National Unity, created in March 1944, felt themselves to be caught between the pressure of public opinion on one side and the silence of the government on the other. As a result, they also set out their programmes, thereby openly challenging and criticising the government. In some of their details, these programmes were somewhat more moderate, but in others (such as agrarian reform and their vision of a state-directed economy) they proposed very radical measures. The programmes of the Nationals, the Sanacja and the Party of Work veered away from this tendency towards political and social radicalism. Instead, they placed the emphasis on private

property as the basis of economic life, on a privileged role for the
Catholic church and on the preservation of the major agricultural
estates and, therefore, also of the local gentry.

Before the war, Poland was a multinational state, with nearly a
third of its population composed of Ukrainians, Jews, Belorussians
and Germans, as well as lesser numbers of other nationalities. The
question of national minorities was, therefore, one of the most
burning issues, both in terms of wartime problems and programmes
for the future. There was no tendency to retreat from the idea of re-
establishing Poland with its 1939 borders, at least with regard to
the east, where the bulk of the non-Polish population was located.
Instead, most programmes, including the one issued by the government in 1942, and those of the parties, assured full civil rights to the
minorities as well as cultural freedom, but sometimes subjected the
exercise of these freedoms to the condition of their loyalty to
Poland. On this issue, too, the Nationals and the Party of Work differed from the others, because they were in favour of the forced
polonisation of the minorities and of forced emigration for the Jews.

In this respect, it seems useful to consider some aspects of the
Jewish problem in the context of the realities of the time. This is
always difficult to do, not least because of the clichéd perception of
the 'inherent anti-Semitism of the Poles' and I do not wish to
become polemical, as I am all too familiar with the arguments and
also, alas, with the resentments of the different parties. As I have
already mentioned, the Jews were the only minority represented on
the National Council and in the government, where there were two
Jewish ministers. In the structures of the Delegation in occupied
Poland, a special service for helping the Jews (code-named 'Zegota')
had been created, funded by the Delegation and by the world Jewish organisations; the funds were sent to Poland by the networks of
'special liaisons' such as messengers and parachute drops. Through
all the possible means of communication, the Polish government
was informed (by the Delegation and the Jewish organisations that,
by means of Delegation radios, sent their calls for help) of the atrocities perpetrated by the Germans against the Jews. The most
accurate information concerning the extermination of the Jews in
Poland was sent by special messenger, Jan Karski, who presented it
to the governmental authorities of the Allied powers and the representatives of the Jewish world organisation, but the information he
conveyed was not taken seriously. The President of the Supreme
Court of the U.S.A., Judge Frankfurter, simply threw him out. It
should also be noted that the directives of the British Political Warfare Executive (PWE) of the time (at the end of 1942 and the
beginning of 1943) had strictly forbidden any reference to the issue

in order not to add fresh fuel to Goebbels' propaganda, according to which the Allies were only waging war in order to protect the Jews' interests. It was to protest against the silence of the Allies concerning the uprising in the Warsaw ghetto that the Jewish representative on the Polish National Council in London, Szmul Zygelbojm[21] committed suicide on 12 May 1943 to draw attention to the suffering of the Jews. His act of sacrifice failed, however, to provoke a commensurate reaction on the part of those to whom it was addressed.

It should be noted here that Poland was the only country in occupied Europe in which anyone who helped the Jews, even only by giving them a chunk of bread, was threatened with death, very often together with their entire family. Without citing the number of people saved, I shall simply confine myself to noting that the most numerous group of 'trees of the just men' in the gardens of Yad-Vashem are those of Poles. Their number certainly exceeds those of the crosses erected nowadays by zealots at Auschwitz-Birkenau. Acting on his own initiative and with the approval of the London Government-in-Exile, the representative of the government in France, with the help of the TOPF, also tried to help the Polish Jews, many of whose nationality papers were not in order.[22] He co-operated with the Jewish organisations active in France (only of course in the Southern zone!) and he tried to make use of his personal connections with the Vichy authorities. Initially, these interventions were rather limited, but, with the threats of deportation in 1942, they were carried out on a much larger scale (the provision of papers, money, parcels and hiding-places, for example), notably in the French internment camps. They also tried to discover ways of helping the Jews to emigrate, but the steps taken by the Polish embassies and consular services to grant visas were resisted in the U.S.A., Britain, Latin America and even the Belgian Congo. Some people, albeit not very many, were helped to escape from France to Switzerland and Spain through the clandestine routes established by the Polish Resistance in France. All in all, the truth was tragic. One could help and even save individuals, but not the thousands of Polish Jews living in France, who formed the majority of the victims of the Shoah in the country.

A very painful incident in Polish-Jewish relations took place in 1944, caused by the desertion of a group of Jewish soldiers serving in the Polish units in Britain. This event triggered off a major campaign in the Jewish press that denounced anti-Semitism in the Polish army, and which was taken up by the English and American newspapers. Even today, it remains unclear how far this affair was based on facts and to what extent it was inspired by groups external to the army.

As for the other minorities, not a single representative of the Ukrainians could be found who would be prepared to commit himself to collaborating with the Polish authorities. The intensive negotiations with the representatives of the Ukrainian nationalist movement did not result in a positive outcome. From the spring of 1943 until the massive resettlement of the Polish population after 1945, the eastern borderlands of former Poland had become the scene of an atrocious fratricidal war between Poland and the Ukraine, comparable with the ones in Yugoslavia during World War II and in the 1990s. The Poles did not emerge victorious, and the aftermath of the war is still imprinted in the Poles' conscience and in the reciprocal images that both nations have of one another. Relations with the Belorussians were uncomplicated, but attempts were made at arriving at a settlement with the Lithuanians on the basis of the history of Polish-Lithuanian collaboration. The Lithuanian party, however – which was also engaged in collaboration with the Third Reich – refused. On the battlefields, the Polish partisans emphatically defeated the Lithuanian regular military formations. This did not improve the relationships, either political or emotional, between the two nations and left a strong feeling of resentment among the Lithuanians.

Twilight

The last ministry of the government in London headed by Tomasz Arciszewski found itself isolated. Its authority became virtually non-existent in Poland after the tragedy of the Warsaw insurrection. The installation of the authorities of the Polish Committee of National Liberation and the presence of the Red Army in Poland, as well as the ever stronger and natural tendency of the population to adapt to the new living conditions and, above all, to recover a more or less normal life, militated against the government recovering its former power. In addition, the negotiations of the three great powers about the fate of Poland, which took place without Arciszewski's Government's knowledge or participation, did not offer it much hope for the future. Neither the arrest of sixteen leaders of the clandestine state in February 1945 nor their trial and subsequent conviction in Moscow during the Potsdam Conference caused any reaction on the Allies' part, except perhaps of some relief. The eventful history of the Polish clandestine state had in effect come to an end.

In the days between 3 and 5 July 1945, the fate of the government was sealed by the declaration of the Allied governments. The issue of the fate of hundreds of thousands of Poles was, however, still pending, including soldiers as well as civilians who were concentrated on the British Isles (about 150,000 of them in 1945–46) in Germany (30,000 soldiers and about 280,000 civilians in the displaced persons camps) and in France. Churchill had promised them after Yalta 'the Citizenship and freedoms of the British Empire...'. But the Labour Government did not feel bound by this statement, even though it acknowledged its responsibility for their fate. This might be settled by repatriation (the favoured solution of the British) or by their settling to live and work in Britain and elsewhere, in other words, by emigrating. In 1945–46, nearly 40,000 people returned home from Britain, but they were replaced by successive influxes of Polish immigrants, notably from Africa, the Middle East, France, Germany and Italy.

The cases of military personnel – in total around 250,000 men – were in the hands of the Cabinet Polish Forces Committee (headed by Hugh Dalton, and later on by Sir Francis Newsam) created in March 1946, which organised the Polish Resettlement Corps (Polski Korpus Przysposobienia i Rozmieszczenia, PKPR) dependent on the Home Office and not the War Office. The unpaid volunteers were given two years to secure a job and learn English. Some very difficult and sometimes shameful problems arose because of the attitude of the recalcitrants (15,000 in 1947) who did not accept any of the solutions proposed to them. Some of them were even imprisoned and many were deported to Germany and demobilised. A number of these cases were raised in Parliament, but a change had taken place in British public opinion. The Poles had become burdensome foreigners and, even worse, troublemakers who were not liked. The Trades Union Congress viewed them with suspicion and regarded them as competitors for jobs. The speech of a Labour M.P., J.B. Hynd, on 1 December 1944 in the House of Commons reveals the essential nature of this situation:

> I would refer to the peculiar change in the attitude of the Government and political circles generally to our own Ally Poland during the last two or three months. We find the Poles, who after all played such a tremendous part in the Battle of Britain, and formed such a considerable portion of those few to whom so many owed so much [an allusion to Winston Churchill's words in 1940], those Poles for whom we understood we went to war in the first instance, who were defending a mighty tradition of independence and democracy and national integrity, are now being toned down, and in our Press and political circles those great emotions which inspired them to put a tremendous stand against the Nazi menace are now becoming a romantic conception, which they really should be prepared to lay aside and see the realities of politics and the realities of dependence on neighbouring Governments . . .

After the recognition of the Polish Government was withdrawn, responsibility for Polish civilians was taken over by the Interim Treasury Committee for Polish Questions (ITC) which made considerable use of Polish staff. It managed all the possessions of the government and its institutions and its subsidiaries. In particular, the educational branch of the ITC dealt with the Polish educational system with very evident success.[23] At first, the Polish civilian population in Britain was settled in the camps administered by the National Assistance Board (in 1949 there were still 459 refugee camps left with about 100,000 inhabitants). They tried to help the people in these camps to adapt to living in Britain or other countries, mainly by providing technical training through the courses organised by the Committee for Education of Poles. All of this activity however came to an end in 1954, however.

As a result, one would not be mistaken in asserting that the real Polish exile started after the war. Very little research has been carried out into this process of readjustment as regards the people who were repatriated as well as the others who chose emigration, to employ the terms used in Poland. For many, especially the regular soldiers or civil servants, it was very often synonymous with social and moral debasement, the sad, humiliating and sometimes tragic evidence of which is often evoked in reports and in the press today. In 1956, a survey was carried out among the academics who had remained expatriated. Out of 185 living in Britain, only fifty-four had found a job closely related to their profession – in most cases they were mathematicians or technicians – whereas those who dealt with the social sciences were in a genuinely difficult position. Those in other countries fared little better: those who had achieved success did not amount to more than 40 percent of the total, with the highest success rate being in the U.S.A.. By contrast, the intellectuals, artists and scientists who had returned to so-called 'People's Poland' were, for the most part, welcomed back as prodigal sons. However, that is quite another story.

The numerous Polish organisations and institutions that had survived in exile on government subsidies now had to adapt to completely different conditions and live on their own financial means or disappear. Many of them have been successful, and there remain numerous social and cultural institutions, newspapers and publications, the origins of which date back to the war period. Several of them, such as the Parisian Kultura, the Polish Library in Paris[24] and the Józef Pilsudski Institute in New York, became well integrated in Polish culture and their existence is still highly appreciated.

The Polish Government-in-Exile continued to exist, but as an institution outside international politics, deprived of diplomatic privileges and preferences and undergoing several conflicts and schisms. The Polish exile during the war changed into a successive but quite separate and sometimes even rather isolated layer of the Polish diaspora, whose attitude towards the government took different forms and evolved in response to the more or less liberalising evolutions of the political regime in Poland.[25] What united these new immigrants to Britain was the solidarity of military veterans, a nostalgia for the Poland of days gone by, as well as hatred for Soviet Russia and an uncompromising animosity against People's Poland. Damaging attempts to launch political or other initiatives in Poland sometimes led to tragedies. Any clandestine activity in Poland, initiated from a foreign country, came within the scope of the civil-war actions from 1944 to 1948 or of the Cold War. As time passed, the evolution and differentiation of the attitudes of the Polish diaspora – which is traditionally known as the Polish emigration in Poland – also influenced this war-emigration in its relations with People's Poland. But that again is another story.

According to the memoirs of Lord Moran, Churchill, who was once again at the head of His Majesty's Government in 1951, took an interest in the fate of the Poles who had remained in Britain, especially in that of those whose situation was not very prosperous, such as the highly-decorated airmen who were working as porters in restaurants, or generals who were employed as manual workers. He was conscience-stricken, Lord Moran wrote, and wanted to repair some of the injustices they had suffered, which he indeed managed to do in some cases . . . *Si non e vero, e bene trovato* . . .

Notes

* Translated by Christine Arthur.

1. The 'great Polish literature' which plays an essential part in Polish culture, was created in exile; the father of modern Polish historical sciences, Joachim Lelwel, worked in Brussels after the failure of the November insurrection in 1830; and Frederic Chopin left his country for France at the same time.

2. The reports of the Soviet police, the NKVD, give the figure of 389,382 former Polish citizens on the territory of the USSR in September 1941. But, by selecting this particular date, these reports avoid any mention of the mortality rate, which had been at its height in the previous period, especially during the disastrous winter of 1940–1941, when it reached approximately 15 percent. It improved slightly the following year, varying from 5 to 10 percent, depending on the area. The total figure included the 81,217 Jews whose Polish citizenship had been disputed for a long time by the Soviet authorities, but did not include the Ukrainians, Belorussians and other minorities or the Polish citizens who had been conscripted against their will into the Red Army in 1940 and 1941.

Consequently, I shall avoid proposing any approximate figures here. In recent years, figures in the region of 650,000 have been quoted, but – like all the others – they are only based on rough estimates.

3. President I. Moscicki, who had been interned in Romania, appointed through a predated decree, M.W. Raczkiewicz, the political representative of the Sanacja and President of the World Organisation of Poles abroad, as his successor. Raczkiewicz designated, as had been previously agreed, Sikorski as the Prime Minister and Commander-in-Chief of the Polish armed forces abroad.

4. The Workers Party (SP), which was very close to General Sikorski and I. Paderewski and was actively involved in the creation of the Polish Government-in-Exile, was far from being a *travailliste* party. It was rather right-wing and could be described as a Christian-democratic party. The strongest was the PSL, the Peasants party. The Socialists and the National parties underwent numerous schisms.

5. The GG was created in the central part of Poland, which was divided into districts and extended after June 1941 to the Galician district on the furthest south-eastern boundaries of pre-war Poland.

6. Several radio transmitters were captured by the Germans, but not by the Funkspiele.

7. There were several routes served by bases in Hungary, Romania, Istanbul, Switzerland, France, Sweden and Portugal.

8. Between 1939 and 1945, through various channels, the country received the total sum of 27 million US dollars, 350,000 of which were in gold, 2,000 in pounds sterling, and 4,000 in Deutsche Mark in gold, 4 million in DM and 90 million of so-called 'occupation money' as well as 1,500 roubles in gold. Most of this sum went to the AK but the so-called 'forest detachments' (the partisans), both from the AK and from other groups, tended to live on resources they found on the ground. The annual budget of the Delegation was the equivalent of 400,000 pounds sterling. The losses amounted to approximately 12 percent.

9. The community of Polish immigrants in the United States had demonstrated distinctive characteristics since before the First World War. It was mainly composed of people – essentially poor and illiterate peasants – who came from regions of former Poland that had been annexed by Russia, Prussia and Austria, and who therefore had citizenship of these countries. It was once they were settled in the United States as immigrants that, as a society, they became aware of their national consciousness, over and above their administrative nationality. This consciousness was impregnated with some very characteristic traits, notably a mixture of various complexes that included a parochial sense of religion that expressed itself in the belief that 'Polish=Catholic' and a pride in 'those who have succeeded' in their parents' eyes, which was very characteristic of the Polish countryside. Before 1918, they considered themselves to be 'the fourth part of Poland', the part that was 'free' compared with the others that were under the yoke of the three oppressing powers.

10. The community of Polish immigrants in France, which was fairly uniform in terms of its socio-professional criteria, nevertheless had profoundly different origins. One section, called the 'Westphalians', came to France from Germany after 1918, after being invited by the French to revive the coal and heavy industry, which had been devastated by the war. The 'Westphalians' had already experienced a hard life as immigrants in a foreign and hostile society, and were used to fighting for their rights, their customs and their religion. They came to France with their organisations, their priests, elites, press and, above all, with their very conservative attitude, typical of the 'Polish-Catholic' immigrants, and to some extent sympathetic to the appeals of the government. The influential

chief editor of the newspaper representing this community, *Narodowiec* (The National), M. Kwiatkowski escaped from France in 1940 and joined the National Council.

11. The Lycée carried on the traditions of the old Polish 'Ecole Batignole' in Paris. Its students and teachers behaved heroically in the tragic battle of the FFI Resistance forces on the Vercors plateau in July 1944; many fell in the battle or were shot afterwards.

12. Almost all of the finances of the Polish Government-in-Exile came from loans: at the outset, from France (600 million francs) which were not fully used; from Britain (5 million pounds, renewed annually); and from the United States (12.5 million dollars in 1942, renewed annually). The gold reserves of the Polish bank, which had been evacuated in 1939, were 'interned' by the Vichy government at Dakar, but, in retaliation, the Poles were able to impound legally the French gold in the U.S.A., which was transported to Communist Poland after the war. The repayment of the loans gave rise to many difficulties.

13. There were four principal periods of deportation: 10 and 14 February, 28–29 June 1940, 28 May and 12 June 1941. The first two were part of a large operation that took place in all of the territories which had been annexed by the USSR in 1939 and 1940. During the third one, there was a greater number of Jews. During the 1941 deportation, affecting the Polish regions, the large proportion of Ukrainians that lived there was also deported. This also encompassed the Baltic populations.

14. The deportees who were administratively classed as 'special displaced people' (*specpieriesielency* in Russian) were deprived of their rights as citizens: their identity cards (the so-called 'passports') were taken away, as well as other documents essential to daily life. Tied to the places where they lived and worked, they were subjected to the supervision and the will of the commandants of the NKVD.

15. Following the Sikorski-Mayski agreement, the Polish Government received a loan of 100 million roubles from the Soviet Government in order to finance aid for the Polish citizens who had benefited from the amnesty. Between January 1942 and May 1943, expenses amounted to: 107,284,573 roubles for general social aid; 25,962,347 roubles for social organisations; and 56,561,629 roubles (according to the records of the Polish Embassy in Kuybychev, Hoover Institution, Document No. 35/136) for allowances. There were therefore two different sources for financing this action: the Soviet loan, only a part of which was used, and the means of the Polish Government itself. It is impossible to assess exactly the costs of this social operation, because, for various reasons, the reports do not tally.

16. I make this point as an historian, but also as a witness, as I experienced the situation at first hand.

17. On this point too, I can rely on my own experience.

18. To simplify the situation, it could be presented as follows: the Soviet authorities warned the Polish Government that if they found one single Jew on the train, they would stop the train. They explained to the representatives of the Jewish population that it was the Poles who refused to take the Jewish evacuees onboard. Despite the Soviet action, 4–5,000 Jews were evacuated with the army, among whom were some Zionist militants (such as M. Begin, the future Israeli Prime Minister) and a few hundred members of the religious organisation. Nearly 3,000 left the army in Palestine, very often by deserting, and were generally not pursued by the Polish army. Several later found themselves in the Zionist organisation, the Haganah, and in the Israeli army (for instance General Dayan). Around 1,000 fought bravely in the units of the Anders army in Italy.

This affair left a bad legacy in the history of relations between the Jews and the Poles. The explanations given in this contribution cannot and do not attempt to omit antisemitism, which was not rare in this army, and they do not tackle the issue – which was frequently mentioned at the time – of the pro-Soviet attitudes displayed by some Jewish social classes between 1939 and 1941.

19. The word 'return' was also used, which was highly significant.
20. There was some support for this idea. People even talked about the possibility of appointing the Duke of Kent as a candidate to the Polish throne.
21. Read 'Chmoul Siegelboym'.
22. There were many reasons for this. The most difficult cases were those of the people who had come to France shortly after 1918 and who had arrived from places newly included within the borders of Poland, but who had not bothered about the regularisation of their current nationality. Many other problems were caused by the obstructiveness of the consular services.
23. During the 1946–47 school-year, there were twenty-one schools of all levels, with 1,607 students; in 1949, fifty-seven schools with nearly 5,500 students and grant-holders; near the end of the ITC, in 1954, in the twenty-nine schools there were still 2,360 students and grant-holders. Later on, this structure was taken over by the United Nations Refugee Programme.
24. This Polish institution, dating back to the nineteenth century, was run for many years by the son of Adam Mickiewicz, the greatest Polish poet. During the Occupation, it was devastated by the Germans, but after being restored after the war, it played a great part as the centre of cultural life for Poles living in France as well as for historic research in its archives.
25. At the time, people used to joke about 'Poland being the merriest barracks in the Socialist camp'.

References

Z. Blazynski, ed., *Wladze RP na obczyznie podczas II Wojny Swiatowej 1939–1945*, London, 1994.

Ibid, *Materialy do dziejów polskiego uchodzstwa niepodleglosciowego, 1939–1990*, London, 1996.

E. Duraczynski, *Rzad polski na uchodzstwie, 1939–1945*, Warsaw, 1993.

E. Duraczynski and R. Turkowski, *O Polsce na uchodzstwie: Rada Narodowa Rzeczypospolitej Polskiej, 1939–1945*, Warsaw, 1997.

Y. Gutman, 'Jews in General Anders' Army in the Soviet Union' in *Yad Vashem Studies* 12 (1977): pp. 231–96.

M. Hulas, *Goscie czy intruzi? Rzad polski na uchodzstwie, wrzesien lipiec 1939–1943*, Warsaw, 1996.

W. Jedrzejewicz, ed., *Poland in the British Parliament, 1939–1945*, vol. 3 (Summer 1944–Summer 1945), New York, 1962.

L. Klisiewicz, ed., *Mobilizacja uchodzstwa polskiego do walki Politycznej, 1945–1990*, London, 1995.

B. Korzec and J. Buzko, *Le gouvernement polonais en exil et la persécution des Juifs en France en 1942*, Paris, 1997.

M. Kridl, M. Malinowski and J. Wittlin, ed., *Polska mysl demokratyczna w ciagu wieków. Antologia*, Warsaw, 1983.

J. Michel, 'La Seconde Guerre Mondiale et l'évolution de la communauté polonaise du Nord de la France', in *La Revue du Nord* 57 (1975): pp. 403–20.

S. Lewandowska, *Prasa polskiej emigracji wojennej, 1939–1945*, Warsaw, 1993.

W. Pobóg-Malinowski, *Najnowsza historia polityczna Polski*, vol. 3, London, 1960.

P.J. Potichnyi, ed., *Poland and Ukraine – Past and Present*, Edmonton-Toronto, 1980.

T. Prekerowa, *Konspiracyjna Rada Pomocy Zydom w Warszawie, 1942–1945*, Warsaw, 1981.

Ibid, *Zarys zydów dziejów zydów w Polsce w latach 1939–1945*, Warsaw, 1992.

K.R. Sword, '"Their Prospects will not be Bright": British responses to the problem of the Polish "Recalcitrants", 1946–1949', in *Journal of Contemporary History* 21 (1986): pp. 367–90.

A. Szkuta, ed., *Kierownictwo obozu niepodleglosciowego na obczyznie, 1945–1990*, London, 1996.

R. Torzecki, *Polacy i Ukraincy: sprawa ukrainska w czasie II wojny swiatowej na terenie II Rzeczypospolitej*, Warsaw, 1993.

E. Trela, *Polskie placówki oswiatowe i wychowawcze w Zwiazku Radzieckim w latach 1943–1946*, Wroclaw, 1981.

M. Turlejska, ed., *Deklaracje i rozwazania programowe organizacji konspiracyjnych, 1940–1944*, Warsaw, 1967.

T. Wolsza, *Rzad RP na obczyznie wobec wydarzen w kraju, 1945–1950*, Warsaw, 1998.

J.E. Zamojski, 'Polskie formacje wojskowe w ZSRR w latach II Wojny swiatowej', in *Mniejszosci Polskie w ZSRR*, Krakow, 1992, pp. 83–86.

J.E. Zamojski, 'The Clandestine Military College of the Academic Camp of the Polish 2nd Infantry Riflemen Division in Freiburg (Switzerland), 1941–1944', in *Universities during World War II*, Krakow, 1984, pp. 99–115.

Ibid, *Polacy w ruchu oporu we Francji, 1940–1945*, Warsaw, 1975.

Ibid, 'La presse clandestine polonaise en France pendant la Seconde Guerre mondiale', in *Acta Poloniae Historica* 56 (1987): pp. 85–126.

Z. Zaremba, *Wojna i konspiracja*, London, 1991.

P. Zaron, *Kierunek wschodni w strategii wojskowo – politycznej gen. Wladyslawa Sikorskiego, 1940–1943*, Warsaw, 1988.

12

France in Exile: The French Community in Britain, 1940–1944

Nicholas Atkin

Much of the history of French exiles in Britain has been written from the perspective of high politics. Inevitably, these accounts have focused on the personality and politics of de Gaulle; the evolution of *la France Libre* and its uneasy relationship with the British Government, typified by the events surrounding the arrest of Admiral Muselier; the intellectual life of exiles such as André Labarthe and Raymond Aron; and the unsuccessful efforts of semi-official Vichy emissaries, notably Professor Rougier, to open a line of dialogue with Churchill.[1] Generals, admirals and professors thus occupy the centre stage to the neglect of those other French exiles, the 'Forgotten French', who also sought refuge in Britain during the *années noires*.[2] Crudely speaking, this disparate community comprised the following: refugees, albeit small in number; servicemen, principally sailors, marooned in Britain after the Franco-German Armistice; Vichyite representatives and consular officials; and a long-established French colony, largely settled in London and the South-East. The purpose of this chapter is to examine the nature of these groups and how they adapted to life in exile. At the same time, it considers how the British authorities monitored the welfare and outlook of French nationals. The picture that emerges is one of an extremely fragmented community: one that struggled to acclimatise to life abroad; one which was bitterly divided on ideological grounds; and one which frequently exasperated and bemused both the British Government and public.

I

Of the groups making up the French community in exile, it is the refugees that have received the least attention, partly because the whole issue of the reception of these unfortunate civilians in 1940 has been neglected by historians and partly because the quantity of French refugees was small, never totalling more than 4,000, roughly a tenth of all refugees that entered this country.[3] The reasons why so few French escaped to Britain are not difficult to fathom. There was first the speed of the German invasion which quickly cut off any escape routes from northern ports. Bewildered and frightened, the majority caught up in the *exode* headed inland, some making for southern resort towns, which, as Roderick Kedward reminds us, they had first known as part of the 'paid holidays' introduced by the Popular Front.[4] The Armistice of 22 June, the division of France into two principal zones and the subsequent creation of the Vichy Government further stemmed the flow of civilians, as did the appeal of Pétainism which effectively 'immobilised' much of the population. Although the defeat was greeted with dismay, many men and women looked to the marshal, the ultimate symbol of patriotism and courage, as their saviour, a man who would protect them in these desperate hours.[5] In any case, what was the point of trying to make the difficult and dangerous journey to Britain, no friend of France since Mers-el-Kébir, and a country soon to be defeated by Germany?

Across the Channel, Britain had naturally supposed that the overwhelming numbers of refugees would be from the Low Countries; the French would look after their own, as had happened in the last war.[6] Yet the rapidity of the German advance and the sweeping aside of the Dutch, Belgian and French governments threw British calculations into confusion. Initially, French refugees were caught up with other nationalities, and were processed in much the same way by the authorities, notably through the Central Committee for War Refugees from Holland, Belgium and France and the local war refugee committees. It was not long, however, before a bewildering array of organisations had been formed to look specifically after the welfare of French civilians, supplanting the efforts of such bodies as the Women's Royal Voluntary Service, an indicator perhaps that even in these dark hours the French community in Britain retained a strong sense of national pride. Among these bodies, may be counted the Comité d'Assistance aux Familles des Soldats Français; Les Français de Grande-Bretagne (FGB), allied closely to the Free French; the Société de Bienfaisance, dealing with the French colony; the Société des Anciens Combattants et Mutilés, handling veterans of the Great War; and the Comité d'Entr'aide aux Français en Grande Bretagne (CEAF).[7]

Of these groups, it was the last of these that became the most influential in the provision of welfare. As an undated Foreign Office memo recalled, it had been founded in the first week of August 1940, and was one of the many organisations that fell under the aegis of the Comité Central Permanent de la Colonie Française de Londres.[8] Its objectives, outlined in an open letter of August 1940, were to provide French refugees with financial and material assistance, shelter and lodging, meals at reduced prices, medical and hospital services, offers of employment, education, help over communications with the mother country and even advice on repatriation.[9] Although originally very much a creation of the French colony, CEAF was soon presided over by the indomitable Lady Warwick and enjoyed amicable dealings with Lord Bessborough's Committee on French Welfare, a sub-department of the Foreign Office the remit of which was to examine all questions affecting French nationals in the British Isles. Interestingly, CEAF also worked well with the French Consulate in Bedford Square, and advised all French nationals to make contact with this Vichy outpost.[10] As the war progressed, Lady Warwick's organisation took on broader responsibilities, looking after men demobilised from de Gaulle's forces, civilians of *la colonie française*, and the employment rights of French nationals working in Britain. Following the D-Day landings, it held glorified bring-and-buy sales at the Grosvenor Hotel to help the needy across the Channel.[11]

It is largely thanks to the efforts of CEAF that we have some insight into the social composition of French refugees in Britain. Whereas the Home Office despaired at the failure of these visitors to register through the proper channels, Lady Warwick composed a detailed card index of all French refugees stranded in Britain.[12] She counted 2,046 with addresses and a further 1,693 for whom there were no addresses, making a total of 3,739. While she was unable to obtain addresses for these 1,693, she was able to uncover other details about their lives. As one would expect of any refugee community, it was extremely eclectic in nature, comprising men, women and large numbers of children and students. Three groups, however, stand out. First, there was a sizeable quantity of fishermen, 106 in number, based in Devon and Cornwall. According to the Committee on French Welfare, many of these men had begun to arrive after 19 June having left Boulogne and the Breton coast 'in a panic', some being transferred to particularly unsuitable housing in Tottenham, London, before being returned to Penzance and Newlyn.[13] Not surprisingly, they proved to be an impermanent community: some left for France, while others went to work in Cornwall, where concerted efforts were made to look after their welfare. A second feature of Lady Warwick's list was the number of priests and novices, some fifty in total. While evidence remains fragmentary, this might reflect the fact that the Catholic Church was one of the few institutions in France to stand by the population during the *exode*. As W.D. Halls has emphasised, while many state officials fled their posts, the clergy remained to give moral and material sustenance to those on the roads, only to be caught up in the general maelstrom.[14] The third striking category in the list was the large number of males between the ages of 17 and 35, some 740 in total, who had somehow managed to evade concerted Home Office and MI5 attempts to enrol them into either the Free French forces or the British armed services. Such men were deemed a drain on resources and dangerous, in the sense that their morale was poor.[15]

If government sources are to be believed, French refugees adapted well to life in exile, being warmly welcomed by local populations who went to some lengths to accommodate these unfortunate visitors.[16] Tales of British charity are legion. Joan Delin, in a wide-ranging thesis on Franco-British relations in the course of 1940, cites several examples from the Southampton area, where many refugees were landed.[17] This generosity notwithstanding, the suspicion remains that French exiles aroused the same sorts of popular suspicions and prejudices as did their Dutch and Belgian counterparts, perhaps even more so. As Philip Bell has demonstrated, during the 'phoney war' British propaganda had celebrated the Anglo-French alliance and the expectation was that this would endure until victory was attained.[18] The quarrels that raged within the French communities also influenced the public's impressions. Susan Briggs relates how Londoners considered that the French had brought France, 'including its quarrels', across the Channel with them.[19]

To be fair, evidence of political squabbling among refugees is scarce, and largely stems from British sources, the fear being that any lingering Vichyite sympathies might be harmful to de Gaulle's movement and public opinion in general. It was concluded early on, however, that French refugees constituted no real threat. A report of early 1941 observed that, while most kept out of politics, 'A number of the more intellectual ... had adopted an attitude which, while violently anti-Vichy, approved of the FFL [i.e. De Gaulle's organisation] only as a military government, and did not associate themselves with it or with the Français de Grande Bretagne.'[20] It was also thought desirable that some greater coordination should be achieved between the various French committees charged with caring for their countryfolk. Yet, as Bessborough's Committee on French Welfare commented, this was difficult, because each society reflected a different political standpoint.[21] Whereas the FGB was Gaullist-dominated, CEAF was known to be loyal to the Allied cause, but not to de Gaulle. Members of the French Red Cross adopted a similar stance, frequently complaining about the behaviour of the Gaullist authorities in Carlton Gardens.[22] Indeed, FGB activists, anxious to muscle in on all aspects of the care of refugees, often created friction with other charitable societies. Trouble especially flared in the Liverpool and Manchester areas, where it was rumoured that the French colony, prominent in the Catholic Women's League, was Pétainist in affiliation.[23] In London, the FGB fell out with the Home Office when it made several demands for the names of all refugees living in Britain, purportedly for information purposes, but clearly for a recruitment drive. Free French officials were particularly disgruntled that some 500 refugees had been granted the right to repatriation. Aware of what was afoot and anxious to preserve the rights of privacy, the Home Office declined all Gaullist requests for information.[24] Such quarrels were nothing, however, compared to the battles that raged over French soldiers and sailors.

II

Reflecting on its first six months in existence, the Committee on French Welfare concluded that the most serious problem it had confronted was not the arrival of refugees, but the question of what to do with those French soldiers, sailors and merchant seamen who had arrived in this country and who had expressed little interest in joining the Free French.[25] This was, in fact, the majority of servicemen – only a paltry few signed up to serve de Gaulle.[26] The soldiers were those rescued from Narvik and Dunkirk and not immediately returned to France. Many were convalescing after injury. French Welfare reported that 1,650 such men were housed in temporary accommodation at White City, London, while 70 of their officers were placed in the York Hotel, in Bermens Street, largely because they were known to be Pétainist in outlook.[27] The sailors mainly belonged to French ships seized in British ports immediately after the Armistice and before the bombing of Mers-el-Kébir. Exact figures for the numbers of seamen are hard to come by. Some were quickly repatriated; a few joined de Gaulle; others simply absconded from the camps in which they were being held, and wandered around the countryside before being picked up by the authorities. Nonetheless, on 26 September 1940, Western Command, responsible for the welfare of these seamen, reported that there were 341 officers and 6,206 sailors of other ranks in its charge. In addition, there were 268 colonial veterans who had arrived in the autumn and who were housed alongside the sailors.[28]

If the preparations for the arrival of refugees had been improvised, those for servicemen were even more makeshift. While soldiers were housed at athletic and dog tracks at Crystal Palace and White City in London, sailors were accommodated in camps, usually race courses, situated mainly in the North-West and the Midlands: Aintree (13 officers, 380 sailors); Haydock (52 officers, 1,305 men); Arrowe Park (55 officers, 140 men); Trentham Park (49 officers and 1,829 men); Doddington (51 officers, 307 petty officers, 880 men); Oulton Park (33 officers, 959 men); and Barmouth (6 officers and 500 men).[29] Strictly speaking, Barmouth and Arrowe Park were not camps: at Barmouth the men were billeted in the town; Arrowe Park was essentially a detention centre, housing several unruly elements, not all French.

Conditions in the camps were not good. Accommodation was a particular gripe, many men being forced to sleep in tents on ground that was not especially suitable. At Aintree, ratings were placed in riding stables. This provoked an outcry from their commanding officer, yet on inspection it was discovered that the new homes were dry, lit by electricity and, in some cases, provided with heaters.[30] Food was another problem. Despite the efforts of such charities as the YMCA and the Catholic Women's League, kitchens were primitive, cooking utensils scarce and menus unappetizing, although there was a suspicion that, in some instances, Pétainist officers were ordering the destruction of food in order to ferment anti-British feeling.[31] More troubling was the lack of medical supplies. Health care was generally left in the hands of French doctors who were grossly overworked and badly equipped. One British visitor, Beryl Fitzgerald, of the United Association of Great Britain and France Solidarity Committee, described the infirmary at Trentham Park as a 'scandal', adding that she felt 'ashamed of being a British woman every time I go to the camp'. [32]

Given these problems, it is no surprise that discipline was a problem. Whereas at Haydock morale was described as good and the men 'neat',[33] camps in the Liverpool area presented a different picture with 'waste material and rubbish' strewn across the ground, and the officers generally demoralised and lacking in authority.[34] At Trentham Park, there had been problems with 'deaths among ornamental geese and deer'.[35] At Arrowe Park, which it will be recalled was a detention centre, it was rumoured the men had threatened mutiny, although such claims proved exaggerated. As Major Spears, a British observer, reported, 'a salutary respect for authority' had settled in after guards had fired at a Frenchman who had wandered too near to the wire.[36] Elsewhere, however, the men were not so closely supervised, often being left to drift out of the camp gates, thanks to the shortage of guards and, on occasion, the lacklustre leadership of British commandants. The Free French recruiting officer based at Stoke-on-Trent was appalled by this lack of discipline, especially 'the carrying on with the girls' that resulted.[37] Paradoxically, locals in the Camberley area made exactly the same complaint about the libidinous behaviour of Free French troops billeted near the town.[38]

It had been hoped that the exiled French servicemen would constitute a fertile recruiting ground, yet among the 1,600 or so troops at White City only 152 men signed up with de Gaulle, a further 34 with the British army and another 36 with the Royal Navy.[39] It is not hard to explain this reluctance. Among the sailors, there was a traditional Anglophobia, nursed by centuries of Anglo-French naval rivalry, and hardened by events at Mers-el-Kébir. Among the troops, or at least among the officer class, there was a strong Pétainist sentiment. It was always going to be difficult to recruit among such circles, and the British did themselves no favours by providing poor conditions in the camps and distributing inept propaganda. When the Ministry of Information newspaper, *France*, was distributed, it provoked a lacklustre response, many men viewing it with intense suspicion.[40] Another problem was that few of the French spoke any English and interpreters were scarce and often of a poor quality.[41] According to Carlton Gardens, Vichy propaganda was far more effective: the Free French accused officials of the Vichy Consulate at Liverpool of helping men return to France, a charge almost certainly true.[42] Suspicion also fell on the Catholic chaplains, often members of French orders, assigned to the camps. One Irish priest, based at Trentham Park, came under particular scrutiny; he vigorously denied that he was a *maréchaliste*, citing Pétain's marriage to a divorcee as one of many reasons why he could not support Vichy.[43]

As winter approached and German air raids intensified, the concern of the British authorities was less to recruit among these marooned sailors, than to arrange for their repatriation.[44] This was no easy matter, involving delicate negotiations with Vichy and protracted discussions with the Ministry of Shipping, which was responsible for arranging the necessary transport. Ironically, one batch of men returning to France was torpedoed by a German U-boat. Rather than being sent back to the camps, they were held in

Plymouth, Portsmouth and Skegness before a further, and this time
successful, attempt was made to transfer them to French metropolitan soil.[45] By Christmas 1940, 6,574 officers and men had been
repatriated. On 16 December, the camps were closed.[46]

III

Another group of men was shortly to follow these soldiers and
sailors: officials of the Vichy consulates in Britain. The embassy, of
course, had been closed at the time of the establishment of the Vichy
Government and, while most countries recognised Pétain as the
legitimate head of state this was not a courtesy extended by either
the British or the Free French. Inevitably, however, it was important
to keep some lines of communication open, and as R.T. Thomas
and more recently Robert Frank have revealed, the Foreign Office
pursued a discreet line of dialogue with Vichy, often to the disap-
proval of the Prime Minister's office.[47] What has been overlooked is
the fact that French Consulates were left active in Britain, dealing
with the everyday concerns of French nationals, including Gaullists.
According to a Foreign Office report of June 1941, consulates
existed in London, Manchester (transferred from Liverpool for
security reasons), Newcastle-on-Tyne, Cardiff, Swansea and Edinburgh, the latter transplanted from Glasgow, again for security
purposes. The liquidation missions, responsible for the tidying up of
financial matters agreed between London and Paris in preparation
for war, also stayed in business, employing some 35 people.[48]

Inevitably, the presence of Vichy officials, albeit few in number,
caused concern to the British Government and excited the already
feverish imagination of the Free French. Action was quickly taken
against any Vichy official thought to be hostile, resulting in a rash
of expulsions in the course of 1940 and a series of prolonged
enquiries on the part of MI5. In June 1941, however, with British
forces fighting Vichy troops in Syria and the Darlan Government
seemingly intent on active, and possibly military, collaboration with
Germany, the time came to question whether a majority of the consulates and missions should be closed down. MI5 was particularly
keen on this course of action, speaking of the way in which these
outposts provided a 'focal point' for disaffected Frenchmen and
financial and material sustenance for those who might otherwise
join de Gaulle.[49] So it was that the Foreign Office enquired of the
various government departments dealing with the missions for their
views on closure. After lengthy correspondence, it transpired that
most of the missions were deemed 'useful'.[50] In the opinion of the

Foreign Office, three options were open: to expel all consuls and members of the missions; to expel the consuls but leave the missions; or to expel the provincial consuls leaving only the Consulate General in London with its staff and the missions nominally attached to it. In the event, the Foreign Office plumped for a mixed option, banishing the provincial consuls and granting a stay of execution to the missions.[51]

There ensued protracted negotiations, in which, perhaps significantly, the masthead of the letter-paper of the Consulate General in London changed from 'La République Française' to the 'Etat Français'.[52] The first to go was Chartier, head of the Consulate General, thrown out in May. On leaving, he produced a nine-page document, seized by the British on 7 June 1941, which was clearly written for the consumption of the technocratic cabinet of Admiral Darlan, and, as outraged Foreign Office officials observed, was designed to tar the British state with the same brush as the Third Republic, although interestingly it was admitted that some of the comment on scandals in the British Government might have 'foundation'.[53] The report began with a critique of British preparations for war, which were deemed to have been inadequate. Such arrangements, Chartier insisted, had misled the French, and it was only after the Armistice that the British made any real military effort, and even then this was muddled and inefficient. Moving on to political matters, Chartier claimed that many intellectuals and members of the middle classes were opposed to Churchill, and stressed the fragility of the National Government, bitterly criticising the way in which M.P.s were often elected without opposition when seats fell vacant. As to the war cabinet itself, Chartier concluded that it was not of the calibre of the First World War and lacked a Lloyd George. Churchill himself was singled out for particular criticism, being chastised for his autocratic tendencies. At least some praise was reserved for the working classes, yet it was maintained that they, and the Labour Party, were being hoodwinked by both the forces of capital and the government. Much of the war effort – the arrangements for rationing, censorship and working practices, described in some detail – was to the detriment of the *classes ouvrières*, and Chartier concluded with another snipe at the British government, accusing parliamentarians of financial misdealings. Curiously, however, on departing London, Chartier requested not to be sent back to France, but to Australia to take up office at the French Consulate in Sydney.[54] This was a strange request to come through the British channels, and a suggestion, perhaps, that he was not viewed as being 'sound' at Vichy.

Other consular officials also appear to have been reluctant to

leave, occasionally writing plaintive letters to the Foreign Office tes-
tifying to their Anglophilia, some being married to Englishwomen
with their children well-settled in English schools and waiting to sit
examinations. While such requests were greeted with scorn, they
were not necessarily treated unsympathetically,[55] and a handful of
diplomats, together with officials of the missions and a skeleton
staff at the Consulate General in London,[56] were allowed to remain,
even though they continued to arouse the suspicions of the Foreign
Office, MI5 and the Free French. So ended an inglorious episode in
Franco-British diplomatic relations.

IV

There remained those French men and women who had chosen the
British Isles as their home: *la colonie française*. Whereas Italian and
German immigrants, among others, have recently attracted the
attention of historians, the composition of the French community
and the lives of its members have been studied little.[57] Thanks to
Home Office statistics, we at least have a guide to how many French
nationals were resident in Britain during the Second World War, the
majority being based in London. Out of a total of 11,463 French
aliens, 7,089 were settled in the metropolitan area and 4,374 elsewhere.[58] Nonetheless, these figures should be treated with caution.
As the Home Office acknowledged, the Central Register of Aliens
did not include children under the age of 16, British-born wives and
many temporary visitors who had failed to register properly. Nor
did it include those who had been granted certificates of naturalisation.[59]

Given the fragmentary nature of this evidence, any evaluation of
the social make-up of the French colony must be impressionistic,
and it is inevitable that we know most about the wealthy and artic-
ulate. For example, there was a respectable business community
that had long made London its base. This included such individuals
as Monsieur Petit, formerly President of the French Chamber of
Commerce, Monsieur Espinasse, a member of the United Associations of Great Britain and France, and Etienne Bellanger, head of
Cartier jewellers, who famously offered his services as a chauffeur
to de Gaulle.[60] There were also significant numbers of lawyers,
including Dr Picarda, a member of the Middle Temple, and of journalists: Monsieur Bret, an English-based reporter for the Havas
agency; Monsieur Massip, the London correspondent of *Le Petit
Parisien*; and Elie J. Bois, the former editor of Massip's paper. Other
members of the French colony were less prosperous and less

conspicuous. A sizeable proportion appear to have been governesses, schoolteachers, chefs and au pairs who had been working temporarily in Britain, only to find themselves here on a more permanent basis.

Indeed, the community comprised several transient elements, including some 75 boys between the ages of 14 and 18, who, through arrangements with the French authorities, were pursuing their studies in England prior to the war; their education was to continue in camps on the Welsh hillsides.[61]

Inevitably, there were concerns about the political attitude adopted by the French colony, especially as Britain maintained relations, officially, with de Gaulle and, unofficially, with Vichy. In a report submitted in early September 1940 to the Morton Committee, a body concerned with the supervision of British-based French nationals, it was reported that the majority of *colons* were 'on the fence' about supporting the war effort, many of them fearing that any other position would have 'unfavourable effects' for their relatives in France.[62] Indeed, only a small number, maybe 600 or so, immediately rallied to de Gaulle, helping to found the Français de Grande Bretagne (FGB), a civilian organisation that became the civil wing of the Free French and that, as already noted, engaged in an enthusiastic recruitment drive, badgering both the Home Office and the Foreign Office for the names and addresses of French residents in this country.[63] Irritated by this type of behaviour, Whitehall was always uncomfortable with this branch of the Free French, apprehensive that it was trying to hoodwink the British Government into recognising de Gaulle as an official head of state. Nor did the FGB enjoy cordial relations with other Allied communities in London, the Norwegians taking particular offence at its conduct. Further antagonism arose between the FGB and the French colony, and it was not long before a rival organisation was formed, the Union des Français d'Outre Mer (UFOM). Supportive of the Allied war effort but not de Gaulle, the UFOM never matched the membership of the FGB.[64]

The majority of *colons*, however, did not busy themselves with either the FGB or the UFOM. Their general attitude may be summed up by an intercepted letter from one prominent resident: 'I consider, and I still consider, that it is quite possible for French men to be devoted to the English cause, obedient to the laws of England, and at the same time loyal to the French government and its representatives. I do not know any French government other than that called the government of Vichy'.[65] Such attitudes were a concern to the British government, yet it was concluded at a very early stage that the French colony, along with French refugees, did not constitute a security threat. Rather than being fascist sympathisers, their *attentiste* attitude was put down to a dislike of the 'rebel' de Gaulle, a respect for Pétain and a desire to safeguard their businesses and livelihoods in England.[66] The fact that certain left-wing personalities had allied themselves to the Free French was also seen as a factor, hinting at the conservative make-up of the colony, or at least of its most prominent representatives.

Nonetheless, while the British Government might not have regarded the French colony as a threat, it was understood that a close watch needed to be kept on its activities. In early September 1940, the Morton Committee considered making all French men and women sign a declaration of allegiance, a strategy quickly abandoned as it was thought such a move was likely to put off recruits to de Gaulle.[67] Bemoaning the gentlemanly and Victorian practices of the Home Office, the War Cabinet was also keen on tough measures, especially in 1941 when it appeared likely that a Weygand government might be formed in North Africa and a Laval government in Paris. If this happened, it was argued, legal niceties should be thrown aside and internment introduced for all Frenchmen who refused to support the Allied cause openly.[68] Characteristically opposed to such draconian action, and intent on defending individual liberties even in wartime, the Home Office settled on a compromise, whereby in the event of a Laval government no general internment would take place, but unreliable elements would nonetheless be arrested.[69] Instructions were thus issued to MI5 and local police authorities to investigate the attitudes of the *colons*. The results, or at least those which are accessible, suggest few subversives were at large. Typical of the response was the following from the police in Eastbourne: '9 French nationals in the district: 4 males and 5 females. All are elderly and have resided here for many years. I have no reason to regard any of these persons with suspicion.'[70] As the Home Office appreciated, perhaps the greater threat came not from French nationals long since established here, but from new arrivals who might well be enemy agents. To safeguard against such dangers, all aliens arriving in Britain were processed through the Royal Victoria Patriotic School at Wandsworth. Few savoured this experience and it was a source of bitter resentment among Free French volunteers who had often risked life and limb to reach London and who believed they had been escaping oppression rather than seeking it out.[71]

Although evidence is piecemeal, the overriding impression is that the French colony kept its head down, retaining a loyalty towards Britain and expressing a growing dislike of Vichy, but retaining a suspicion of de Gaulle and his intentions. That the colony did not pose any real security threat is illustrated in the fact that the British

Government remained eager to involve its members in the war effort and eventually exempted several categories of French citizens, along with Danish nationals, from certain clauses in the Aliens Restrictions Order, although in August 1944 Carlton Gardens and the FGB were complaining that their volunteers still suffered too many civil constraints.[72]

V

Many of the findings of this necessarily brief study are impressionistic, but certain conclusions present themselves. To begin with, it is clear that the French community in Britain was fragmented, seemingly having little to do with either de Gaulle or the indigenous population. Exiles struggled to adapt to life abroad, and it is not surprising that some, predominantly soldiers and sailors, were eager to return to France, at least during the early stages of the war before the full weight of German oppression and true extent of Vichy cowardice had become apparent. It is also apparent that a majority of exiles, especially refugees and the London colony, expressed similar sentiments to their cousins on metropolitan soil: a respect for Pétain, but not necessarily for his government; an initial suspicion of de Gaulle; and a general desire to keep their heads down and avoid politics. They were, however, fortunate in that their *attentiste* position was never seriously challenged in the same way as it was across the Channel. Being subject to an Aliens Restrictions Order was not the same as being subject to the antisemitic and discriminatory legislation of Vichy. Being drafted to work in a British factory was not the same as being enlisted to work in Nazi Germany as part of the *Service du Travail Obligatoire*. Aware of this liberty, French exiles – with the obvious exception of the soldiers and sailors who were to be repatriated – never became Anglophobes, a point quickly appreciated by both the British Government and public opinion. While Whitehall and the many charitable agencies charged with looking after the welfare of French nationals might have despaired at the interminable internecine quarrels that afflicted the French community, it was widely understood that these exiles posed no threat to national security and, ultimately, were fighting for the same cause.

Notes

1. Among the vast literature on de Gaulle, see especially J. Lacouture, *De Gaulle: Le Rebelle, 1890–1944*, Paris, 1984; on the Free French, J.-L. Crémieux-Brilhac, *La France Libre*, Paris, 1995; on intellectual life, M. and J.-P. Cointet, *La France*

à Londres, 1940–1943, Brussels, 1990; and on contacts between London and Vichy, R.T. Thomas, *Britain and Vichy, 1940–1942*, London, 1979.

2. One of the few studies to examine the broader French community is A. Gillois, *Histoire secrète des français à Londres, 1940–1944*, Paris, 1973. The present author is engaged in writing a study entitled *The Forgotten French. Exiles in Britain, 1940–1944*.

3. On British policy towards refugees, see the important article M.L. Buck, 'Feeding a Pauper Army: War Refugees and Welfare in Britain, 1939–1942', *Twentieth-Century British History*, forthcoming. I am grateful to Matthew Buck for permission to consult this essay before publication.

4. H.R. Kedward, 'Patriots and Patriotism in Vichy France', *Transactions of the Royal Historical Society*, 5th series, 32 (1982), pp. 175–92.

5. See H.R. Kedward, *Occupied France: Collaboration and Resistance, 1940–1944*, Oxford, 1985, for the impact of Pétainism.

6. See the correspondence between the Home Office and Ministry of Health for the period June 1936–May 1939 in the Public Record Office (PRO) , London, HO 213 464 203/2/1.

7. French Welfare, 'Report for 1941', PRO FO 1055 8.

8. 'Comité d'Entr'aide', undated, PRO FO 1055 7.

9. 'Comité D'Entr'Aide aux Français en Grande-Bretagne', 7 August 1940, PRO FO 1055 7.

10. Comité D'Entr'Aide, 'Points for the Foreign Office', undated, PRO FO 1055 7.

11. Eric Chetwood Aiken, Secretary of Comité D'Entr'Aide, to Captain Williams, French Welfare, 10 November 1944, PRO FO 1055 7.

12. 'Comité d'Entr'aide', undated, PRO FO 1055 7.

13. 'Report of Visit of Mr H. Astor to West Country Re Breton Seaman, October 18th-26th, 1940, Inclusive', and letter from Lady Warwick to Captain Williams, French Welfare, 11 October 1940, PRO FO 1055 4.

14. W.D. Halls, 'Catholicism under Vichy', in *Vichy France and the Resistance*, eds H.R. Kedward and R. Austin, London, 1985, pp. 133–46.

15. 'Note' by Hankey, 11 June 1941, PRO FO 371 28366 Z3936/123/17.

16. 'French Community in the United Kingdom. Note by French Welfare', 5 February 1941, PRO FO 371 28365 Z822/123/17.

17. J. Delin, 'L'Opinion britannique et les français en Grande-Bretagne pendant l'année 1940' (Ph.D. diss., Université de Lille, 1993). I am grateful to the author for permission to consult this thesis.

18. P. Bell, *A Certain Eventuality. Britain and the Fall of France*, London, 1974, p. 109.

19. S. Briggs, *The Home Front. The War Years in Britain, 1939–1945*, London, 1975, p. 130.

20. 'The French Community in the United Kingdom. Report to the Committee on Foreign (Allied) Resistance', 20 February 1941, PRO FO 371 28365 Z822/123/17.

21. French Welfare, 'Report for 1942', PRO FO 1055 8.

22. 'Report by the Sub-Committee on Welfare and Security of the French Community in the United Kingdom', February 1941, PRO FO 1055 8.

23. Sir Evelyn Wrench of the Liverpool Overseas League to Duff Cooper, 16 August 1940, PRO 1055 1, remarks on 'anti-British propaganda' in the district.

24. Memorandum of 14 September 1940, PRO HO 213 1744 204/15/6.

25. 'Work of French Welfare', 29 January 1941, PRO FO 371 28365 Z629/123/17.

26. 'Memorandum on the French Armed Forces in Britain', undated [1940], PRO FO 1055 8, suggests that between 2,000 and 3,000 men had joined de Gaulle's

army and that some 300 had enlisted in the Free French Air Force. No figures are given for the navy.

27. 'Work of French Welfare', 29 January 1941, PRO FO 371 28365 Z629/123/17.
28. Edward Knoblock, 'Report on French Camps', undated [October 1940?], PRO FO 1055 1.
29. 'Work of French Welfare', 29 January 1941, PRO FO 371 28365 Z629/123/17.
30. Edward Knoblock, 'Report on French Camps', undated [October 1940?], PRO FO 1055 1.
31. 'Report on Visit to French Camps in the Liverpool Area by Dame Rachel Crowdy, 29th-31st July 1940', PRO FO 1055 1.
32. Beryl Fitzgerald to Sir Aidan Baillie, French Welfare, 10 September 1940, PRO FO 1055 1.
33. Edward Knoblock, 'Report on French Camps', undated [October 1940?], PRO FO 1055 1.
34. 'Report on Visit to French Camps in the Liverpool Area by Dame Rachel Crowdy, 29th-31st July 1940', PRO FO 1055 1.
35. Dame Rachel Crowdy to Lord Bessborough, French Welfare, 16 August 1940, PRO FO 1055 1.
36. Major Spears, 'Report on the situation in the camps occupied by French Sailors in the Neighbourhood of Liverpool', 31 July 1940, PRO FO 1055 1.
37. Hon. Sylvia Fletcher-Moulton to Lady Reading, 13 October 1940, PRO FO 1055 1.
38. Jean Hesse, Association des Volontaires Français to Lord Bessborough, 29 May 1941, to which are attached several reports on the Free French forces at Camberley, PRO FO 1055 10.
39. 'Work of French Welfare', 29 January 1941, PRO FO 371 28365 Z629/123/17.
40. 'Report on Trentham Park sent in by Mr John Christie, Teacher of English', 14 October 1940, PRO FO 1055 1.
41. Report from Rear Admiral G.R.S. Watkins to H.Q., Western Command, 9 September 1940, PRO 1055 1.
42. 'Communication Sheet', by Rear Admiral G.R.S. Watkins, 30 September 1940, PRO 1055 1.
43. Father X to Lady Peel, early September 1940, PRO FO 1055 1.
44. Unsigned letter from French Welfare to Committee on Foreign (Allied) Resistance, 5 September 1940, PRO FO 1055 8.
45. 'Memorandum on the French Armed Forces in Britain', undated [1940], PRO FO 1055 8.
46. 'Work of French Welfare', 29 January 1941, PRO FO 371 28365 Z629/123/17.
47. R.T. Thomas, *Britain and Vichy* and R. Frank, 'Vichy et les britanniques, 1940–1941: double jeu ou double langage?' in *Vichy et les français*, eds J.-P. Azéma & F. Bédarida, Paris, 1992, pp. 144–63.
48. R.L. Speaight, 'Action Against French Officials in the United Kingdom', 10 June 1940, PRO 371 28423 Z5154/179/17.
49. MI5 officer to Miss Davies, Home Office, 20 May 1941, PRO FO 371 28424 Z5701/179/17.
50. Much of this correspondence is contained in PRO FO 371 28424 Z5821/179/17.
51. R.L. Speaight, 'Action Against French Officials in the United Kingdom', 10 June 1941, PRO 371 28423 Z5154/179/17.
52. Jalenques to Speaight, 7 October 1941, PRO FO 371 28426 Z9127/179/17. Interestingly, as the Liberation approached, officials at the Ministry of Education at Vichy began to use letter-paper bearing the mast head La République

Française rather than *Etat Français*. Occasional examples may be found in 'Papiers provenant du cabinet d'Abel Bonnard' in Archives Nationales (AN), Paris, F17 13336–13367 and 'Papiers de M.Roy', in AN F17 13378 and F17 13390.

53. The Foreign Office commentary and the Chartier letter of 7 June 1941 are both contained in PRO FO 371 28423 Z5037/179/17.
54. G. Kimber, Downing Street, to R.R. Sedgwick, Foreign Office, 14 July 1941, PRO FO 371 28424 Z6007/179/17.
55. Such correspondence is contained in PRO FO 371 28423 Z5282/179/17.
56. W.H.B. Mack, Foreign Office, to Jalenques, 18 June 1941, PRO 371 28423 Z5154/179/17.
57. The best introduction is C. Holmes, *John Bull's Island: Immigration and British Society, 1871–1971*, London, 1988.
58. 'French Community', figures supplied to French Welfare, PRO FO 1055 8. These are also included in 'The French Community in the United Kingdom. Report to the Committee on Foreign (Allied) Resistance', 20 February 1941, FO 371 28365 Z822/123/17.
59. 'Tabular Statement for period 1932–41', PRO HO 213 315 42/1/61.
60. Some insight into this community is provided in A. Gillois, *Histoire secrète*.
61. 'Paper A', 29 August 1940, prepared for the Welfare and Security Sub-Committee of French Welfare, PRO 1055 8.
62. 'Attitude of the French Colony', report submitted for the Morton Committee meeting on 2 September 1940, PRO FO 1055 3.
63. For much that follows on the FGB, see PRO HO 213 1744 204/15/6.
64. 'Note of an interview with M. de Bellaing, 15 August 1940, by Brennan', PRO FO 1055 2.
65. 'The French Community in the United Kingdom. Report to the Committee on Foreign (Allied) Resistance', 20 February 1941, PRO FO 371 28365 Z822/123/17.
66. Ibid.
67. 'Attitude of the French Colony', report submitted for the Morton Committee meeting on 2 September 1940, PRO FO 1055 3.
68. Le Mesurier, War Cabinet, to Brennan, 25 February 1941, PRO FO 1055 8.
69. Miss Davies, Home Office, to Le Mesurier, War Cabinet, 28 February 1941, PRO FO 1055 8.
70. Note of Chief Constable, Police Headquarters, Eastbourne, 9 June 1941, PRO HO 213 1724 200/271/5.
71. Circular of 5 June 1941, PRO HO 213 1981 203/2/141.
72. W.H.B. Mack, Foreign Office, to F. Newsam, Home Office, 11 August 1944, PRO HO 213 2098 411/3/16.

13

DUTCH EXILES IN LONDON

N. DAVID J. BARNOUW

Anglo-Dutch relations have a long and competitive history that was frequently dominated by efforts to rule the waves in order to control lucrative overseas trade. But the British and the Dutch have also a tradition of working together; for instance during the Dutch Revolt against Spanish rule. After the Treaty of Nonsuch in 1585, between the United Provinces and Elizabeth I, Lord Dudley, Earl of Leicester was sent as Governor-General to the Low Countries. As the leader of the puritans, the radical Protestant party in England, he came with an army to protect the Protestant faith – or was it simply an army of occupation? England has also been a place of refuge for the Dutch, notably Dutch Calvinists who found refuge and even established a refugee church in London until the Roman Catholic Queen Mary came to power.

But more powerful Dutch have also crossed the North Sea, and on three occasions during the last four hundred years Dutch heads of state from the House of Orange went to England. Two of them arrived as refugees, while one was explicitly invited to make the crossing. This was Prince William of Orange, Stadholder in the Low Countries and the son of William II and Mary Stuart, who arrived in 1688 to restore and protect the Protestant order in Britain. He became King of England, and one can still see a legacy of this Dutch adventure in the politics of Northern Ireland. The second occasion was in 1795, when Prince William IV, Stadholder of the Low Countries, fled to England when the revolutionary armies of France swept over Europe and the old structure appeared to have collapsed. His son returned after Napoleon's defeat and in 1813 he became the first King of the Netherlands. The third time a Dutch head of state fled to England was in 1940, when Queen Wilhelmina and her government fled from the German invasion of her country.

Was this twentieth-century exile much different from the previous exiles? In this article, we shall examine the impact of the war in general, the difficult relations between the government-in-exile and the occupied country, the ideas of post-war reconstruction, the loss of empire and, above all, the role played by the House of Orange in London.

The House of Orange and Queen Wilhelmina

For more then two centuries the Netherlands had been a republic, starting with the Golden Age of the early modern era and developing into an empire much too large for such a small country. The House of Orange has been a constant factor in its history, but never by acting as absolute rulers; the proud citizens would not have permitted that. But after the defeat of Napoleon the country became a kingdom, as part of the anti-revolutionary restoration of Europe. The House of Orange provided three kings before a queen assumed the throne: Queen Wilhelmina. She was only eighteen in 1898 when she was crowned in Amsterdam after her father William III had died eight years previously. She was his only child and had been raised in almost strict isolation, in a 'golden cage', as she said later, to prepare her for her responsibilities as queen. She was not a strict Calvinist, but was convinced that she had a divine task, although she recognised that she had to respect the constitution. She also had a deep belief in the important role of her country in the world and wanted to ensure a well-maintained army and navy, not least in order to protect the Dutch colonies in the west and, above all, in the east. The power of a king or queen in the Netherlands is limited, but she tried, just as her father and grandfather had done, to influence members of the government. In 1924, for instance, she refused to allow the recognition of the USSR, largely because she could not forgive the murderers of her relatives, the Romanovs. It was only in July 1942 that the government-in-exile decided to send a Dutch envoy to Moscow.

Wilhelmina reigned over a traditionally conservative country that had escaped the horrors of the First World War. The Netherlands refused after that war to hand over the Kaiser who had taken refuge in the country. But it was also a divided country, in which Protestants and Catholics on one side and socialists on the other had constructed tightly-knit strongholds of organisations that precluded contacts with members of the other groups. Only the leaders of these groups maintained the contacts rendered necessary by, for instance, the electoral system of proportional representation, which ensured that a coalition was always needed to govern the country. It was 1939 before the Socialists were permitted to supply any ministers, even if, at a lower level, they had already exercised considerable administrative responsibility.

The Depression hit the Netherlands as severely as it did others, but despite the privations of the time a fascist or national-socialist solution to the problems had never made significant headway, if we exempt a limited National Socialist success in 1935, when this party gained 8 percent of the votes in provincial elections. This was partly a consequence of the attitude of the churches, who warned their flocks that fascism was not an acceptable choice for Christians, and partly because the foreign, German nature of national socialism did not attract the Dutch. Unlike many of her fellow countrymen, Wilhelmina had a realistic view of the rise of Hitler and the aggressive nature of the Third Reich, and she anticipated that the Netherlands would be embroiled in the coming conflict. The House of Orange, exemplified by Wilhelmina, seemed to act as a unifying factor in a divided country, but this was not entirely the case. The enormous distance between the Queen and 'her' people remained, and the political left was not very royalist, even if it was realistic enough not to fight for a republic. The marriage in 1937 of the Queen's only daughter, Juliana, to a German prince, Bernhard von Lippe-Bisterfeld, was a desperate step to consolidate the House of Orange, and the birth of their first daughter Beatrix was greeted with much enthusiasm. But the gap between Queen and nation remained.

It was the war that changed this situation completely. Wilhelmina became 'the only man in the Cabinet'; one could hear her broadcast from time to time on the Dutch radio from London, Radio Orange; and she bolstered morale among all the Dutch people, Calvinist and Communist alike. Meyer Lisser, a Communist Jew in hiding, wrote in his diary in August 1943:

> The birthday of the Queen. What is the matter with me? It was very poignant, more then I thought. Is the Rotterdammer [a popular Dutch newsreader in London] right in saying that everybody in Holland is waiting impatiently for the return of the Queen? . . . Yes, I have felt the same way secretly and I have not told anybody. I want to be liberated, but I am against the monarchy. But I am a communist and that is difficult to reconcile. Yes, I am a staunch communist and an ardent supporter of Stalin and the Soviet Union. But I want to see the Queen as a fine Dutch woman resisting the Nazi attack. That is why I have to be shoulder to shoulder with her. That has nothing to do with the fact that she happens to be Queen.[1]

He was not the only one who changed his mind in this way during the war.

Preparation for War and the German Invasion

Hitler's attack came as a complete surprise to most Dutch people; Holland had been neutral during the First World War, so why not in this new World War? This neutrality also reflected the prevailing mood of large sections of the population, summed up in an expression often used at the time: 'Wij willen onszelf zijn en blijven' ('We wish to be and remain ourselves').[2] But the Low Countries were less naive than tended to be thought during and after the war. In 1937 the government had issued ordinances on how civil servants should conduct themselves in the event of an enemy occupation, taking as a model the decrees issued by Belgium during the First World War. The most important aspect of these was that the civil servants were ordered to remain at their posts only so long their services were of greater benefit to the general public than to the enemy.[3] Moreover, a Committee for Economic Defence Preparation had been established a year earlier, and the unofficial Agricultural Crisis Centres were brought under the authority of the State Office of Food Supply after the general mobilisation was proclaimed in 1939. *Kernbureaux* (key offices) and *Rijksbureaux* (state offices) were established, the latter to control the shortages of raw materials that would inevitably occur in the event of war. The *Kernbureaux* were composed of a mixture of civil servants and businessmen in order to make the business community assume equal responsibility for the drastic measures expected. 'In the framework of Economic Defence Preparation, the Dutch Government created an apparatus that in times of emergency had far-reaching powers to control economic life'.[4]

The Dutch National Bank had shipped half of its gold reserves to London and New York and major companies had made war preparations. The Philips Company had been very active in this field, and had prepared the evacuation of staff members and their families to England. Officially, since April 1940 the Philips Corporation had had its head office in Curaçao,[5] while Unilever founded a holding company in South Africa in case of a German occupation. Dutch trade unions were less active in the preparations for war, although they knew what had happened in Nazi Germany, where the unions were banned and robbed of their assets.[6] Preparations were also taken to protect the general population; Cecil Hamilton wrote in *Holland To-day*:

> Utrecht, it was obvious, had realised the wisdom of preparedness: the city had opened an air-raid exhibition [in the second half of 1939], complete with that paraphernalia of civilian defence which was soon to be in actual use. Shelters and searchlights; gas masks and

decontamination equipment; groups of waxen figures rendering realistic first aid; fire-fighting devices and instructive leaflets – the promotors of the show had done their work with detailed thoroughness.[7]

The Dutch General Staff had been in contact with their British and French counterparts to discuss what help they might offer if Hitler should strike, so one cannot speak of absolute neutrality. They knew that the Dutch armies were no match for the Germans in the long run, and the strategic idea was to retreat after a German attack to the 'Vesting Holland' ('Stronghold Holland'), the area protected by water between Utrecht, Rotterdam, The Hague and Amsterdam. There they would wait for Allied support. In fact, the Dutch armies were not so badly prepared as was claimed after the war and there were no acts of treason by Dutch Nazis during the German invasion. Nevertheless, it took Hitler's armies only four days of Blitzkrieg to conquer the Netherlands, where the use of paratroopers was new, although not quite in the way Columbia University Professor A.J. Barnouw wrote in the USA in his *Monthly Letter* that month: 'It has been raining men from the sky in the Low Countries, men in Dutch and Belgian uniforms, German men seeking shelter in disguise'.[8] The bombing by the Luftwaffe of the centre of Rotterdam (with 800 casualties) marked the end of the war in the Netherlands. There was some Allied support: French troops arrived in the southern provinces and English demolition teams blew up some petrol reserves. The Germans, however, missed only one of their aims: the capture of the Queen and her government.

The only child of Queen Wilhelmina, Princess Juliana, and her husband Prince Bernhard and their two children (one of whom is the present Queen), had travelled to England on the third day of the invasion. The cabinet also decided that the Queen should follow them as quickly as possible. She departed the next day aboard the British HMS *Hereward*, and the entire cabinet, along with a few senior civil servants, left on another ship. The Queen was met in London by King George VI and Queen Elizabeth, and the first proclamation by the Dutch Government-in-Exile was released from Buckingham Palace:

> After it had become abundantly clear that We and our Ministers could no longer freely continue Our Government, it was necessary to make the difficult decision to move the seat of the government abroad for so long as was unavoidable, with the intention of returning to Holland as soon as possible.
>
> The Government is now located in England. In this way they will forestall a Government capitulation. In this way the territory of the Netherlands, whether in Europe, the East or West Indies, remains one

sovereign state, whose voice, as a full-fledged member of our allies, can continue to be heard.

The military command, and in the highest position, the Commander-in-Chief, will take such measures as are necessary from a military point of view.

There, where the usurper dominates, local civil authorities must continue to do what is necessary to further the public interest, and primarily, cooperate for the maintenance of peace and security.

Our heart goes out to our countrymen in the fatherland who will experience hard times. But Holland, with God's help, shall one day reconquer its European territory.

You will recall earlier disasters centuries ago, out of which Holland arose. That shall happen this time once again.

Do not despair. Do, all of you, what is in the national interest. We will do ours. Long live the fatherland!

Wilhelmina.[9]

The retreat, or flight, of the Queen and her cabinet came as a shock to the Dutch, especially for the soldiers who were supposed to fight on. After five days a partial surrender was achieved, the exception being in the Zeeland province in the south-west, mostly because there were still French troops there. Only a few hundred soldiers escaped being taken prisoner, and these travelled to England as guardians of 1,200 German POWs, most of whom were paratroopers. It was easy for the navy to sail its twenty-six ships to England, and its 2,700 sailors could immediately contribute to the war effort. Forty fishing-vessels also went over to be used as mine-sweepers (more then 700 fishing vessels stayed behind and a number of them were used by the Germans for the same purpose). In addition to the members of the navy, about 1,600 Dutch civilian refugees arrived in England in the first weeks after the invasion, some of them directly from the Dutch coast, others by way of France. Approximately 570 ships of the merchant marine, 200 coasters and twenty-five sea tugs as well as their personnel of 18,500 men were at the disposal of the Dutch Government. Moreover, there were still the colonies: the West Indies and Dutch Guyana (Surinam), but above all the Dutch East Indies.

Together with the 6,000 Dutchmen already living in Britain, these few civil servants, soldiers and civilian refugees formed the Dutch village in London. Later on they were joined by some 1,800 Dutch who were able to flee the Netherlands and to reach England. In Dutch memory they are 'England-Farers', daredevils who crossed the North Sea by boat or even by canoe. But in fact only a very small group (approximately 150 strong) reached England this way. The remainder went a much longer, but safer, way, overland via Spain or Switzerland.[10]

Refugees from an empire or from a small country?

The Dutch Constitution states in article 21 that 'In no case can the governmental seat be transfered to a place outside the empire'; in this case, 'empire' means the Netherlands itself. Nevertheless, the government-in-exile acted as a real government, was accepted by the Dutch colonies and was de jure recognised by most countries in the world. They had soldiers, a navy, Radio Orange to broadcast news to the occupied homeland, and the government even issued its own stamps.

The political power of a queen or king in the Netherlands is almost non-existent, because of the country's structure of parliamentary democracy. Only after parliamentary elections and during cabinet crises can the head of state exercise any real power by appointing the person charged with forming a new government. But the situation was different in London during the Second World War: the cabinet had no parliamentary support or opposition, and the role of Queen Wilhelmina could therefore increase. It was a very positive one during her first six months in London; she was the one who wanted to fight on, taking a contrary view to that of some cabinet ministers. They had seen the fall of Poland, Denmark, Norway, their own country, Belgium, the British retreat at Dunkirk and the fall of France. They felt helpless and did not believe that Germany could be defeated, and some of them advocated a separate peace with Germany. A few of them also had the idea that a peace settlement would place the Netherlands in a better position to retain its colonies in the east. Prime Minister D.J. De Geer was a defeatist himself and wanted to strike a deal with Hitler, so the Dutch image in London was initially very poor. With royal help De Geer was dismissed after three months and succeeded in returning home. At first the cabinet had tried to find an overseas posting for him, but from Lisbon he defected more or less to the Netherlands. The Germans were, of course, very pleased with this, and De Geer published in 1942, with German consent, a pamphlet in which he proposed peace by mutual agreement.

Only his spirited successor as prime minister, the strict Calvinist P.S. Gerbrandy, could try – with a considerable degree of success – to restore the idea that the Dutch were respectable Allies. Just like his Queen, he wanted to fight on, and he was fond of Churchill. In the autumn of 1941 he delivered a speech in Oxford, 'The contribution of the churches to the reconstruction of European life', in which he glorified 'the Almighty God, who created everything: the Kingdom of the Netherlands, the British Commonwealth of Nations and the great brain of Winston Churchill'.[11] The prime minister and the Queen had similar ideas concerning the war effort, namely to do as much as possible, but not about the future post-war reconstruction of the Netherlands. This was the division between simple reconstruction and reconstruction with renewal.

The Dutch Cabinet could hardly do anything about the war itself; there was a navy and a merchant navy that worked for the Allied war effort and there were still the colonies. British and French troops landed, with Dutch consent, in Curaçao and Aruba to protect the oil refinaries. Furthermore, around 8,000 American troops landed in Surinam to protect the very important bauxite mines, a raw material for aluminium and therefore necessary for the warplane industry. But not all of the cabinet ministers supported these actions; they feared that the British would keep those colonies for themselves after the war. So the colonies in the West Indies were placed under the control of the Allies, while those in the East Indies remained under Dutch control. Although rich, the Dutch East Indies could hardly contribute to the war effort, because they were preoccupied with protecting themselves against the southward Japanese expansion. After Pearl Harbour (7 December 1941), the Dutch Government declared war on Japan, but it was only a matter of time before the Japanese reached the Dutch colony. In March 1942 the Dutch Colonial Army surrendered to the Japanese invader and the Netherlands was no longer an empire, but had reached 'a position like Denmark': a very marginal one.[12]

The members of the government-in-exile did not initially see themselves as refugees and beggars as the Dutch East Indies (and the much smaller West Indies) were still in Dutch hands. Holland was not a small nation, but much bigger: a colonial power! This view was dispelled in March 1942, when the Dutch East Indies surrendered to the Japanese. The Netherlands was a small country once again and the cabinet could concentrate on the post-war future of the Netherlands in all of its dimensions. Prominent among them was, of course, the political and social future of the country. Broadly speaking, there were two different attitudes towards this problem, both in London and in occupied Holland. On the one hand, there were those who saw reconstruction primarily in terms of the recreation of the pre-war world; on the other, there were those who wished to combine reconstruction with renewal. This debate dominated discussion both in London and in the clandestine press in the Netherlands, but it was one which transcended the conventional conservative-progressive division in politics.

In London it was Queen Wilhelmina who saw the future as lying in the hands of the 'heroes of the resistance' headed by a much more powerful head of state – in other words, herself. She did not like politicians in general, and the members of her cabinet in particular; instead, she was fond of the young and inexperienced 'England-farers', whom she frequently invited for tea and a biscuit. Almost all these people agreed with Her Majesty that renewal was necessary, that the pre-war politics were detested by the overwhelming majority of the Dutch people and that they did indeed want a stronger head of state. Wilhelmina did not realise that most of her guests did not dare to speak against her or that she was still seen as a demi-goddess and 'the mother of the resistance'. She was absolutely convinced that she would have to get rid of the old politicians, the old generals and the entire pre-war establishment, but she did not seem to realise she was part of that same establishment.

Her government-in-exile consisted of representatives of the different political parties in the Netherlands and they saw no reason at all to change the political system. But Queen Wilhelmina tried to find ways to have her say in a 'renewal' of the Netherlands, proposing for example that after the war there would have to be a three-year period without party-political activities. During that time a new constitution could be prepared that would accord less power to the politicians and more to herself. Moreover, she intended that after the war she should return to the Netherlands without her government, which she wanted to be free of as soon as possible. All of these plans were very monarchical and not entirely constitutional, even if none of them became reality. Nevertheless, they were sufficient to make the members of her government nervous, not least because the Queen also wanted to make her son-in-law, Prince Bernhard, the head and commander of the Dutch Armed Forces. He was one of the few men she trusted and he was full of admiration for her. Because of this and also in order to tighten the bond between the House of Orange and the Dutch during the war, she tried to give him high-ranking positions. Prince Bernhard, who had been a member of the German Nazi party[13] and the SS[14] before his marriage in 1937, and had worked for IG Farben in Paris, was not trusted by the British authorities. Moreover, his behaviour in London, where he indulged himself with fast cars and beautiful women, led them to fear that he was a security risk. With his wife and children safely in Canada and with no parliamentary control or critical press, he seemed intent on having a good time. He performed meaningless military functions, but wore beautiful uniforms and surrounded himself with the daredevils from the Netherlands, the 'England-farers'.[15]

In August 1944, Prince Bernhard became Commander of the Netherlands Forces of the Interior, a loosely-knit organisation of the different resistance groups. It was not a situation his new supreme commander, General Eisenhower, liked at all. In common with the other Allied commanders, he did not see the Prince as a real military leader. The south of the country had been liberated as a result of Operation Market Garden in September 1944, but the rest of the country had to wait for more than half-a-year before the Germans surrendered completely. In the liberated zone Prince Bernhard played his role as Commander with zest and everybody seemed to like him. Together with his mother-in-law, the Prince was responsible for the very pro-royalist feeling in the Netherlands, shared even by the Communist Party which won 10 percent of the vote in the elections in 1946. They were both seen as the great inspirers of resistance. Nobody knew about the affairs of Prince Bernhard, of course, and hardly anybody knew about the very conservative and sometimes undemocratic actions of the Queen in London. After the war a parliamentary investigation was set up to examine the actions of the government-in-exile in London. No questions were asked about the role of the Queen (or of the Prince). This was quite understandable, because the ministers were (and are) politically responsible for the actions of the royal family; nevertheless, it was a pity for historians.

The Dutch and the war

What could the Dutch do to become a real partner in the war? It was obvious that it was up to the major countries, such as the United Kingdom, Canada and later the United States, to conquer Fortress Europe and it was clear once Operation Barbarossa had started that the Red Army had to contribute as much fighting power as it possessed. The most important contribution that the Dutch could make was, without doubt, the Dutch merchant marine, because all the military and non-military resources for the United Kingdom, and, later, for the Soviet Union, had to come by ship. German U-boats and raiders hunted merchant ships on the Atlantic, and the Dutch lost almost half of their ships and half of the entire tonnage. To raise an army was almost impossible; the majority of the able men were in the Netherlands. The government tried to call up Dutchmen living in Britain, the United States, Canada and South Africa, but its success was limited. Most of the Dutchmen living abroad had left their native country for different reasons and there was hardly any willingness to fight. In South Africa, for example, the Queen's envoy tried to persuade reluctant Dutch construction workers to fight. He said that the Germans were plundering Holland and feared that he would not see again the paintings in his family's mansion in the east of the country. The construction workers yelled that they did not want to fight for his family's paintings.[16] But some conscripts did arrive, and the Dutch were able to form the Princess Irene Brigade (named after the second daughter of Juliana) and to form No. 2 (Dutch) Troop of the Commandos. Others opted to serve in the RAF and some even volunteered to be sent back to the Netherlands as intelligence agents.

One of the main problems for the Dutch Government was the lack of information, both military and non-military, from the occupied homeland. This was also, of course, a problem for the Allied military commanders. It was already difficult to know what the German occupying forces were doing, although information generally reached London, albeit sometimes very late. But it was almost impossible to know if there was any resistance and, if so, what kind of clandestine actions were taking place. Only with this knowledge could they try to support the Resistance, but in the Netherlands the Resistance groups were annoyed, both at how little was known about their activities in London and the misinformation broadcast by Radio Orange. The Dutch Government received information from people who had left the Netherlands clandestinely, but unless these individuals had been in contact with one of the major Resistance groups their information was not very valuable. In mid-1942, an intelligence line was set up that ran from the north of the Netherlands to Sweden. The Germans allowed some coastal traffic to that neutral country and some of the Dutch captains were willing to smuggle information into Sweden and back into the Netherlands. This 'Swedish Route' operated for a little more then a year before it was stopped as a result of counter-intelligence work by the Germans. A second route was the 'Swiss Route', where Switzerland as a neutral country played the same role as Sweden. The Dutch General Secretary of the World Council of Churches in Geneva, Dr W. A. Visser 't Hooft had originated this line and he protected it against competition from others.

But both the Dutch Government and the Allies wanted more. It was Churchill who stated that it was necessary 'to set Europe ablaze'. Britain had been on the defensive since the outbreak of the war, and it was only at the end of 1942 that German troops were forced to retreat in North Africa. The bombing of Germany was not very successful, so the notion of internal uprisings in occupied Europe was an attractive one. But how could one boost such uprisings; how could one sabotage the German war effort? Our ideas about armed resistance and sabotage have been formed mostly by post-war films and especially by French cinema.[17] *La Bataille du rail* (1945) by René Clément was one such film, but it was only the start

of an abundant stream of Resistance films of a highly romanticised
nature, with brave fighters and stupid German soldiers or cruel
Gestapo officers. But what was the reality of life under the first for-
eign occupation of the Netherlands since that of Napoleon? Unlike
Belgium and France with their German military administrations, the
Netherlands had a civilian administration, headed by the Austrian
Dr A. Seyss-Inquart. He was appointed by Hitler and he remained
his ardent follower until he was hanged after the Nuremberg trials.[18]
He controlled the whole administrative structure as can be clearly
perceived from one of his first Orders, issued on 21 June 1940:

> By order of the Reich Commissioner for the occupied Dutch territory,
> regarding the authority of the Secretaries-General of the ministries of
> the Netherlands.
>   In accordance with Paragraph 5, of the Führer's decree regarding
> the competence of governmental authorities in the territory of the
> Netherlands, dated 18 May 1940, I hereby order:
>
> Paragraph 1.
> (1) The Secretaries-General of the Dutch ministries are empow-
> ered, within the limits of their responsibility, to take such measures as
> are necessary for the maintenance of public order and safety; in par-
> ticular they are authorised to charge their subordinates with such
> responsibilities.
> (2) If the authority granted in (1) is exceeded, those responsible are
> liable to the most severe punishment.
>
> Paragraph 2.
> (1) The Reich Commissioner for the occupied Dutch territory
> reserves the right, in particular circumstances, to reduce or take away
> the authority delegated in Paragraph 1.
>
> Paragraph 3.
> (1) This order becomes effective immediately

There was no Queen, no government and no parliament, but life
continued nevertheless and it was difficult for everybody to take a
stand against the occupier. From *attentisme*, 'Pétainisme' to complete collaboration on the one hand,[19] or from *attentisme* to
full-scale resistance on the other, everything was possible. Possibilities included helping people in hiding, both Jews and non-Jews;
forging or stealing identity cards, ration cards and stamps; espionage and sabotage; and rescuing Allied airmen and trying to
smuggle them back to Britain. And last, but not least, around
30,000 people were involved in writing, printing and distributing
illegal newspapers and pamphlets. Two of the six daily newspapers
currently published in the Netherlands started as illegal newspapers. One must bear in mind that there was no overall organisation

of the Resistance; there was competition, just as in peace-time, and there were serious quarrels about the social and political future of the Netherlands.

The Dutch Government in London knew only a little about these activities, and it was decided to create a Bureau Inlichtingen (Intelligence Bureau) which would try to send agents to the Netherlands. This bureau was also responsible for the information arriving from the Swiss and Swedish routes. More than forty agents, often accompanied by a radio operator, were dropped in the Netherlands. Their mission was always to contact an intelligence-gathering group and to assist them, or to found such a group. More than half of the agents were subsequently arrested by the Germans. It is very difficult to evaluate the usefulness of the intelligence gathered by these groups and the agents. Moreover, even if they had good information, it could be ignored. For instance, Major-General R.E. Urquhart, the First Airborne's commanding officer at the disaster of Arnhem in September 1944, subsequently wrote:

> . . . already, however, Dutch resistance reports had been noted to the effect that 'battered [German] panzer remnants have been sent to Holland to refit', and Eindhoven and Nijmegen were mentioned as reception areas. And during the week an intelligence officer at SHAEF, poring over reports and maps, came to the conclusion that these panzer formations were the 9th and possibly the 10th Panzer Divisions.[20]

Alas, other intelligence officers took another view, but the panzers were indeed there and the Allied paratroopers were no match for them.

One of the recent historians of the Resistance in the Netherlands, C.M. Schulten, has come to the conclusion that the significance of the Resistance in the liberation of the Netherlands was, in fact, very slight.[21] Certainly a joint Dutch-English operation known as Plan Holland proved to be a complete failure. It was intended that agents should be parachuted into the occupied country to train Resistance fighters who would become active at the time of an Allied invasion. Things went wrong from the first drop, and German counter-intelligence, the Abwehr and Sicherheitsdienst, succeeded in making contact with London, pretending that they were the Dutch agents who had landed safely and were ready to work. Altogether, in this so-called *England-Spiel* or *Fall Nordpol*, fifty-nine agents and 570 containers of weapons fell into the hands of the Germans. Approximately 1,000 people lost their lives directly or indirectly as a result of this *Spiel*. In the light of this and other disasters, John Woodruff has written that:

To Resistance workers in Holland London was distant, inept, igno-
rant of their aims, problems and accomplishments. Requests for aid
or recognition were likely to be met with indifference or even silence.
From London's vantage point it saw a mass of unknown Resistance
organisations, staffed by faceless persons of varying degrees of competence, some with unrealistic aims, who often approached the
Government with grandiose claims of strength not based on fact.[22]

The Destruction of the Jews

One could say that two wars were fought by the Nazis: one against
the Allies and one against the Jews. In the latter war, the Holocaust
or Shoah, there was no victory over Hitler. And the statistics on the
Netherlands 'tell a chilling story', as Bob Moore has written:

> Of more then 140,000 Jews living in pre-war Netherlands, approxi-
> mately 107,000 were deported to the east and at least 102,000 were
> murdered or worked to death in the Nazi camps. Horrific enough on
> their own, the impact of these figures was compounded by two other
> statistics. Firstly there was the fact that the deported Jews constituted
> around 40 percent of the total civilian casualties for the country as a
> whole. This made it abundantly clear that the Jews had suffered out
> of all proportion to their non-Jewish compatriots. While this could
> be partly explained by the low levels of mortality suffered by Dutch
> civilians as a result of German occupation policies and the relatively
> short periods of fighting on Dutch soil in 1940 and 1944–45, a far
> more telling comparison emerged when the 73 percent Jewish mor-
> tality of the Netherlands was compared with the figures for Belgium
> (40 percent) and France (25 percent). How could such a huge differ-
> ence have arisen between apparently similar states, and, more
> importantly, how could the Netherlands compare so unfavourably
> with her nearest Western European neighbours?[23]

Strangely enough, scholars have only recently begun to take an
interest in this phenomenon.[24] And until recent years, the role of the
Dutch themselves in the destruction of the Jews has hardly been discussed; the Germans have been presented as the persecutors and the
Dutch as their victims. Guus Meershoek, however, explained in his
dissertation on the war-time Amsterdam police how Dutch policemen became involved in the Holocaust,[25] while Aalders showed in
his book *Roof* how Jews were plundered by the Germans with the
help of the Dutch.[26] Controversy recently flared up in the Netherlands over a book by Nanda van der Zee about the destruction of
Dutch Jewry.[27] She claimed that, although it was quite obvious
what would happen to the Jews both before and during the war,
nobody in London acted. The Queen, in particular, should have

said more on Radio Orange about the persecution of the Jews and she should have encouraged the Dutch to help their Jewish neighbours. Although no-one would deny the importance of this element of her book, it is, however, hardly novel.

In the decades following the war, everyone said that no-one knew anything about the persecution of the Jews, certainly not before and hardly during the war: 'Wir haben es nicht gewusst'. In 1989, however, Frank van Vree demonstrated in his dissertation on the Dutch press between 1930 and 1939[28] that this idea of 'not knowing' was nonsense. The public was well informed about the National Socialist dictatorship on the other side of the border, and knew about the persecution of the Jews. As for the extent to which information was available during the war years themselves, one need only consult the diary of Anne Frank. She wrote, on Friday 9 October 1942:

> Our Jewish friends are being rounded up by the dozen . . . If it is as bad as this in Holland, whatever will it be like in the distant and barbarous regions they are sent to. We assume that most of them are murdered. The English radio speaks of being gassed; perhaps that is the quickest way to die.[29]

But the real disaster, it seems – the killing of more than 100,000 Jews from the Netherlands – was not clear to London. The Commission for Repatriation, established in London, stated that some 70,000 Jews would have to be repatriated from Poland after the war; in reality the figure was less than 6,000. Moreover, no special measures were envisaged for the Jews, the strange assumption being that the Germans had discriminated against the Jews and that the Dutch would therefore not do so after the war.

Van der Zee, however, advanced a more controversial thesis. She argued that because the Queen (and the government) had fled the country, it was possible for the Germans to install a civilian administration under Seyss-Inquart, and this was why more Jews than in other western countries were rounded up and murdered in the east. History, however, is more complex than that; for instance, we do not know yet why Hitler installed a civilian administration so quickly. Furthermore, the behaviour of King Leopold III of Belgium, who remained in his own country, does not seem to offer an encouraging counter-example. It is true that Queen Wilhelmina did not frequently protest openly on Radio Orange against the persecution of the Jews, but that was the case for all of the Allies. Winning the war was the overriding priority; all the other issues, including the camps at Auschwitz and Sobibor, were at that time regarded as of minor importance.

The Loss of Empire

The future of the Dutch East Indies occupied a very important place in the eyes and hearts of the Dutch in London. Since the 'golden age', and after the four so-called 'English wars' over mastery of the sea, the Netherlands had an enormous colony and no intention of giving it up. The initial intention in London was to liberate the East Indies from the Japanese, but the government knew, of course, that it would be the British and the Americans who would have to perform this role – even if nobody could know that two atomic bombs would prove necessary to achieve this goal. The politicians in London also realised that there were calls for independence within the colony, but before the war it was run like a police state and freedom fighters were safely interned in concentration camps on New Guinea. It therefore came more or less as a blessing in disguise that the Japanese tried to give those fighters for independence a free hand at the beginning of the Japanese occupation. It was now easy for the Dutch to label people, such as Sukarno as Quislings.

On 7 December 1942, Queen Wilhelmina made a famous speech in which she spoke about the occupied colony. In popular memory it is often claimed that she spoke about the possibility of independence, but the opposite was in fact true. The first task, she stated, was to restore the Kingdom of the Netherlands completely, including the colonies. Maybe (but only maybe) in the future one could discuss the right for independence, but certainly not at that moment.

Because of the shortsightedness of the politicians, not only in London but also in the Netherlands, there were two colonial wars: one from July 1947 until the end of that year; and a second one that began in December 1948 and ended in mid-1949. Officially these wars are still termed 'Police Actions', as if the freedom fighters in the East Indies were children who had to be punished. In the Netherlands it still seems difficult to confront the colonial past completely, and during the last decade debates have begun to arise about so-called 'war crimes' committed by Dutch troops in the East Indies. Some of these troops were people who had been deeply involved in the Resistance in Holland, and they thought they were doing the same thing in the East Indies: fighting for freedom. This was therefore one of the most important consequences of the Second World War for the Netherlands: the loss of its colonies. The country also became firmly embedded in European and international organisations; neutrality was no longer a viable option. With these two exceptions – the loss of colonies and the abandonment of neutrality – it was, however, the continuities rather than the changes which seemed most prominent in the Netherlands after the war. Seen in the long term, the war did not mark a major break in Dutch history.[30]

Notes

1. M. Lisser, *Dagboek 1940–1943*, Diary collection, Netherlands Institute for War Documentation, Amsterdam.
2. G. Hirschfeld, *Nazi Rule and Dutch Collaboration. The Netherlands under German Occupation, 1940–1945*, Oxford/New York/Hamburg, 1988, pp. 12–13.
3. J.H. Woodruff, *Relations between the Netherlands Government-in-exile and occupied Holland during World War II*, Boston, 1964, pp. 8–9.
4. D. Barnouw and J. Nekkers, 'The Netherlands: "State Corporatsim against the State"', in *Organising Business for War. Corporatist Economic Organisation during the Second World War*, eds W. Grant, J. Nekkers and P. van Waarden, New York/Oxford, 1991, p. 141.
5. I.J. Blanken, *Geschiedenis van Philips Electronics N.V.*, vol. 4, *Onder Duits Beheer*, Zaltbommel, 1997, pp. 111–44.
6. L. de Jong, *Het Koninkrijk der Nederlanden in de Tweede Wereldoorlog*, 14 vols, The Hague,1969–1991, vol. 2, pp. 426–30.
7. C. Hamilton, *Holland To-day*, London, 1950, p. 51.
8. A.J. Barnouw, *Monthly Letters*, Assen, 1969, p. 164.
9. Woodruff, *Relations*, p. 13.
10. See A. Dessing, 'De Grote Oversteek: Engelandvaarders over de Noordzee', *Oorlogsdocumentatie '40–'45. Jaarboek van het Rijksinstituut voor Oorlogsdocumentatie 7* (1996): pp. 67–89.
11. de Jong, *Koninkrijk*, vol. 9 (1979), p. 137.
12. J.L. Heldring, 'De rang van Denemarken', *NRC/Handelsblad*, 13 April 1999.
13. G. Aalders, *De affaire-Sanders*, The Hague,1996, pp. 130–133.
14. de Jong, *Koninkrijk*, vol. 1 (1969), p. 578.
15. A. van der Zijl, 'De zondagsprins', *HP/De Tijd*, 24 April 1998.
16. de Jong, *Koninkrijk*, vol. 8 (1978), p. 703
17. S. Lindeperg, *Les écrans de l'Ombre. La Seconde Guerre Mondiale dans le cinéma français (1944–1969)*, Paris, 1997.
18. H.J. Neuman, *Arthur Seyss-Inquart*, Utrecht, 1967.
19. See Hirschfeld, *Nazi-Rule*.
20. R.E. Urquhart, *Arnhem*, New York, 1958, p. 9, cited in Woodruff, *Relations*, 120.
21. C.M. Schulten, *'En verpletterd wordt het juk' – Verzet in Nederland 1940–1945*, The Hague, 1995, p. 15.
22. Woodruff, *Relations*, p. 136.
23. B. Moore, *Victims and Survivors: The Nazi Persecution of the Jews in the Netherlands 1940–1945*, London, 1997, p. 53.
24. P. Griffioen and R. Zeller, 'Jodenvervolging in Nederland en België tijdens de Tweede Wereldoorlog: een vergelijkende analyse', *Oorlogsdocumentatie '40–'45. Jaarboek van het Rijksinstituut voor Oorlogsdocumentatie 8* (1997): pp. 10–63.
25. G. Meershoek, *Dienaren van het gezag. De Amsterdamse politie tijdens de bezetting*, Amsterdam, 1999.
26. G. Aalders, *Roof*, The Hague, 1999.

27. N. van der Zee, *Om erger te voorkomen. De voorbereiding en uitvoering van de vernietiging van het Nederlandse jodendom tijdens de Tweede Wereldoorlog*, Amsterdam, 1997.

28. F. van Vree, *De Nederlandse pers en Duitsland 1930–1939 – Een studie over de vorming van de publieke opinie*, Groningen, 1989.

29. A. Frank, *The Diary of Anne Frank – The Critical Edition*, eds D. Barnouw and G.P. van der Stroom, London, 1989, p. 273.

30 See J.C.H. Blom, 'The Second World War and Dutch Society: Continuity and Change', *Britain and the Netherlands*, vol. 6, *War and Society*, eds A.C. Duke and C.A. Tamse, The Hague (1977): pp. 228–48.

14

THE SOCIALIST INTERNATIONALE: SOCIETY OR COUNTER-SOCIETY?

HERMAN BALTHAZAR

At no moment in its history did the Socialist Workers Internationale (IOS), founded at Hamburg in May 1923, prove able to develop as a supranational political force. More than had been the case even before 1914, the IOS was obliged to take into account 'the national geography of the socialist movement' (a phrase invented by Ernest Labrousse and taken up by George Haupt). The various shocks and ideological conflicts did not prevent the development of strong bonds of solidarity and regular contacts, but, once the Great Depression and the Nazi seizure of power had come to dominate events, the IOS fell into an apparently terminal crisis. The nature of this crisis was clearly apparent at the meeting of its ruling body, the Bureau, on 14 May 1939. On this occasion, the two great figures of socialist internationalism, Louis de Brouckère (Belgium) and Friedrich Adler (Austria) resigned as president and secretary respectively. On 17 June a further brief meeting was held at which the Dutch Socialist J.W. Albarda, a moderate and anti-Marxist was appointed as the new president. Shortly afterwards, however, the Dutch Socialist Party, the SDAP, entered government for the first time and C. Huysmans assumed the post of president. Who would replace Adler was not, however, resolved. After 10 May 1940 the situation became highly confusing. The meeting of the Bureau initially due to be held in Brussels on 26–27 May and subsequently relocated to Paris was postponed indefinitely. Adler left for the United States and declared in an interview with *Call* (the organ of the American socialist party) that 'the Labour and Socialist International is no longer in existence, since the great majority of its component parties no longer function legally and cannot provide satisfactory representatives for an international association'. This marked the apparent death of the long-weakened IOS. In terms of how representative they were, their means and their positions in the military conflict, the member parties of the IOS had nothing in common and were in no position to meet together.

At this tragic moment, London became the only place in which new initiatives were possible, because of the influx of émigrés, the establishment of numerous recognised exile governments and, lastly, the dominant position in the international socialist movement of the Labour Party. In all aspects of international affairs, the activities of the Labour Party's International Department (ID) within the National Executive Committee (NEC) increased considerably, even though Labour had never had a particularly internationalist attitude. Within the ID, William Gillies was the principal figure: a man of the bureaucracy, a dedicated and determined worker, he had opinions that were not exactly of the left. The presence of Gillies made the ID a centre of intense interest both for the socialist émigrés and for Labour, now sharing power in the War Cabinet.

In addition to the Labour leadership, the British left also participated very actively in the debate on the possibilities of socialist international co-operation. One forum for debate was the Fabian Society, which possessed considerable moral authority. Another, further to the left, was the Left Book Club, founded in 1935 and possessing 75,000 members and more than 1,200 local branches by 1939. There was also the Socialist Clarity Group, editor of *Labour Discussion Notes*, and the Independent Labour Party (ILP), which since 1925 had been the motor behind international contacts between the radical non-communist left.[1] Finally, there was the important role played by the trade unionists grouped in the Trades Union Congress (TUC).[2] The complex history from July 1940 of the restructuring of the Socialist Internationale or, more exactly, of a panoply of initiatives intended to bring together the socialists present in Britain must be considered in this context.[3]

The first meeting to try to achieve this restructuring took place, at the official initiative of Labour, on 13 July at St Ermins, a vast Victorian-style hotel. Present, apart from George Dallas, Hugh Dalton, Harold Laski and William Gillies, as members of the NEC and its ID, were twenty-one carefully selected guests: two Norwegians, one Dane, three Frenchmen, four Poles, three Czechs, one Slovak, two Sudeten-Germans and four Belgians. All were members of the bureaux of their respective parties. Gillies tried to limit the discussion to highly vague agreements and ruled out the possibility of creating either a definitive or provisional organisation of an international secretariat. Instead, it was to be a consultative group: 'The group of international friends who meet at St Ermins on the second Friday of each month under the chairmanship of George Dallas', was the standard formula used for summoning meetings issued on the headed note paper of the Labour Party and signed, throughout the war, by W. Gillies. Two months later, another invitation, almost identical in nature, summoned 'socialists of good faith' to 'the International Group which has been constituted with C. Huysmans as President'. Huysmans, who was not a man to keep silent, had already written on 30 July to Gillies: 'Believe me, let it not be said later that we have quietly strangled the Second Internationale. I kept it alive through the 1914–1918 conflict. I will keep it alive, I hope, through the present conflict and I will not allow anyone to prevent it from living, even if it must do so modestly'.

Huysmans moreover passed up no opportunity to represent the Internationale abroad. In his position as president, he sent a telegram to President Roosevelt on 28 September requesting that he intervene in favour of the former French socialist prime minister Léon Blum. His equivocal initiatives provoked irritation on the part of the British and many other socialists. That his efforts were nevertheless partially successful was possible only because the Labour leadership believed it to be useful to bring together some socialists who did not form part of the Allied governments accredited with London. In this way, the Huysmans committee was allowed to come into existence on the condition that its deliberations remained confidential, the names of those invited were not published and Huysmans worked in collaboration with and under the leadership of Labour. Moreover, Gillies remained the secretary of the new organisation. Among those invited to the meetings of the Huysmans committee were the German Hans Vogel and the Austrian Oscar Pollak, both émigrés from the Reich. The issue of contacts with such people was a highly sensitive one among the socialists.[4]

Distrust towards German-speaking socialists, or at least towards most of them and their organisations was mingled with hatred towards Germany. The highly influential and widely distributed ideas of Lord Vansittart excluded any possibility of considering the war as an ideological conflict. As he wrote in his book *The Roots of Trouble*, published in 1940:

> There is no such thing as Hitlerism. It is only a projection of nationalism and militarism, conducted on a lower and more popular plane ... but many – including some who would prefer a 'fresh and joyous' class-war to this one – have forgotten the ugly role of the German Left at the Stockholm Conference in the last War, its approval of the

atrocious Treaty of Bucharest, its dark complicities in Weimar's failure. Trust no Germany till this one is gone for ever.[5]

Those socialists who believed that the complete military defeat of
Germany was at that moment in the war the only objective to be
pursued therefore distrusted the attitude and actions of some Ger-
man or Austrian socialists such as Julien Braunthal, the former
assistant of F. Adler in the bureau of the Austrian party before the
Anschluss, and Richard Löwenthal of the group *Neu Beginnen* (a
group in opposition to the SPD). Supported by the periodical *The
Left News*, these figures had launched the idea of an International
Socialist Forum based on the primacy of the ideological conflict in
May 1941. The evolution of the war, especially after the entry of the
Soviet Union into the Allied camp, gave rise to other problems and
priorities that reinforced the conflicts and divergences of view
among the émigré socialists. At the opposite pole from the initiative
of the International Socialist Forum, one must also mention the creation at the end of 1941, by the German Walter Loeb, of the
publishing house Fight for Freedom, an initiative that rapidly grew
into an influential and effective pressure group. Loeb deserves particular attention in this respect for he drew to him major figures
both from Labour and from the world of the émigré socialists.
Among them figured, somewhat surprisingly, President Huysmans,
whose change in attitude can be explained by reference to this
extract from a long letter that he wrote to Gillies, dated 13 February 1942:

> My conviction of today is not the result of impulsive abstraction; it
> is the conclusion of a deceived socialist who is convinced now that
> the German nation is infected by the spirit of violence ... that this
> German nation will follow obediently and heartfully Mr. Hitler as
> long as he may be able to speak as a victorious man ... that, if he
> could remain victorious, the great majority of the German nation
> would consider him as a national hero, even if he destroys liberty,
> even if he murders all people around him, even if he makes a Europe
> of one Herrenvolk and numerous slave countries. For this reason, I
> am thinking, very strongly that I was in error twenty years ago, and
> that I should be a poor socialist spirit if I took the risk to be deceived
> a third time.

All this helps to explain the confusion and prevarication that were
characteristic of the milieu of the socialist émigrés. Francis Carsten
recounts in his autobiographical memoir that he arrived in London
in the spring of 1939 as a member of the group New Beginnen.[6]
Once a left-wing socialist, active at Oxford in the Democratic
Socialist Group, his political philosophy shifted to incline towards

the ideas of Loeb. Perhaps this was also because in 1942 he obtained a post in the secret service of the Political Warfare Executive, where he was responsible for writing a manual for British officers who would have to administer the British zone after the German defeat.

This example shows the importance of not underestimating the mundane material needs of the émigrés, which often had a major impact on the evolution of their political attitude. Another important determinant was the multiple conflicts that existed within and between groups of émigré socialists, differences that very often were not the product of ideological divergences. A good example is the comparison between the numerous Belgian socialists and the few Dutch socialists in England. The Belgians had their own organisations, dissident groups and antipathies;[7] they engaged in many attempts at international liaison and from 1943 maintained regular contact with the socialists acting illegally within occupied Belgium. The Dutch socialists, by contrast, were not very active in London and they do not feature in the literature on the role of the socialists in London during the war.[8]

Labour and the British left never broke off their contacts with this microcosm of socialist émigrés during the war. However, it is impossible to say that they exercised a real influence over the British agenda. After the great turning-point of the war, with the collapse of the Mussolini regime in July 1943, the Labour leadership gave Hugh Dalton the task of establishing within the ID a first blueprint of a post-war society. His report was presented on 12 November; on 27 November Gillies invited the members of the Dallas group to take note of it and to decide its stance on ten issues concerning post-war measures. The major themes of the Dalton report were taken up in the manifesto 'The International Post-war Settlement', which was presented to the 43rd annual Labour Party conference held from 10 to 14 December 1944. Between the publication of the report in November 1943 and the conference in December 1944, Labour intensified its efforts to bring about a structured rapprochement between the social democratic parties and groups.

The first consequence of these efforts was the decision of 13 September 1944 to establish an International Labour and Socialist Preparatory Committee, with an almost identical composition to that of the Dallas Group. This committee can therefore be considered to have been a first step towards a formal restructuring of the Socialist Internationale. It was specifically stated to be a provisional committee without real powers and without the right to publish declarations so long as the parties were not formally reconstituted in their respective countries. The most critical, and also significant, response came from Stockholm where a group of socialists from fourteen countries had constituted itself into a 'Little Internationale', which in 1944 was entitled the Internationale Gruppe democratischer Sozialisten, Arbeitskreis fur Friedensfragen. Operating in a neutral country, and less dominated by governmental policy, this Stockholm group was free to devise projects for the reform of the Socialist Internationale. This was evident in their manifesto of 5 November 1944, 'Wiederrichtung der Sozialistischen Internationale', signed by, among others, the German Willy Brandt, the Austrian Bruno Kreisky and the Norwegian Martin Tranmael.[9] Their appeal for a wider union at the geopolitical and ideological level (around questions of unity, of anti-communism and of class struggle) was not accepted by the British Labour Party, but that does not render the comparison between what happened in London and Stockholm any less interesting.

Between the legacies of the crisis of the 1930s and the challenges of the post-war era, rapidly defined by the Cold War, the debates that took place among the émigrés foreshadowed their engagement and struggles in the post-war world.

Notes

1. See W. Buschak, *Das Londoner Büro – Europäische Linkssozialisten in der Zwischenkriegzeit*, Amsterdam, 1985.
2. See in particular T. Kushner, 'Their Brother's (and Sisters') Keeper? Refugees from Nazism and British Labour', in *Racism and the Labour Market*, eds M. Vanderlinden and J. Lucassen, Berne and Vienna, 1995, pp. 581–620.
3. Concerning the wider history of these initiatives there exist to my knowledge only two studies: H. Balthazar, 'L'Internationale socialiste – Les débats de Londres en 1940–41', in *Cahiers d'histoire de la Seconde Guerre Mondiale* 2 (1972): pp. 191–210, and O. Dunkelmann, 'Zwischen S.A.I. und Sozialistischer Internationale – Zur Genesis des International Labour and Socialist Preparatory Committee in London, 1940–1945', in *Zeitschrift für Geschichtswissenschaft* 24:12 (1976): pp. 1394–1913.
4. Much of the historical literature has been devoted to this issue. For analysis of it, see *Exile in Great Britain – Refugees from Hitler's Germany*, ed. G. Hirschfeld, New Jersey, 1984; A.J. Sherman, *Island Refuge – Britain and Refugees from the Third Reich 1933–1938*, Ilford Essex, 1994 (originally published in 1973); H. Gruber, The German Socialist Executive 1933–1939 – Democracy as International Contradiction, in *Chance and Illusion – Labour in Retreat – Studies on the Social Crisis in Interwar Western Europe*, eds W. Maderthaner and H. Gruber, Vienna and Zurich, 1988, pp. 185–245; and A. Glees, *Exile Politics during the Second World War – The German Social Democrats in Britain*, Oxford, 1982.
5. Lord Vansittart, *The Roots of Trouble*, London, 1940, pp. 37–42.
6. F. Carsten, 'From Revolutionary Socialism to German History', in *Out of the Third Reich: Refugee Historians in Post-War Britain*, ed. P. Alter, London and New York, 1998, pp. 25–40.

7. See, for example, J. Gotovitch, *De Belgische Socialisten in London*, G. Huysmansdocumenten vol. 8, Antwerp, 1981.
8. See L. De Jong, *Het Koninkrijk der Nederlanden in de Tweede Wereldoorlog*, vol. 9, The Hague, 1979 and A. Klijn, *Arbeiders- of Volkspartij? Een vergelijkende studie van het Belgisch en Nederlands Socialisme, 1933–1946*, Maastricht, 1990.
9. See the analysis of O. Dankelmann and the following series of studies: E. Paul, *Die 'Kleine Internationale'*, Stockholm, 1960; W. Brandt, *Draussen, Schriften wahrend der Emigration*, Munich, 1966; H. Müssener, *Exil in Schweden – Politische und kulturelle Emigration nach 1933*, Munich, 1974; and K. Misgeld, 'Die Internationale Gruppe demokratischer Sozialisten Stockholm, 1942–1945', in *Studia Historica Uppsaliana*, Uppsala, 1976.

Note on Archival and Bibliographical References

The archival research for this contribution is primarily based on: the archives of the *International Department* of the Labour Party (at the time of my research housed in Transport House, London); the C. Huysmans archives (Antwerp), mainly series d and f, which contains a rich correspondence with most of the prominent socialist leaders in exile; and the Fonds Heyse in CEGES-SOMA, Brussels, which houses a rich collection of brochures edited in Great Britain by various socialist groups (British and exiles).

For a discussion of the Belgian case, which apart from the German-speaking groups formed the most numerous group and were also important because of the position and influence of Huysmans as President of the Socialist Internationale, see:

J. Gotovitch, *De Belgische Socialisten in Londen*, C. Huysmans-documenten, vol. 8, Antwerp, 1981.

Regarding the participation of German-speaking Socialists from the Reich, Austria and the Sudetenland, see:

G. Hirschfeld, ed., *Exile in Great Britain – Refugees from Hitler's Germany*, New Jersey, 1984;
A.J. Sherman, *Island Refuge, Britain and Refugees from the Third Reich 1933–1938*, Ilford, Essex, 1994;
H. Gruber, 'The German Socialist Executive 1933–1939 – Democracy as International Contradiction', in *Chance and Illusion – Labour in Retreat: Studies on the Social Crisis in Interwar Western Europe*, eds W. Maderthaner and H. Gruber, Vienna and Zurich, 1988, pp. 185–245;
A. Glees, *Exile Politics During the Second World War – The German Social Democrats in Britain*, Oxford, 1982;
H. Mommsen, 'Die Sozialdemokratie in der Defensive', in *Sozialdemokratie zwischen Klassenbewegung und Volkspartei*, ed. H. Mommsen, Frankfurt, 1974, pp. 106–33;
T. Prager, *Bekentnisse eines Revisionisten*, Vienna, 1975;
W. Jaksch, *Potsdam 1945 ou l'histoire d'un mensonge*, Paris, 1966.

On the role of the Left, see:

W. Buschak, *Das Londoner Büro – Europäsche Linkssozialisten in der Zwischenkriegszeit*, Amsterdam, 1985.

General information on the history of the Internationale is provided in:

F. van Holthoon and M. Vanderlinden, *Internationalism in the Labour Movement, 1830–1940*, Leiden, 1988;

J. Braunthal, *Geschichte der Internationale*, 3 vols, Hannover, 1961–71;

G. Callesen (ABA, Copenhagen), *Bibliography of the Social-Democratic Internationals 1914–2000* (Preliminary Report for the IALHI-project presented at the IALHI conference 1990, Milan, unfinished paper for internal circulation).

On the influence of the Trade Union Movement, see:

T. Kushner, 'Their Brothers' (and Sisters') Keeper? Refugees from Nazism and British Labour', in *Racism and the Labour Market*, eds M. Vanderlinden and J. Lucassen, Berne and Vienna, 1995, pp. 581–620.

15

LEGACIES OF EXILE: THE EXILE GOVERNMENTS IN LONDON DURING THE SECOND WORLD WAR AND THE POLITICS OF POST-WAR EUROPE

MARTIN CONWAY

Exile is the experience of impotence. This, at least, would seem to be the lesson of the mid-twentieth century. The heterogeneous groups of Russian exiles scattered across Europe after the Bolshevik seizure of power and the opponents of Franco forced to flee from Spain in the 1930s all had plenty of time to brood on Karl Marx's dictum that exile was no more than 'a school of scandal and of meanness'.[1] If the causes they espoused were eventually in some limited sense vindicated, this victory owed almost nothing to their efforts, and few of the original exiles had the ambivalent pleasure of living long enough to witness the downfall of their opponents. More recently, the central European exiles who found refuge in Britain in the 1940s and 1950s followed a largely similar path: unable to shake Soviet communist rule in their erstwhile homelands, they were obliged to survive on the long-term exile's meagre diet of propaganda, ritual, rumour and intrigue. Even London's latest exile communities, the diverse and often fiercely contradictory groups from Iran, Iraq, Saudi Arabia and Algeria, who have transformed London into the principal centre of Middle Eastern exile during the 1980s and 1990s, seem all too likely to undergo a similar experience, as proud boasts of their influence and imminent success turn remorselessly into internecine intrigue and disillusionment.

At first sight, the exile populations and regimes in London during the Second World War would appear to be the striking exception to this rule. Their beginnings were indeed unpromising. Only the Dutch and Norwegian governments could claim the sanction of royal approval; and all faced significant rival contenders for power, either in exile or, more threateningly, within their native lands. Their resolve to continue the war was uncertain, while the resources they possessed, in material, human and financial terms, were often little more than derisory. When the British journalist and official, Bruce Lockhart, paid his first visit to the erstwhile President of Czechoslovakia, Edvard Benes, in London, it was at his new and distinctly unofficial residence at 26 Gwendolen Avenue in Putney.[2] And yet within a few years the fortunes of war and their own determined efforts had transformed these exiles from the irrelevant flotsam of lost battles into the recognised leaders of their countries, cloaked in the improvised trappings of legitimacy and the more substantial apparel of Allied military and diplomatic support. With the important exception of the Poles, those in London proved able to return to their native lands, not as reviled *fuyards* but as custodians of the national honour and highly convenient retrospective incarnations of unwavering opposition to Nazi Germany.

The means of their rapid and often implausible transition from comic-opera gesture politics to the reality of power had been several. The willingness of the Churchill government in Britain, and, subsequently and distinctly more cautiously, of the United States to sponsor and assist these exiles, proved to be an inestimable benefit. Attendance as the accredited representatives of a government-in-exile at a Buckingham Palace garden party might have seemed a rather insubstantial attribute of statehood in an era of world war, but it was often all that the exiles in London could cling to in the early 1940s. Other factors also played a role. Colonies, in the case of the Belgian Government and subsequently the Free French, provided a distant opportunity to act out the rituals of sovereignty and contribute, however obliquely, to the Allied war effort. Expatriate populations in the United States and Latin America also supplied much needed injections of personnel and finance. Above all, the creation of armed forces in exile, however slow and painful, formed the most tangible means of claiming their place as participants in the Allied war effort. With the important exception of the Polish Army, none of the London regimes possessed the resources to add substantially to Allied military strength, but the amorphous and multi-faceted character of the Allied campaigns on land, sea and air during the Second World War offered fortuitous opportunities by which many of these improvised armed units could become something more than mere *soldats de propagande*.[3]

The success of these exile groups was certainly not solely of their own making. Allied sponsorship, the political errors of rivals and the accidents of battle were in many respects the decisive factors. Yet, it would be unduly mean to deny men such as Sikorski, Benes or de Gaulle a part in their own success. Their obstinate determination to construct the diplomatic, political and military constituents of statehood out of the unpromising resources of 1940 amounted, in the judgement of Henri Michel on the Free French, to something close to a 'miracle'.[4] If Sikorski was deprived by death of the opportunity to return to Poland, the return of the Dutch and Norwegian monarchs to their liberated homelands, of Benes to the Hradcany Castle in Prague and, above all, De Gaulle's self-consciously triumphant procession down the Champs Elysées in August 1944 constituted the reward for their single-minded determination to seize the chances provided by the rapidly evolving political and military situation.[5] Even the German Socialists in London, succeeded, in the words of Anthony Glees, not merely in rising 'phoenix-like' from the ashes of the Nazi era but also in influencing significantly the political orientation of the SPD in the Federal Republic.[6]

And yet this miraculous or 'phoenix-like' interpretation of the London regimes is not the whole story. Even for these most successful of European exiles of the mid-twentieth century, the war years had a much darker side of frustration and failure. Two factors above all always served to circumscribe the degree of success experienced by the exile groups and governments: their dependence on Allied favour and their limited control over 'their' citizens within Axis-occupied Europe. The first of these factors, Allied policy, constituted the most obvious and initially most immediate constraint. At its most basic level, the exiles could do or say nothing of significance either to the outside world or to their native lands without the approval of their British minders.[7] British surveillance, including the use of intelligence agents among the exiles, remains a murky subject, but it was clearly substantial.[8] That this British watchfulness was often resented is scarcely surprising: Benes, for example, was always keen to maintain back-channel contacts with the Soviet Union of which the British were only partially aware;[9] while the Free French seized enthusiastically on the opportunity to establish their headquarters in Algiers in 1943, at a relative distance from Allied control. Even so, the freedom of the Gaullist regime to develop an independent foreign policy, for example, towards Francoist Spain was always strictly circumscribed by its need to follow British 'guidance'.[10]

Broadly speaking, relations between the British (and Americans) and the exile groups evolved in an inverse relationship to Allied military fortunes. When the military situation was perilous, relations between the exiles and the British tended to be 'warm and relatively uncomplicated';[11] past, often bitter, disagreements were subsumed in a bond of urgent mutual need. Subsequently, even if the willingness of the British to assist the exile groups remained in many respects remarkable, a host of other calculations began to complicate relations. The German socialist exiles, for example, after having initially been welcomed as allies in an anti-fascist alliance, found themselves shunned by the British as the war became redefined as one against Germany.[12] Most obviously, from June 1941, the British were obliged to prioritise the building of a close alliance with the Soviet Union. Churchill and his inner circle of advisors recognised this imperative with characteristic directness, as well as its unwelcome consequences for the Polish and Czechoslovak exiles. In July 1941, the British harried a suspicious Polish Government into concluding a treaty with the Soviet Union that avoided any commitment to the pre-1939 Polish boundaries.[13] Henceforth, the British and the Americans did everything to make the Polish exiles accept the need to work with the Soviet Union, even after the revelation of the Katyn massacre and the establishment of the Soviet-controlled Polish Committee of National Salvation in Lublin had made it apparent that such a policy could only lead the London Poles into political or even personal oblivion. The British policy towards the Polish exiles was not a cynical one, but it was pursued without compromise. In the case of the Czechoslovak regime, the dictates of British policy were less a constraint than an opportunity. For reasons that in part remain obscure, Benes had decided as early as the spring of 1939 to seek a close alliance with the Soviet Union. He maintained this policy throughout the era of the Nazi-Soviet pact, and it reached its culmination in the wide-ranging and decisive Soviet-Czechoslovak Treaty concluded by Benes and Stalin in Moscow in December 1943. In this way, the British-Soviet military alliance became a convenient tool that was manipulated by Benes to impose his pro-Soviet policy on the less convinced elements within the Czech exile community.[14]

The bonds of dependence on the Allies were not, however, felt only by central European exiles. If de Gaulle's often strained dealings with the British and Americans provide the most striking example of the conflict between exile strivings for sovereignty and Allied diplomatic and military *Realpolitik*,[15] the wartime relations between the British and all of the London regimes were replete with points of tension that sharpened as the twin but distinct events of Allied invasion and national liberation drew closer. The refusal of the Allies to guarantee pre-war borders or to reveal their (largely non-existent) plans for post-war Europe exacerbated the nationalist sensibilities of exile. Above all, the extraordinarily secretive atmosphere that pervaded

Anglo-American military planning right up until the spring of 1945 created ample opportunities for misunderstanding, disagreement and simple conflict. The Allies were trying to win a war; the exile regimes were on the whole much more concerned to win the peace. This basic difference helps to explain the many bitter 'paper wars' between the British and their exile allies, such as the one that arose between the British and the Belgian Government in 1942 over the efforts of SOE to subordinate the Belgian Resistance to its strategic control.[16] Similarly, relations between the British and the Norwegian Government-in-Exile, broadly the most successful wartime alliance, were bedevilled by British use of Norwegian soldiers for raids on Norwegian territory and by the refusal of the Allies to accord priority to the invasion of Norway during the closing phases of the war.[17]

The legacy of these tensions undoubtedly overshadowed subsequent relations between Britain and post-war Europe. If one of the most obvious features of the end of the war was an emotional outpouring of gratitude to the English-speaking liberators among the populations of Europe, the elites who had spent the war in London were left with more complex feelings. Certainly, as the war drew to a close, expressions of mutual respect proliferated, accompanied by commitments to the 'special relationship' that the war had forged between Britain and its wartime European allies.[18] Yet, there were few practical consequences of these effusions, and within a few years a process of European integration had begun that reinforced Britain's detached status from the other states of western Europe.[19] On both sides, perhaps, one of the less tangible legacies of the war years was a process of mutual distancing on the part of the political, military and bureaucratic elites. For the British, their dealings with the exile groups had served as a reminder of the costs and complexities of European entanglements. For the former exiles, the London years remained not only an essential tool of patriotic legitimation but also an awkward memory of a time when dependence on British favour and largesse had threatened to turn co-operation into collaboration.[20]

The other constraint on the success of the exile governments was their limited ability to control and direct the populations of occupied Europe in whose name they claimed to speak. In 1940, such claims were rarely more than vainglorious posturing; at the end of the war they still remained something less than an established fact. Certainly, the exile regimes had made considerable strides during the intervening years in turning their pretensions to leadership into reality. Radio and leaflet propaganda, agents sent into occupied Europe and emissaries spirited from Europe to London had all helped to consolidate their control. So too had the inchoate and necessarily clandestine nature of much of political life within occupied Europe. Once the refusal of the Germans to tolerate anything other than emphatic collaboration had become evident in 1941, a vacuum was created that the London governments were well placed to fill.[21] Consequently, in the superficial terms of popular sympathy, most if not all of the exile regimes had acquired popular legitimacy by 1944.[22] In organisational terms, however, the process was far from complete. The success of the exile governments in exercising leadership over their populations depended, as they were very much aware, on their ability to tie the disparate political, social and economic organisations within their occupied territories into unitary structures that acknowledged loyalty to the government over the water in London.

Some succeeded in this difficult task better than others: the Norwegian Government, aided by the peculiarly homogenous nature of the 'homefront' organisations within Norway and by the symbolic presence of King Haakon in London, was able to exercise significant control over the home country.[23] So too, in very different circumstances did the Polish regime. The peculiarly brutal German occupation of Poland left no space for a domestic civil society, and the establishment of the clandestine Government Delegature within Poland and subsequently of the Armia Krajowa (Home Army), though certainly not a mere tool of the London regime, brought much of mainstream Polish nationalist opinion into a clandestine structure that acknowledged the authority of London.[24] Others, however, were less successful. Capitulation to the Munich Agreement of 1938 cast a long shadow over the ability of the Benes regime in London to exercise authority over the fractured territories of the former Czechoslovakia. Even after the failure of collaboration had discredited its initial domestic rivals, many Czechs refused to acknowledge the Benes regime as their present and future government, while the Slovak national uprising of 1944 demonstrated the limits to the loyalty felt in Slovakia to the predominantly Czech exile leadership.[25] The most complex difficulties were, however, undoubtedly encountered by the Belgian Government and by the Free French. Both, in essence, pursued a twin policy of seeking to prevent alternative leaders from emerging (be they King Leopold III in Belgium or Darlan and Giraud in French North Africa) while also multiplying their efforts to bring Resistance groups, political movements and social organisations into umbrella organisations under their direction. In the French case, the establishment of the Provisional Government of the French Republic in Algiers in June 1944 and the Conseil National de la Résistance within France were the two expressions of de Gaulle's eventual and hard-won partial success.[26] In Belgium, the absence of equivalent institutions equally demonstrated the Pierlot regime's partial failure.[27]

Whatever the degree of control achieved by the exile governments over their populations, their capacity to project that control into the post-liberation period remained tenuous. The Europeans accepted back their exile leaders 'on approval' only, and their willingness to accept their leadership was always conditional on the returning exiles acknowledging domestic sensibilities and fulfilling domestic aspirations. On the whole, this tolerance proved to be short-lived. Ill-judged attempts by former exiles to give lessons in patriotism to their compatriots were strongly resented, and accusations that the exiles did not understand the changes wrought in popular attitudes by the hardships of the years of occupation rapidly became a prominent theme of post-liberation politics.[28] The subsequent careers of the exiled political leaders were mixed. If the political isolation of Mikolajczyk and his subsequent renewed exile from Poland must be regarded as primarily the consequences of Soviet policy, the lack of influence of former exiles such as Benes and Jan Masaryk in the turbulent materialist politics of Czechoslovakia between 1945 and 1948 indicated a more deep-rooted mismatch of mentalities.[29] In Norway and the Netherlands, the returning governments rapidly surrendered power to new coalition regimes dominated by 'men of the interior'. In Belgium, the post-liberation government of Hubert Pierlot collapsed ignominiously in February 1945, and was replaced by a new governmental coalition in which the Foreign Minister Paul-Henri Spaak was the sole survivor from the exile regime. De Gaulle was, of course, as always a special case, but his resignation from office in January 1946 was expressive of the broader failure of Free French exiles – Pierre Mendès-France and André Philip were perhaps the two most notable exceptions – to become major political figures in the Fourth Republic. Whoever the rulers of post-war Europe were, they were not primarily the men of London.

This personal marginalisation was also symbolic of a broader and, in many respects, more profound failure of the exile regimes: their inability to mould significantly the subsequent development of their countries. Despite, or perhaps because of, their wartime success in establishing themselves as the legitimate representatives of their nations, their legacy to the post-war history of Europe would seem to have been meagre indeed. Certainly a superficial historical literature, much influenced by the predominantly self-serving memoirs of former exiles,[30] has tended to portray the war years in London as key ones in the making of a new Europe. According to such accounts, the years of exile were a decisive period of preparation, during which new models of welfare provision and economic planning were developed that subsequently came to fruition after the war. Little if any of this London-centred interpretation does, however, bear serious historical examination. Indeed, perhaps the most striking feature of recent historical writing on post-war Europe is how little reference it makes to wartime exile.[31] Instead, the focus of historical attention has moved towards the internal history of Europe, and in particular towards the underlying realities that determined the course of politics during the immediate post-war years. The Europe that emerged from the Second World War might have once looked new, but it is the continuities with the pre-war world, at least in the areas beyond Soviet control, that now seem most evident to historians. The notion of 1945 as a turning-point has been replaced by a predominant emphasis on the unity of the pre- and post-war eras, accompanied by a concomitant emphasis on the more profound ruptures wrought by the First World War and by the social and political changes of the 1960s.[32]

This continuity was not accidental; it reflected the success of conservative social and political forces in maintaining and even enhancing their power during the war years. The revolution of 1945, it seems, was not defeated; it simply failed to occur.[33] The working class, decimated by the economic sufferings of the war years, lost out to a new and durable social alliance of the bourgeoisie and of rural interests that, aided by the economic bounty provided by the Marshall Plan, were able to dissolve the acute class tensions of the immediate post-war years in what Mike Smith has aptly termed 'the liberalism of abundance'.[34] The real determinants of the course of Europe after the war were therefore not the Allies, or still less the exile politicians, soldiers and bureaucrats, but forces internal to wartime Europe. Even the two major political parties that emerged in most post-war European states, the Communists and the Christian Democrats, were exactly the two groups that had been singularly under-represented, or indeed almost entirely absent, in exile in London.[35]

Post-war Europe was not therefore made in London. The exiles returned from London with a plethora of vague plans but little by way of concrete policies, beyond those intended to secure the immediate consolidation of power.[36] In particular, they failed to establish either pragmatic programmes or a new governing ideology that, regardless of the accidents of their own subsequent careers, could have provided the template for the policies of reconstruction in post-war Europe. There appear to have been several reasons for this underlying failure. The atmosphere of exile, with its distinctive combination of enforced inactivity, isolation, feuding and strangeness,[37] was not conducive to long-term planning. Confronted by so many imponderables, even the more conscientious officials tended to take refuge in the immediate and pressing tasks of military mobilisation and providing assistance to the civilian refugee populations.[38] Tomorrow would be obliged to take care of itself.

The dictates of foreign policy also served to distract from domestic planning. In the cases of Poland and Czechoslovakia, everything, it seemed to the exile governments, depended on winning Allied backing for the survival of their nation-states. Issues of post-war planning were therefore either neglected or subordinated to these diplomatic goals. This was especially evident in the case of the Czechoslovak regime. Benes' pursuit of the diplomatic and political support of the Soviet Union and the Czech communists caused him to mouth superficial clichés about state planning and social reform, while devoting much of his energies to his only substantial domestic goal: the root-and-branch expulsion of the German-speaking minorities from the Czech lands. Even during the early stages of the war, he lobbied the Allies for approval for these drastic expulsions, comparing them unashamedly to the expulsion of the Greek populations from Asia Minor in the 1920s. Ethnic or linguistic cleansing had, it seems, supplanted in his mind any more substantive vision of post-war reconstruction.[39]

Above all, the wartime governments became obsessed not with the post-liberation era but with the liberation itself, and, more especially, with how they would re-establish their authority. It is almost impossible to exaggerate the extent to which planning for the moment of liberation came to preoccupy the exile regimes during 1943 and the spring of 1944, when the Allied invasion of north-western Europe was seemingly always imminent and yet always deferred. Fears of the popular hostility that they might encounter and of the intentions of other contenders for power, as well as exaggerated predictions of the extent of economic destruction, all served to render the enforcement, in de Gaulle's uncompromising words, of 'l'ordre républicain sous l'autorité de l'État,' the all-absorbing goal.[40] 'Order,' in its manifold forms, was the key word in much planning for the liberation, embracing not merely the re-establishment of food and energy supplies, but, more especially, the rapid imposition of structures of public administration and of justice capable of forestalling the emergence of the dreaded power vacuum.[41] That, broadly speaking, these goals ultimately were achieved without excessive difficulty does not detract from the almost obsessive pre-eminence that they acquired in the minds of the exile governments.

The absence of longer-term planning for post-war reconstruction was also to some extent the result of a conscious decision. De Gaulle, with his instinctive sense of political realities, knew the power of making resonant but vague promises of the substantial changes which would follow the liberation,[42] but for a long time he seems to have deliberately prevented any discussion in London of the actual content of such changes. He probably feared that any discussion would expose the heterogeneous ideological tendencies of the Free French exiles, and, though he did finally allow study commissions to consider social and political reforms in London and Algiers during 1942 and 1943, he carefully distanced himself from their recommendations.[43]

Given this combination of constraining factors, it is not surprising that, when the exile regimes did, nevertheless, turn their attention to post-war policy-making, the results tended to be unimpressive. The Belgian Government, for example, established the grandly-titled Commission pour l'Etude des Problèmes d'Après-Guerre (CEPAG) in 1941, which subsequently published an imposing corpus of reports on a wide variety of political, social and economic issues.[44] Like much wartime planning, however, it tended to recycle ideas that had already been current in many European states during the 1930s, supplementing them with ritual exhortations about the need to learn from British and American models.[45] Few, if any, of the reforms proposed by CEPAG or by its equivalents in the other exile regimes were subsequently implemented, not least because the circumstances of their production in exile rendered them suspect in the eyes of those of their compatriots who had remained within occupied Europe. In 1943, for example, André Philip, as the Free French commissaire for post-war reforms had devised a *Charte Economique et Sociale* that he submitted to the internal Conseil National de la Résistance. The Resistance council rejected the charter's radical plans for post-war reform, and yet, when a few months later the internal communist-led Front National proposed very similar reforms to the Conseil, they were accepted without debate. More than one factor explains the different receptions accorded to the two documents, but it would seem that proposals that emanated from within the country possessed a legitimacy that those produced in exile lacked.[46]

In the major areas of post-war policy-making, it was therefore not the exiles' plans but the programmes and agreements constructed within occupied Europe that were the dominant influence. This is particularly evident in the important twin fields of welfare reform and post-war socio-economic corporatism. In both areas, outside influences certainly played a role: the Beveridge Report, which circulated not merely among exiles but was even parachuted into occupied Europe, served as an obvious stimulus for discussion of welfare provision. Similarly, the wartime structures of tripartite consultation between trade unions, employers and the state in Britain and the United States were widely admired. These external stimuli, and the imitative planning that they provoked within the exile regimes, were, however, less important than the convergence that occurred during the war years between the principal socio-economic forces within many European countries. Agreements such as the *Stichting van de Arbeid*, concluded between employers and trade unions in the Netherlands, the Social Pact of April 1944 in Belgium and the accord between the employers and the single trade-union organisation in Norway in 1944, proved to be more than transient alliances of convenience.[47] Instead, they marked the coming to fruition of structures of socio-economic corporatism, already prefigured in pre-war agreements such as the so-called Main Agreement of 1935 in Norway, that recognised employers and trade unions as partners in negotiations, often under rather nominal state supervision, concerning a wide range of social and economic issues.

The post-war structures of corporatist negotiation and welfare provision that emerged from these wartime agreements differed markedly from British-American models and from the ideas of the exile governments. The autonomy that they accorded to the social partners, and, in particular, the devolved framework of welfare provision that they established were in many respects the antithesis of the Beveridge model of public-sector welfare.[48] Indeed, in a number of states, the years after the Second World War witnessed a retreat in the role played by the state in welfare provision in favour of an enhanced importance for pillarised, corporatist trade unions, insurance leagues and welfare organisations.[49] This subsidiarity matched the political hegemony achieved in many states by the Christian Democrats, who, unsurprisingly, protected the autonomy of Catholic social organisations as well as using state revenues to subsidise improved welfare provision for their middle-class, self-employed and rural electorates.[50]

If it would be wrong to construct anything more than a very indirect connection between exile discussions and the post-war corporatist welfare structures established in most European states, it would be similarly incorrect to exaggerate the impact of the London regimes on subsequent economic planning. Exile regimes frequently voiced their commitment to an enhanced role for the state in the direction of the economy. But so too did many other groups, including not least the New Order regimes of German-occupied Europe. Both the apparent success of state-directed wartime mobilisation (by all the major belligerents, both east and west) and the widespread conviction that the post-war era would witness enhanced competition for access to markets, made a belief in the essential role of the state as the director of economic activity one of the clichés ritually invoked in almost all wartime planning.[51] Given the prevalence of such ideas, it is perhaps less remarkable that the post-war years witnessed some rather limited steps towards state-directed economic planning, than that capitalist economic freedoms were re-established extraordinarily rapidly. As is well known, in almost all of Europe economic controls were dismantled soon after the end of the war, prompted by popular pressures and by the lobbying of agricultural and industrial interests. Wartime dreams of rational planning gave way to the chaotic exuberance of a primitive free market, as a variable cocktail of factors, including pent-up demand for consumer goods, state budget deficits, American aid and the high salaries made possible by labour shortages in certain sectors, fuelled high levels of growth in most of the economies of western Europe.[52]

Moreover, those forms of planning that did emerge successfully in the post-war era owed little to exile influence. The Monnet Plan in France, for example, as Philippe Mioche's careful study has clearly demonstrated, was in many respects the antithesis of the statist economic planning envisaged by wartime exiles such as André Philip and Pierre Mendès-France. While Philip and Mendès-France envisaged 'socialisations' of the key sectors and a careful policing of the allocation of raw materials, the Monnet Plan offered little more than state investment in key sectors. Drafted initially in order to justify unrealistic French requests for huge volumes of American aid in 1946, it was a document that essentially adopted an American vision of the re-establishment of capitalist economic structures supplemented by state injections of capital.[53] Reinforced by the Marshall Plan of 1947 and the European Coal and Steel Community (ECSC), launched in 1950, this use of public funds to enhance private enterprise rapidly became the model that predominated in post-war Europe. Even in Norway, where exceptionally state planning retained a more central role in economic reconstruction, it was less the plans of wartime exiles that were important than the ability of the Labour government to maintain in the name of the superior national interest the wartime alliance of the trade unions and the employers' organisations.[54]

The process of limited European integration provides another area of policy-making in which wartime plans were rapidly supplanted by post-war realities. Certainly, an 'idealist' history of European integration has long tended to accord a privileged role to wartime exile in London.[55] The distance that London afforded from narrow national concerns, as well as, conversely, the almost promiscuous proximity that it imposed with other exile groups, provided a context in which the Europeanist ideas often latent in the multilateral diplomatic and economic agreements of the interwar years[56] could finally come to the fore. The impulses of emotional solidarity were reinforced, too, by the necessities of the time. Fears of the future economic and political viability of the smaller nation-states, as well as a retrospective recognition of their failure to unite against pre-war German expansionism, prompted the exiled elites to advocate some form of future European federation. The Belgian Foreign Minister, Paul-Henri Spaak, for example, eager as always to leap upon any passing bandwagon, became an advocate as early as the end of 1940 of a 'fédération des Etats d'Occident' and participated with the other exiled foreign ministers of Europe in earnest wartime discussions about post-war European co-operation.[57]

To seize upon such essentially circumstantial statements to make them into one of the foundations of the subsequent process of European integration would be, however, excessively teleological. As Alan Milward has demonstrated well, the origins of European integration lay not in the gestures and discussions of exile but in the pragmatic decisions, taken by European political leaders in the later 1940s and more especially the 1950s, to pool certain circumscribed attributes of national sovereignty in order to guarantee all the better the continued economic viability of their nation-states.[58] In this 'realist' account, the wartime declarations in London, far from laying the basis of subsequent measures, were no more than aberrant statements, untypical of the careful calculations of national interest that determined both the extent and, more especially, the limits of post-war integration. In its more polemical forms, the Milward account, with its almost entire neglect either of the London exiles or of Resistance 'Europeanism', no doubt verges on over-simplification. But it is nevertheless convincing in its broad outlines, especially when one examines more closely the very limited measures of co-ordination agreed in London. The Benelux Agreement, signed in September 1944, was, for example, much less a step towards European integration than an exercise in 'realist economic statecraft'[59] prompted by a mutual desire to pre-empt destructive economic competition during post-war reconstruction. Sketched in no more than outline terms in London, its subsequent development into a fully-fledged economic union was the product of the post-war willingness of the Belgian and Dutch governments (and of the economic lobby-groups within each state) to sustain this alliance of common interest.[60] Indeed, building on this example of Benelux, one might argue that, if a contribution to the process of European integration is to be found in the London years, it is less in vacuous declarations of good intent than in the model that the difficult wartime negotiations between the exile regimes provided for the complex mutual compromises that facilitated the subsequent creation of the ECSC and EEC.

Welfare reform, corporatism, economic planning and European integration would, thus, all seem to constitute false trails in an examination of the consequences of exile for post-war European politics. In each case, direct lines of cause and effect give way on closer inspection to a much more complex and tangled web of influences, in which forces internal to wartime Europe and the interplay of post-war political and social forces seem far more important than the ineffectual and muddled attempts of exiles to plan the future. Indeed, rather in the manner of some recent historical writing on the Resistance movements, it is tempting to dismiss the exile regimes as no more than an *épisode entre parenthèses*, remarkable not for what they subsequently achieved but for the fact that they existed at all. And yet the experience of exile was perhaps not entirely without consequences. The direct and immediate impact of the London years on the politics of liberation and reconstruction was, indeed, emphatically meagre. But this may be to adopt the wrong frame of reference. If a legacy of exile is to be found in post-war Europe, it lies perhaps less in the immediate post-war years than in the indirect and even unintended consequences of exile that became evident less in the short term than in the longer term.

One such legacy might be termed the opportunity that exile provided to re-configure the nature of the relationship between state and society. At least in the residual parliamentary regimes of interwar Europe, the relative weakness of the state and the difficulties that it encountered in imposing its policies on the major social forces had been a prominent theme of the 1930s, as well as the stimulus to manifold projects of authoritarian constitutional reform. The abdication of state power provoked by military defeat, and its replacement during the years of occupation by a combination of notable leadership, ad hoc Resistance movements and the informal power of social organisations, in effect marked a further retreat by state authority tht carried over into the mass politics and social corporatism of liberation. In the longer term, however, the new state structures that emerged in the 1950s and 1960s, characterised by a larger and more self-confident bureaucracy and bolstered by an enhanced share of national revenues, brought about an abrupt resurgence in state power. This process no doubt had many causes. Nevertheless, it would not seem too fanciful to locate one of the sources of this state power, and, more especially, of the new bureaucratic ethos, in the experience of exile. The London bureaucracies were liberated, however artificially, by their enforced exile from the constraints and pressures of civil society. Officials learned to act in isolation, freed from the constraints of lobby-groups and parliaments. A plethora of exceptional powers and the omnipresent model of military command-structures encouraged them to adopt a more activist and less deferential attitude. Something of the arrogance that this sometimes fostered was evident in the unsuccessful manner in which these bureaucracies attempted to impose their policies in the very different circumstances of the post-liberation era. The mentality, however, perhaps proved more durable than particular policies. Exile injected into the ethos of Europe's civil servants a spirit of autonomy from their political and social masters that, though subsumed in the immediate post-war years, re-emerged in the planning and *dirigisme* of the 1960s.[61]

The political ideology that, at least in much of northern Europe, identified most closely with this activist use of state power was, of course, social democracy. Here again, it is possible to see the years of wartime exile as one of the elements that contributed to the gradual consolidation during the 1950s and 1960s of a social democratic ideology. Socialists returned from London determined to bring about reforms in the structures and mentalities of their socialist parties. On the whole, these hopes were frustrated. The new Partij van de Arbeid in the Netherlands, for all of its proud boasts, was primarily the pre-war Socialist Party under a different name. In Belgium, the aspiration of Spaak and of those around him to create a *travailliste* progressive party modelled on the British Labour Party were destroyed not merely by Catholic suspicions but by socialist traditionalism.[62] Similarly, in France, control of the resuscitated SFIO remained firmly in the hands of pre-war leaders such as Léon Blum and of new men, notably Daniel Mayer, Guy Mollet and Gaston Defferre, who had emerged within France during the occupation.[63] Even in Germany, it was a figure of the interior, Kurt Schumacher, who was able to seize the political initiative before the SPD exiles were permitted to return from London.[64]

Short-term failure did not, however, exclude long-term influence. Though it would be simplistic to equate exile socialism with social democracy, the years of exile did lead many socialists in London to adopt two of the principal attributes of the subsequent social democratic ideology: the instrumental use of the state to create a more just and equal society, and an uncompromising anti-communism. The first of these was to come belatedly to the fore in the late 1950s and 1960s, and was symbolised most directly by the role played by an erstwhile German SPD exile in London, Willi Eichler, in the drafting of the social-democratic Bad Godesberg programme of 1959.[65] The second, however, had a more immediate impact. Exile was above all an education in anti-communism for European socialists. The apprehensions that they imbibed from their British hosts about Soviet intentions in east and central Europe, as well as their own intense fears of Communist political advances at their expense within occupied Europe, combined to forge a political mentality in which a wartime popular front of all left forces was seen as undesirable if not positively dangerous.[66] This rejection of the communists as potential political allies in anything other than the broadest national coalition extended into the post-war years and, after the exclusion of a number of communist parties from government in 1947, helped to contribute to the consolidation of a European socialism that, even before the Cold War fully took shape, knew on which side of the fence it stood. Much emphasis has been laid in recent years on the internal European origins of the Cold War;[67] perhaps in this respect we should also begin to pay attention to its exile origins.

The resurgence in state power, the construction of a social democratic ideology and, most directly, the reinforcement of the anti-communist choice of western Europe in the Cold War are therefore perhaps all ways in which the experience of exile had an impact that was wider, more diffuse and above all more delayed than might initially be suspected. Returning from London, the exiles were overwhelmed by the volatile materialist politics they encountered, and marginalised by internal contenders for power. Exile in that sense proved all too often to be a personal dead end. Yet the Europe that took shape in the later 1950s and 1960s was one that resembled much more closely the tenor and mentalities of the war years in London. The Europe of the Treaty of Rome, of the Bad Godesberg programme, of Gaullist modernisation in the 1960s and of the *doorbraak* (breakthrough) in the Netherlands that eroded confessional pillarisation was one in which the exiles could not merely recognise their aspirations but even, in some tangled way, identify their belated contribution.

Notes

1. Cited in R.H. Bruce Lockhart, *Comes the Reckoning*, London, 1947, p. 64. On Russian and Spanish Republican refugees, see C.C.L. Andreyev, *Vlasov and the Russian Liberation Movement*, Cambridge, 1987; M. Miller, *Shanghai on the Metro*, Berkeley, 1994, pp. 128–44; D. Wingeate Pike, *In the Service of Stalin: the Spanish Communists in Exile*, Oxford, 1993; A. Angoustures, 'Les réfugiés

espagnols en France de 1945 à 1981', *Revue d'histoire moderne et contemporaine* 44 (1997): 457–83.

2. Lockhart, *Comes the Reckoning*, p. 62. See also Z. Zeman (with A. Klimek), *The Life of Edvard Benes 1884–1948*, Oxford, 1997, p. 143.

3. In contrast, the International Brigades in the Spanish Civil War and the collaborationist units that fought alongside the German armies on the Eastern Front rarely had the opportunity to act as anything more than supplementary infantry.

4. H. Michel, *Histoire de la France Libre*, Paris, 1967, p. 125.

5. The unadvertised and fearful return of the Pierlot government to Brussels in September 1944 betokened an entirely different political situation: M. Conway, 'The Liberation of Belgium, 1944–1945', in *The End of the War in Europe 1945*, ed. G. Bennett, London, 1996, pp. 117–38.

6. A. Glees, *Exile Politics during the Second World War*, Oxford, 1982, p. 3 and 'The German Political Exile in London 1939–1945. The SPD and the British Labour Party', in *Exile in Great Britain. Refugees from Nazi Germany*, ed. G. Hirschfeld, Leamington Spa and Atlantic Highlands NJ, 1984, p. 85.

7. Access to the radio in London was often the focus of tensions between British officials and the exile regimes. See, for example, the incidents recalled in Lockhart, *Comes the Reckoning*, especially pp. 300–4.

8. See, for example, the interesting material on British recruitment of German Socialists as intelligence agents in L. Eiber, 'Verschwiegene Bündnispartner. Die Union deutscher sozialistischer Organisationen in Grossbritannien und die britischen Nachrichtendienste', in *Exilforschung. Ein internationales Jahrbuch Band XV Exil und Widerstand*, Munich, 1997, pp. 66–87.

9. Zeman, *Edvard Benes*, especially p. 177.

10. M. Catala, 'La France Libre et l'Espagne 1940–1944', *Relations internationales* 93 (Spring 1998): 64–83.

11. J. Coutouvidis (and J. Reynolds), *Poland 1939–1947*, Leicester, 1986, p. 73.

12. Glees, *Exile Politics*, pp. 124–84.

13. Coutouvidis, *Poland 1939–1947*, pp. 70–1 and 75–6.

14. Zeman, *Edvard Benes*.

15. Michel, *France Libre*.

16. E. Verhoeyen, 'La résistance belge vue de Londres. Ententes et divergences entre Belges et Britanniques', in *La Résistance et les Européens du Nord*, Brussels, 1996, pp. 163–75.

17. O. Riste, 'Relations between the Norwegian government in exile and the British government', in *Britain and Norway in the Second World War*, ed. P. Salmon, London, 1995, p. 46; O.K. Grimnes, 'The Resistance and the Northern Europeans. The Case of Norway', in *La Résistance et les Européens du Nord*, p. 57. See also C. Mann's contribution to this volume.

18. See for example Lockhart's description of a dinner attended by Anthony Eden and Free French and Belgian officials in September 1944: Lockhart, *Comes the Reckoning*, p. 319.

19. D. Reynolds, 'Britain and the New Europe. The Search for Identity since 1940', *Historical Journal* 31 (1988): 223–39.

20. De Gaulle above all was aware of the dangers of dependence, remarking in 1942: 'Why do you think the *émigré* governments play such a melancholy role in history? It is because in the long run they adopt the attitudes of their hosts and become an object of contempt for their own people' (cited in Riste, 'Relations between the Norwegian government in exile and the British government', p. 49).

21. The example of the *Nederlandse Unie* is significant in this respect. It was its failure to emerge as a viable political organisation in the occupied Netherlands

which caused many Dutch to turn towards London: M. Smith, 'Neither Resistance nor Collaboration: Historians and the Problem of the Nederlandse Unie', *History* 72 (1987): 251–78.

22. See, for example, Paul Struye's comments on the evolution in attitudes to the London government within occupied Belgium: P. Struye, *L'évolution du sentiment public en Belgique sous l'occupation allemande*, Brussels, 1945.

23. Grimnes, 'The Resistance and the Northern Europeans – The Case of Norway', pp. 52–68.

24. Coutouvidis, *Poland 1939–1947*, p. 84. See also the contribution of J. Zamojski to this volume.

25. Zeman, *Edvard Benes*, pp. 211–12.

26. J-P. Azéma, *From Munich to the Liberation, 1938–1944*, Cambridge, 1984, pp. 158–76 and 182–5. The difficult early relations between the Free French and the internal Resistance are well conveyed in L. Douzou and D. Veillon, 'Les relations entre les résistances intérieure et extérieure françaises vues à travers le prisme des archives du BCRA (1940–1942)', in *La Résistance et les Français*, eds J. Sainclivier and C. Bougeard, Rennes, 1995, pp. 13–27.

27. Verhoeyen, 'La résistance belge vue de Londres', pp. 178–82; P. Lagrou, *Patriotic Memory and National Recovery – The Legacy of Nazi Occupation in Belgium, France and the Netherlands 1945–1965*, Cambridge, forthcoming.

28. Zeman, *Edvard Benes*, p. 244. Resentment at the actions and attitudes of those referred to pejoratively as 'les londoniens' was frequently voiced in post-liberation Belgium. See for characteristic examples *L'Appréciation*, 16 September 1944, pp. 12–16, 'Premier coup d'oeil'; *L'Avenir du Luxembourg*, 29–30 November 1944, p. 1, 'L'inévitable malaise'.

29. K. Kaplan, *The Short March – The Communist Takeover in Czechoslovakia, 1945–1948*, London, 1987, especially pp. 33–49 and 121–2.

30. The memoirs of Spaak are a classic example of this genre: P-H. Spaak, *Combats inachevés*, Paris, 1969.

31. Three examples are: R. Vinen, *Bourgeois Politics in France 1944–1951*, Cambridge, 1995; D. Rogers, *Politics after Hitler – The Western Allies and the German Party System*, Basingstoke and London, 1995; and *De democratie heruitgevonden*, eds L. Huyse and K. Hoflack, Leuven, 1995.

32. See, for example, the interpretations of the history of the Netherlands in the twentieth century advanced in: M.C. Brands, '*The Great War* die aan ons voorbijging. De blinde vlek in het historische bewustzijn van Nederland', in *Het belang van de tweede wereldoorlog*, eds M. Berman and J.C.H. Blom, The Hague, 1997, pp. 9–20; J.C.H. Blom, 'The Second World War and Dutch Society: Continuity and Change', in *Britain and the Netherlands*, Vol. 4 – *War and Society*, eds A.C. Duke and C.A. Tamse, The Hague, 1977, pp. 228–48.

33. M. Mitchell, 'Materialism and Secularism: CDU Politicians and National Socialism, 1945–1949', *Journal of Modern History* 67 (1995): 278–308; Vinen, *Bourgeois Politics*, pp. 1–11; A. Shennan, *Rethinking France – Plans for Renewal 1940–1946*, Oxford, 1989, pp. 287–9.

34. M. Smith, 'Introduction' in *Making the New Europe – European Unity and the Second World War*, eds M. Smith and P. Stirk, London and New York, 1990, p. 5.

35. The impact of communist wartime exile in Moscow is of course an entirely different story and one that is only now beginning to be studied. The limited extent and importance of Christian Democrat exile politics is well displayed in W. Kaiser, 'Cooperation of European Catholic Politicians in Exile in Britain and the United States during World War II', *Journal of Contemporary History*, forthcoming.

36. See the dismissive comments of Jean Monnet on Free French planning cited in P. Mioche, *Le plan Monnet. Genèse et élaboration 1941–1947*, Paris, 1987, p. 36.
37. Glees, 'The German Political Exile in London', p. 83.
38. See, for example, M. Buck, '"Feeding a Pauper Army"': War Refugees and Welfare in Britain, 1940–1942', *Twentieth Century British History*, forthcoming.
39. Zeman, *Edvard Benes*, pp. 182, 186, 189, 225–6 and 247. See also the text of Benes' radio broadcast to Czechoslovakia from Moscow after the conclusion of the Soviet-Czechoslovak Treaty in December 1943 cited in H. Ripka, *East and West*, London, 1944, p. 137.
40. De Gaulle cited in Michel, *France Libre*, pp. 120–2.
41. Shennan, *Rethinking France*, pp. 61–4; A. Bourneuf, *Norway – The Planned Revival*, Cambridge Mass., 1958, pp. 14–15.
42. For example, his declaration on 1 April 1942 to the National Defence Public Committee in London: 'c'est une révolution, la plus grande de son Histoire, que la France, trahie par ses élites dirigeantes et par ses privilégiés, a commencé d'accomplir' cited in C. Andrieu *et. al.*, *Les nationalisations de la libération*, Paris, 1987, p. 231.
43. Michel, *France Libre*, pp. 29–30; Shennan, *Rethinking France*, pp. 53–68.
44. B. Henau, 'Shaping a New Belgium: The CEPAG – The Belgian Commission for the Study of Post-War Problems, 1941–44', in Stirk and Smith, eds, *Making the New Europe*, pp. 112–132. See also the contribution of D. de Bellefroid to this volume.
45. See the comments on the post-war planning by the Free French in Shennan, *Rethinking France*, pp. 67–8 and Michel, *France Libre*, pp. 110–11.
46. Andrieu *et. al.*, *Les nationalisations*, pp. 56–9.
47. Blom, 'The Second World War and Dutch Society', pp. 237–8; *Het Sociaal Pact van 1944. Oorsprong, betekenis en gevolgen*, eds D. Luyten and G. Vanthemsche, Brussels, 1995; Bourneuf, *Norway*, pp. 15–17; S. Kuhnle, 'Norway', in *Growth to Limits – The West European Welfare States since World War II*, ed. P. Flora, Berlin and New York, 1986 vol. 1, p. 122.
48. P. Baldwin, *The Politics of Social Solidarity – Class Bases of the European Welfare State 1875–1975*, Cambridge, 1990, pp. 158–62.
49. For example, E.R. Dickinson, *The Politics of German Child Welfare from the Empire to the Federal Republic*, Cambridge Mass., 1996, pp. 247–9.
50. H.L. Wilensky, 'Leftism, Catholicism and Democratic Corporatism: The Role of Political Parties in Recent Welfare State Development', in *The Development of Welfare States in Europe and America*, eds P. Flora and A.J. Heidenheimer, New Brunswick and London, 1981, pp. 345–82.
51. For example, Ripka, *East and West*, p. 137; Henau, 'Shaping a New Belgium', p. 119; Shennan, *Rethinking France*, pp. 236–44.
52. I. Cassiers, P. De Villé and P.M. Solar, 'Economic growth in post-war Belgium', B. Van Ark, J. De Haan and H.J. De Jong, 'Characteristics of economic growth in the Netherlands during the post-war period' and W. Carlin, 'West German growth and institutions' in *Economic Growth in Europe since 1945*, eds N. Crafts and G. Toniolo, Cambridge, 1996, pp. 180–2, 302–5 and 463–8.
53. Mioche, *Le plan Monnet*; Andrieu *et al.*, *Les nationalisations*, p. 123.
54. Bourneuf, *Norway*, pp. 16–22.
55. W. Lipgens, *A History of European Integration* (Oxford, 1982) vol. 1, pp. 66–7; *Documents on the History of European Integration*, eds W. Lipgens and W. Loth, Berlin, 1985, vol. 2. (*Plans for European Union in Great Britain and in Exile, 1939–1945*).
56. See, for example, the excellent analysis of European inter-war trade agreements

in E. Buissière, *La France, la Belgique et l'organisation économique de l'Europe 1918–1935*, Paris, 1992.

57. T. Grosbois, 'L'action de Józef Retinger en faveur de l'idée européenne', *European Review of History* 6 (1999): pp. 59–82. See also M. Dumoulin, *Spaak*, Brussels, 1999, 276–81.

58. A. Milward, *The European Rescue of the Nation-State*, London, 1994, especially pp. 15–16 and 27. Agricultural policy provides a characteristic example of the combination of national pragmatism and lobby-group pressure that influenced the development of a common European agricultural policy: G. Noël, *France, Allemagne et "Europe verte"*, Berne etc., 1995.

59. P-H. Laurent, 'Reality not Rhetoric: Belgian-Dutch Diplomacy in Wartime London', in Stirk and Smith, eds, *Making the New Europe*, p. 139.

60. Ibid., pp. 133–41.

61. J.C.H. Blom and W. ten Have, 'Making the New Netherlands?: Ideas about Renewal in Dutch Politics and Society during the Second World War' in Stirk and Smith, eds, *Making the New Europe*, p. 110.

62. J. Bosmans, 'Het maatschappelijk-politieke leven in Nederland 1945–1980', in *Algemene geschiedenis der Nederlanden* vol. 15, Bussum, 1982, p. 273; 'A propos d'un meeting socialiste', *Cahiers socialistes* 3 [January 1945]: pp. 51–2.

63. B.D. Graham, *Choice and Democratic Order. The French Socialist Party, 1937–1950*, Cambridge, 1994, pp. 259–365.

64. Glees, *Exile Politics*, pp. 235–41.

65. Ibid., p. 242.

66. Hence, for example, the refusal of the SPD exiles in London to work with the communist-inspired Committee for a Free Germany: Ibid., pp. 212–26.

67. For example, *The Origins of the Cold War in Europe: international perspectives*, ed. D. Reynolds, New Haven and London, 1994.

INDEX

Abersoch 89
Adler, Friedrich 247, 250
Aerial, Operation 167–8
Ainsztein, Reuben 23–4
Albarda, J.W. 247
Albert I, King 42
Amigo, Archbishop 58
Anders' Army 196, 198, 199
Anderson, Sir John 18
Anglo-Belgian Employment
    Exchange 60–1, 75
Anspach, Maurice 147
Antwerp 86, 90, 146, 147
Arciszewski, Tomasz 204
Ardennes 91–2
Arnhem 86, 91, 241
Aron, Raymond 213
Aruba 236
Association of Polish Patriots
    198–9
Atlantic, Battle of the 159, 160
Auschwitz 203
Australia 20, 221
Austria, refugees in Britain 15, 20,
    249, 250–1

Barmouth 218
Barnouw, A.J. 233
Bassompierre, Baron de 41
Bastin, Charles 56–7
Belgian Institute 56
Belgian Military Mission (BMM)
    136, 137, 139, 146

Belgian Red Cross 71, 75, 76, 78
Belgium
    air force 85–6, 96
    armed forces in World War II
        81–96
    and Boer War 36–7, 39
    commandos 88–90, 92
    education policy 59–60
    enfranchisement of women 79
    and European integration 109,
        131, 267
    foreign policy 42–48, 106–113,
        130
    government in exile 55–7, 74–5,
        82–3, 100, 107, 122, 135,
        136, 259, 260–1, 264
    inter-war governments 128–9
    liberation in 1944 95
    merchant navy 96
    military planning 99–120
    navy 86–7, 96
    paratroops 90–2
    post-war politics 261, 269
    pre-war attitudes to Britain
        35–48
    refugee community in Britain
        53–63, 67–80
    return of refugees to Belgium 61
    security in liberated Belgium
        135–49
    socialists in exile 251
    trade unionists in exile 125, 126
    and USA 108

and USSR 111–2
welfare policy 128–9, 265
Belgrade 189
Bellanger, Etienne 222
Belorussia 199, 202, 204
Benelux Agreement 267
Benes, Edvard 172, 173–4, 177,
        178, 179, 256, 257, 258,
        260, 261, 263
Bermuda Conference 18
Bernard, Major Henri 94
Bernhard, Prince 231, 233, 237–8
Bernier, Colonel 143, 145
Bessborough, Lord 215, 217
Beveridge, Sir William 129, 264–5
Bigwood, Professor 126
Billet, Lieutenant Victor 86
Bir-Kadem 89
Bloch, Jean 87
Blondeel, Eddy 87
Blum, Léon 269
Bois, Elie J. 222
Bondas, Joseph 126
Borremans, Louis 57
Boyle, Archibald 169
Bracken, Brendan 195
Braemar 60
Brandt, Willy 252
Braunthal, Julien 250
Bricman, Lucienne 142
Britain, Battle of 86
British Broadcasting Corporation
        100
British Council 60, 175–6
Brittain, Vera 42
Brixham 55
Brussels, University of 144, 146,
        147, 148, 149
Buls, Charles 39–40
Burma 86
Buset, Max 107, 111, 123
Bute, Isle of 186
Buxton 60

Caisse Belge de Prêts et d'Epargne
        60
Cambier, Major Emile 82
Cammaerts, Professor 100

Canada 20, 86, 87, 157, 160, 191,
        237
    armed forces in World War II 90
Capelle, Baron Robert 47
Carmarthen 87
Carsten, Francis 250–1
Cartier de Marchienne, Emile 85,
        100–1, 104–5, 110, 112
Carton de Wiart, Count Henry 46
Casement, Roger 40–1
Catholic Church (in Britain) 58–9
Catholic War Refugees Spiritual
        Committee 58, 59
Cattier, Félicien 40
Cattoir, François 139, 142, 143,
        147, 149
Centres de recrutement de l'armée
        belge (CRABs) 83
Chamberlain, Austen 44
Chamberlain, Neville 45–6, 172
Charles, Prince Regent of Belgium
        90
Cholmondeley Park 170
christian democracy 262, 265
Churchill, Sir Winston 163,
        170–1, 205, 207, 213, 221,
        239, 258
Ciliax, Admiral 159
Civil Affairs 137, 138, 139
Clacton-on-Sea 94
Clément, René 239
Commission pour l'étude des
        problèmes d'après-guerre
        (CEPAG) 101, 106–7, 113,
        121–33, 264
Congo 38–41, 45–7, 203
Crèvecoeur, Jean 143, 144, 147
Crickhowell 87
Cuba 3
Cumont, Major Charles 87, 92
Curaçao 232, 236
Curzon, Lord 44
Cycle, Operation 167–8
Czechoslovakia
    air force 168–70, 174, 176–9
    armed forces in World War II
        167–79
    army 170, 171–2, 178

authorities in exile 172–4, 256, 258, 260, 263
and Great Britain 169, 256, 258
post-war politics 261
and USSR 257, 258

Dahl, Colonel 163
Dallas, George 248–9
Dalton, Hugh 205, 248, 251
Danielsen, Admiral 164
Danloy, Lieutenant Georges 82, 84, 89
Daufresne de la Chevalerie, General Raoul 88, 92
Deauville 95
de Brouckère, Louis 110–1, 123, 125, 131, 247
Defferre, Gaston 269
De Gaulle, Charles 93, 187, 257, 258, 261, 263, 264
De Geer, D.J. 235
de Gruben, Hervé 107
Delacroix, Léon 43
de Lavelaye, Victor 105, 107
Delvoie, General 101, 102, 105, 106, 111, 112
De Man, Henri 125, 126, 128, 129
De Paepe, Major Edmond 85
De Schryver, Auguste 35
De Staercke, André 35
Deswarte, Willem 144
Deton, Albert 88
Devèze, Michel 145–6
De Vleeschauwer, Albert 62
de Voghel, abbé 58
Dewandre, Roger 88
Dewé, Walthère 42
Dieppe Raid 86, 161, 177
Dunstable, Operation 192
Dutry, Armand 56

Eden, Anthony 46, 101, 104, 168, 177
Edinburgh 194, 195
Edward VII, King 37
Eichler, Willi 270
Eisenhower, General Dwight D. 238

Erkes, Major 146
European Coal and Steel Community (ECSC) 266, 268
European integration 266–8, 270

Fabian Society 248
Finnmark 163, 164
Fitzgerald, Beryl 218
Fleischer, Major-General Carl 155, 157
Fontaine, Georges 146
France
armed forces in World War II 82–3, 217–20
and Belgium 42–4
exiles in Britain 213–25
Free French authorities 216–7, 219, 223, 257, 260–1, 264
Polish community in 191–3, 203
post-war politics 261, 266, 269, 270
resistance in 192–3, 203, 264
Vichy regime 2, 220–2
Frank, Anne 243
Freiburg 194

Ganshof van der Meersch, François 146
Ganshof van der Meersch, Walter 135, 136, 137, 139, 141, 143, 145, 146, 147, 148, 149
Gent 146
George VI, King 47, 233
Gérard, Auguste 145
Gerbrandy, P.S. 235–6
Germany
Belgian occupation of 102, 105–6, 111
and colonies 45–6
occupation of Norway 153, 155, 159, 163–4
occupation of Netherlands 232–3, 240–1
post-war politics 257, 269, 270
refugees in Britain 249–51, 257, 258, 269–70

Gevers, Jean 146, 147
Gillies, William 248–9, 250, 251
Glasgow 195
Grassett, General 102
Great Britain
    appeasement 45–7
    and Belgium 41–2, 43–5, 103–4
    and Czechoslovakia 172–4,
        177, 179, 258
    internment 19–20
    labour mobilisation 71–3
    and Poland 20–1, 258
    and Polish refugees 205–7
    popular attitudes towards
        refugees 26–8, 176, 187,
        216
    propaganda 17, 72, 73, 202–3
    refugees in armed forces 75,
        88–9, 154–8, 168–79
    and refugees from Europe
        11–34, 53–4, 57–8, 68–9,
        71–3, 74–5, 168, 214, 256,
        257
    scientific work in wartime
        16–17
Great Yarmouth 94
Gréban de Saint-Germain, Frédéric
    84
Greenwood, Arthur 110
Grisar, William 87
Guérisse, Albert 84
Gutt, Camille 55, 62, 85, 87, 88,
    96, 101, 124, 128, 131

Haakon VII, King 153–4, 260
Halifax, Lord 45, 173
Haller, General J. 191
Hambro, Sir Charles 156–7
Hamilton, Cecil 232–3
Harasowska, Jadwiga 195
Harboort, Pierre 82
Henderson, Sir Neville 46
Hereford 88
Herrera, Denise 69
Heydrich, Reinhard 177
High Commissariat for National
    Security 135–49
Hillary, Richard 15

Hinsley, Cardinal 58
Hoare, Sir Samuel 23
Horton, Max 159
Hoste, Julius 125, 126, 131
Huddleston, Air Vice Marshal 162
Hungary, refugees in 18–19,
    195–6
Huysmans, Camille 144, 247,
    249, 250
Hymans, Paul 42–3, 44
Hynd, J.B. 205

Iceland 163
Independent Labour Party (ILP)
    248
India 199
International Socialist Forum 250
Internazionale Gruppe democratis-
    cher Sozialisten 252
Iran 196, 197, 199
Ireland 40–1
Ismay, General Hastings 156
Italy
    battles in 89
    refugees in Britain 20, 22

Janousek, Karel 176–7, 179
Janson, Paul 39
Jaspar, Henri 44
Jaspar, Marcel-Henri 83, 84, 85
Jews
    in the Netherlands 242–3
    refugees in Britain 13, 16, 22,
        69
    refugees in Hungary 18–19
    refugees in Palestine 19
    refugees in USSR 199
    relations with Poles 187, 199,
        202–3
Joassart, Gustave 126

Kalla, Josef 168–9
Karski, Jan 202
Keyes, Admiral 48
Kingston (GB) 60
Kirschsen, Lieutenant 91
Kleinzeller, Arnost 24–5
Koht, Halvdan 154, 155

Krebs, Dr. Hans 24
Kreisky, Bruno 252
Kuczynski, Jürgen 26

Labarthe, André 213
Labour Party, relations with exiles
    248–52
Laski, Harold 248
Lecomte, Colonel 92
Left Book Club 248
Left News, The 250
Légion Etrangère 85, 92, 93
Legrand, Louis 85
Leith-Ross Committee 125
Leopold II, King 36, 38
Leopold III, King 47–8, 54, 81,
    107, 243
Lerot, Jules 140, 141, 142, 143
Leroy, Jean 129
Lévy, Paul 125
Lie, Trygve 155–6
Limpens, Major 146
Linge, Captain Martin 155–6
Lisser, Meyer 231
Lithuania 204
Liverpool 39–40, 217–8
Lloyd George, David 43
Locarno, Agreements of 44
Lockhart, Bruce 256
Loeb, Walter 250, 251
Lofoten Islands 155
Louvain, University of 35
Löwenthal, Richard 250
Lunden, Captain Baron René 84
Luxembourg, Grand Duchy of 42,
    43, 44, 93

Maiersdorf, Léon 84
Malvern 87, 88, 90
Marchal, André 84
Marshall Plan 262, 266
Masaryk, Jan 177, 261
Mayer, Daniel 269
Mechelen-sur-Meuse, incident at
    48
Medhurst, Air Commodore Sir
    Charles 169, 170
Mendès-France, Pierre 261, 266

Meny, Adolphe 84
Mexico 3, 199
Mikolajczyk, Stanislaw 261
Mohr, Wilhelm 160
Mollet, Guy 269
Monnet, Jean 266
Moore, Admiral 164
Moran, Lord 207
Morel, E.D. 38, 40
Morgan, Lieutenant General 162
Motzfeldt, Colonel 161–2
Muselier, Admiral 213
Myers, Monseigneur 59

Narvik 153–4
Netherlands 92, 96, 108, 162, 247
    armed forces in World War II
        95, 233, 236, 238–9
    colonies 236, 244
    exiles in Britain 230–45, 251
    government in exile 233–4,
        235–7, 239, 241, 256, 267
    invasion of 232–4
    persecution of Jews in 242–3
    post-war politics 261, 265, 269,
        270
    pre-war politics 230–1
    resistance in 236–8, 239, 240–2,
        244
    royal family 230–1
Neu Beginnen 250
Newman, Cardinal 35
Newsam, Sir Francis 205
Nicod, Paul 84
Normandy Campaign 85, 86, 91,
    94–5, 161–2
Norway
    air force 159–62
    armed forces in World War II
        153–65, 259
    army 162–3
    and Britain 154, 259
    government in exile 153–8, 160,
        164, 256, 259, 260
    liberation of 163–4
    navy 158–9, 164
    post-war politics 261, 265,
        266

Oakeshott, Walter 27
Øen, Captain Bjorne 159–60, 161
Olav, Crown Prince of Norway
    163
Orkneys, The 161
Orwell, George 12
Ostende 146
Oujda 85
Oxford 235, 250

Palestine 19, 196
Philip, André 261, 264, 266
Philips 232
Pierlot, Hubert 36, 58–9, 61–2,
    83, 87, 92, 101, 102, 107,
    122, 125, 136, 148, 261
Pilsudski Institute 191, 206
Piron, Major Jean-Baptiste 92,
    93–6
Plan Holland 241
Poland
    armed forces in World War II
        15, 89, 92, 94, 168, 169,
        198–9, 203, 256
    assistance for Polish Jews 202–3
    clandestine state in 188–91,
        197, 200–2, 260
    cultural life 195–6
    education 194, 198
    exile community in USA 185,
        191
    government in exile 186–93,
        197, 198, 199, 200–1, 203,
        204, 206–7, 258, 260
    political life in exile 200–2
    refugees in Britain 14, 26–7,
        184–5, 187, 205–7
    refugees in France 185, 191–3,
        195, 203
    refugees in USSR 14–15, 185,
        197–9
    trade unions in exile 188
    volunteers in Spanish Civil War
        192
    welfare policies 196–200
Polish Red Cross 192, 194, 197
Political Warfare Executive (PWE)
    202–3, 251

Pollak, Oscar 249
Potsdam Conference 204
Pound, Admiral Sir Dudley 158
Prevention and Relief of Distress
    Scheme 68

Quebec Conference 162

Rathbone, Eleanor 25
Rens, Jef 107, 122–3, 125, 126,
    131
Richard, Raoul 125–6, 131
Riiser-Larsen, Admiral 161
Roberts, Frank 170, 172
Roch, Roger 131
Rolin, Henri 45, 92
Rolland, Romain 40
Roman, Pierre 96
Romania 186, 196
Rothschild, Robert 46
Rougier, Professor 213
Ruge, General Otto 155
Ruhr, occupation of the 44
Ruzette, Baron 126

Scaillet, Renée 142
Scotland 162, 187, 194, 195
Service Central des Réfugiés 57–8,
    61
Seyss-Inquart, Dr. Artur 240
Sheffield, University of 24–5
Sikorski, General Wladyslaw 186,
    187, 191, 197, 257
Simpson, Esther 24
Sipido Affair 37–8
Slovakia 168, 178, 260
Smekens, Lieutenant Richard 82
Snoy, Charles 107
Socialist Clarity Group 248
Socialist Workers Internationale
    247–52
Society for the Protection of Sci-
    ence and Learning 24
South Africa 238–9
Soviet Union (USSR)
    intelligence activities 15
    and liberation of Norway 163
    place of refuge 3, 197–9

policy towards Poland 190–1,
    199, 204, 258
policy in wartime Europe 3, 14,
    112, 178–9, 257, 258
wartime image of 21, 111–12
Spaak, Paul 37
Spaak, Paul-Henri 36, 37, 46–7,
    48, 62, 87, 100, 101, 104,
    105, 107–8, 113, 124–5,
    126, 130, 131, 261, 267,
    269
Spain 2, 23, 93, 234
Spears, Major 218
Special Air Service (SAS) 90–1
Special Operations Executive
    (SOE) 155–7, 192, 259
Surinam 236
Sweden 2, 93, 239, 252
Switzerland 2, 93, 194, 234, 239

Tenby 81, 82, 84, 87
Terlinden, Léon 84
Thorpe, Sir Andrew 164
Torp, Oscar 156–7
Trades Union Congress (TUC) 248
Tranmael, Martin 252
Tromsø 164
Truffaut, Georges 82, 84, 88

Ukraine 187, 199, 202, 204
Umberto, Crown Prince of Italy 37
Unilever 232
Unité Combattante Belge 84–5, 87
United States of America (USA)
    2–3, 87–8, 191
Urquhart, Major-General R.E. 241

Vågsøy 155, 156
Van Acker, Achille 131
Van Cauwelaert, Frans 95, 108
Van de Perre, Hugo 144
Vanderheyden, Captain 91
Vandervelde, Emile 36, 38, 40
Van de Vloet, Captain-Commandant
    142

Van Dorpe, Joseph 144–5
Van Kleffens, E.N. 108
Van Langenhove, Fernand 42,
    108–9, 112
Van Leirberge, Major 146
Van Overstraeten, General 47, 48
Van Severen, Joris 145
Vansittart, Lord 249–50
Van Strydonck de Burkel, Lieu-
    tenant General Victor 81,
    88
Van Zeeland, Paul 122, 124–5,
    126, 128, 129, 131
Vermeylen, Pierre 84, 100
Villars de Lans 194
Vis 89
Visser 't Hooft, Dr. W.A. 239
Vogel, Hans 249

Walcheren 90, 163, 164
Wanty, Jacques 83–4
War Refugee Committees 54
Ward, J.G. 170
Warwick, Lady 215, 216
Wauters, A.J. 40
Weald, North 161, 162
Weyemberg, Paul 100
White Cross 194
Wibier, Lieutenant General Albert
    83
Wilhelmina, Queen 230–1, 233–4,
    235, 236–7, 238, 243
Women's Auxiliary Air Force
    (WAAF) 76–7, 78
Women's Voluntary Services for
    Civil Defence 54, 214
World Council of Churches 239
Wouters, Colonel Louis 85

Yeu, Isle of 89–90

Zealand 90
Zygelbojm, Szmul 203